lonely planet

Cyprus

**Kyrenia (Girne) &
the North**
p184

**North Nicosia
(Lefkoşa)**
p171

**Famagusta (Gazimağusa)
& the Karpas
Peninsula**
p206

**Nicosia
(Lefkosia)**
p147

**Troödos
Mountains**
p75

**Pafos &
the West**
p97

**Larnaka &
the East**
p121

**Lemesos &
the South**
p56

**Joe Bindloss,
Jessica Lee, Josephine Quintero**

Contents

RUINS AT ANCIENT KOURION, P71

OLLIE TAYLOR / 500PX ©

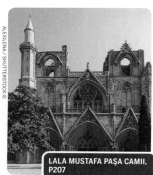

LALA MUSTAFA PAŞA CAMII, P207

ALEX LENA / SHUTTERSTOCK ©

Contents

FIG TREE BAY, P143

Welcome to Cyprus

Strike out beyond the sun-soaked stretches of sand to discover an island of compelling culture and landscapes, steeped in myth and riddled with ancient riches.

Crossing the Line

Crossing the line between the South and the North allows you not only to gain some understanding of the island's complex and painful modern-day history, but also experience the two Cypriot communities. Greek Cypriot and Turkish Cypriot societies are intrinsically different yet incredibly similar, linked by the still-strong role of traditional family life and a rich history where food cultures and folk customs have intermingled, but divided by belief. One thing's for sure wherever you are on the island: the naturally warm Cypriot hospitality is much in evidence on both sides of the Green Line.

The Great Outdoors

The landscape and Mediterranean climate mean that outside is where it's at – and where you should be. Sun-soaked stretches of sand are Cyprus' calling card and there's a beach for everyone here, from wild and windswept to family-friendly and packed. Every conceivable water sport is on offer, from scuba diving to skimming the surface on a kite- or windsurf board. And if you tire of all that blue, strike out into the interior, where wildflower-studded meadows and valleys of densely planted vineyards sweep up to a pine-clad mountain spine offering hiking, biking and, yes, even winter skiing.

A Sense of the Past

Steeped in myth, coveted by every conqueror with an eye for a prize, Cyprus' tumultuous and multilayered past has left ancient riches strewn across this island. Neolithic dwellings, Bronze Age and Phoenician tombs, remnants of once-mighty city-kingdoms, Roman mosaics, mountaintop castles and Byzantine churches lay scattered through the countryside. Cyprus may welcome you to flop out on the beach, but dig into the past here and you'll unearth the entire history of the Mediterranean.

A Culinary Feast

Meze is a delicious way to acquaint yourself with the local cuisine, tantalising the taste buds with a feast of small dishes, from creamy hummus to kebabs or *afelia* (pork cooked in red wine) and everything in between. Heavily influenced by Turkish, Greek and Middle Eastern food cultures, Cypriot cooking has some of its own culinary stars, including haloumi (hellim in Turkish) and kebab favourite *sheftalia* (*şeftali kebap* in Turkish; grilled sausages wrapped in caul fat). And don't forget the desserts. Flavoured with almonds, rose water and pistachios, sweet treats range from comforting rice puddings to gloriously sticky baklava.

Why I Love Cyprus

By Jessica Lee, Writer

For a girl not big on beach time, Cyprus' appeal may seem strange. But just like Aphrodite's ability to lure in the lovers, this island has exuded a magnetic charm on all who've washed up here across the centuries. Whether hiking between time-warp villages and ruins, over hillsides strewn with Jerusalem sage and wild fennel, or admiring crumbling castle ramparts and the golden glint of richly saturated Byzantine frescos, for me, Cyprus encapsulates the convoluted and fascinating history of the eastern Mediterranean, all wrapped up in one bite-sized package.

For more about our writers, see p288.

Above: Kato Drys village (p125)

Cyprus

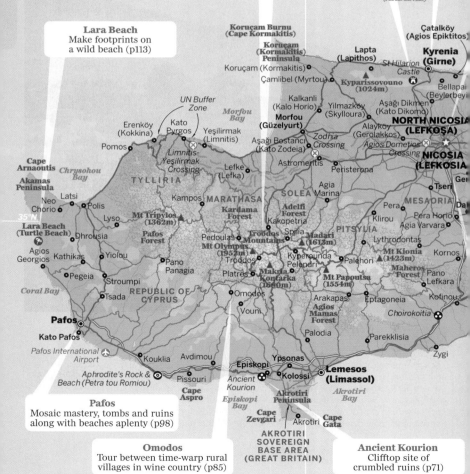

ELEVATION

- 1500m
- 1000m
- 500m
- 0

Kyrenia
Stroll the postcard-pretty
Old Harbour (p188)

St Hilarion Castle
A storybook castle with
views to match (p194)

Troödos Mountains
Fresco frippery, lush rolling hills
and great trekking (p75)

Lara Beach
Make footprints on
a wild beach (p113)

MEDITERRANEAN SEA
(AKDENİZ)

Koruçam Burnu
(Cape Kormakítis)

Koruçam
(Kormakitis)
Peninsula

Koruçam (Kormakitis)

Çamlıbel (Myrtou)

Lapta
(Lapithos)

St Hilarion
Castle

**Kyrenia
(Girne)**

Çatalköy
(Agios Epiktitos)

Bellapais
(Beylerbeyi)

Kyparissovouno
(1024m)

*UN Buffer
Zone*

Erenköy
(Kökkina)

Kato
Pyrgos

Yeşilırmak
(Limnitis)

*Morfou
Bay*

Kalkanlı
(Kalo Horio)

Yılmazköy
(Skylloura)

Aşağı Dikmen
(Kato Dikomo)

**NORTH NICOSIA
(LEFKOŞA)**

Pomos

*Limnitis-
Yeşilırmak
Crossing*

Aşağı Bostancı
(Kato Zodeia)

Zodhia
Crossing

Alayköy
(Gerolakkos)

**Morfou
(Güzelyurt)**

Lefke
(Lefka)

Astromeritis

Agios Dometios
Crossing

**NICOSIA
(LEFKOSIA**

**Cape
Arnaoutis**

*Chrysohou
Bay*

TYLLIRIA

Kampos

MARATHASA

Peristerona

SOLEA

Agia
Marina

MESAORIA

Ger

Tseri

**Akamas
Peninsula**

Neo
Chorio

Latsi

Polis

Lyso

Mt Tripylos
(1362m)

**Pafos
Forest**

Kardama
Forest

Kakopetria

Adelfi
Forest

Spilia

PITSYLIA

Pera

Klirou

Pera Horio

Agia Varvara

**Lara Beach
(Turtle Beach)**

Dhrousia

Pedoulas

**Troödos
Mountains**

Madari
(1613m)

Lythrodontas

Mt Kionia
(1423m)

Kornos

Agios
Georgios

Kathikas

Yiolou

Pano
Panagia

Mt Olympus
(1952m)

Troödos

Kyperounda

Pelendri

Palehori

**Maheros
Forest**

Pano
Lefkara

Coral Bay

Pegeia

Stroumpi

Tsada

**REPUBLIC OF
CYPRUS**

Platres

Makria
Kontarka
(1660m)

Mt Papoutsa
(1554m)

Lefkara

Omodos

Arakapas

Eptagoneia

Kofinou

Vouni

**Agios
Mamas
Forest**

Choirokoitia

Palodia

Parekklisia

Zygi

Pafos

Kato Pafos

*Pafos
International
Airport*

Kouklia

Avdimou

Ypsonas

Episkopi

Kolossi

**Lemesos
(Limassol)**

*Akrotiri
Bay*

Aphrodite's Rock &
Beach (Petra tou Romiou)

Pissouri

**Cape
Aspro**

*Epískopi
Bay*

Ancient
Kourion

Akrotiri
Peninsula

**Cape
Zevgari**

**Cape
Gata**

Akrotiri

**AKROTIRI
SOVEREIGN
BASE AREA
(GREAT BRITAIN)**

Pafos
Mosaic mastery, tombs and ruins
along with beaches aplenty (p98)

Omodos
Tour between time-warp rural
villages in wine country (p85)

Ancient Kourion
Clifftop site of
crumbled ruins (p71)

33°E

35°N

N 0 — 50 km
0 — 25 miles

34°E

North Nicosia
Twisted alleys and preserved
architecture (p171)

Karpas Peninsula
Remote, wild and beautiful with
swaths of golden sand (p221)

Zafer Burnu
(Cape Apostolos
Andreas)

Kleides

Dipkarpaz
(Rizokarpaso)

Ancient Salamis
Vast, evocative archaeological
site (p217)

Yenierenköy
(Yiallousa)

**Karpas
Peninsula**

Kaleburnu
(Galinoporni)

Yedikonuk
(Eptakomi)

Ziyamet
(Leonarisso)

Kaplıca
(Davios)

Kumyalı
(Koma tou Gialou)

Büyükkonuk
(Komi)

**Cape
Elaia**

Esentepe

**NORTHERN
CYPRUS**

İskele
(Trikomo)

Boğaz (Bogazi)

Alevkaya
Forest
Station

Yialias
▲(935m)

KYRENIA RANGE

*Famagusta
Bay*

Famagusta
Gothic splendour within
Venetian walls (p207)

Değirmenlik
(Kythrea)

Serdali
(Kiados)

Geçitkale
(Lefkoniko)

**Yeniboğaziçi
(Agios Sergios)**

Ercan Airport

Dörtyol
(Prastio)

⊛ *Ancient Salamis*

Vadili (Vatili)

**Akdoğan
(Lysi)**

*Agios Nikolaos
Crossing*

**Famagusta
(Gazimağusa)**

MESARYA

Athienou

*Pergamos
Crossing*

⊗ **Deryneia**

*UN Buffer
Zone*

Avgorou

Frenaros

Paralimni

Pernera

Xylotymvou

Sotira

Protaras

Oroklini

Ormidia

Liopetri

Agia
Napa

**Cape
Greco**

*Larnaka
Bay*

Xylofagou

**Cape
Pyla**

Cape Greco
Kayak around the
limestone cliffs (p142)

Kalo Horio

⊙ **Larnaka**

Dromolaxia

*Larnaka
International
Airport*

**DEKELIA
SOVEREIGN
BASE AREA
(GREAT BRITAIN)**

Anglisides

Kiti

**Cape
Kiti**

Mazotos

Larnaka
Dive one of the top five
wreck dives in the world (p123)

Nicosia
Contemporary cafe life and
fascinating museums (p147)

MEDITERRANEAN SEA

(AKDENİZ)

34°E

35°N

Cyprus'
Top 18

Troödos Byzantine Churches

1 From the outside, the rural churches of the Troödos appear insignificant, but don't be fooled – that's just a front for the spectacular frippery inside. From the 11th to the 16th centuries, skilled artisans went to town in isolated hill chapels such as Panagia Forviotissa (pictured; p92) creating some of the most vivid fresco finery of the late-Byzantine and post-Byzantine periods, as a wave of artistic vision rippled through these secluded hills. Today, 10 of these churches appear on the Unesco World Heritage Site list, truly crowning Cyprus as the 'island of the saints'.

Exploring the Karpas Peninsula

2 With its spine of cliffs tapering out to fields filled with wildflowers and rare orchids edged by beaches where loggerhead turtles nest, the Karpas (p221) is Cyprus at its most rural, wild and woolly. Just a handful of villages are scattered across the skinny peninsula, which stretches up the island's most easterly point where the Monastery of Apostolos Andreas faces the sea. Hike the trails here, laze on the vast stretch of dune-rimmed sand of Golden Beach or simply take time out from modern life.

NEJDET DUZEN / SHUTTERSTOCK ©

Pafos Archaeological Site

3 One of the island's most mesmerising archaeological sites (p98) is in the southerly resort of Pafos. A vast, sprawling site, the ancient city dates to the late 4th century BC and what you can see today is believed to be only a modest part of what remains to be excavated. The major highlight of the ruins are the intricate and colourful Roman floor mosaics at the heart of the original complex, first unearthed by a farmer ploughing his field in 1962.

Magnificent Meze

4 Loosen your belt buckle. Grab a few friends. This small-plates feast, made to be shared, is a taste-bud tour of the island's culinary heritage. Sweep up familiar favourites of hummus, tzatziki and tara-masalata with bread, and savour seasonal vegetables doused in lashings of garlic, lemon and olive oil. Then get ready for the parade of meat or fish dishes waiting in the wings. It adds up to a lot of food, so *siga, siga* (slowly, slowly) does it. Sample meze at its best at long-time favourite Zanettos Taverna (p160) in Nicosia.

Kyrenia's Old Harbour

5 Backdropped by jagged mountains and overlooked by a golden-stoned castle, Kyrenia's Old Harbour (p191) evokes an aura of bygone Cyprus. Where merchant ships once fought for space, an armada of bobbing gülets (traditional wooden ships) now moor. Hugging the waterfront, tall stone-cut buildings which once stored raw carob have been reinvented as cafes and restaurants. On a blue-sky day, with sunlight sparkling on the mirror-calm water, it may just be the most photogenic spot on the island. Kyrenia Castle (p188)

Navigating North Nicosia

6 Crossing the Green Line from Nicosia (Lefkosia) into North Nicosia (Lefkoşa; p171), the Turkish Cypriot side of the capital, is an extraordinary experience. Leave the smart shops of the Republic's Ledra St behind and enter the altogether more ramshackle world of Arasta Sokak, lined with scruffy bazaar stalls. Here lies some of the city's best-preserved architecture, including the soaring Gothic Selimiye and Haydarpaşa Mosques and the trade-caravan remnants of the Büyük Han (pictured).

WILDSTRAWBERRY / SHUTTERSTOCK ©

Roaming Cape Greco

7 Southeast of Agia Napa, the beach-party music fades away and trails lead out along the rocky limestone headland of Cape Greco National Park (p142). Kayaking around the cape gets you up-close-and-personal with dramatic cliff faces, whittled away by wind and sea, while the coastal walks and cycling tracks, rimmed with wild thyme and low-lying scrub, lead to church ruins, sea caves, beaches and natural rock formations. To cool off afterwards, head down to Konnos Beach, the prettiest strip of white sand in the area.

Ruins of Ancient Kourion

8 Founded in neolithic times and gloriously perched on a hillside overlooking the sea, Ancient Kourion (p71) flourished under the Mycenaeans, Ptolemies, Romans and Christians. This is the most spectacular of the South's archaeological sites, including some well-preserved mosaics, an early-Christian basilica and a theatre with sweeping views that still hosts opera under the stars. After exploring the site, take a dip in the sea at nearby Kourion Beach, where you can find ruins of a port basilica dating from around the 6th century.

Historic Famagusta

9 Enclosed within the mammoth bulk of its Venetian walls, Famagusta's Old Town (p207) is a ghost of its once grand and gilded past. Wind your way down narrow rickety alleyways roamed by rowdy chickens to find shells of churches, with still-standing walls holding on to scraps of faded frescos. Rising above the dilapidated remnants is the swaggering Gothic spectacle of the Lala Mustafa Paşa Camii (originally St Nicholas Cathedral), standing like a lonely sentinel to the lavish excess of the Lusignan era.

Hiking in the Troödos

10 The Troödos Mountains (p75) offer an expanse of flora, fauna and geology across a range of pine forests, waterfalls, rocky crags and babbling brooks. The massif and summit of Mt Olympus, at an altitude of 1952m, provide spectacular views of the southern coastline and the cool, fresh air is a welcome respite from summer heat. Ramblers, campers, flower-spotters and birdwatchers alike will be absorbed by the ridges, peaks and valleys that make up the lushest and most diverse hiking and nature trails on the island.

SANCHIK / SHUTTERSTOCK ©

St Hilarion Castle

11 Local lore says St Hilarion (p192) was created by a fairy queen who spent her spare time seducing unwitting shepherds. With its crumbled walls snaking up the craggy cliff, peppered with half-ruined towers, it does indeed look like the castle of your imagination. Keeping a watchful eye over the Mediterranean for centuries, it was built by the Byzantines with sprinkles of Gothic pomp applied by the later Lusignans. Puff your way up precipitous staircases right to the top for sweeping views across the sea to the Anatolian coast.

Lovely Lara Beach

12 The Akamas Peninsula is largely unburdened by development and access to Lara Beach (p111) is via a rough road, backed by desertlike scrubland, studded with gorse, bushy pines and seasonal wildflowers. This beach is widely considered to be the Republic's most spectacular, and thankfully remains relatively untouched by tourism. Cupped by limestone rocks, the sand is soft and powdery and the sea is warm and calm. It's a magical place at sunset. Tread carefully though – this is prime turtle-hatching ground.

Windsurfing

13 With this much coastline, and every kind of wind and wave condition a water-sports junkie could want, it's no surprise that Cyprus has become a top windsurfing spot. For total beginners Pissouri Bay (p73), with its calm, sheltered waters, is one of the best places on the island to learn the ropes. Once you've conquered wind-god Aeolus' lighter blows though, the high wind conditions off Lady's Mile Beach make it the local in-the-know place for serious flat-water-blasting fun.

Shipwreck Diving

14 Thanks to silted-up ancient ruins, old shallow ports and plain old dodgy navigating, the waters surrounding the Cypriot coastline are a wreck-diving dream. The battered husks of sunken ships which never made it to port are now patrolled by shoals of flitting fish and the occasional octopus acting as crew. Larnaka Bay's Zenobia (pictured; p125), which capsized in 1980, is rated as one of the world's top-five wreck dives. Exploring its innards, complete with cargo decks of trucks, is one of the island's eeriest adventures.

Neolithic Site of Choirokoitia

15 Unesco World Heritage Site Choirokoitia (p132) is one of the most important and best-preserved prehistoric settlements in the Mediterranean. It dates to around 7000 BC and offers an incredible insight into the lives and living conditions of some of the first Cypriots. Visitors can wander the ruins of the cylindrical flat-roofed huts, which sit on a protected hillside within the boundaries of an ancient wall. Using original methods, archaeologists have helped construct five replica huts on-site, which further enliven the experience.

Seaside Salamis

16 The once-proud beacon of Hellenic civilisation and culture on the island, Ancient Salamis (p217) was the most famous and grandiose of the ancient city-kingdoms. Today the vast site, set beside the sea, is scattered with the debris of all who set their sights on Cyprus; through Mycenaean Greek settlers up to Byzantine rule. Roam the trails which branch out from the grand columned gymnasium to explore Roman villas, mosaic-floor scraps, Byzantine basilicas and a vast reservoir and ponder the passing of empire. Roman theatre (p217)

Wine Villages

17 The far-reaching vineyards of the *krasohoria* (wine villages) dominate the surrounding slopes of Omodos (p85). Navigating this region, where every house was once said to have its own winemaking tools, is an adventure that requires discipline and good use of the spittoon. Boutique wineries now number over 50 here, spread across six or seven traditional villages, with a vast array of wines and grapes for the connoisseur's choice. The most famous indigenous varieties derive from the mavro (dark-red grape) and xynisteri (white grape) vines, along with another 10 varieties. Omodos village

Petra tou Romiou

18 Also known as Aphrodite's Rock & Beach (p74), this is where myth says the goddess of love emerged from the sea before setting off on her bed-hopping romps. Unsurprisingly, the romantic connections and cliff-fringed coastal view make it possibly Cyprus' most famous photo stop, particularly at sunset. Take the time to stroll along the pretty pebble beach, lapped by delightfully cool water and loomed over by its striking sea stack, to admire Aphrodite's dramatic choice of an entrance up close.

Need to Know

For more information, see Survival Guide (p257).

Currency
Republic of Cyprus:
euro (€)
Northern Cyprus:
Turkish lira (TL)

Language
Republic of Cyprus:
Cypriot Greek, English
Northern Cyprus:
Turkish

Visas
Generally no restrictions
for stays up to three
months in the Republic
and in Northern Cyprus.

Money
Credit cards are
accepted in most
hotels, restaurants and
larger shops throughout
Cyprus and ATMs are
widely available.

Mobile Phones
If you don't want to pur-
chase a local SIM card,
pay-as-you-go mobiles
with credit are available
from €25.

Time
Eastern European Time
(GMT/UTC plus two
hours)

When to Go

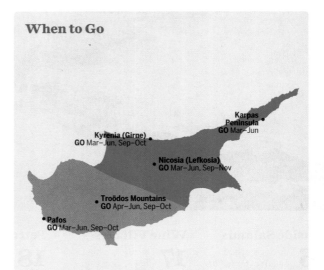

Karpas Peninsula
GO Mar–Jun

Kyrenia (Girne)
GO Mar–Jun, Sep–Oct

Nicosia (Lefkosia)
GO Mar–Jun, Sep–Nov

Troödos Mountains
GO Apr–Jun, Sep–Oct

Pafos
GO Mar–Jun, Sep–Oct

 Dry climate
Warm to hot summers, mild winters

High Season (Jun–Aug)
➡ Accommodation
books out; prices
increase by up to
30%.

➡ Beach resorts are
crowded, especially
with families.

➡ Marked increase
in local tourism.

➡ Temperatures
can reach up to 40°C
inland (30°C to 35°C
on the coast).

Shoulder (Mar–May & Sep–Oct)
➡ Ideal time to
travel; pleasant
weather and fewer
crowds.

➡ Perfect for
outdoor activities,
particularly hiking
and cycling in the
Troödos.

➡ April and May
display a dazzle of
wildflowers inland.

Low Season (Nov–Feb)
➡ Skiing in the
Troödos.

➡ Can be wet and
cool or pleasantly
mild.

➡ Some hotels and
restaurants in the
main resorts close
for winter.

Useful Websites

Cypnet (www.cypnet.com) Decent round-up of destinations and tourist sites in Northern Cyprus.

Cyprus Tourism Organisation (www.visitcyprus.com) Official website of the Republic's Cyprus Tourism Organisation (CTO); useful for general tourist information.

Lonely Planet (www.lonely planet.com/cyprus) Destination information, hotel bookings, traveller forum and more.

My Cyprus Insider (http://mycyprusinsider.com) Travel inspiration and tips, culture, what's-on guide and reviews for the Republic.

Welcome to North Cyprus (www.welcometonorthcyprus.co.uk) General visitor information for Northern Cyprus.

Important Numbers

Country code (Republic of Cyprus)	☑357
Country code (Northern Cyprus)	☑90 392
International access code	☑00
Ambulance	☑199 or 112
Police	☑155

Exchange Rates

Republic of Cyprus

Australia	A$1	€0.65
Canada	C$1	€0.65
Japan	¥100	€0.80
New Zealand	NZ$1	€0.63
UK	£1	€1.15
US	US$1	€0.89

Northern Cyprus

Australia	A$1	TL2.65
Canada	C$1	TL2.64
Japan	¥100	TL3.15
New Zealand	NZ$1	TL2.55
UK	£1	TL4.46
US	US$1	TL3.50

For current exchange rates see www.xe.com.

Daily Costs

Budget: Less than €60

➡ Budget hotel room: €25–35

➡ Street food (souvlaki, felafel pitta): €2.50–4

➡ Bus ticket: €4

➡ CTO guided city tours: free

Midrange: €60–120

➡ Double room in midrange hotel: €60–70

➡ Meze spread for dinner: €15–21

➡ Car rental per day: €20–30

➡ Admission to top museums and sights: €5

Top End: More than €120

➡ Top-end hotel room: €120

➡ Fine dining for dinner: €40–60

➡ Bottle of wine at restaurant: €17–35

➡ *Zenobia* wreck two-dive scuba package: €84

Arriving in Cyprus

Pafos International Airport (Republic of Cyprus) Pafos Buses run roughly hourly from the airport to Pafos harbour in Kato Pafos (€1.50, 40 minutes) from 7am to 12.30am. A taxi to either Ktima or Kato Pafos costs around €30.

Larnaka International Airport (Republic of Cyprus) Buses run half-hourly from the airport to the central Finikoudes bus stop from 5.55am to 11.25pm (€1.50, 25 minutes). A taxi costs approximately €15.

Ercan Airport (Northern Cyprus) Kibhas airport shuttle has 12 services between Ercan and the bus station on Cemal Gürsel Caddesi daily (35 minutes). A taxi from the airport to Lefkoşa old city costs around 70TL.

Etiquette

If you are offered a cup of Turkish/Cypriot coffee, accept. It is considered impolite to decline.

Wait to be invited before using someone's first name.

If invited to a Cypriot's house, bring a consumable gift such as pastries.

Do not give white lilies as they are used at funerals.

For much more on **getting around**, see p265.

What's New

Cyprus' Modern-History Museum

The Centre of Visual Arts & Research (CVAR) weaves the story of modern Cyprus, from the early European travellers who were beguiled by this island up to the British colonial era, told through art galleries and fascinating exhibits of documents and artefacts of the era. (p151)

Famagusta's Old Town Guesthouses

Sleeping within the Venetian-walled Old Town is finally an option – and a tempting one at that, with a clutch of quirky, intimate guesthouses now open for business in Famagusta (Gazimağusa). (p207)

Troödos Geopark

An old asbestos mine gets a new, and much more environmentally friendly, lease of life, transformed into a geological garden with plenty of information on the flora and fauna of the Troödos region. (p84)

Microbrewing in Nicosia

We love a cold Keo as much as the next person. But handcrafted, nonfiltered beers, brewed on-site in Nicosia's Old City? Yes please. Craft beers finally hit the capital with Pivo Microbrewery. (p161)

Fengaros

Rock, jazz and alternative folk. The village of Kato Drys now plays host to one of the coolest summer music festivals in the Med. (p129)

Roman Theatre, Pafos

The 11-year excavation on Fabrica Hill has finally finished, to reveal what's thought to be the oldest Roman Theatre on the island, along with fragments of the Roman city including a Roman road and nymphaeum (public fountain). (p104)

North Nicosia's Old City Rejuvenation

A handful of hip cafes are breathing new life into North Nicosia's Old City centre, while two utterly charming boutique hotels have opened in the alleys within the Venetian walls. The restoration of Arabahmet's Armenian Church is now open to the public. (p180)

Monastery of Apostolos Andreas, Karpas Peninsula

The four-year restoration of this major pilgrimage site, right at the island's eastern tip, was completed in 2016. (p222)

Jeep Tours, Kyrenia

See the lesser-seen sights of the northwest, with plenty of scenic views along the way, on these fun jeep tours which run out of Kyrenia. (p191)

Buffer Fringe

This new festival is a celebration of cutting-edge and innovative performance art, held in the UN Buffer Zone between Nicosia and North Nicosia. (p158)

For more recommendations and reviews, see lonelyplanet.com/cyprus

If You Like...

Archaeology

The wealth of ancient sites in Cyprus makes it one of the most rewarding destinations for archaeology and history enthusiasts.

Ancient Salamis Hike through the mind-boggling sweep of ruins left over from the island's grandest ancient city-kingdom. (p217)

Ancient Kourion Coastal views from the theatre, well-preserved mosaic floors and fascinating column-strewn Hellenistic and Roman remains. (p71)

Pafos Archaeological Site An exquisite collection of mosaics and remains which rumble back to the 4th century BC. (p98)

Tombs of the Kings Evocative and well-preserved underground tombs and chambers. (p102)

Ancient Vouni Atmospheric, lonely clifftop site with panoramic views. (p205)

Hrysopolitissa Basilica & St Paul's Pillar Large and fascinating site which encompasses foundations of a 4th-century basilica and more. (p102)

Choirokoitia Modest-looking but incredibly significant neolithic site dating to 7000 BC. (p134)

Beaches

Deciding on a beach depends on how you want your sand-between-the-toes day out...

Lara Beach The Republic's most spectacular beach, cupped by limestone rocks, with golden, powdery and pristine sand. (p113)

Aphrodite's Rock & Beach Also known as Petra tou Romiou, this is Cyprus' most famous stretch of sand. (p74)

Golden Beach (Nangomi Bay) The longest beach on the island, with miles of sand, curving dunes and wild donkeys. (p222)

Konnos Beach Curvy strip of white sand with plenty of pedalo fun and water sports. (p142)

Fig Tree Bay Busy, fine-sand beach. Supershallow at the shoreline, so great for families with little ones. (p143)

Alagadı Beach A wild sweep of sand where sunbathers are few and far between. (p196)

Arts & Crafts

From Byzantine frescos and contemporary art spaces, to traditional craftwork which still thrives today, Cyprus' proud artistic heritage is worth exploring.

Byzantine Art Museum Icon-tastic. The best place to take in the full scope of Byzantine-era artistry. (p150)

Lefkara Traditional lace-making lives on in this cobblestone village. (p135)

Loukia & Michael Zampelas Art Museum Permanent collection of contemporary Cypriot art plus temporary exhibitions by upcoming artists. (p155)

Skala Larnaka's Skala is prime hunting ground for Cypriot ceramics, both traditional and contemporary. (p127)

Agios Ioannis Lambadistis Monastery Vivid late-Byzantine and post-Byzantine frescos, all with deep-navy-blue backgrounds. (p89)

Büyük Han Shop in a restored Ottoman caravanserai now chock-a-block with traditional craft workshops. (p173)

Municipal Folk Art Museum This tiny Lemesos museum holds some seriously stunning pieces of *tornaretto* embroidery. (p60)

Cyprus Handicrafts Centre Watch local craft artisans at work at this reliable one-stop souvenir-shopping choice. (p165)

Wine

The island's winemaking tradition goes back to antiquity. Pick up the local Republic of Cyprus tourist information booklet outlining six wine routes and hit the trails.

Lemesos Wine Festival Taste a range of local tipples at this annual festival. Dionysus would be proud. (p63)

Around Omodos Explore the wine villages that surround Omodos on the southwest flank of the Troödos Mountains. (p85)

Pitsylia Cyprus' sweet Commandaria wine at Pelendri's Tsiakkas Winery and award-winning tipples at Kyperounda. (p93)

Cyprus Wine Museum The place to come if you fancy tasting (and learning about) the local tipple. (p70)

Being Pampered

Having your partner rub sunscreen on your back is a start but not quite in the same indulgence league as a having a chocolate massage in candlelight.

Hamam Omerye Indulge in a traditional soak, scrub and massage in this 16th-century hammam (Turkish bath). (p156)

Büyük Hamam Ease tired travelling muscles with a pummelling from the masseurs at this Ottoman-era bath. (p175)

Hamam Inn Bar You've had a hammam massage, now enjoy a sunset drink inside a 17th-century Turkish bath. (p216)

Limassol Marina Even if you don't have your own yacht, you can live the high life with the nautical set at the swanky Lemesos marina. (p64)

Top: Limassol Marina, Lemesos (p64)

Bottom: Tombs of the Kings, Pafos (p102)

Cyprus Yacht Charters Contact these pros if you want to seriously splash out on a private yacht with captain and crew. (p105)

Tantalising the Taste Buds

Cyprus is home to a culinary culture which fuses Greek, Turkish and Middle Eastern influences to create a cuisine that sums up the sun-drenched days of the Mediterranean.

Seafood meze At **Trata Fish Tavern** enjoy a smorgasbord of the tastes of the sea, from red mullet to prawns and octopus. (p64)

Kleftiko Lamb and potatoes, slow-cooked in a marinade of garlic, lemon and olive oil at **Hondros**. (p107)

Full kebab At **Niazi's**, kebab and meze collide in carnivore heaven. (p192)

Haloumi (in Greek; hellim in Turkish) Made from goat's or ewe's milk. The homemade version at **Mousikos Tavern** kicks shop-bought out the window. (p144)

Koupes Have the perfect midafternoon snack at **Alasia**; spiced mincemeat wrapped in cracked wheat and deep-fried. (p130)

Molohiya Try this viscid jute-leaf and meat stew at **Saraba**. You'll either love it or hate it. (p177)

PLAN YOUR TRIP IF YOU LIKE...

Month by Month

January

Weather-wise January is generally mild, but the Troödos Mountains can be snow-capped so remember to pack your skis. Tourism is down and some resort-based restaurants and hotels are closed.

Epiphany

On 6 January, religious processions celebrating Jesus' baptism wind their way to the shore at Agia Napa, Larnaka, Lemesos, Pafos and Polis where the holy cross is ceremonially thrown into the sea and then retrieved by young male divers.

February

The weather is mild, so good for cycling and hiking the trails (although it can be wet). It's also fiesta time with the high-octane annual carnival.

Lemesos Carnival

Fancy-dress parades, festive floats and carafe-loads of partying on the streets, the Lemesos Carnival is a fabulous family-geared celebration. (p63)

Green Monday

The first day of Lent is marked throughout the South by Greek Cypriots taking the day off and flocking to the countryside for a meat-free picnic, an unusual feast for an island of carnivores.

March

Enjoy wildflowers, particularly orchids, with more than 32 endemic varieties. Birdwatching, hiking and the occasional sunbed on the sand make this a good month for a spring break.

Marathon Season

Like some coastal views with your run? Both the **Limassol Marathon** (www.limassolmarathon.com.cy), along the Lemesos coastline, and the **Logicom Cyprus Marathon** (https://logicomcyprusmarathon.com), with a route stretching from Petra tou Romiou to Pafos harbour, are on this month.

Cyprus Walking Festival

Pack your hiking shoes. Geared towards all levels of fitness, the Cyprus Walking Festival offers a program of walking tours in the Akamas, Troödos Mountains and Cape Greco with free transport to boot.

April

The temperature can be perfect but expect crowds and a hike in flight and accommodation prices; it's school-holiday time during the Easter break.

Easter Parades

Chocolate eggs take a back basket during Easter week, when there are solemn parades with religious floats adorned with elaborate floral decorations, culminating in a spectacular firework finale. This is the most important religious festival for Greek Cypriots.

☆ Cyprus Film Days

Movie fans get a treat with this festival's 10-day program of award-winning films, screened in both Nicosia (Lefkosia) and Lemesos.

May

A great month to visit, with plenty of towel space on the sand, an average temperature of 26°C and warmer evenings for dining alfresco.

☆ Bellapais Music Festival

The arches of Bellapais Abbey are an atmospheric and fittingly regal venue for this feast of classical music and choirs which runs across May and June. (p200)

☆ International Pharos Chamber Music Festival

This swag of chamber-music concerts by internationally acclaimed classical musicians is held in both Nicosia (Lefkosia) and Kouklia village, in the Pafos district. (p156)

☆ Classic Cars

Grab the tweed cap and don the shades – in May the **Historic Car Rally** (www.lespafipa.org) takes place, covering 300km across the island.

☆ Street Life Festival

Live music and street performers take over town and there's plenty of arty fun to be had at this one-day festival in Lemesos. (p63)

June

The weather is a delight with an average of 11 hours of sunshine daily. Book accommodation well ahead: it's the start of serious summer hols.

☆ Kataklysmos Festival

Particularly appropriate for this sunny time of year, *kataklysmos* (meaning 'deluge' in Greek) is a traditional celebration of Noah and his escape from the flood. Rather the opposite takes place, however, with good-humoured water fights and water-based activities in Larnaka. (p129)

☆ Güzelyurt Orange Festival

Running since 1977, the Güzelyurt Portakal Festivali at the end of the month offers a street-party atmosphere and a schedule of activities and tournaments for kids, plus music concerts in the evenings.

☆ Shakespeare at Curium

Every June one of the Bard's famous plays has a three-night run in the wonderfully dramatic location of Ancient Kourion's theatre (www.shakespeare atcurium.com).

July

The mercury is rising but the average temperature in the southern resorts is still a tolerable 32°C. This is the best month for music lovers, with several world-class festivals.

☆ International Famagusta Art & Culture Festival

The North's biggest festival is the International Famagusta Art & Culture Festival, with a program of concerts ranging from orchestras to modern rock taking place across July in Ancient Salamis' theatre and at Othello's Tower in Famagusta's old town. (p214)

☆ International Festival of Greek Drama

One of the Republic's major annual events, the International Festival of Ancient Greek Drama brings classical theatre to life. Productions by local and international drama troupes take place throughout the month at Ancient Kourion, Pafos and Nicosia (Lefkosia).

☆ Larnaka Summer Festival

Plenty of musical concerts, dance performances and theatre come to town when Larnaka hosts its long-running summer festival. (p129)

August

This is the month you use your umbrella – for shade: the sun is at its hottest, though it still rarely sizzles above 35°C. This is peak tourist season; expect crowded beaches and higher prices.

RAMADAN

The most important Muslim annual event is the holy month of Ramadan (Ramazan in Turkish) in which pious Muslims fast during daylight hours. As the Islamic calendar is based on the lunar year, religious holiday dates shift by 11 days annually. Many Turkish Cypriots do not strictly adhere to Ramadan fasting, and businesses and restaurants open as normal, meaning travellers in Northern Cyprus at the time are not affected. At the end of Ramadan, the (usually three-day) public holiday of **Şeker Bayram** is a time of family get-togethers and feasting, with banks and offices closed during this period.

Village Festivals

August is a popular month for village festivals. Keep an eye out for posters and ask at the local tourist offices. These annual fiestas have a real carnival atmosphere with live music, traditional dance and plenty of food and drink.

Mehmetçik Grape Festival

The village of Mehmetçik (Galateia) on the Karpas Peninsula celebrates its vineyards with food feasting, folk dancing, concerts and a King and Queen of Grape contest at their festival, held annually for over 50 years. (p223)

Lemesos International Documentary Film Festival

Screenings of the latest top independent documentary picks from across the globe, with a focus on innovative films and socio-political issues; as well as workshops and lectures (www.filmfestival.com.cy).

Fengaros

The teeny village of Kato Drys is the setting for the Republic's big modern music event. Organised by Louvana Records, Fengaros brings three days of rock, pop, dance, blues and folk to the hills above Larnaka. (p129)

September

This is still a hot and hectic month. Escape the clamour of the coastal resorts by heading inland to the Troödos Mountains for wine tasting, picnicking or gentle autumnal strolls.

Lemesos Wine Festival

Raise a glass to Dionysus. Locals and tourists alike celebrate the Lemesos Wine Festival in the Municipal Gardens with plenty of sniffing, swirling, spitting – and tasting. (p63)

Pafos Aphrodite Festival

Sneak a bit of culture into the evening after a long day at the beach. Opera performances are staged under the stars at Pafos Castle during the Pafos Aphrodite Festival. (p107)

Cyprus International Film Festival

Held over two weeks in Pafos, the Cyprus International Film Festival (http://cyiff.cineartfestival.eu) celebrates independent shorts and feature films both by local directors and from across the world, all competing for the Golden Aphrodite award for best film.

Kypria International Festival

September and October host a swag of theatre and orchestral productions at venues across the Republic as part of the Kypria International Festival.

Agia Napa Festival

Agia Napa's long-running festival brings folk dancing, concerts and a program of cultural events highlighting traditional Cypriot customs and crafts to town in late September.

October

Enjoy autumn golds and reds in the leafy Troödos with temperatures hovering around 27°C – perfect for striding out...

Kyrenia Olive Festival

Held in Kyrenia (Girne) and nearby Zeytinlik, this festival has folk dancing, shadow theatre, local crafts and other eclectic performances. You can taste olives and even help plant the trees.

☆ Pharos Contemporary Music Festival

The Pharos Foundation bring 10 days of recitals and concerts to Nicosia (Lefkosia), shining a light on talented upcoming composers and classical musicians. (p158)

November

Expect a mix of weather, including clear summer days. It's a quiet month for annual festivities and many hotels and restaurants pull down their shutters for the winter break.

🏃 Calling All Runners

The annual Cyprus International 4-Day Challenge (www.cypruschallenge. com) has four races, ranging from novice to marathon level, with routes set around the stunning Akamas Peninsula.

☆ Cultural Winter

An annual program of free concerts, recitals, theatre and dance performances is rolled out between November and March in Agia Napa and Larnaka.

☆ Buffer Fringe Festival

Just the zaniest little festival on the island. The Buffer Fringe, held in the UN Buffer Zone between Nicosia and North Nicosia, hosts three days of cutting-edge and experimental performing arts. (p158)

December

A month for family reunions, with Cypriots returning home to celebrate the festive season. The weather is changeable but overall mild with the occasional beach day – though the sea is very cold!

🎆 New Year's Eve

Fireworks and music into the night around Nicosia's Plateia Eleftherias and in other towns around the island.

Plan Your Trip
Itineraries

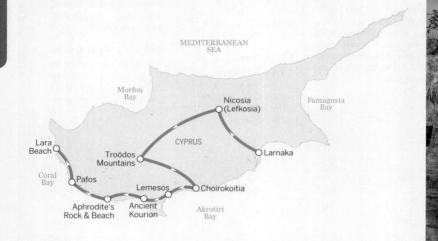

MEDITERRANEAN SEA

Morfou Bay

Nicosia (Lefkosia)

Famagusta Bay

Lara Beach

CYPRUS

Troödos Mountains

Larnaka

Coral Bay

Pafos

Lemesos

Choirokoitia

Aphrodite's Rock & Beach

Ancient Kourion

Akrotiri Bay

2 WEEKS

Top Spots in the Republic of Cyprus

Take in beaches, wide-arcing history, mountain vistas, rural villages and urban buzz, all in one swoop.

Fly into **Larnaka** for a day of beach time. Brush off the sand to discover the history behind this beach resort by checking out the Agios Lazaros and Pierides Archaeological Foundation. Afterwards, head for **Nicosia (Lefkosia)** via the cobblestone villages of Kato Drys and Lefkara. In the capital, delve into the historic Old City, framed by Venetian walls and crammed with art galleries, museums and contemporary cafe life.

Next head for the hills. The slopes of the **Troödos** hide a clutch of churches, home to fabulous frescos which fizz with Byzantine-era flair. While here, pull on your hiking boots to traverse a mountain trail or two. Roll back to the coast, stopping at neolithic **Choirokoitia** on your way to **Lemesos** (Limassol). Base yourself here while exploring the spectacular hillside perch of **Ancient Kourion** and the Commandaria region's village idylls.

Beach promenande, Lemesos (Limassol; p56)

Then veer west, getting your best goddess-of-love strut on beside **Aphrodite's rock** at Petra tou Romiou, as you hop to **Pafos**. Check out the swag of mosaics and ruins here before escaping the crowds to flop on the sand at **Lara Beach**.

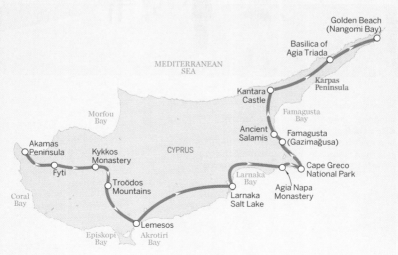

Beach promenande, Lemesos (Limassol; p56)

Then veer west, getting your best goddess-of-love strut on beside **Aphrodite's rock** at Petra tou Romiou, as you hop to **Pafos**. Check out the swag of mosaics and ruins here before escaping the crowds to flop on the sand at **Lara Beach**.

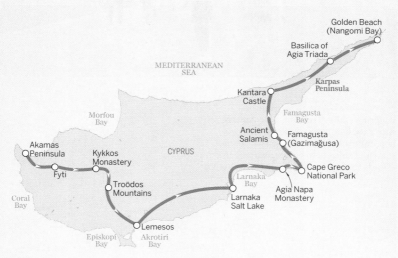

Golden Beach
(Nangomi Bay)

Basilica of
Agia Triada

MEDITERRANEAN
SEA

Karpas
Peninsula

Kantara
Castle

Famagusta
Bay

Morfou
Bay

Ancient
Salamis

Famagusta
(Gazimağusa)

Akamas
Peninsula

Kykkos
Monastery

CYPRUS

Fyti

Cape Greco
National Park

Troödos
Mountains

Larnaka
Bay

Agia Napa
Monastery

Coral
Bay

Larnaka
Salt Lake

Lemesos

Episkopi
Bay

Akrotiri
Bay

Spanning the Peninsulas

Stretching from western tip to eastern tail, this evocative journey encompasses crumbled ruins, rural vistas and white-sand stretches as it sweeps across the island.

Head up to the rugged **Akamas Peninsula** from Pafos airport. Hike in the footsteps of Greek gods on the Aphrodite and Adonis trails and throw your towel down on strips of wild and windswept beach. Then make a beeline east inland, stopping at traditional villages such as Ineia and Dhrousia on the way to charming **Fyti** to revel in the slow pace of Cypriot rural life.

Dive onwards into the sylvan backwoods of Cedar Valley to visit ornate **Kykkos Monastery** before heading to the **Troödos Mountains** to stride out on the nature trails meandering through the hills. After a few days of birdsong, forest walks and frescoed church frippery, hightail it to **Lemesos** (Limassol) to explore the nearby archaeological sites and feast on meze while overlooking the castle within the compact old town. Scoot along the coast all the way to Protaras; stopping to say hi to the flamingos at **Larnaka Salt Lake**, and calling in to **Agia Napa Monastery** and **Museum of the Sea** en route. Kick back on **Konnos Beach** for a day and discover the dramatic limestone cliffs of **Cape Greco National Park** on foot or by kayak while hanging out at the Republic's most easterly point.

Cross the border to the North to spend the night amid shattered church shards in the old city of **Famagusta (Gazimağusa)** and then crane your neck at the Gothic glory inside the Lala Mustafa Paşa Camii. Devote a day to tootling around the Famagusta hinterland, delving far back into the island's mind-boggling past at the nearby ruins of **Ancient Salamis**, **Ancient Enkomi** and the beautiful **Church of Apostolos Varnavas**. Then unplug from modern life with a journey up the Karpas Peninsula. On your way up the island's eastern tail, climb the ramparts of **Kantara Castle** and view the mosaic remnants of the **Basilica of Agia Triada** before basing yourself near teensy Dipkarpaz (Rizokarpaso) for some serious downtime soaking up the long swath of sand at **Golden Beach (Nangomi Bay)**.

From here you could zoom back down to Larnaka to fly out, or turn west along Northern Cyprus' coast to Kyrenia.

PLAN YOUR TRIP ITINERARIES

Top: Street scene in Platres (p84)
Bottom: Mosaic, Pafos Archaeological Site (p98)

Essential Northern Cyprus

2 WEEKS

Take a week to traverse the highlights of Northern Cyprus, capped by castles, scattered with lonely ruins and monuments and rimmed by beaches.

Make your first stop **Kyrenia (Girne)** to take in the old-fashioned Mediterranean vibe of this picturesque harbour town loomed over by a Byzantine castle. Base yourself here while you explore the Augustinian splendour of **Bellapais Abbey** just inland. Here you'll capture a sense of simple village life while meandering the narrow alleys which spindle up the hillside beyond. Afterwards take to the water to swim, fish and soak up coastal views with an afternoon aboard a gület (traditional wooden ship with raised bow).

Head west to the fairy-tale crumbled ramparts of **St Hilarion Castle**, where, if you puff your way up to St John's Tower, you'll be rewarded with vistas which can stretch all the way to Turkey's Taurus Mountains on a clear day. Then scoot coastwards to Lapta (Lapithos) for the night. From here, road-trip through the northwest, heading through citrus country with stops at the remarkable blue-toned frescos of **Agios Mamas Church** in Morfou (Güzelyurt) and the lonely coastal ruins of **Ancient Soloi** and scattered clifftop remnants of **Ancient Vouni**, before hitting the road to **North Nicosia (Lefkoşa)**.

Take a full day to wind your way through North Nicosia's old-town alleys, checking out the layers of history preserved in the architecture of the Büyük Han and Selimiye Mosque, then scoot east, via the ruined towers of **Buffavento Castle** sitting high on a mountaintop, to **Famagusta (Gazimağusa)**. Wander the crumbled remnants of Gothic glory of this once-mighty Lusignan stronghold and head even further back in time amid the vast ruins of **Ancient Salamis** just to the north. From here, take a drive up the remote **Karpas Peninsula** to enjoy the beaches and raw vistas all the way along this thin finger of land, capped by the lonely **Monastery of Apostolos Andreas** watching over the coast on the eastern tip. Spend the night in one of the peninsula's rustic hotels, then it's time to backtrack west towards Kyrenia, stopping at the golden sweep of Kaplıca beach and wild **Alagadı Beach**, with its official turtle-hatching program, along the way.

Top: Kyrenia Harbour (p188)
Bottom: St George of the Greeks Church (p214)

MEDITERRANEAN
SEA

Monastery of
Apostolos Andreas

Karpas
Peninsula

Kyrenia
(Girne)

Alagadı
Beach

Famagusta
Bay

Agios Mamas
Church

St Hilarion
Castle

Bellapais Abbey

Ancient
Salamis

Morfou Bay

Buffavento
Castle

Ancient
Vouni

North
Nicosia
(Lefkoşa)

Famagusta
(Gazimağusa)

Larnaka
Bay

Coral
Bay

Akrotiri
Bay

Episkopi
Bay

Off the Beaten Track: Cyprus

KORUÇAM (KORMAKITIS) PENINSULA

The last refuge of Cyprus' dwindling Maronite community, with deserted beaches and dusty villages that see few outside visitors. (p204)

KATO PYRGOS

A sleepy backwater tucked against the north-south border, where locals come to escape the hubbub, away from the coach-tour crowds. (p118)

STAVROS TIS PSOKAS

Loved by Cypriots, but rarely explored by visitors, this Tyllirian forest reserve is home to the last mouflon (wild sheep) on the island. (p119)

MEDITERRANEAN SEA
(AKDENİZ)

KORUÇAM
(KORMAKITIS)
PENINSULA

Lapta
(Lapithos)
○

Kyrenia
(Girne)
○

Çatalköy (Agios Epiktitos)
○

UN Buffer
Zone

*Morfou
Bay*

Morfou
(Güzelyurt)
○

NORTH NICOSIA
(LEFKOŞA)

KATO ○
PYRGOS

NICOSIA
(LEFKOSIA)
✪

*Chrysohou
Bay*

TYLLIRIA

Geri ○

*Akamas
Peninsula*

Tseri ○

STAVROS
TIS PSOKAS ○

MARATHASA

SOLEA
Adelfi
Forest

MESAORIA   Dali
○

*Pafos
Forest*

PANAGIA TOU
○ MOUTOULLA

PITSYLIA

○ TREIS ELIES

*Maheros
Forest*

Coral Bay

REPUBLIC OF
CYPRUS

○ LANEIA

Pafos ○
Kato Pafos ○

ANOGYRA
○

Ypsonas
○

Episkopi ○
Kolossi

Lemesos
○ (Limassol)

*Akrotiri
Bay*

*Episkopi
Bay*

Akrotiri
Peninsula

ANOGYRA

Just inland from Lemesos, this sleepy carob-producing village is a reminder of the old Cyprus – just sleepy streets of stone-walled houses and lovely peace and quiet. (p72)

AKROTIRI SOVEREIGN
BASE AREA
(GREAT BRITAIN)

LANEIA

The postcard vision of a Cypriot village, with flower-filled streets, rustic tavernas and a handful of traditional village enterprises. (p74)

0
N
0
━━━━━━━━━━━ 50 km
━━━━━━━━━━━ 25 miles

AGIOS FILON

A lovely, lonely outpost on the north coast of the Karpas Peninsula, where ruined basilicas back onto empty sands. (p224)

PANAGIA TOU MOUTOULLA

One of the least visited of Cyprus' painted churches, set in the pocket-sized village of Moutoulla. (p89)

ZAFER BURNU (CAPE APOSTOLOS ANDREAS)

AGIOS FILON

Karpas
Peninsula

NORTHERN
CYPRUS
KYRENIA RANGE

Famagusta
Bay

ZAFER BURNU (CAPE APOSTOLOS ANDREAS)

Pointing like a spear towards Syria, the tip of the Karpas feels like the end of the earth, and in Cyprus, it is. (p222)

Yeniboğazici
(Agios Sergios)

Akdoğan
(Lysi)

Famagusta
(Gazimağusa)

MESARYA

Athienou

UN Buffer
Zone

Deryneia

KOKKINHORIA
Paralimni

Xylofagou

Larnaka
Bay

Larnaka

Dromolaxia

Kiti

DEKELIA
SOVEREIGN
BASE AREA
(GREAT BRITAIN)

KOKKINHORIA

Despite their proximity to Paralimni and Agia Napa, the red villages of the Ammochostos region are a million miles from the commercialism of the coast. (p144)

*MEDITERRANEAN
SEA*

TREIS ELIES

A hidden pocket of the Troödos Mountains, where the ruins of medieval bridges are dotted through the scented forests. (p91)

Accommodation

Accommodation Types

Cyprus has a wide range of accommodation and in high summer season it is advisable to book at least two months in advance, especially at the larger hotels which are often block-booked by tour companies.

Camping The island has a handful of inexpensive campsites; facilities tend to be simple, but most are close to beaches with trees for shade.

Agrotourism Increasingly popular accommodation, typically in traditional stone-built houses; many place offer extras such as cooking courses, guided walks and horse riding.

Hotels Range from simple, stripped-back accommodation to the truly luxurious – with a commensurate range in prices. As a rule, the South offers a wider choice and better facilities than the North.

Apartments Cyprus has hundreds of apartments for rent, most with a private kitchen for self-catering, including some gorgeous apartments in traditional stone village houses.

Villa rentals Holidays villas have been built all over Cyprus, from the beach resort towns to the mountains; most come with a kitchen and access to a pool, but the minimum stay is usually one or two weeks.

Booking Accommodation

Many expats have holiday homes on Cyprus: listings of apartments and villas for rent can be found through Rent Cyprus Villas (www.rentcyprusvillas.com), Rentvillacyprus (www.rentvillacyprus.net), AirBnB (www.airbnb.com), Owners Direct (www.ownersdirect.co.uk), HomeAway (www.homeaway.com) and Booking.com (www.booking.com). You can also find lots of accommodation on www.lonelyplanet.com/hotels.

Where to Stay

With the ease of crossing the border, you can stay in the North or the South and still easily explore the whole island. In the South, families are drawn to Larnaka, Lemesos and Pafos, while Agia Napa is the heart of the clubbing scene. For culture and history, look to the villages of the Troödos Mountains or the cultured capital, Nicosia (Lefkosia). In Northern Cyprus, Kyrenia is the main hub, but you'll find more peace and seclusion around Famagusta (Gazimağusa) and the Karpas Peninsula.

Top Choices

Best on a Budget

Pyramos Hotel, Kato Pafos (www.pyramos-hotel.com; s/d from €40/50) Mosaic-tiled bathrooms add a splash of class at this cosy hotel near Hrysopolitissa Basilica.

Nostalgia, Kyrenia (www.nostalgiaboutiquehotel.com; dm/s/d 60/90/170TL) An ancient house full of higgledy, piggledy clutter, with comfy budget rooms in the heart of the old city.

Lusignan House, Famagusta (r €40, house €80) A medieval house with bright, white interiors and a courtyard full of trailing vines.

Bunch of Grapes Inn, Pissouri Bay (www.thebunchofgrapesinn.com; s/d €30/50) Country-style rooms look out over a flower-filled courtyard shaded by a mulberry tree.

ANDRIY MARKOV / SHUTTERSTOCK ©

Village, Troödos Mountains (p75)

AGROTOURISM

Agrotourism (accommodation in rural properties) took off in Cyprus in the 1990s when the **Cyprus Agrotourism Company** (CAC; www.cyprusagrotourism.com.cy), was established to stem the exodus of people from rural villages. Some 100 properties are now part of the scheme (see the website for details) and many offer guided walks and other outdoor activities and the chance to participate in village traditions such haloumi cheesemaking and olive picking.

Best for Families

Okeanos Beach, Agia Napa (www.okeanoshotel. com.cy; r from €70) A bright, clean family-friendly favourite, with balconies overlooking the pool and beach.

Brilliant, Protaras (www.brillianthotelapts.com; apt from €100) Close to the beach action and brilliantly set-up for families, with two pools and activities and entertainment for kids.

Amarakos Inn, Kato Akourdalia (www.amarakos. com; apt from €70) Air-con apartments in a wood and stone complex with a courtyard, pool and fun activities for families.

Nicki Holiday Resort, Polis (www.nickiresort. com; apt from €45) Three pools including one for tots make this a great choice for families in relaxed Polis.

Best Agrotourism

Gabriel House, Kato Drys (apt €70) Village-style cosiness, with two apartments decked out with local lace and ceramics.

To Spitiko tou Arhonta, Treis Elies (apt €75-130) An enthusiastic host offers cooking courses at this village home overlooking Treis Elies.

House of Eleni, Kathikas (www.houseofeleni. com; r from €45, house per week from €380) An old stone home with wooden beams, stone fireplaces and oodles of rustic charm.

Leonidas Village Houses, Goudi (www.leonidas villagehouses.com; apt from €50) Five traditional village homes, upgraded with a real eye for design and aesthetics.

Best for Beach Lovers

Josephine, Larnaka (www. thejosephinehotel,com; s/d from €65/75) Right in the action at Finikoudes Beach, with smartly stylish rooms and a rooftop pool and bar.

Cavo Maris Beach, Protaras (www.cavomaris. com; r from €65) A family-friendly hotel with all the trimmings, right on its own strip of Protaras beach.

Atlantic Aeneas, Agia Napa (www. atlantichotels,com; r from €140) The full Mediterranean hotel package, with balconies overlooking a giant pool, just steps from Nissi Beach.

Oasis at Ayfilon, Agios Filon (d from €40) A minimalist escape built onto the cliff above crashing waves at Ayios Filon in the Karpas.

Getting Around

For more information, see Transport (p265).

Travelling by Car

Driving in Cyprus is easy and hassle-free, though the condition of the roads deteriorates once you leave the coast, particularly in the mountains and in the north of the island.

Car Hire

Hiring a car is by far the easiest way to explore the island. However, car-hire companies are often reluctant to allow their vehicles to be taken across the border in either direction – it's usually easier to cross the border on foot and rent a car on the other side.

If you book a car before you arrive, it will be waiting for you when you reach Larnaka or Pafos (in the Republic of Cyprus) or Ercan Airport (in Northern Cyprus). Consider renting a 4WD for trips to the Karpas and Akamas Peninsulas and Troödos Mountains.

Driving Conditions

Cyprus has a handful of motorways connecting major cities, but to reach the interior of the island and remote beaches, you'll have to navigate winding country lanes. Facilities for drivers are few and far between in the remote Karpas and Akamas Peninsulas.

➡ Don't let the laid-back island mood lull you into a false sense of security – Cyprus has a high rate of road accidents so drive defensively.

➡ Both sides of Cyprus drive on the left, as in the UK. Seatbelt use is mandatory, and children under five years are banned from the front seats. Drink-driving rules are strictly enforced.

RESOURCES

Cyprus Automobile Association (www.caa.com.cy) Useful advice on road safety and legal information. Southern Cyprus only. The 24-hour road-side assistance number is ☑2231 3131.

Cyprus Driving (www.cyprusdriving.net) Extensive information on all aspects of driving in Cyprus.

Cyprus Ski Federation (www.cyprusski.com) Posts updates on winter driving conditions in the mountains.

➡ Watch for erratic driving by buses and minibuses in the North; these often stop without warning to pick up and drop off passengers.

➡ Always keep sunglasses to hand to deal with the Mediterranean glare.

➡ Note that cars can become dangerously hot in the sun. A beach towel will help insulate hot seats. Never leave children unattended in a hot car.

➡ During the winter, roads in the Troödos Mountains can be closed by snow; the Cyprus Ski Federation website (www.cyprusski.com) posts regular updates.

➡ Public car parks are found in most large towns; in villages, free on-street parking is the norm.

No Car?

Bus

Bus services between major cities are regular and inexpensive in both North and South, but few services run on Sundays, and most companies run reduced services outside the June-to-October tourist season. Less frequent local bus services connect the cities to rural areas.

Intercity Buses (www.intercity-buses.com) links larger cities in the South; private companies provide the same service in the North. The website www.cyprusbybus.com provides a useful overview.

➡ **Airport Buses** Shuttle buses connect Nicosia, Lemesos and Larnaka town to Larnaka airport. In the North, a shuttle bus runs from Ercan Airport to Kyrenia (Girne) and Famagusta (Gazimağusa).

➡ **Costs** Fares start at €1.50 in the south, or 4TL in the north.

➡ **Luggage** Buses are not set up to carry lots of luggage; a backpack is usually easier to carry than suitcases.

Taxi & Service Taxi

Kombos (shared service taxis) supplement the bus service, running between major cities for a fixed fare per seat. Call ahead to book and arrange a pick-up.

Taxi stands are found in larger towns and drivers are used to taking passengers out to rural villages.

Bicycle

Cyprus can be a rewarding destination for cyclists, with lots of quiet country roads in the interior. In the South, the Cyprus Tourism Organisation (CTO) produces the *Cyprus for Cycling* brochure, listing recommended mountain-bike rides on the island.

Bicycles can be easily hired in the South; local tourist offices can recommend operators. Bicycle hire is limited in the North. Note that cycling is prohibited on motorways. Do not expect to be able to take your bike on Cyprus buses.

PLAN YOUR TRIP GETTING AROUND

DRIVING FAST FACTS

➡ **Right or left** Left

➡ **Top speed limit** 50km/h in built-up areas, 80km/h on major roads, 100km/h on motorways

➡ **Signature car** Suzuki Jimny

➡ **Petrol stations** Common on major roads around the coast, rare in the interior

➡ **Road signs** In Greek and English in the South; only in Turkish in the North.

Road Distances (km)

	Nicosia	Larnaka	Lemesos	Pafos
Larnaka	44			
Lemesos	82	66		
Pafos	150	134	68	
Kyrenia	26	71	93	128

Don't Miss Drives

Picturesque Villages, Beaches & Wine A fine loop from Lemesos, taking in outlying beaches and winemaking villages.

Monasteries & Mountain Villages A chain of ancient monasteries, strung across the pine-scented Troödos Mountains.

Wine Route 6 A drive through mountain wineries that were old when Europe was young.

Wineries, Weaving & Abandoned Villages Dally with artisans and village vintners in the hills around Pafos.

Craftwork of Traditional Villages Meet some of Cyprus' most skilled craftspeople in the villages around Larnaka.

Combing the Northeastern Ridge & Coast Scan the coastline from romantic ruined castles on this tour along Cyprus' rocky spine.

Remote Rural Villages of the Karpas A trip off the beaten track, through the friendly, dusty villages of the Karpas Peninsula.

Plan Your Trip

Eat & Drink Like a Local

One of the best things about Cyprus is its varied and flavoursome cuisine. Cypriots love their food and take it very seriously. Celebrations and family get-togethers are rarely without an army of little plates crowding the long tables: the ubiquitous and irresistible meze.

Food Experiences

Meals of a Lifetime

Zanettos Taverna (p160), Nicosia (Lefkosia)
Where the locals come for delicious traditional meze in a warm, busy atmosphere.

Mandra Tavern (p108), Pafos Enjoy succulent glide-off-the-bone *kleftiko* (oven-baked lamb) and other traditional fare at this longtime favourite restaurant.

İkimiz (p192), Kyrenia (Girne) At this atmospheric spot, enjoy hearty and traditional Turkish Cypriot food, including *kleftiko* kebabs made in a traditional clay oven.

Stou Kir Yianni (p86), Omodos Tucked in the backstreets, this place serves superb Middle Eastern favourites such as *fattoush* (salad with fried pitta), plus moussaka, *kleftiko*...and snails.

Voreas (p130), Oroklini Located in a hilltop village, this restaurant is famed for its fabulous meze.

Cheap Treats

The following are available in both the North and South of Cyprus. In the North look for *kebapči* (small kebab shops), *oakbaş* (fireside kebab shops) or *meyhane* (taverns). In the South, seek tavernas with a traditional charcoal grill. Also look for

The Year in Food

Spring (February–April)

A good season for warming *kleftiko* (oven-baked lamb), while midspring sees the emergence of wild fennel and asparagus, as well as *koupepia* (meat and fish wrapped in young vine leaves). During Lent, traditional fare includes *spanakopita* (spinach and egg wrapped in filo pastry); the main dish at Easter is *souvla* (barbecued meat), along with *flaounes* (savoury cakes) made with cheese, eggs, spices and herbs.

Summer (July–September)

Figs, mangoes, peaches, pears, plums: there's plenty of fresh fruit around, and in September, the Lemesos Wine Festival is an appropriate toast to autumn.

Autumn & Winter (October–December)

Kick-start this serious foodie season with the Kyrenia Olive Festival, then look for freshly harvested wild mushrooms, artichokes and winter greens. Closer to Christmas, bakeries overflow with *kourabies* and *melomakarona* (almond and honey cakes), while on Christmas day, families traditionally make and smoke their own *loukanika* (sausages made from lamb and pork).

street kiosks – generally more common in Northern Cyprus.

Haloumi (hellim in Turkish) Goat's- or ewe's-milk cheese, fried or grilled and simply served often with an accompanying small salad.

Kebab Meat, generally lamb, grilled on a skewer and then served on a plate accompanied by a large salad, dressed with lemon juice.

Souvlaki Barbecued meat (lamb or pork), stuffed into a pitta or rolled in flatbread.

Republic of Cyprus

Spanakopita Spinach-filled flaky pie. Available at bakeries, along with *tiropittes*.

Souvla Large chunks of meat (usually lamb) cooked on a skewer over a charcoal barbecue.

Tiropittes Small pies made from filo pastry traditionally stuffed with local anari cheese.

Northern Cyprus

Charcoal-grilled corn on the cob Sold at street kiosks.

Lahmacun Crispy, flatbread Turkish pizza topped with minced lamb and fresh parsley.

Pide Similar to *lahmacun* but the pastry is more oval in shape and slightly thicker.

Şiş köfte Barbecued meat on a flat skewer.

Dare to Try

Don't worry: if you want to play it safe with familiar ingredients, you can in Cyprus. But if you fancy being just a tad bolder, there's plenty to consider. You could also try Greek or Turkish coffee served *sketos* (in Greek) or *şekersiz* (in Turkish), which is without sugar, so very bitter and strong.

Amelitita hirina vrasta (boiled pig testicles) Cooked with onions and celery and served with a dressing of garlic, cloves, thyme, olive oil and lemon juice.

Karalous keftedes (fried snail balls) Minced and boiled with chopped onions, potatoes and eggs, then coated in flour and deep-fried.

Karaolous me pnigouri (snails with bulgur wheat) Boiled snails which are then fried with chopped onions and tomatoes and served on a bed of bulgur wheat.

Kokorets (offal wrapped in intestines grilled over charcoal) Lamb liver, lungs, heart, spleen, glands – you get the picture – chopped into

medium-size pieces, wrapped in intestines and grilled over charcoal for approximately 1½ hours.

Mialle arnisha vrasta (boiled lambs' brains) Halved and served with olive oil, chopped parsley, lemon juice and salt.

Zalatina (jellied pork) Ingredients include one small pig's head, two pig's trotters, eight oranges and a few red-hot peppers.

Local Specialities
Republic of Cyprus

Look for the following traditional dishes on the menu. Some of these may also be included in your meze line-up.

Dolmades Stuffed vine leaves (other similarly stuffed veggies, including tomatoes, aubergines and marrows, are also popular).

Guvech A combination of meat (traditionally beef or lamb), courgettes, aubergines, potatoes, garlic and onions.

Koupepia Meat and rice wrapped in young vine leaves and baked in a tomato sauce.

Louvia me lahana Greens cooked with black-eyed beans and served with olive oil and fresh lemon juice.

Melintzanes yiahni Tasty bake of aubergines, garlic and fresh tomatoes.

Mucendra Side dish that combines lentils with fried onions and rice.

Ofto A simple meat and vegetable roast.

Pilaf Cracked wheat steamed with fried onions and chicken stock and served with plain yoghurt; generally accompanied by meat and vegetables.

Spanakopita Combination of spinach, feta cheese and eggs, wrapped in paper-thin filo pastry.

Stifado Rich stew made with beef or rabbit and onions, simmered in vinegar and wine.

Tava Lamb and beef casserole with tomatoes, onions, potatoes and cumin cooked in an earthenware pot.

Trahana Mixture of cracked wheat and yoghurt; traditionally eaten for breakfast.

Yemista Courgettes stuffed with rice and meat.

Top: Haloumi (hellim in Turkish) with olives

Bottom: Coffee shops on Ledra St, Nicosia (Lefkosia; p148)

KIRILL MAKAROV / SHUTTERSTOCK ©

SWEET DELIGHTS

Cypriot desserts reflect the rich flavours of Turkey and the Middle East. But despite these sweet delights, fruit is the most common Cypriot dessert on both parts of the island.

Baklava Filo pastry layered with honey and nuts.

Galatopoureko Sweet, sticky pastry filled with custard.

Irmik kurabiyesi Nut-stuffed semolina pastries.

Kandaifi (in Greek; *kadaif* in Turkish) Strands of sugary pastry wound into a roll.

Katméri A kind of crêpe filled with bananas, honey and cream.

Lokma Doughnuts in syrup.

Mahalepi (in Greek; *muhallebi* in Turkish) An aromatic Middle Eastern rice pudding sprinkled with rosewater and pistachios.

Shammali Yoghurt and semolina cake.

Tahinli Tahini buns.

Northern Cyprus

In more touristy resorts such as Kyrenia (Girne), be discerning with your restaurant choice; if you're opting for seafood, watch the cost: menus in the resorts frequently quote the price in grams.

Adana kebab Kebab laced with spicy red pepper.

Adana köfte Spicy, grilled ground veal or lamb patties with parsley, cumin, coriander and onions.

Dolmades The Turkish variety is meatless, stuffed with rice, currants and pine nuts.

Kebab Meat (usually lamb, although there are also chicken and fish variations) wrapped in flatbread with salad; often accompanied by *ayran*, a cool, salty, refreshing yoghurt drink.

Patlıcan Meatball and aubergine kebab.

Urfa kebab Kebab with plenty of onions and black pepper.

The Meze

Prepare yourself for an assault by food: a pleasant assault, a sampling of and gorging on around 30 dishes. The small plates may look unthreatening, but they keep on coming, promising a night of indigestion laced with wonderful taste-bud-tantalising memories.

The word meze is short for *mezedes* ('little delicacies') and is shared by the Greeks and the Turks equally. Meze is almost never served for one: two is the minimum and three's never a crowd but the beginning of a beautiful feast. Try to dine in a larger group, since sharing meze is as integral to the experience of eating it as the variety of the dishes themselves. All the passing this and passing that and shouting across the table for more tahini or bread is a true bonding experience that Cypriots share many nights a week.

First on the table are shiny olives, a salad and fresh bread, along with tahini, taramasalata, *talatouri* (tzatziki) and hummus for dipping. Pace yourself, go easy on the bread, suck on an olive or two, and crunch on a salad leaf.

Next are the vegetables. Some are garnished with lemon, some are raw, a few are pickled or served with haloumi. Sausages and Cyprus' own *lountza* (smoked loin of pork) follow. Again, eat the vegies, sample a coin of sausage and a strip of cheese, but remember, a bite of each will suffice because the biggies are still to come.

The next course is the meat (vegetarians may be able to order vegetarian meze). A meat meze is a parade of lamb, chicken, beef, pork, souvlaki, *kleftiko, sheftalia* (spiced, grilled sausage), meatballs and smoked meat. If you're having fish meze, then expect everything from sea bass to red mullet, prawns, octopus and, of course, calamari (squid).

Finally the waiter will bring fresh fruit and pastries. You will doubtless be on your last belt notch by now but, if possible, try some prickly pears – they're a real delicacy.

The best advice is to be sure not to have any lunch before you go for a meze dinner. Pace yourself and eat slowly and, as with every good meal, a nice wine is recommended, so choose a bottle and *kali orexi* – bon appétit!

How to Eat & Drink

When to Eat

Cypriots generally eat three meals daily; dinner is the main meal.

Breakfast Eaten around 8am; normally a combination of olives, grilled or fresh haloumi, bread and tomatoes and, of course, coffee. It's a wonderful combination to start your day.

Lunch Usually eaten at around 2pm or 3pm; meals don't usually last for more than an hour or so. Sunday lunch is the exception: on both sides of the island, this is when you will find entire families gathering, either at home or in restaurants, and staying for a good three to four hours, eating, drinking and chatting.

Dinner Generally eaten late, from around 9pm, which is when restaurants start to seriously fill up. This is the meal where the meze is typically served. Always shared between at least two – it's usually more like 10 – and dishes are passed around vociferously, so don't be shy to ask if you're dining with Cypriots and want to try something from the other end of the table.

Where to Eat

The taverna is where Greek Cypriots go to eat whenever they don't eat at home, and there is one in every Cypriot town and village. A taverna can be a no-frills village eatery, or a more upmarket restaurant with a leaning towards the traditional. The *psistaria* specialises in souvlaki, while the *psarotaverna* mainly serves fish.

The *kafeneio* is central to any self-respecting Greek Cypriot village's existence. Traditionally, *kafeneia* serve coffee and snacks of haloumi, tomatoes and olives, and are frequented only by (older) men.

Meyhanes are Turkish taverns where you can enjoy meze, meat, fish and anything else, swilled down with plenty of *raki* (Turkish aniseed liquor). In the North, a *lokanta* is an informal restaurant and a *restoran* is a more upmarket version. *Hazir yemek* ('ready food') restaurants specialise in dishes that are best eaten earlier in the day when they're fresh. You'll see signs for *kebapçi* (kebab shops) and *oakbaş* (fireside kebab shops) where you can watch your kebab being prepared.

Don't miss the *pastanes* (patisseries) selling sugary treats, such as *kiru* (biscuits), cakes and sweet, sweet baklava.

VEGANS & VEGETARIANS

Vegetarianism is slowly gaining attention in Cyprus, particularly in Nicosia (Lefkosia) with its more cosmopolitan populace. Many tavernas will also have an option for a vegetarian meze and, even if they don't, a traditional meze typically includes both vegetarian and vegan options. Throughout the island, Middle Eastern mainstays such as hummus, felafel and tabbouleh are readily available.

Beware of the difference between *pasta* (pastry) and *makarna* (noodles).

Drinking

Don't miss the fabulous juice bars. Mango, papaya, strawberry, guava: endless combinations are whizzed up on the spot and packed full of all those five-a-day fresh-fruit essentials, at a very reasonable price.

If you are after something stronger, locals drink at bars and generally accompany their meal with locally produced wine. Cyprus produces a wide range of red, white and rosé wines, as well as a famous sweet dessert wine, Commandaria. Spirits are also popular, particularly the famous anise-laced ouzo and the stronger grape-based *zivania*.

The most popular cocktail is Cypriot brandy sour, often cited as being the national drink and with a somewhat bizarre history. Apparently the young (and Muslim) King Farouk of Egypt, who frequented the Forest Park Hotel in Platres, used to drink this as it resembled iced tea.

Beer drinkers normally go for the inexpensive local brew Keo, although imported beers are also available, as well as the Yorkshire-style bitters produced by the craft brewery Aphrodite's Rock Brewery (p112).

Tap water is safe to drink and can be requested at any restaurant without raising an eyebrow. Locals, however, prefer the bottled variety as the local water is very hard. It is advisable to drink bottled water in North Nicosia.

Plan Your Trip
Activities

Small it may be but Cyprus punches above its weight in terms of outdoor pursuits. Whether it's sun, sand and sea on the coastline that tempts you or the rugged mountain terrain inland, this island has activities that suit every age and energy level.

Best Outdoors

Best Wreck Dive
Zenobia, Lemesos; *Vera K*, Pafos; Helicopter Wreck, Larnaka; M/Y *Diana*, Lemesos

Best Wind- & Kitesurfing Spots
Pissouri Bay, Lemesos; Protaras, Agia Napa district; Makenzy Beach (including Cape Kiti), Larnaka

Best Hiking Zones
Aphrodite Trail and Adonis Trail, Akamas Peninsula; Avakas Gorge, Akamas Heights; Kyrenia Mountain Trail, Kyrenia; Mt Olympus, Platres and the Troödos Mountains; Stavros tis Psokas forest reserve trails, Tylliria

Best Riding Centres
George's Ranch, Pafos; Moonshine Ranch, Protaras; Curium Beach Equestrian Centre, Kourion Beach

Best Cycling Routes
Troödos cycling route; Cape Greco national park, Agia Napa; Lemesos to Pano Platres cycling route, Lemesos

Beaches

The azure-blue waters of the Mediterranean are Cyprus' biggest drawcard and it's not difficult to see why. From May to late October sea temperatures rarely dip below 20°C. While during the peak summer months of July and August, water temperatures average between 24°C and 27°C, making Cyprus the perfect place to plunge right in.

In the South most beaches are well equipped with all the facilities you'd need for a day on the sand. Even quieter, less developed beaches will have one or two tavernas on hand for supplies and sunlounger and sunshade hire. From April to October the popular beaches have lifeguards on patrol. The South has 57 beaches that have been awarded Blue Flag status and 11 beaches that are fully accessible for wheelchairs right down to the waterfront; visit www.blueflag.org for more information.

Some of the safest swimming on the island is in the calm sheltered waters of Coral Bay (Pafos) and Fig Tree Bay (Protaras). Konnos Bay on Cape Greco (Agia Napa) is also an excellent strip of sand for those more interested in swimming than sunning themselves.

Although the beaches of the North have lagged behind on the development front they are fast catching up. Northern Cyprus beaches are divided into public and private. The private beaches have an entrance fee (though between October and May they are usually free) and, unsurprisingly, have the most facilities on offer. Even the public

since been used as a romantic background for underwater photography; its submerged arches are particularly special. It's also an ideal dive for beginners.

Officially called the Helicopter Wreck, this former British Army Air Corps helicopter is located 15 minutes by boat off Larnaka's shore. With excellent visibility to 25m, it attracts many divers and is a magnet for sea creatures such as octopus, jack and groper.

M/Y *Diana,* near Lemesos port, is a 15m Russian yacht that foundered in 1996. Now sitting upright on the seabed, it's frequently used for diver training and night dives. Its large squid and many fish make it popular with underwater photographers.

Just off the coast of the Karpas Peninsula, the Ancient Wreck site is just that: the excavation site of a Greek merchant ship which sank off the coast here in around 300 BC. It is the oldest shipwreck ever to have been recovered from the seabed.

beaches usually have toilets, though, and a restaurant or two which will rent sunshades and sunloungers.

Diving

Cyprus draws flocks of tourists to dive its pristine waters, which offer ancient remains, reefs, sea shelves and shipwrecks. Some of the best diving can be found along the Cape Greco Peninsula and Protaras bay.

Diving centres hiring full equipment and offering certified instruction are in Larnaka, Agia Napa, Protaras, Lemesos (Limassol), Pafos, Coral Bay, Latsi, Kyrenia (Girne) and Yenierenkoy (Yiallousa). And check out www.oceanssearch.com to stay up to date with Cyprus' diving community.

Shipwrecks

Situated off the coast of Larnaka, where it sank in 1980, the *Zenobia* is rated as one of the world's top-10 diving wrecks. The 200m-long Swedish cargo ship is now home to giant tuna, barracuda, amberjack and eel.

The *Vera K* is a fascinating wreck located 5km from Pafos harbour. This Turkish cargo vessel sank in the 1970s and has

Sea Caves & Culture

Beautiful underwater caves such as the Big Country (23m below sea level), a multilevel cave site near Lemesos, and the Akrotiri Fish Reserve (9m below sea level), are ideal dive sites for the inexperienced but enthusiastic. You can expect to see groper and sea bass among shoals of fish.

Serious divers should head to Mushroom Rocks (50m below sea level) near Larnaka; it offers mass fish sightings and canyons sprouting from the sea floor. Many of the rock formations are mushroom-shaped, hence the name.

Ancient history underwater is best found at the Amphorae Reef in Pafos (5m to 10m below sea level). An abundance of pottery and amphorae sit hauntingly on the seabed, shadowed by a wreck beached on the reef.

For marine life, Northern Cyprus' huge Zephyros reef, with its 18m to 28m drop-off, is an exciting dive while the Antique Shop site (25m below sea level) mixes archaeology with spotting shoals of soldier fish.

Wind-, Kite- & Stand-Up Paddle-Surfing

Thanks to the island's steady winds and mild weather, various forms of sea surfing (windsurfing, kitesurfing and stand-up paddle surfing) have become some of the most popular and widespread of all water sports.

The season runs from April to September with peak conditions for all these water sports from June to August.

For novices, the best location is Makenzy Beach, Larnaka, where you can hire everything you need, including an instructor. Expect to pay roughly €75 a day for equipment and tuition.

PARAGLIDING & PARASAILING

For the best bird's-eye view of the island consider paragliding or parasailing. Currently there is just one opportunity for the former, in Northern Cyprus where Highline Tandem (p189) near Kyrenia (Girne) organises tandem flights from a heady altitude of 750m affording stunning panoramic views with serious wow factor. Far more common, if a tad tamer, is parasailing, which is similar except instead of a free-flying, foot-launched glider aircraft, a specially designed, parachute-like canopy is pulled along by a speedboat; waters should be reasonably calm and participants should be good swimmers. Parasailing is offered at several of the larger water-sports centres including Columbia Watersports (p73) in Pissouri and Pafos Watersports (p106).

Experienced windsurfers and kitesurfers rate Pissouri Bay (north of Lemesos) highly for its strong wind conditions in season.

In the North experienced wind- and kite-surfers should head to the beaches on the west coast, along Morfou Bay where the sea and wind conditions are excellent.

Fishing

Over 250 species of fish enjoy Cyprus' warm waters. Many fishing villages along the coastline hire out boats, and at the marinas of the resort towns you'll find plenty of anglers willing to take you on board or on organised fishing excursions (kids welcome). These trips usually include a village lunch.

Deep-sea fishing is also possible, with bluefish, sea bass, barracuda, tuna, jack and amberjack all copious catches. In Northern Cyprus, Kyrenia is the main centre for organised deep-sea fishing trips, while in the South you'll find trips easy to organise in all the main resorts.

Mountain Biking & Cycling

Tracks through terrain that once took pack mules and camel trains are now some of the best-recommended mountain-bike areas on the island. The Troödos Mountains and their valleys take in both surfaced and unsurfaced roads. Long, sweeping and slowly increasing gradients lead up and down the mountains, providing riders with some of Cyprus' most scenic areas. Further west, the Akamas Peninsula offers kilometres of pine-forest trails, rocky tracks and twisting roads worthy of a yellow jersey. Bikes with a good range of gears, puncture kits and maps are essential.

Check out Mountain Bike Cyprus (p106) for information on bike rental, bike service and tours in the Akamas Heights and Troödos Mountains. The Cyprus Tourism Organisation (p263) also carries a handy booklet, Troödos Cycling Routes, which describes three routes and includes comprehensive maps.

The Karpas Peninsula, in Northern Cyprus, offers some worthwhile traffic-free and flat rural roads along its cape. It has the added bonus of isolated beaches along its coastline, always available for a dip in summer. Got to www.cypruscycling.com for information on cycling clubs, races and events.

Hiking

Cyprus has oodles of trails with plenty of wilderness and unspoilt nature to discover. Its many paths span the ages and history of the island, leading to Byzantine churches, picturesque monasteries, Venetian bridges, Gothic arches, crumbling ancient ruins and waterfalls, to name just a few.

In the South hikers can fully immerse themselves in the expanses of the Akamas Peninsula and Troödos Mountains. Cape Greco on the eastern coast also offers wonderful trails, filled with spring flora, leading to its majestic coast of sea caves and natural rock arches. Paths are well marked, making independent hiking perfectly feasible for the less-experienced. For serious through-hikers and ramblers, the South is part of the European Long Distance Path E4.

For those shorter on time, the Aphrodite Circular Route (four hours, Akamas Peninsula), Atalanti Circular Route (five hours) and Kannoures to Agios Nikolaos tis Stegis Church trail (three hours), both in the Troödos Mountains, all offer good walking with a good slice of historic sites thrown in.

Northern Cyprus offers walkers vast tracts of empty trails in the Kyrenia Range and Karpas Peninsula. Many of the paths are part of the way-marked Kyrenia Mountain Trail which stretches for 230km across the full breadth of the coast. The hiking industry here lacks infrastructure and detailed maps are difficult to come by so unless you're an experienced trekker it's generally best to hire a local guide.

Some of the best shorter hikes in Northern Cyprus are in the craggy hills between Buffavento Castle and Bellapais village.

Skiing

One of the most southerly ski resorts in Europe really comes alive over winter from early January to mid-March.

The spectacular 1952m peak of Mt Olympus, part of the Troödos Mountains, is the perfect venue, and its facilities have recently increased in quality and gained in popularity.

There are four ski runs close to Troödos, operated and maintained by the Cyprus Ski Club. On the north face of Mt Olympus you'll find two sweeping runs, one of 350m that's suitable for enthusiastic beginners, and a more advanced run of 500m. In the peaceful Sun Valley, on the southern side of the range, are two faster, shorter runs, each 150m long. One suits beginners and one is for intermediate-level skiers.

There's a ski shop on the southern side of the mountain with an ample supply of items for hire. The newest and best-quality equipment always goes first, though, so be sure to get in early or risk being left with slightly shabbier pieces. Check out www.cyprusski.com for ski-club information and snow updates.

Horse Riding

The island's diverse range of landscapes and scenery make it an exhilarating place for horseback riding. Cypriots' love and respect of the big animal have led to well-organised riding facilities and networks across the south of the island. The various clubs and centres offer everything from sunset rides, scenic treks, skills improvement and kids' lessons to letting you be a cowboy (or cowgirl) for a day.

Rates usually run from €25 to €40 per hour. Trails often take in ruins and the island's ancient history, which makes riding an unforgettable way to get to know Cyprus, so pony up.

Plan Your Trip
Travel with Children

Cyprus is a family-friendly destination with excellent food to satisfy even the fussiest of eaters and a broad range of attractions that appeal to adults and children alike, as well as superb beaches. Visiting as a family does require some planning, but no more than for any other European country.

Best Regions for Kids

Lemesos & the South
The city beaches offer shallow waters and plenty of activities, and horse riding and a water park are options inland.

Pafos & the West
Pafos overflows with watery activities: boat rides, fishing trips, snorkelling and a water park. Or there's the spine-tingling trip to the Tomb of the Kings.

Larnaka & the East
Older kids will really enjoy the underwater activities, plus sandy beaches, sea caves, camel rides and museums.

Kyrenia (Girne) & the North
Fairy-tale castles, deserted beaches, nature strolls, and the hulking shipwreck in the museum at Kyrenia Castle, should blow their little socks off.

Famagusta (Gazimağusa) & the Karpas Peninsula
Famagusta's medieval walled city captures the imagination. On the peninsula, stride out on endless beaches and see turtles in the wild.

Cyprus for Kids

Cyprus is definitely a family-friendly destination. Cypriot culture revolves around the (extended) family and children are adored. Expect your children to be kissed, offered sweets, have their cheeks pinched and their hair ruffled at least once a day!

Stripped back to basics, beaches, castles, ancient sights and virtual year-round sunshine are pretty good raw ingredients. Add to this water sports, museums, parks, boat rides and loads of ice cream, and it becomes serious spoil-them-rotten time. Note that the majority of theme parks and human-made entertainment for children is in the Republic of Cyprus.

Children's Highlights
Activities

Cydive (p106), Ktima Beginner bubble-maker scuba-diving courses for children aged eight years or older.

Zephyros Adventure Sports (p108), Pafos A wide range of organised activities for older kids, ranging from kayaking to trekking.

George's Ranch (p108), Pafos Horse riding for children along the nearby beach.

Theme Parks & Wildlife

Extreme Park (p156), Nicosia An enormous playground, complete with trampolines and obstacle courses.

Parko Paliasto (p138), Agia Napa A traditional funfair with plenty of head-spinning rides.

Lemesos Zoo (p61) A recently renovated small zoo with a large aviary.

Pafos Zoo (p105) A superb zoo and bird park.

Mazotos Camel Park (p138), Larnaka Ride on camels, then freshen up in the swimming pool

Water Parks

Water World (p137), Agia Napa It's big, it's splashy and it's been the recipient of a tidal wave of international awards.

Fasouri Watermania (p61), Fasouri, Lemesos Options range from paddling pools for tots to kamikaze slides for teens.

Aphrodite Waterpark (p107), Pafos Great for all ages with plenty of slides as well as shallow pools.

Museums & History

Natural History Museum (p127), Larnaka Great for kids, with a good playground and peacocks, pelicans and macaws, plus the all-time favourites – creepy crawlies.

Ancient Kourion (p71), Lemesos Let the little ones put on a show in the Kourion amphitheatre.

Kyrenia Castle (p188), Kyrenia The Shipwreck Museum is sure to enthrall kids of all ages.

Fairy-Tale Castles

St Hilarion Castle (p194), Northern Coast Walt Disney apparently drew inspiration from this castle for his *Snow White;* it's that sort of place.

Buffavento Castle (p195), Northern Coast Older kids should enjoy the hilly hike to this lofty castle, with its sensational views.

Kantara Castle (p222), Karpas Peninsula This castle has a real magical appeal with turrets, towers and lookouts.

Planning

Cyprus is an easygoing, child-friendly destination, and little advance planning is necessary. July and August can be very busy with tourists, and everywhere gets crowded during the busy Easter holidays. Late spring is a good time to travel with children, as the weather is warm enough for beach days but not too hot. Consider renting an apartment or villa with a kitchen and pool as a pocket-friendly alternative to staying in a hotel.

Beaches

Overall, beaches in the main resorts have shallow waters, bucket-and-spade-worthy pebbles and sand, various activities (pedalos, boat rides, volleyball or similar), plus family-friendly restaurants and ice-cream vendors within tottering distance of the sand.

Dining & Mealtimes

Children are generally made very welcome at restaurants, but nappy-changing facilities are rare. Cypriots like to eat late, but tourist restaurants will be open for earlier supper-times. Most restaurants have a children's menu, and as Cypriot food is rarely spicy, kids tend to like it anyway. Seek out local patisseries for savoury snacks and sweet treats.

Transportation

Car-hire companies can provide child seats. Be aware that airlines flying into the north of Cyprus have a poor record for mislaying pushchairs and child seats. Take a towel in the car to put over hot car seats, and never leave a child unattended in a hot car.

Regions at a Glance

Yes, you could just head to the beach. But there's so much more to see once you venture away from the shore. History buffs can ponder big-hitter archaeological sites around Famagusta (Gazimağusa), Pafos and Lemesos, a trove of fresco finery in the Troödos and mountaintop castles in the North. While the ridiculously underrated divided capital of Nicosia (Lefkosia) and North Nicosia (Lefkoşa) serve up architectural gems from multiple eras and contemporary culture in equal measure.

On both sides of the Green Line there are vast opportunities for outdoor pursuits, from paragliding off a peak near Kyrenia (Girne) to exploring a cargo-ship carcass on a wreck dive in Larnaka Bay. From a rural retreat in the Karpas Peninsula to easy-breezy holiday fun in Protaras, this island may be small in stature but it punches well above its weight.

Lemesos & the South

History
Food
Villages

Into the Past

Ancient Kourion is the star archaeological site with views as majestic as its past. Nearby Kolossi is a doll's house of a castle. Lemesos has Ancient Amathous on its doorstep plus its own fortress.

Cultured Cuisine

Lemesos is famed for its innovative culinary scene, particularly around the historic centre. Check out the expertly renovated Old Carob Mill.

Life in the Foothills

Some of the region's prettiest villages lie near Lemesos in the foothills of the Troödos Mountains. Enjoy picturesque cobbled streets, traditional architecture, atmospheric tavernas and fascinating monasteries tucked away in the hills.

p56

Troödos Mountains

Hiking
History
Nature

Striding Out

The Troödos is hiking heaven, with an ever-expanding number of signposted nature trails, whether you're looking for an easy half-hour ramble to a tumbling waterfall, or tackling the climb to Mt Olympus' peak.

Lavish Frescos

The vivid frescos decorating the churches hidden within these hills are an artistic triumph. Their unique state of preservation makes them one of the world's most important collections of Byzantine art.

Nature Pursuits

Cycling, birdwatching, or horse riding, or just road-tripping the villages – this region's appeal lies in its lack of commercialism, compounded by its natural beauty.

p75

Pafos & the West

Beaches
History
Nature

Sand & Sun

Pafos is all about easygoing sun-and-sand resort fun. For full facilities with beach bar on hand, stick close to town. Or head away from the crowds on the Akamas Peninsula, where you'll find stretches of sand without a sun lounger in sight.

Magnificent Mosaics

Off the sand, the haul of mosaics at the Pafos Archaeological Site should be your first stop but don't make it your only one; there are tombs, catacombs and a castle too.

Wild Countryside

For a glimpse of untamed Cyprus, head out on a hike in the Akamas Peninsula, visit the villages in the western foothills or wonder at the towering trees in the bucolic Cedar Valley.

p97

Larnaka & the East

Beaches
Water Sports
Villages

Golden Sand

West and east of Agia Napa you'll find some of the prettiest sweeps of golden sand Cyprus can offer. This is serious sand-between-your-toes country for the beach connoisseur.

Sea Scene

One of the world's top-five diving wrecks is just off the coast at Larnaka. Get up-close-and-personal with Cape Greco's sea caves via kayak or snorkelling, or try boat rides, windsurfing and kiteboarding...or just go for a swim.

Hillside Hamlets

Sample traditional life with cobblestone-alley strolls and local produce shopping (including that famous lace) amid the tiny villages of Vavla, Lefkara and Kato Drys.

p121

Nicosia (Lefkosia)

Museums
Culture
Food

Museums & Galleries

Nicosia is the cultural heartbeat of the island. The Cyprus Museum and the Byzantine Museum host a swag of riches while a bundle of small, private museums walk you through Cypriot history 101.

Cafe Culture

Street life is big in Nicosia thanks to a vibrant cafe-culture. Independent art spaces create a buzz and once the sun goes down this tiny capital punches far above its weight in a nightlife scene.

Capital Dining

Dining out is a way of life. This is a foodie city with everything from rustic home-style tavernas to industrial-chic-styled bistros serving up modern-Med menus.

p147

North Nicosia (Lefkoşa)

Architecture
Culture
History

Iconic Buildings

The Selimiye Mosque was once a Gothic cathedral and the Büyük Han showcases typical Ottoman caravanserai style. The British colonial law courts still stand and fulfil their original use today.

Local Experiences

Watch the dervishes whirl, get a rub-a-dub scrub down in an old hammam, or simply sit down with a *çay* (tea) and watch the city at work.

Abundant History

Wander towards the eastern walls to spot Ottoman houses slouching into ruins. Twist your way through Arab-ahmet for some of the best-preserved townhouses on either side of the Green Line.

p171

Kyrenia (Girne) & the North

History
Beaches
Activities

Castle Ruins

Run rampant on the ramparts at Kyrenia's castle, soak up the ruined glory atop the lonely crag of Buffavento and spiral your way up seemingly never-ending stairs to the very top of mighty St Hilarion Castle.

Beach Bonanza

For wild deserted beaches head for the coastal tip of Koruçam. Just west and east of Kyrenia there are more stretches of sand, including one of the Mediterranean's prime turtle-nesting spots.

Mountain Strolls

The Kyrenia Mountain Trail is an epic hike through the entire North, but if that's a little too rugged, the Kyrenia Range has plenty of day-hiking options offering sweeping coastal views.

p184

Famagusta (Gazimağusa) & the Karpas Peninsula

Nature
History
Architecture

Wild Landscapes

The Karpas Peninsula is Cyprus at its most remote. The beaches are wild, intrepid hikers and cyclists can enjoy rugged trails and during spring rare wildflowers bloom across the hills.

Toppled Temples

Ancient Salamis is one of the island's prime and most extensive archaeological sites and the most significant of the 10 ancient city-kingdoms in Cyprus.

Architectural Legacy

Once seen, never forgotten, the historical centre of Famagusta is an extraordinary landscape of Frankish and Venetian ruins.

p206

On the
Road

Kyrenia (Girne) &
the North
p184

Famagusta (Gazimağusa)
& the Karpas
Peninsula
p206

North Nicosia
(Lefkoşa)
p171

Nicosia
(Lefkosia)
p147

Troödos
Mountains
p75

Pafos &
the West
p97

Larnaka &
the East
p121

Lemesos &
the South
p56

Lemesos & the South

Places to Eat

➡ Mayirio Sykaminia (p64)

➡ Dino Bistro Cafe (p64)

➡ Trata Fish Tavern (p64)

➡ Kastro (p73)

➡ Kyrenia Beach Restaurant (p73)

Best Historic Sites

➡ Ancient Kourion (p71)

➡ Kolossi Castle (p69)

➡ Ancient Amathous (p68)

➡ Sanctuary of Apollon Ylatis (p72)

Why Go?

The south coast is Cyprus at its most diverse. Beaches hem the shore and offer relaxed holiday fun, while impressive sites such as Ancient Kourion showcase the island's rich history. Travellers seeking vestiges of traditional rural life are charmed by the gentle pace of the villages scattered on the slopes of the Troödos Mountains. At the heart of it all is cosmopolitan Lemesos (Limassol) and its developing reputation as a rising star in Cyprus' foodie scene.

Hotel developments may have taken over much of the coast, but drive a little further afield and the natural beauty of the region reveals itself. Beaches around Episkopi Bay nestle in against verdant farmland and dramatic bluffs, while inland the countryside rolls upward in hilly waves, with roads edged by olive and almond trees and vineyard rows.

When to Go

➡ Spring is ideal for hiking in the Troödos Mountains when the foothills are blanketed by a riot of wildflowers.

➡ July and August are the height of the holiday season, so beaches are busy. Enjoy the full gamut of coastal facilities and water sports then escape to the hills to catch a breeze in picturesque villages.

➡ Catch one of the city's annual festivals, such as the famed Wine Festival in September when Dionysus' favourite tipple takes centre stage; or the annual carnival (50 days before Easter), a wonderfully festive event with family-friendly parades and traditional music and dance.

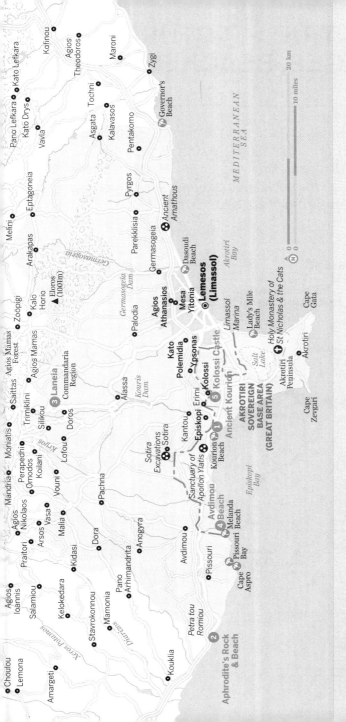

Lemesos & the South Highlights

1 Ancient Kourion (p71)
Exploring the tumbled columns and intricate mosaics, then sitting on your lofty Roman-theatre perch to enjoy the sweeping coastal view.

2 Aphrodite's Rock & Beach (p74) Going all Aphrodite and taking a dip at the legendary spot where the ancient patron goddess of Cyprus emerged from the sea.

3 Laneia (p74) Having lunch at the Walnut Tree, a typical taverna in this beautiful hillside village of honey-toned stone houses and meandering cobbled streets.

4 Avdimou Beach (p73)
Relaxing on the sand before enjoying a seafood meal at one of the beachside restaurants.

5 Kolossi Castle (p69)
Playing king or queen of the castle at this impressive historic fortress.

ROAD TRIP > PICTURESQUE VILLAGES, BEACHES & WINE

Downtown Lemesos (Limassol) might seem every inch the tourist resort, but there's a whole hinterland to explore, complete with winemaking villages and beaches where you can escape the package-tour crowds. This loop from Lemesos roams from the hills to the tip of the Akrotiri Peninsula.

1 Kourion Beach

From Lemesos, head west towards Pafos on the E602, passing the KEO winery and turning left to the signposted **Lady's Mile Beach**

(p69). After a quick dip in the sea, follow the long loop with the beach on your left to visit the **Holy Monastery of St Nicholas of the Cats** (p70). Explore the exquisite small chapel and pick up some fruit or biscuits

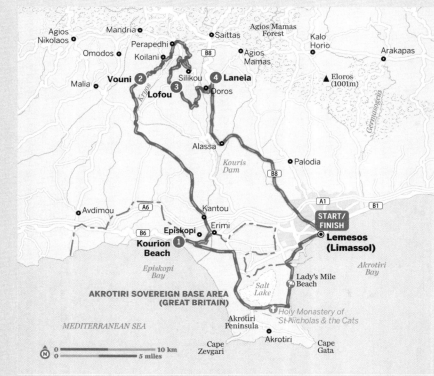

• •

for your onward journey. Continue past the salt lake to the dramatically located **Kourion Beach** (p72) for a coffee and a mid-morning snack. A visit to **Ancient Kourion** (p71) takes a good two to three hours, so you may want to save this for another day. You can get an inkling of what's to come by checking out the remains of the 6th-century port basilica backing Kourion Beach.

② Vouni

Next, double-back towards Lemesos on the B6 and take the Erimi E601 exit heading north towards Omodos, passing Kouris Dam to the east. Follow the signs to your next stop, Vouni. Take a stroll around this pretty town and enjoy lunch in one of the simple tavernas. Continue north for 5km and swing by the **Ayia Mavri Winery** (☑ 2547 0225; www.ay-iamavriwinery.com; Archimandriti Kypriano 8, Koil-ani; ⏰10am-5.30pm) on the outskirts of Koil-ani; the winery does an excellent cabernet sauvignon and its sweet muscatel has won the prestigious French Moscats du Monde award four times.

③ Lofou

Roughly 2km after this hiccup of a detour, turn towards Silikou and Lofou; the road passes through dramatic mountain scenery and terraced agriculture with distant sea views. Wander the streets of Lofou, where cobbled lanes are bordered by traditional warm limestone buildings.

④ Laneia

The next stop is lovely **Laneia** (p74), arguably the prettiest village in these parts. Enjoy a Cypriot coffee and a slice of delicious wal-nut pie in the leafy courtyard of the Walnut Tree restaurant, followed by a leisurely stroll through the cobbled backstreets. Peruse the paintings of local landscapes at the **Michael Owen Gallery** (p74) before returning to Le-mesos on the speedy, well-signposted B8.

LEMESOS (LIMASSOL)

POP 101,000

Still known to many as Limassol, Lemesos is one of Cyprus' most underrated cities. Although fringed on its eastern edge by a glut of bland-looking developments, the core is full of character. Wrapped around a castle, the historic centre radiates out in a web of lanes where old, shuttered houses and modern boutiques lie cheek by jowl. It's an area buzzing with cafes, bars and restaurants that are as popular with locals as with visitors.

This is Cyprus' international business centre and, despite the financial woes of recent years, there's again a sense of optimism in the air. Its flashy marina has introduced an atmosphere of glamour and opulence, and grittier areas of town are being tagged for a revamp. For travellers looking for a holiday that takes in more than sun and sea, Lemesos lies at the very heart of one of the island's richest areas for exploration.

History

In 1191 the crusader king Richard the Lionheart put Lemesos on the map when he defeated the then ruler of Cyprus, Isaak Komninos, and took Cyprus and Lemesos for himself.

The city prospered for more than 200 years under a succession of Knights Hospitaller and Templar as its rulers until earthquakes, marauding Genoese (1373) and Saracens (1426) reduced Lemesos' fortunes to virtually zero. The city was still creating a bad impression in the mid-20th century: Lawrence Durrell, writing in 1952 in *Bitter Lemons of Cyprus,* noted upon arrival in Lemesos that 'We berthed towards sunrise in a gloomy and featureless road-stead, before a town whose desolate silhouette suggested that of a tin-mining village in the Andes.'

Lemesos grew up quickly following the Turkish invasion of Cyprus in 1974, replacing Famagusta (Gazimağusa) as the nation's main port. It also needed to expand to keep up with the Republic's growing tourist boom. Originally comprising what is today known as the old town, around the historic fishing port, Lemesos has outgrown its original geographic limits to now encompass a sprawling tourist suburb. Signposted as the 'tourist centre', this is a riotous confusion of hotels, bars and restaurants, and you could be excused for forgetting that the sea is there at all. Not so at the city's sophisticated marina, which was finally completed in 2017 and is situated right on the waterfront on the site of the former fishing harbour.

◉ Sights

Lemesos' city beaches are popular enough and decent for a quick swim but they don't possess any particular wow factor. For a quieter and more picturesque strip of sand, look a little further afield, particularly due east towards Larnaka where you will find a fine choice of golden sands.

★ **Lemesos Castle** CASTLE
(☑ 2530 5419; Richardou; adult/child incl Medieval Museum €4.50/free; ☺8am-5pm Mon-Fri, 9am-5pm Sat, 10am-1pm Sun) This 14th-century structure, built over the remains of a Byzantine castle, has been utilised by conquerors throughout Cyprus' turbulent history. The Venetians vandalised it; the Ottomans gave it a facelift for military use; and the British used it as a colonial prison. It is said that Richard the Lionheart married Berengaria in the chapel of the original castle in 1191, where he also grandly crowned himself King of Cyprus and his wife Queen of England.

In the courtyard surrounding the castle walls there's an old olive press that dates from the 7th to 9th centuries.

The interior of Lemesos Castle contains a series of chambers on various levels that are home to the Medieval Museum. Don't miss the views from the ramparts.

Medieval Museum MUSEUM
(☑ 2530 5419; Lemesos Castle, Richardou; adult/child incl castle €4.50/free; ☺8am-5pm Mon-Fri, 9am-5pm Sat, 10am-1pm Sun) This museum is an interesting hotchpotch of Byzantine and medieval artefacts, including tombstones, weaponry, Ottoman pottery, religious objects and a suit of armour (sadly a copy).

Municipal Folk Art Museum MUSEUM
(Agiou Andreou 123; adult/child €2/free; ☺8am-2.30pm Mon-Fri) Spread over six rooms and a past winner of the prestigious Europa Nostra Award (EU prize for cultural heritage), this museum hosts beautiful ethnographical displays of traditional costumes, furniture and agricultural implements as well as some stunning examples of *tornaretto* embroidery (a traditional style of silk needlework) and other textiles. The museum is set in a finely restored stone house that showcases the typical architecture of old Lemesos.

Archaeological Museum
MUSEUM

(☑ 2530 5157; cnr Vyronos & Kaningos; adult/child €2.50/free; ☺ 9am-4.30pm Mon-Sat) This museum includes an extensive collection of pottery, and a selection of items dating from neolithic and chalcolithic times through to Mycenaean pottery. A multitude of terracotta figures on show are thought to be the remains of votive offerings. There is a display of classical pottery, jewellery and oil lamps, as well as curiously modern-looking glass bottles and vials, and a touchingly mundane pair of tweezers. At the other extreme are the Greek and Roman statues from Ancient Amatheus.

Although it pales in comparison to Nicosia's Cyprus Museum, this museum is well worth a browse for anyone interested in the region's fascinating history.

Grand Mosque
MOSQUE

(Kebir Camii; Ankara) At the heart of the old Turkish quarter, the Grand Mosque is surrounded by palms almost as tall as its minaret. It is used by Lemesos' remaining Turkish Cypriot population and resident Muslims who have come from the Middle East. As with any mosque, visitors are requested to dress conservatively; leave shoes by the door and avoid visiting at prayer times. There are no fixed opening hours; if the gate is open, step within and take a look.

Recent excavations have revealed the architectural remains of the 10th-century cathedral of Agia Ekaterini below the east side of the mosque.

Cyprus Theatre Museum
MUSEUM

(☑ 2534 3464; www.cyprustheatremuseum.com; Pano Solomonides 8; adult/child €3/1; ☺ 9am-1pm Mon-Fri, 4-7pm Tue & Fri) This former private collection belonging to an enthusiastic amateur actor offers a fascinating glimpse into the history of theatre in Cyprus through photographs, scale models, costumes, posters and audiovisual exhibits. The collection stretches back to the ancient theatres of the Hellenistic and Roman periods and ends with the current theatre culture in Cyprus, which is happily thriving.

Lemesos Zoo
ZOO

(☑ 2558 8345; www.limassolzoo.com; Municipal Gardens; adult/child €5/2.50; ☺ 9am-noon & 3-7pm May-Sep, 9am-6.30pm Oct-Apr; ☐ ☐) This small zoo is well maintained and has a selection of animals ranging from giraffes to crocodiles. Pony rides are available for kids (€3) and there's also a handy large playground right next door. The zoo is within Lemesos' leafy Municipal Gardens, 1.5km from the central old town by walking along seafront Christodoulou Hatzipavlou.

Natural Sea Sponge Exhibition Centre
MUSEUM

(☑ 2587 1656; www.apacy.com; Old Port Exhibition Centre, Agias Theklis; ☺ 9am-7pm Mon-Fri, to 3pm Sat; ☐) This exhibition goes through the process of sea-sponge harvesting, and how the living creatures become the soft things we use in our baths. The cartoon, duly dedicated to a talking sponge, will amuse younger kids. Naturally enough, you can purchase sponges here too.

🏃 Activities

Crest Dive Centre
DIVING

(☑ 2563 4076; www.crestdive.com; St Raphael Marina, Amathous; ☺ 9am-6pm) This five-star Professional Association of Diving Instructors (PADI) centre offers the gamut of PADI courses as well as a good range of diving and snorkelling trips. Discover scuba, for beginners, is €75.

It is worth noting that most of the dive sites just offshore from Lemesos are perfect for beginners, including Marina Wall (a favoured night-diving spot) and Julie Reef (where you'll usually be surrounded by shoals of barracuda and sea bream). For more experienced divers the major site is the *Diana* wreck and its plethora of resident sealife.

Dive-In Limassol
DIVING

(☑ 2531 1923; www.dive-in-limassol.com; Four Seasons Beach Hotel, 67/69 Amathountos Ave; ☺ 9am-5.30pm) This PADI centre offers the full range of PADI, British Sub-Aqua Club (BSAC) and Divers Alert Network (DAN) diving courses, including Advanced Open Water and Wreck Diving.

Fasouri Watermania
WATER PARK

(☑ 2571 4235; www.fasouri-watermania.com; Fasouri; adult/child €30/17; ☺ 10am-6pm Jun-Aug, to 5pm Sep, Oct & May; ☐) A 15-minute drive out of Lemesos in the Fasouri area, this place has all the usual watery options, including a kamikaze slide, a 'big orange wet bubble', a 'lazy river', a wave pool, and pools for both kids and adults. There are also sunbeds and parasols for run-off-their-feet parents.

If you're driving, the park is off the Lemesos–Pafos highway, 5km northwest of

Lemesos (Limassol)

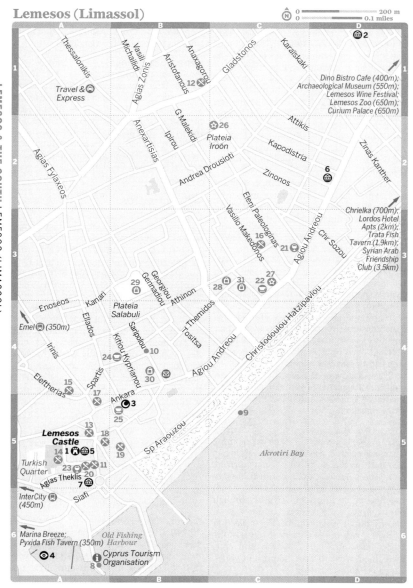

town. If you don't have your own wheels, there's a shuttle to the park; check the website for pick-up times and location.

☞ Tours

Cyprus Tourism Organisation   WALKING
(CTO; ☎ 2536 2756; www.visitcyprus.com; Syntagma Sq, Old Fishing Harbour) The CTO organises

Lemesos (Limassol)

three walking tours. These are free, but it's wise to book in high season.

The Historic Limassol Walk, at 10am on Monday, takes you around Lemesos' historic centre, monuments, markets and main sights.

At 10am every Wednesday, from October to April, there are alternating tours. The first, Germasogeia: A Village Blessed by Water, goes to Germasogeia village, with a visit to the village dam. You also get to see the architecture and street life of the village itself. The second, Discover the Natural Environment of Germasogeia, is a walk in the hills (some fitness required) along a nature trail laid out by the forestry department.

🎊 Festivals & Events

Lemesos Carnival   CARNIVAL
(www.limassolmunicipal.com.cy/carnival) Lemesos is the only town in Cyprus with a full-blown carnival atmosphere, which is enjoyed particularly by children. The 11-day carnival, held 50 days before Easter, starts with the 'King of the Carnival' entering town, escorted by a motley parade. There's also a children's carnival parade. Festivities close with a fancy-dress extravaganza.

Street Life Festival   ART
(www.facebook.com/streetlifefest; Saripolou; ⊙early May; ⊛) This one-day festival on a Saturday in early May celebrates street art

with the chance to contribute to a giant graffiti mural (bring your own paints), plus brings live music, jugglers and craft stores.

Kataklysmos Festival   RELIGIOUS
(Flood Festival; www.cyprusevents.net; ⊙mid-Jun) Lemesos is one of the best places in Cyprus to experience the Kataklysmos festivities, commemorating both the biblical flood of Genesis and the Greek myth of Deukalion. Celebrations take place over three days in mid-June on the seafront and include boat races and folk dancing.

Lemesos Wine Festival   WINE
(www.limassolmunicipal.com.cy/wine; Municipal Gardens; ⊙Aug & Sep) Held annually from 30 August to 11 September, this festival provides a chance to sample a wide range of local wines. As you might predict, the festival is extremely popular with young, fun-seeking tourists, here for the Cypriot food, traditional music and dancing, and did we mention the wine?

Musical Sundays   MUSIC
(www.visitcyprus.com; Limassol Coastal Rd; ⊙Feb-May, Nov & Dec) Throughout spring, autumn and winter the CTO organises a series of free concerts every Sunday at the Onisilos Seaside Theatre in the tourist area. It's a great way to experience traditional Cypriot music.

LIVING THE MARINA LIFE

After years of delays and funding problems, Lemesos' decrepit former fishing harbour has undergone a €300-million facelift. The visionary behind the massive **Limassol Marina** (☑ 2502 0020; www.limassolmarina.com; Lemesos; ⊘ 24hr; [P]) project is French architect Xavier Bohl, who based the design of the marina on St Tropez' Port Grimaud and Monte Carlo's Hercule Harbour. The result is a slick, contemporary and luxurious marina with little that looks essentially Cypriot. No worries: the deluxe apartment blocks are here; the landscaping is meticulous; and the designer boutiques are gradually moving in, together with glamorous bars and gourmet restaurants. The long-term aim of the marina is to bring life to the city centre all year round; so when the high-tourist season wanes in the early winter months, the harbour will transform into a vibrant conference and lecture centre.

To get a feel for the scale of the place, which can be hard at ground level, take a look at the model in the property sales office near the main entrance, and check out the marina's flashy website.

✖ Eating

Lemesos' culinary scene combines variety, quality and modernity, particularly in the old town; most of the tourist area's eating options are fairly forgettable. The aesthetically restored Old Carob Mill near the castle is home to several restaurants and bars sharing a cool, sophisticated vibe. For quick bites head for the pedestrian Plateia Salabuli, next to the municipal market, which is surrounded by inexpensive kebab houses, traditional coffee shops and similar.

★ **Mayirio Sykaminia** CYPRIOT **€**
(☑ 2536 5280; Eleftherias 26; mains from €6) This is an unwaveringly authentic local restaurant with a daily menu chalked up on the wall (in Greek only), paper tablecloths and faded pics of yesteryear Lemesos on the walls. The food is as close to home cooking as you will get in this town. The owner speaks some English so can help you decipher the dishes.

★ **Dino Bistro Cafe** INTERNATIONAL **€€**
(☑ 2576 2030; www.dinobistro.com; Gladstonos 137; mains from €8; ⊘ 7.30am-11.45pm; 🛜) Now in a new venue, Dino's continues to attract a loyal local following thanks to its smart but unpretentious decor, friendly owner Dino Kosti and palate-pleasing dishes. The menu ranges from east to west, including fresh sushi, pasta and a selection of innovative salads. Relax your belt a notch further and sample one of the art-on-a-plate house-made desserts

★ **Trata Fish Tavern** SEAFOOD **€€**
(☑ 2558 6600; Ioanni Tompazi 4; seafood meze €21; ⊘ 7-11pm) This is arguably one of Lemesos' best fish restaurants, particularly famed for its seafood meze. Despite the plain decor and unassuming atmosphere, the place attracts shoals of locals, particularly at weekends. It's located close to Debenhams department store, around 400m east of the Municipal Gardens.

Meze Taverna TAVERNA **€€**
(☑ 2536 7333; Athinon 209; mains €10-15, meze €10.50-13; ⊘ 11am-2pm & 7.30-11pm) This charming family-run taverna is a timeless classic serving up a traditional comfort-food menu of Greek dishes. Expect uncomplicated, fresh flavours in classics such as moussaka, or go for the old-school meze. Gracious service, red-and-white checked tablecloths and jugs of (just about drinkable) local wine complete the picture. Not to mention the steady stream of regulars.

Bono Bar & Restaurant INTERNATIONAL **€€**
(☑ 2537 8800; www.bonorestaurant.com; Gladstonos 69; mains €8-10; ⊘ 8am-11.30pm Mon-Sat; 🛜) Bono's owner spent several years in the US, where he learned how to whip up serious cowboy-size burgers and cheesecake that's reputed as the best in town. Now at a larger locale, Bono retains a global menu of curries, Tex-Mex and pasta. It also claims to have the largest beer selection in town – and serves the appetisers to go with it.

There's live music on Fridays.

Syrian Arab Friendship Club MIDDLE EASTERN **€€**
(SAFC; ☑ 2532 8838; Iliados 3; meze €15; ⊘ 7pm-11.30pm; [P]) A delight for all lovers of Arab cuisine, the SAFC puts on some of the best meze in Cyprus. Have a nargileh (water

pipe) afterwards for the full experience. On the downside, service can be a little slack and the belly dancing on Saturday night is accompanied by very loud music, which could make whispering sweet nothings to your beloved a little tricky.

To find the Syrian Club (as it's known), head east of the centre via the coast road for around 3.5km. The restaurant is located just behind the Apollonia Beach Hotel.

Il Castello　　　　　INTERNATIONAL €€
(☑2535 6222; Irinis 22; sandwiches & salads €7-14, mains €15-25; ☺10am-11pm; 🎅🍴) Don't be put off by the touristy look of this place. There is a refreshing lack of chips and a huge choice of salads, as well as some tasty sandwich and wrap combos, such as vegetables with avocado and sour cream. It's a great lunch spot for after viewing the castle. The serving staff are charming.

Stretto Cafe　　　　INTERNATIONAL €€
(☑2582 0465; www.carobmill-restaurants.com; Old Carob Mill, Vasilissis; light meals €6-12, mains €12-25; ☺10am-11pm; 🎅) This snazzy cafe attracts Lemesos' hipster set with its menu of pasta, sushi, steaks and light bites. It caters well for a thirsty clientele, with a vast selection of smoothies, milkshakes, iced coffees and cocktails, and has comfy sofas, great streetside tables and superb people-watching potential.

Noodle House　　　　　　ASIAN €€
(☑2582 0282; www.thenoodlehouse.com; Ankara 3; mains €10-15, lunch menu €10; ☺11.30am-midnight; 🎅🍴🍺) Noodle House's menu fuses Singaporean, Thai and Chinese favourites for a trip through Asia. If you like spicy – ask; the kitchen tends to tame the heat for Cypriot palates. Sunday lunch is kids' time, with face-painting and balloons. The daily lunch menu is great value.

Rizitiko Taverna　　　　　TAVERNA €€
(☑9911 1212; Tzamiou 4-8; mains from €7; ☺noon-11pm) Tucked away by the mosque on a pedestrianised street, this is a reliably good, low-key establishment with tables that spill out onto the cobbles at night. The *afelia* (pork cooked in red wine and coriander) and *kleftiko* (oven-baked lamb) are of homemade quality – or better.

★Karatello　　　　　　CYPRIOT €€€
(☑2582 0464; www.carobmill-restaurants.com; Old Carob Mill, Vasilissis; mains €12-16; ☺11am-2pm & 7.30-11pm; 🎅) A modern take on Cypriot classics is the name of the game at this stylish restaurant with a vast outdoor terrace, part of the Old Carob Mill complex. The hearty traditional taverna food here has been given a thorough touch of finesse for modern foodie palates. Be warned: the floor-to-ceiling wine display in the dining room may make you very thirsty indeed.

Pyxida Fish Tavern　　　SEAFOOD €€€
(☑2505 1200; www.pyxidafishtavern.com; Limassol Marina; mains €15-20, fish meze €24; ☺11am-10pm; 🅿🎅) Enjoy ocean views twinned with an elegant interior of white linen and fresh flowers at Pyxida, an upmarket seafood tavern and oyster bar that consistently delivers on fish dishes. Of particular note is the excellent fish meze. Complimentary desserts are generally along the lines of homemade baklava with mango ice cream.

Ousia　　　　　　MEDITERRANEAN €€€
(☑2510 9040; Irinis 30-32; mains €11-25; ☺11.30am-11pm; 🎅🍴) Set in the former stables of the castle, Ousia has a varied and contemporary menu that's far from medieval. Choose from dishes such as vegetable tagine and seafood ravioli, and Cypriot staples including haloumi (hellim in Turkish) fried with sesame seeds and topped with gooey carob syrup. Desserts are excellent too; the chocolate soufflé in particular has diners swooning.

Artima Bistro　　　　MEDITERRANEAN €€€
(☑2582 0466; www.carobmill-restaurants.com; Old Carob Mill, Vasilissis; mains €18-25; ☺noon-11pm Sun-Thu, to 11.30pm Fri & Sat; 🎅) A fashionable, upbeat restaurant with Italian-inspired cuisine. The menu includes lots of zesty pasta choices, plus sushi and seafood options with exciting innovative tweaks. Muted lighting, sexy jazz on the soundtrack and a contemporary-chic interior with lofty ceilings and exposed-brick walls equal an inviting ambience. It is busy with well- (and high-) heeled regulars at weekends.

🍷 Drinking & Nightlife

Most places in Lemesos are quiet until at least 10pm. Bars on the seafront strip are predictably tourist-geared, with bitter on tap and football on the big screen. For a more authentic Cypriot experience, head for bars in and around the Old Carob Mill and the historic centre. The city also has a handful of boho-chic cafes where you can get online, drink frappé and check out the local scene.

Antithesis
CAFE

(☑ 2536 9479; http://antithesiscoffeeshop.blog spot.com.cy; Agiou Andreou 201; ☺ 9.30am-7pm Mon, Tue, Thu & Fri, to 3pm Wed & Sat; ☎) This snug cafe whips up a mighty fine slice of cake as well as some great coffee, pots of tea and delicious smoothies. If you're peckish there's a small menu of pies, pitta pockets and soups for a tasty lunch. The owner also runs the chic homeware-cum-furniture shop next door.

Draught
BAR

(www.carobmill-restaurants.com; Old Carob Mill, Vasilissis; ☺ midnight-late; ☎) This lively place mixes up killer cocktails in cool industrial-chic surrounds, and although it's not quite the microbrewery it claims to be (there is only one craft beer on tap), it serves up a healthy selection of national and international ales. Food is also served, including platters to share.

7-Seas
CLUB

(☑ 2527 8000; www.7seaslive.com; Columbia Plaza, Agiou Andreou 223; ☺ 10.30pm-late; ☎) This hip club and venue attracts a roll-call of Cyprus' best DJs and hosts live-music events. The regular Tuesday Latin nights and Friday DJ nights are free entry. Put your gladrags on if you want to get in. Strictly no beachwear allowed.

Tepee Rock Bar
BAR

(☑ 2532 8222; www.facebook.com/tepeerock; Ampelakion; ☺ 11am-11pm) Chomp on Mexican burritos while enjoying live rock bands at this popular restaurant-bar with a great foot-stomping atmosphere. It's located in the tourist centre, around 4km east of the historic quarter on the coastal road.

Marina Breeze
LOUNGE

(☑ 2505 1230; www.breeze.com.cy; Limassol Marina; ☺ 10am-2.30am; ☎) Push the boat out and enjoy an evening of cocktails and shared platters at this chic spot overlooking the water at the heart of the marina. After dusk it morphs into clubbing mode with a nightly DJ and theme nights that range from retro '60s to chill-out smoochy.

Xoyzoypi
COFFEE

(☑ 9945 1996; Genethliou Mitella 5; ☺ noon-2am) In the shadow of the Grand Mosque's towering minaret, this traditional, dark and brooding coffee shop is frequented by a youthful local crowd. It serves drinks as well as platters of meat and cheese.

Guaba Beach Bar
CLUB

(☑ 9668 2865; www.facebook.com/guababeach bar; Agia Varvara Beach; ☺ 10pm-late May-Sep) This popular bar located 5km east of the historic centre has kick-back seating right on the beach. It hosts parties, as well as relaxed evenings, with DJs who play anything from reggae to electro, depending on the night and their fancy. It's next to the Aquarius Hotel.

Pi
CAFE

(☑ 2534 1944; Kitiou Kyprianou 27; snacks €5; ☺ 10am-11pm) A relaxed, gay-friendly cafe with a lovely garden, light meals, excellent salads, a 10-plus choice of beer, good (mainly Italian) wines and elaborate cocktails.

Entertainment

Rogmes Live Music
LIVE MUSIC

(☑ 2534 1010; Agiou Andreou 197; ☺ 10pm-5am) A highly praised bouzouki bar touting a mad, wonderful tempo on weekend nights, when the musicians stay and play as loud and as late as the crowd wants.

Rialto Theatre
THEATRE

(☑ 2534 3900; www.rialto.com.cy; Andrea Drousioti 19) Exquisitely restored to its former art deco glory, the Rialto is the main venue in town for theatre, concerts and film festivals.

K Cineplex
CINEMA

(www.kcineplex.com; Ariadnis 8; ☺ noon-midnight) The multiscreen K Cineplex shows new-release movies. It's located in the tourist centre, 6km east of the historic quarter. See the website for current screenings.

Shopping

Most of Lemesos' clothes, shoe and appliance shops are clustered along the pedestrian street of Agiou Andreou in central Lemesos. Head for the backstreets for more idiosyncratic gift shops, boutiques and similar.

Municipal Market
FOOD & DRINKS

(Georgiou Gennadiou; ☺ 6am-3pm Mon-Sat) Full of fresh produce, the restored municipal market is a must-visit for self-caterers, and is also an excellent source of foodie-style souvenirs, such as local honey, nuts and scrumptious Cypriot sweets. It's housed in a lovely old stone structure dating from 1917.

Cyprus
Handicrafts Centre
GIFTS & SOUVENIRS

(Themidos 25; ☺ 9am-7pm Mon-Fri, to 2pm Sat) This government-sponsored store is the best place for seeking out authentic, traditional and fairly priced handmade crafts.

Pana's Patchwork   FASHION & ACCESSORIES
(📷 9941 6733; www.panas-creations.com; Saripolou 21; ⊙9am-7pm Mon, Tue, Thu & Fri, to 2pm Wed & Sat) Crammed with a colourful jumble of ornaments, tapestries, dolls and embroidered pieces, all made by the owner, Pana.

Violet's Second Hand Shop   CLOTHING
(Salaminos 10; ⊙9am-6pm Mon-Fri, to 2pm Sat) A great place for clothes and jewellery, including some interesting Cypriot vintage pieces.

❶ Information

Internet access is widely available at hotels, restaurants and cafes throughout the city.

Bank of Cyprus (www.bankofcyprus.com; Agiou Andreou; ⊙8.30am-1.30pm Mon-Fri) Centrally located and handy for its ATMs and currency exchange.

Cyprus Tourism Organisation (CTO; 📷 2536 2756; www.visitcyprus.com; Syntagma Sq, Old Fishing Harbour; ⊙8.15am-2.30pm & 3-6pm Mon, Tue, Thu & Fri, to 2.30pm Wed, to 1pm Sat Apr-Oct, shorter hours Nov-Mar) Also has a branch in the **tourist centre** (CTO; 📷 2532 3211; www.visitcyprus.com; Georgiou 1, 22a; ⊙8.15am-2.30pm & 3-6pm Mon, Tue, Thu & Fri, to 2.30pm Wed, to 1pm Sat Apr-Oct, shorter hours Nov-Mar). Both centres have helpful staff and good maps.

Post Office (Saripolou; ⊙7.30am-1.30pm & 3-5.30pm Mon-Fri) Centrally located. Note that you can also buy stamps at newsagents.

Salamis Tours (📷 2535 5555; www.salamis international.com; Salamis House, Oktovriou 28; ⊙9am-6pm Mon-Fri) Organises cruises to Greece, and issues tickets to transport your vehicle by boat to Greece or Israel.

❶ Getting There & Away

AIR

Lemesos is more or less equidistant from Pafos and Larnaka Airports. The **Limassol Airport Express** (📷 7777 7075; www.enlimassolair portexpress.eu; Amathussa; adult/child €9/4) runs a regular service from both airports to the Lemesos tourist area (Kanika Elias Beach)

BOAT

Two- and three-day cruises depart from Lemesos year-round. They go to Haifa (Israel), Port Said (Egypt), a selection of Greek islands and sometimes (in summer) to Lebanon. You can book at most travel agencies.

❶ LIFE'S NO CABARET

We don't recommend visiting any of the city's 'cabarets', but if you do decide to go, keep in mind that many of the women working in the clubs may be there under duress. Also bear in mind stories of customers being charged several hundred euros for a couple of beers at the end of the night – and woe betide those who refuse to pay.

BUS

InterCity Buses (www.intercity-buses.com; Limassol Marina) runs regularly to Nicosia (Lefkosia; 1¼ hours), Larnaka (one hour) and Pafos (one hour) from its bus station at Limassol Marina. It also picks up and drops off passengers to Nicosia and Larnaka at the bus stop in front of Agia Napa Church and in front of Debenhams department store (in the tourist area) on the main coast road. To Pafos, the central pick-up point is the roundabout in front of the old fishing harbour.

The local bus company **Emel** (www.limassol buses.com) runs buses around the city as well as services to surrounding villages. Fares cost €1.50 per journey, €5 per day or €15 per week.

SERVICE TAXI

Travel & Express (📷 7777 7474; www.travel express.com.cy; Thessalonikis 21; ⊙6am-7.30pm Mon-Sat, to 3pm Sun) operates service (shared) taxis to Nicosia (€11, 1¼ hours), Larnaka (€10, one hour) and Pafos (€9.50, one hour) every 30 minutes between 6.30am and 6pm Monday to Saturday, and every hour between 7am and 5pm on Sundays. Will also drop you at Larnaka airport (€13) and Pafos airport (€13).

❶ Getting Around

BUS

Emel provides an urban-wide and regional network of buses. Fares cost €1.50 per journey, €5 per day or €15 per week within the district of Lemesos, including rural villages. The main **Emel Bus Station** (Irinis) is located 1km north of the central port area.

Useful regional bus lines departing from this station include the following:

Bus 16 Runs to Episkopi village (45 minutes, roughly every 20 minutes from 6am to 7.30pm with reduced service at weekends).

Bus 17 Runs to Kolossi Castle (40 minutes, roughly every 20 minutes from 6am to 7pm with reduced service at weekends).

Bus 70 Runs to Pissouri Bay (1½ hours, three daily Monday to Friday, two at weekends).

CAR

There are convenient car parks all along the waterfront. You can expect to pay around €1.25 per hour.

AROUND LEMESOS

Lemesos is surrounded by some of the island's top sights. Archaeological must-sees include the Greek and Roman remains of Ancient Kourion and Amathous, and the former Crusader castle at Kolossi; all three are within easy reach of each other. Also here are fabled curiosity Aphrodite's Rock, fine museums and churches, and several of the island's most picturesque villages, where pedestrian cobbles are flanked by caramel-coloured stone houses splashed with vivid blood-red bougainvillea.

This is a region where you should slow down and experience Cypriot village life at an unhurried pace, enjoying traditional coffee houses that are frequented by a local clientele rather than the coach-tour circuit. Keeping to a leisurely note, the area is home to several pristine beaches and is along one of the Cyprus Tourism Organisation's desig-

---

BEACHES AROUND LEMESOS

While the city beaches are nothing remarkable, the coastline around Lemesos is blessed with picturesque sand and pebble coves. Here are the top spots:

Governor's Beach (p69) Dark-sand coves dotted among white chalk cliffs, 30km east of Lemesos.

Lady's Mile Beach (p69) A weekend favourite west of Lemesos on the coast of British-controlled Akrotiri.

Kourion Beach (p72) A wide strip of sand and pebbles below Ancient Kourion; limited development is part of the appeal.

Avdimou Beach (p73) A beach club serves up holiday fun at this relaxing beach west of Kourion.

Melanda Beach (p73) Cliffs back this pretty curve of pebbles and sand.

Pissouri Bay (p73) A cosy cove with resorts, cafes, water activities, sand, sea and sun.

---

nated wine routes, with tastings available at some of Cyprus' better-known wineries.

ℹ Getting There & Around

You can reach Ancient Kourion, Episkopi and Kolossi Castle in the same day using a combination of Emel buses 16 and 17 from Lemesos. Pissouri Bay and Ancient Amathous can also be visited by Emel bus 70; all routes cost €1.50.

East of Lemesos

Although less visited than the coastline west of Lemesos, the highway east is dotted with beaches and ancient sites.

⭐ **Ancient Amathous**   ARCHAEOLOGICAL SITE
(Amathussa; Leoforos Amathountos, Lemesos; adult/child €2.50/free; ⊙ 9am-7.30pm Jul & Aug, to 5pm Sep-Jun; P) The remains at this archaeological site, about 11km east of Lemesos, belie its original importance. Amathous was one of Cyprus' original four kingdoms, along with Salamis, Pafos and Soloi. Founded about 1100 BC, the city had an unbroken history of settlement until about the 12th century AD. Because much of the stone has long been looted for other building projects, imagining the ancient city layout as it was can be baffling. At the entrance, an excellent explanatory pedestal helps interpret the ruins.

Legend has it that the city was founded by Kinyras, the son of Pafos. It is also said that Kinyras introduced the cult of Aphrodite to Cyprus.

Amathous suffered badly at the hands of corsairs during the 7th and 8th centuries, and by 1191, when Richard the Lionheart appeared on the scene, the city was already on the decline. Since its harbour had silted up, King Richard was obliged to disembark on Amathous' beach to claim the once proud and wealthy city. He promptly applied the royal coup de grâce by destroying it, and Amathous was no more.

An interesting aside is that the world's largest stone vase was discovered during excavations here. It dates back to the 6th century BC, weighs a mighty 12.5 tonnes, is 1.85m high, and now stands on display at the Louvre in Paris.

Occasional free summer concerts are held within the grounds. Look for posters at the site or check with the CTO tourist office in Lemesos.

Governor's Beach
BEACH

(P) Lemesos' tourist appeal starts 30km east of the city at Governor's Beach, which features several coves of dark sand contrasting with white, chalky rocks. On the downside, the Vasilikos power station looms 3km to the east, blighting the otherwise seamless sea views. The restaurant here, **Panayiotis** (2563 2315; www.panayiotisgovernorsbeach. com; Governor's Beach; mains €9-20; ⊙11am-10pm; P), is popular for its fish meze.

West of Lemesos

Most of the action is south and west of Lemesos on the way to Pafos.

Akrotiri Peninsula

Once a separate island and now part of the Cypriot mainland, the Akrotiri Peninsula is an intriguing corner of Cyprus. Most of it is occupied by the British Sovereign Base Area (SBA), but the only indication that you are on 'foreign soil' is the odd sight of British SBA police, who patrol the territory in special police vehicles. To the west of the peninsula, you'll come across green playing fields, cricket pitches and housing estates more reminiscent of Leicester than Lemesos. There isn't a whole lot to see here, aside from the excellent environmental centre, which celebrates the peninsula's geological and environment significance, and a historic monastery. The village of Akrotiri is the only true settlement within the SBA and home to a good traditional Cypriot restaurant.

The southern part of the peninsula is out of bounds as this is a military area, and the sovereign territory of the British government. When Cyprus finally received its independence from colonial administration in 1960, Britain negotiated terms that saw the newly formed Republic of Cyprus ceding 158 sq km of its territory to the British Army, now known as the Sovereign Base Areas (SBAs), comprising Akrotiri and Dekelia, near Larnaka.

◉ Sights

Akrotiri's salt lake is an important habitat for migratory birds including flamingo, crane and ibis. Just south of Akrotiri village you can stop in at the **Akrotiri Environment Centre** (2582 6562; http://english.akrotirienvi ronment.com; Akrotiri; ⊙8am-5pm Mon-Fri, 10am-

5pm Sun; P) FREE, which has exhibits on the area's flora and fauna, a wildlife observation kiosk and a short cultural trail.

The area is also known for its **Fasouri plantations**, a swath of citrus groves across the north of the peninsula, interwoven with long, straight stretches of road overhung by tall cypress trees. The plantations create wonderfully cool and refreshing corridors after the aridity of the southern peninsula.

Lady's Mile Beach
BEACH

(Akrotiri Peninsula) This 7km stretch of hard-packed sand and pebbles is a popular weekend beach. Named after a horse belonging to a colonial governor who exercised his mare here, it runs south beyond Lemesos' New Port and along the eastern side of the British-controlled Akrotiri Peninsula. Keep driving away from the blight of cranes at the port; the beach and the view improve the further south you go. That said, it's not the prettiest stretch of sand in these parts.

At summer weekends, the citizens of Lemesos flock here in large numbers to relax in the fairly shallow waters. A couple of beach tavernas serve the crowds and provide some respite from an otherwise barren beach-scape. Bring your own shade if you plan to sit on the beach all day, as well as mosquito repellent if you are staying until dusk – the nearby salt lake provides a ripe breeding ground for these little nippers.

Kolossi Castle
HISTORIC SITE

(7777 7204; Agiou Antoniou 1, Kolossi; €2.50; ⊙8.30am-7.30pm Apr-Sep, to 5.30pm Oct-Mar; P) This doll's house of a castle (more like a fortified tower) perches on the edge of Kolossi village. It's an interesting reminder of the rule of the Knights of St John in the 13th century, who started producing wine and processing sugar cane at a commandery that stood on this land. The current structure dates from 1454 and was probably built over the older fortified building.

Kolossi Castle is approached via a drawbridge. Look up from here to imagine where the parapet would have been located, high above, and from where boiling oil was poured on top of any enemies who dared to approach. On entering the castle you will see two large chambers, distinctive for the original mural of the crucifixion, a large fireplace, and a spiral staircase that leads to a further two chambers on the second level and then beyond to the battlements, restored in 1933.

To the east of the castle is a large outbuilding, now called the sugar factory, where cane was processed into sugar.

Holy Monastery of St Nicholas of the Cats
MONASTERY

(☑ 2595 2621; entry by donation; ⊙8am-2pm & 3-6.30pm) This monastery was founded in AD 327 by the first Byzantine governor of Cyprus, Kalokeros, and patronised by St Helena, mother of Constantine the Great. A delightful small chapel here dating from the 13th century has noteworthy icons painted by the two original nuns in residence. The actual monastery building has received a modern (and somewhat bland) refurbishment. You can buy the sisters' preserves, jams, honey and sweets, plus bags of oranges when in season.

There's a curious story behind the monastery's name. At the time of construction, the Akrotiri Peninsula, and indeed the whole of Cyprus, was in the grip of a severe drought and was overrun with poisonous snakes, so building a monastery was fraught with practical difficulties. A large shipment of cats was therefore brought in from Egypt and Palestine to combat the reptilian threat. A bell would call the cats to meals and the furry warriors would then be dispatched to fight the snakes. These days, the many cats you'll find snoozing in the shade of the monastery colonnades far outnumber the handful of solitary sisters who now look after the place.

Positioned on the edge of the salt lake with its back to the SBA fence, the monastery can be reached by a good dirt road from Akrotiri or via a not-so-obvious route west from Lady's Mile Beach.

✕ Eating

Il Gusto
ITALIAN €€

(☑ 2529 2638; Timiou Stavrou 6, Akrotiri; mains €10-18; ⊙11.30am-11pm) Definitely something to write home about, Il Gusto serves superb cuisine that's an innovative twist on classic Italian cooking. Try the roast pork stuffed with ricotta and figs. It's easy to find, situated among the strip of restaurants on Akrotiri's main street, wedged in between Chinese, Indian and fish-and-chip restaurants – it's vastly superior to them all. Reservations are essential.

Episkopi & Around

Episkopi is built on the hill above Ancient Kourion and is sometimes confused with 'the other' Episkopi, which is a rural village 12km inland from Pafos to the southwest. Episkopi in Greek means 'Home of the Bishop' and the village dates back to the AD 1192–1489 Frankish (Lusignan) period. A pleasant enough place, its main attractions include the excellent Kourion Museum and the sweep of sand that is the **Agios Ermogenis Beach**, complete with its own bar and restaurant. The simple **Agios Ilarion church** in the centre of the village dates to the Lusignan period. The popular Cyprus Wine Museum is also located in the vicinity, just 4km east of town on the B6.

Note that part of Episkopi lies within the confines of the SBA.

⊙ Sights

★ Kourion Museum
MUSEUM

(☑ 2599 1049; Episkopi; adult/child €2.50/free; ⊙8am-7.30pm Jul & Aug, shorter hours rest of year; **P**) History buffs should not miss this excellent museum signposted off the Lemesos–Kourion road and marked from Episkopi. The collection includes terracotta objects from Ancient Kourion (p71) and the Sanctuary of Apollon Ylatis (p72) collected by late archaeologist George McFadden and housed in his former private residence. Among more harrowing exhibits are the skeletal remains of city inhabitants who lost their lives in the 4th-century earthquakes that devastated this area, found in situ in their houses.

Cyprus Wine Museum
MUSEUM

(☑ 2587 3808; www.cypruswinemuseum.com; Odos Pafou 42, Erimi; €4-7; ⊙9am-5pm) Located 4km east of Episkopi, off the B6 Lemesos–Pafos highway, the Cyprus Wine Museum offers an insight into the history of Cypriot winemaking. There are three guided-tour options, some including wine tasting after viewing the winemaking exhibits. Displays include medieval drinking vessels and jars, as well as explanatory information on all aspects of winemaking. There's also a short audio-visual presentation.

✕ Eating

Old Stables
CYPRIOT €€

(☑ 2593 5568; B6, Episkopi; mains €10; ⊙6-11pm Mon-Sat) Run by a mother-and-daughter team, Old Stables is the place to try *tavas* (lamb stew with cumin, potatoes, onions and tomatoes), a speciality here. It's out on the Lemesos–Pafos road opposite the Eko petrol station; it looks like it was established generations before there were roads here, and its small and shady front terrace deserves a better view than this.

Ancient Kourion

The area's most famous sight is 13km west of Lemesos, rising dramatically above the coastal plain.

⊙ Sights

★ **Ancient Kourion**   ARCHAEOLOGICAL SITE
(☑ 2593 4250; Episkopi; adult/child €4.50/free; ⊙ 8.30am-7.30pm Apr-Oct, to 5pm Nov-Mar; Ⓟ) Defiantly perched on a hillside, with a sweeping view of the surrounding patchwork fields and the sea, Ancient Kourion is a spectacular site. Most likely founded in neolithic times due to its strategic position high on a bluff, it became a permanent settlement in about the 13th century BC, when Mycenaean colonisers established themselves here.

There's a small visitors centre where you can see a scale model of the whole site, which will help orientate your visit.

The ticket office is at the entry gate halfway up the hill. From there the road continues to the hilltop to the visitor's centre and ruins.

The settlement prospered under the Ptolemies and Romans, and a pre-Christian cult of Apollo was active among the inhabitants of Kourion in Roman times, as evidenced by the nearby Sanctuary of Apollon Ylatis (p72). Christianity eventually supplanted Apollo and, despite disastrous earthquakes in the region, an early Christian basilica was built in the 5th century, testifying to the ongoing influence of the religion on Kourion by this time.

Pirate raids 200 years later severely compromised the viability of the Christian bishopric; the Bishop of Kourion was obliged to move his base to a new settlement at nearby Episkopi (meaning 'bishopric' in Greek). Kourion declined as a settlement from that point on and was not rediscovered until tentative excavations at the site began in 1876.

➡ **Early Christian Basilica**

The early Christian basilica at Ancient Kourion displays all the hallmarks of an early church, with foundations clearly showing the existence of a *narthex diakonikon* (a storage area for agricultural products used by priests and monks), various rooms, a bap-

ⓘ TIPS FOR ANCIENT KOURION

➡ Ancient Kourion is firmly on the coach-tour and school-excursion trail. Come early in the morning or late in the afternoon, when the site is usually less crowded.

➡ If you do get there at the same time as a busload, don't fear. Most groups only tour the Roman Theatre and the House of Eustolius. Start your visit at the Northern Plateau Ruins and by the time you get to the theatre the crowds should have dispersed.

➡ Ancient Kourion is close to two other attractions in the immediate vicinity: the **Sanctuary of Apollon Ylatis** (p72) and **Kolossi Castle** (p69); all three can be visited in the same day.

➡ As a cooling break, incorporate a swim at **Kourion Beach** (p72), which spreads out temptingly below the ancient site.

tistery and an atrium. Some floor mosaics are also visible among the remains.

➡ **House of Eustolius**

Originally a palace dating from the early Roman period, this complex was subsequently altered in the 3rd century AD and made a more communal space for the local residents, with the addition of extensive baths, courtyards and halls. Its colourful Christian-influenced mosaic floors are well preserved and make a mention of the builder, Eustolius, and the decidedly non-Christian patron, Apollo. Look for Christian motifs of cross-shaped ornaments and fish.

➡ **House of the Gladiators**

At the northwestern edge of the Ancient Kourion site you come to the House of the Gladiators, so called because of two fairly well preserved floor mosaics depicting gladiators in combat dress. Two of these gladiators, Hellenikos and Margaritis, are shown practising with weapons.

Just to the north is the House of Achilles, where a fragment of a beautifully intricate floor mosaic depicting Achilles meeting with Odysseus has survived.

➡ **Northern Plateau Ruins**

The ruins of Hellenistic and Roman Kourion lie on the northern plateau of the Ancient Kourion site. The Roman agora and the stoa,

ANOGYRA

Just 39km inland west of Lemesos (Limassol), sleepy Anogyra is all solid stone houses, painted window shutters and narrow lanes that twist and turn in lazy squiggles. This is the only village that still produces carob *pasteli* (a Cypriot sweet) the traditional way, and if you're passing through in September, don't miss the annual Pasteli Festival, when the village celebrates the heritage of its sweet-treat industry.

It's a charmingly peaceful place with an unhurried atmosphere far removed from the bustle of the coast. Park by the central plaza, dominated by the stately **Church of the Archangel Michael** (home to some lovely icons), and stroll out to explore from there.

Anogyra and the surrounding area are also home to several interesting foodie-focused sights that are well worth a look (and taste), including the **Oleastro Olive Park** (☑9952 5093; www.oleastro.com.cy; adult/child €3/2; ☉10am-7pm; 🅿), 3km north of Anogyra, the **Pasteli Museum** (☑2522 1500; ☉10am-4pm Jun-Sep, shorter hours rest of year) FREE and **Nicolaidis WInery** (☑2522 1709; www.facebook.com/nicolaides.winery; ☉9am-5pm Tue-Sun).

with its colonnade of 16 marble columns, sit alongside the early Christian basilica.

Just to the north, a wooden walkway leads you over the substantial remnants of the Roman city baths, an irrigation system and the nymphaeum. The foundations of the public baths, with the layout of the frigidarium (cold room), tepidarium (warm room) and caldarium (hot room), can still be clearly seen.

➡ Roman Theatre

More interesting for its lovely coastal views than for its actual structure, Ancient Kourion's Roman Theatre is a reconstruction of a smaller theatre that existed on the same spectacular site, high on the hill overlooking the sea, which was destroyed by earthquakes in the 4th century. Nevertheless, it gives a good idea of how the original would have been at its peak. Today the theatre is often used for cultural events and performances by Cypriot and visiting Greek singers and bands.

★ Sanctuary of Apollon Ylatis   ARCHAEOLOGICAL SITE

(Episkopi; €2.50; ☉8.30am-7.30pm Apr-Oct, to 5pm Nov-Mar; 🅿) About 2km west of Ancient Kourion's main entrance, and prominently signposted off the highway, is the Sanctuary of Apollon Ylatis, which is part of the larger site of Ancient Kourion.

Apollon Ylatis' main sanctuary has been partly restored; the beautiful, imposing columns mark the extent of the restoration. Also discernible are the priests' quarters, a *palaestra* (sports arena) and baths for the athletes, and a rather depleted stadium

500m to the east, which once seated up to 6000 spectators.

The precinct was established in the 8th century BC in honour of Apollo, who was considered god of the woods (*ylatis* means 'of the woods' in Greek). The once woody site now has far less vegetation but retains a good scattering of remains that give a reasonable idea of the layout of the original sanctuary. The remnants that you see are Roman structures that were levelled by a large earthquake in AD 365.

🏊 Beaches

A string of pretty beaches traces the coastline west of Kourion.

Kourion Beach   BEACH

(Akrotiri Sovereign Base Area; 🅿) This is a lovely beach of sand and small pebbles; the area is windy and attracts windsurfers and kiteboarders, as well as those who just want to chill out amid the unspoilt setting and backdrop of white cliffs.

The beach is around 17km west of Lemesos, within Great Britain's Akrotiri SBA, which is the reason for the lack of development. There's no natural shade, but the adjacent tavernas rent sunbeds and parasols for the day (€4.50).

The eastern end of the beach is unsafe for swimming (note the sign), so head west if you fancy a dip. This beach is best combined with a trip to Ancient Kourion. You'll also find the remains of a 6th-century port basilica here, complete with 11 columns, backing on to the centre of the beach.

Locals rate the **Chris Blue Beach Bar & Restaurant** (☑2599 1052; Kourion Beach;

mains €9-15; ⊙ 10.30am-10pm; P ✍ ⬥) as the best on this short culinary strip. You can select your fish or seafood from the large tank near the entrance.

Kourion beach is also home to the well-respected **Curium Beach Equestrian Centre** (✍ 9956 4232; curiumequestrian@hotmail. com; Kourion Beach; classes from €25; ⬥), which offers guided horse treks and classes, including dressage.

The beach can be reached by bus 16a operated by Emel (€1.50, 45 minutes, three daily) from Lemesos. Note that there is a reduced service at weekends.

★ **Avdimou Beach**   BEACH
(Avdimou; P) This lovely stretch of beach is home to the sophisticated **Zias Beach Club** (✍ 2682 8000; www.aphroditehills.com; ⊙ 10am-11pm Apr-Nov) and the Kyrenia Beach Restaurant, which is superb for seafood. The views of the bay are stunning and the crystal-clear waters here are ideal for snorkelling. The restaurant rents out sunbeds and parasols (€4.50). Note that the scenic access road is rough in parts, but passable.

Melanda Beach   BEACH
(off B6, near Avdimou; P) An arc of fine pebbles and sand sheltered by low, white cliffs and backed by olive trees, this is one of the best beaches in the region. It's signposted off the B6; the approach road is fairly rough, but nevertheless accessible, and passes by vines and lush agricultural land. **Melanda Beach Restaurant** (✍ 9956 5336; mains €10-12; ⊙ 9.30am-9.30pm Tue-Sun, to 5pm Mon; P) has a terrace on the beach, and rents sunbeds and parasols (€5). Avoid in busy July and August, but otherwise Melanda's sweeping sands equal a good choice for a beach day out.

Pissouri Bay & Village

Pissouri Bay resort, 10km west of Avdimou, has a delightful arched shingle-and-sand beach backed to the west by olive-dappled hills. It's a popular spot for visitors, with plenty of holiday villas in the surrounding area, as well as a couple of luxury resorts. Despite the holiday overtones (and the fact that Pissouri is a free wi-fi zone), the original village at the top of the hill still has some authentic corners and a couple of outstanding restaurants. The newer part of town lies above the beach and is basically a modern strip of water-sports outfits, bars and small

KYRENIA BEACH RESTAURANT

You won't have to push the boat out too far to enjoy superb catch-of-the-day seafood at the long-standing, popular **Kyrenia Beach Restaurant** (✍ 9967 9451; Avdimou Beach; mains €9-16; ⊙ 11am-10pm; P). Its stunning beach-side setting means shoals of families turn up at weekends, so come early to grab a table; you can't reserve in advance. An insider's tip: try the swordfish simply grilled in tinfoil. Delicious.

stores selling buckets and spades. In short, most visitors come here for the beach life, and very appealing it is too.

🏃 Activities

Divers are well catered for at Pissouri. **Cyprus Diving Adventures** (✍ 9766 1046; www.cyprusdivingadventures.com; Makedonias 40, Pissouri; ⊙ 9am-6pm) and **Pissouri Bay Divers** (✍ 9653 0761; www.pissouribaydivers. com; Pissouri Beach; ⊙ 9am-6pm) offer shore dives, boat dives and 'discover scuba' and bubble-maker sessions for children, as well as PADI certification courses. For certified divers, prices start at €90 for two shore dives.

Columbia Watersports (✍ 9961 2262; www.columbiaresort.com; Ampelonon, Pissouri Bay; ⊙ 8.30am-6pm; ⬥), located on the beachfront near the Columbia Beach Resort, is long-established and operated by enthusiastic couple Yiannos and Dia. It offers just about any water sport you can think of, including windsurfing, parasailing and kayaking. It also operates boat trips to Kourion Bay and beyond, and runs various water-sports classes for children.

🍴 Eating

★ **Kastro**   CYPRIOT €€
(✍ 2522 2211; Ampelonon 73, Pissouri Bay; mains €12-14; ⊙ 11am-9pm Fri-Wed; P) This long-standing family-owned restaurant started life as little more than a beach shack several decades ago. It's a lot smarter today, yet still maximises the view from its sprawling terrace overlooking the surf. Culinary convictions still run deep: opt for one of the traditional Cypriot dishes, or go for the freshly caught seafood.

LEMESOS & THE SOUTH WEST OF LEMESOS

LANEIA VILLAGE

Some of the prettiest Cypriot villages are located in the mountainous region north of Lemesos (Limassol). Vouni, Silikou and Lofou are all worth a visit and within easy distance of each other, but arguably the most photogenic village is Laneia, signposted off the B8 road, just beyond Doros (also picturesque, and centred around a beautiful 14th-century church).

Popular with artists and foreign residents, Laneia's flower-filled cobbled streets and warm limestone buildings have real picture-postcard appeal. This is just the sort of place where the real joy is to simply wander the streets with your camera at the ready, fantasising as you go about buying a hideaway home for regular, annual escapes.

There's a modest **agricultural museum** displaying olive oil and grape presses just off the main square; a charming former cobbler's shop that now displays the history of his craft (look for the sign, 'Shoemaker'); and a couple of good local tavernas, including the **Walnut Tree** (☑ 9956 5976; mains €8-10; ☺ 9am-10pm; P), if you fancy lunch. Leave time to catch Laneia's other highlights on your stroll, including the **Church of the Virgin Mary** (Main Square; ☺ hours vary) and the fine **Michael Owen Gallery** (☑ 2543 2404; www.michaelowengallery.com; ☺ 10am-5pm).

Bunch of Grapes Inn   MEDITERRANEAN €€
(☑ 2522 1275; Ioannou Erotokritou 9, Pissouri; mains from €8; ☺ 11am-late; 🛜) This tranquil, atmospheric place in the village centre offers excellent dining under the thick shade of grapevines and fig and mulberry trees. Feast on dishes such as crispy roast duck in apricot and brandy sauce, and red mullet in garlic. Established by a Dutchman back in the 1970s, it's now Cypriot owned. Foreign residents still flock here, especially at weekends.

Two Friends   CYPRIOT €€
(☑ 2522 2527; Pissouri; mains from €8; ☺ noon-11pm) Two Friends prides itself on its homemade cuisine. Everything is made from scratch, including the cheese ravioli, filled with haloumi cheese and mint, and the tahini dip with freshly ground sesame seeds, garlic and olive oil. It's located on the main road to the beach, just outside the village, with sweeping views that stretch to the sea.

ⓘ Getting There & Away

Emel bus 70 runs from Lemesos to Pissouri (€1.50, 1½ hours, three daily Monday to Friday, two at weekends).

Petra tou Romiou (Aphrodite's Rock & Beach)

Possibly the most famous beach in Cyprus, Aphrodite's Beach is distinctive for its two upright rocks, which are easy to spot, particularly as you'll generally find swimmers perched somewhat precariously on top of them. To get here, take the old B6 road from Lemesos to Pafos (a recommended scenic journey).

The English moniker Rock of Aphrodite comes from the legend that Aphrodite, ancient patron goddess of Cyprus, emerged from the sea at this point in a surge of foam before, no doubt, going off to entertain some lovers. The same thing is claimed by the residents of Kythira island in Greece. But who's to say she didn't do such a thing in both places?

Most visitors either stop midtrip to have a swim or come for the sunset, which is best seen from either the Petra tou Romiou tourist pavilion or from a roadside car park about 1.5km further east. Skip any kind of eating at the tourist-pavilion cafeteria, where you'll be overcharged for indifferent snacks; bring your own food and have a picnic instead.

A pedestrian underpass leads to the beach from the kiosk and car park on the other side of the road, around 500m further on towards Pafos from the tourist pavilion; it's well signposted.

Troödos Mountains

Best Places to Eat

➡ Mylos Restaurant (p93)

➡ Mimi's Restaurant (p85)

➡ Elyssia (p88)

➡ Stou Kir Yianni (p86)

➡ Loutraki (p89)

Best Churches & Monasteries

➡ Kykkos Monastery (p90)

➡ Panagia tou Moutoulla (p89)

➡ Panagia Forviotissa (p92)

➡ Archangelos Michail (p88)

➡ Agios Ioannis Lambadistis Monastery (p89)

Why Go?

Home to Mt Olympus (1952m), the island's highest peak, this stunning mountain range provides visitors with a forested flip side to the coastal resorts and big-city clamour. Overlooking the valleys of Lemesos (Limassol), Larnaka and the greater Mesaoria plain, this region covers over 90 sq km and is a protected natural park which safeguards its wildlife, ecology and geology. In winter, skiers and snowboarders populate the ski resorts of the northern slopes, while at other times of the year the park is ideal for camping, picnicking, hiking, cycling and birdwatching.

In addition to the natural beauty of the landscape, the Troödos Mountains are home to a variety of postcard-pretty villages with cobbled streets, terraced slopes and vernacular architecture. The region's peaks and valleys also hide some of the island's most important medieval frescoed churches, along with unexpected monasteries, museums and some of the Republic's finest wineries.

When to Go

➡ From January to April, you can experience the wintery pleasures of skiing and snowboarding the slopes by day, and enjoying a hearty tavern meal by night.

➡ April to September is ideal for wine tasting; explore some of the superb wineries hidden among the sprawling vineyards and steep, breezy valleys.

➡ In early summer ramble over 65km of diverse nature and hiking trails across the region, ranging from simple strolls to more arduous hikes.

➡ Beat the July and August heat by camping 1000m above sea level at verdant sites in the ranges.

Troödos Mountains Highlights

1 Panagia Forviotissa (p92) Wondering at this extraordinary Byzantine painted church in the Solea Valley.

2 Troödos Botanical Gardens (p82) Exploring this fragrant and beautiful botanical garden.

3 Kykkos Monastery (p90) Marvelling at the treasures of the island's most opulent and imposing monastery.

4 Venus Rose (p94) Shopping in Agros for rose-related products for and, if you're there in May, experiencing the annual Rose Festival.

5 Treis Elies (p91) Enjoying peaceful forest hikes over ancient bridges, far from the madding crowds.

6 Archangelos Michail (p88) Ogling the fabulous 15th-century frescos at this tiny church in picturesque Pedoulas.

7 Kyperounda Winery (p96) Sipping on award-winning wines at this delightful winery in the heart of the Troödos Mountains.

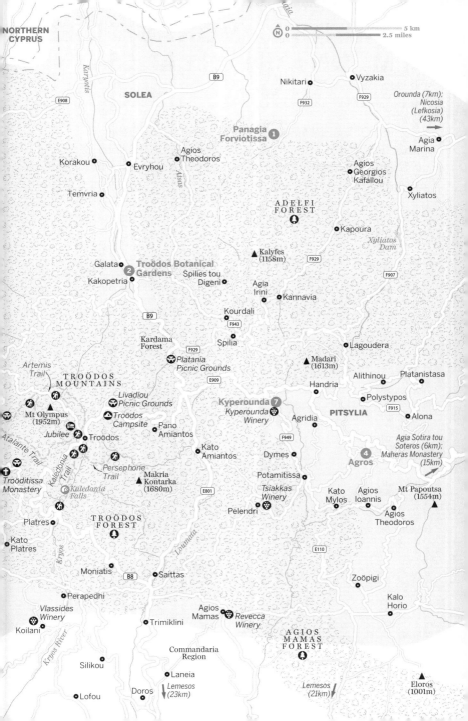

ROAD TRIP > MONASTERIES & MOUNTAIN VILLAGES

A different way of life endures in the Troödos, only superficially touched by the modern age. The pine-clad hills are dotted with ancient villages and even more ancient monasteries, and this drive links the best of them, starting in peaceful Platres.

① Troöditissa Monastery

First stop is the **Platres Chocolate Workshop** (p85) in Platres to pick up a bag of scrumptious handmade chocolates for the trip. Next, take the E804 from Platres for a peek at some of the valley's hidden villages. This route includes the 13th-century **Troöditissa Monastery**, located amid thick pines at the top of a steep gorge, founded after the

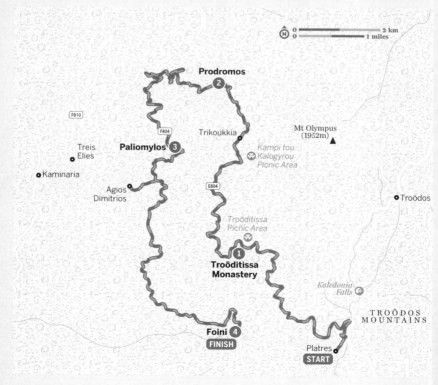

discovery of a priceless silver-plated icon of the Virgin that was brought from Asia Minor. Believed to assist fertility, the icon had been guarded in a nearby cave by two hermits until their deaths. The monastery's existing church, built in 1731, is currently closed to the public as it is part of a working religious order. However, if you are polite and patient the monks may well let you in.

② Prodomos

Continuing along the mountain road, you pass the shaded picnic areas of **Troöditissa** and **Kampi tou Kalogyrou** in the cool pine forests. From there you reach the village of **Prodromos**. This small village still has some hill-station clientele but is not as well known as Troödos and Platres. At 1380m, it's Cyprus' highest village and is surrounded by lush orchards with apple, peach, plum, almond and chestnut trees.

③ Paliomylos

Looping back towards the south brings you to **Paliomylos** and **Agios Dimitrios**, a pair of timeless villages barely touched by tourism, buried beneath the greenery and grapevines. In Paliomylos (population 40), duck into the church for a look at the 17th-century murals. Both villages date from the Byzantine period.

④ Foini

A little further on is **Foini**, a great place to stop for some *loukoumades* (similar to Turkish delight, but flavoured with bergamot rather than traditional rose water) and a strong coffee. It's also very popular for its handmade pottery and *pitharia* (earthenware storage jars). For lunch, a good choice is the fresh trout at **Neraida**. Located on the western side of the village, near the stream, it's open Thursday to Tuesday for lunch, and for dinner Friday and Saturday.

ROAD TRIP > WINE ROUTE 6

What keeps the sleepy villages of the Troödos looking so peaceful and bucolic? It might be the full-blooded red wines and Commandaria that have been fermented in the mountains since at least Byzantine times. This drive links some of the best wineries, strung out between Platres and Agros.

① Tsiakkas Winery

Wine Route 6 takes in over 14 villages, two wineries and some of the best family-owned vineyards in the region. It is well signposted the whole way: look out for the green and burgundy signs with a grape symbol and the number six on them. The route is one long, winding loop, so make lots of rest stops, allocate a designated driver and watch the

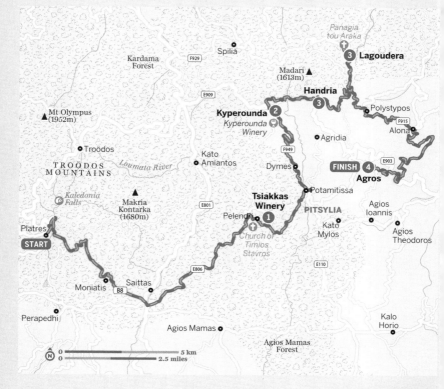

amount of wine you consume. Visiting times at the wineries are fairly flexible, so it's a good idea to call beforehand. The wineries offer vineyard tours and are happy for you to taste freely. You ought to buy at least one bottle, though, which isn't much of a hardship.

Take the B8 south from Platres, then turn onto the E806 towards Pelendri. Look for the signs to the **Tsiakkas Winery** (p96) and make a stop to taste some excellent dry whites and a commendable Cabernet Sauvignon. Just before you come to Pelendri, take the right-hand turn to the **Church of Timios Stavros** (p95), one of the region's most magnificent painted churches, home to rare 12th-century frescos.

② Kyperounda

Continue on the F949 past Potamitissa, one of the highest villages on the island with traditional stone houses, natural springs and nature trails, and then Dymes, a village with two historic churches. Next stop is Ky-

perounda and the **Kyperounda Winery** (p96). This contemporary winery has a large range of whites and reds and a particularly palatable red blend called Andessitis.

③ Handria & Lagoudera

Next stops are the high-altitude villages of Handria and Lagoudera, on the F915, with abundant vineyards. Here you can stop and see the Unesco-listed 12th-century Byzantine church of **Panagia tou Araka** (p95).

④ Agros

Double back a short way to the F915 then wind past Polystypos, one of the highest villages in the region, famed for its natural springs and nature trails, and Alona, with traditional stone houses and two historic churches. Turn on to the E903 to reach the village of Agros, home of many mavro grapevines and shops selling Troödos wines and products made from locally produced rose water.

TROÖDOS

POP 24

Located near the summit of Mt Olympus, Troödos village is the focal point for all hiking, cycling and snow-related activities in the region. At over 1900m above sea level, it's far cooler than the plains below and offers superb views of the surrounding valleys.

The village, known as Central Troödos (Kentriko Troödos in Greek), is minimal and centred on a simple *plateia* (square). The square has a playground with some benches and a handful of souvenir shops selling everything from wind chimes to *soujoukko*, a traditional sweet made from almonds and sun-dried grape juice.

Opposite the park is the Troödos Hotel, with a couple of neighbouring restaurants and cafes. A further 200m downhill to the west is the Troödos Visitor Centre. The skiing facilities (open in winter) are just to the north near the Jubilee Hotel.

History

The Troödos ocean crust, created over 90 million years ago, was the first part of the island to emerge from the sea around 15 million years ago. Rocks such as serpentinite, dunite, wehlite, pyroxenite, plagiogranite, gabbro, diabase and volcanic rock can be found at high altitudes in the region.

According to Strabo, the Greek geographer (63 BC), Mt Olympus was the site of a temple to the goddess Aphrodite during the Hellenistic period. It was said to be not only unapproachable by women but completely invisible to them.

In AD 1571, Venetian generals built a fort on the mountain to keep invading Ottomans at bay, according to Cypriot nobles who visited the surrounding monasteries and summer recreation areas.

In the late 1800s Troödos became the summer residence of the island's British governors, who came to avoid the scorching sunshine, and the area was considered the summer seat of government during British rule. At different points in its history it has provided a refuge for religious communities, freedom fighters and outlaws, as well as the wealthy of the Levant.

Nowadays, nature lovers, natural-history buffs and activity-seekers flock here for camping, hiking trails and skiing during the winter months.

Sights

⭐ **Troödos Botanical Gardens** GARDENS
(☑ 2555 0091; Archiepiskopou Makariou III 62, Amiantos Old Mine; ⏰ 8am-2pm Mon-Fri; **P**) **FREE**
Part of the excellent **Troödos Geopark**, this is a small but well-laid-out botanical garden with a lily pond and other water features, including a tumbling waterfall. Species in the park include common, rare and endangered flora, with the garden split into thematic sections including aromatic, endemic and traditional garden plants. There's a short audiovisual presentation about the local flora, and a photographic exhibition covering the history and restoration of the site's former (somewhat alarming) asbestos mine.

Activities

Hiking

Troödos has 13 nature trails, varying in length from a novice-friendly 1.6km to 14km for the more experienced. Together they provide an excellent insight into the diversity of the region. Most trees and plants on the trails are marked with their Latin and Greek names, and there are frequent wooden benches positioned beneath trees to allow you to take breaks and admire the views.

Booklets outlining the flora, fauna and geology of each trail are available from the Troödos Visitor Centre (p84).

Kaledonia Trail HIKING
A perfect summer hike, the Kaledonia Trail is well shaded and well marked. Around 3km long, it starts approximately 1km downhill from Central Troödos and ends just outside the town of Platres. The last kilometre brings you to picturesque **Kaledonia Falls**, a 15m drop of cascading water from an immense gabbro-rock precipice. Allow yourself two hours for an uplifting and relaxing hike.

The trail winds down through a thickly wooded valley alongside the Kryos River, a gurgling stream with stepping-stone crossings and log bridges. The track is steep in parts and is best tackled from north to south, as it drops about 400m in altitude. It offers a variety of vegetation, including black pines and Cyprus mint, and an abundance of small birds, such as Cyprus and Sardinian warblers and nightingales.

Artemis Trail HIKING
(Chionistra Circular Trail) Ideal for a first hike, this 7km trail goes around the summit of Mt Olympus in a roughly circular loop, begin-

ning and ending in the small car park off the Mt Olympus summit road. The trail is fairly flat and takes three to four hours to complete. It runs alternately through shaded and open areas with spectacular views to the south.

The trail takes in such vegetation as St John's wort, Troödos sage, alyssum and barberry, and geological features including a chromite pit and veins of pyroxenite and dunite. The route also features the 'Walls of the Old Town', which legend says are remnants of a 1571 Venetian fort. The ski lift is conveniently located on this trail, should you come in winter. Come prepared with drinking water and a hat.

Persephone Trail   HIKING
Named after the mountain it ascends, this trail takes you on an attractive out-and-back hike through tall pines, rich vegetation and open areas with views to the horizon. The trail is 3km long and takes about an hour and a half to complete.

There's a lookout at the top of Makria Kontarka, where you can see the spread of vineyards and wine villages as far as Lemesos port to the south. On the northern side, look for the enormous scar in the earth left by the now-closed asbestos mine at Pano Amiantos.

Atalante Trail   HIKING
Starting at the Troödos square, this 12km trail is relatively easygoing and well marked. Named in honour of forest nymph Atalante, it runs at a lower altitude than the Artemis trail but follows nearly the same route. While the views are not as spectacular as those from the higher trail, it's still an enjoyable walk.

To get back to the village, take the main Prodromos–Troödos road. Allow around five hours.

There's a fresh spring with drinking water about 3km from the trail's beginning.

Birdwatching
Cyprus is blessed with nearly 400 bird species, and many visitors come to Troödos for its tranquillity, excellent visibility and variety of habitats. Birds found here include griffon vultures, warblers, wagtails and pipits. Contact **Cyprus Birding Tours** (📞9955 8953; www.cyprusbirdingtours.com) for more birding information.

Cycling
Troödos has a growing number of routes dedicated to cycling and mountain biking, including several forest tracks. The booklet *Troödos*

Cycling Routes is available at the Troödos Visitor Centre (p84) and Cyprus Tourism Organisation (CTO) offices, and has detailed information on bike tracks in the mountain range. Troödos' most common cycling route comprises three tracks making up one large circular run of the Mt Olympus summit:

Psilo Dendro (Platres)–Karvounas A 16.2km flat ride through easy terrain, including good quality tarmac, forest and dirt track.

Karvounas–Prodromos A 22.7km ride with a decent incline, a medium to hard degree of difficulty and good all-surface conditions.

Prodromos–Psilo Dendro An 18.2km simple ride downhill with good roads mixed with stony tracks that can be tough on tyres.

Check out www.cypruscycling.com for information on bike runs and events held on the island.

Picnicking
With nine well-organised sites ranging in capacity from 250 to 2000 visitors, **Troödos Forest Park** attracts flocks of picnickers. You can set up practically anywhere and all sites have facilities such as wooden tables, fresh drinking water, toilets, playgrounds and parking. Barbecuing is allowed in the pits provided, if you wish to join the locals in grilling chops or spit-roasting *kontosouvli* (chunks of lamb).

Kampos tou Livadiou, a great little picnic ground among the pine trees, is located 3km down the Troödos–Nicosia (Lefkosia) road (B9). A further 8km along this road is the popular **Platania** (Plane Trees) picnic ground and campsite. It can get busy with weekend visitors, but it offers plenty of shade and includes a children's adventure park, making it ideal for families.

✖ Eating

Choice here is not great unless you're after a simple snack. Otherwise, head for Platres, where there are many more restaurants offering a variety of cuisine to suit various budgets.

Fereos Park Restaurant   CYPRIOT €€€
(📞2542 0114; Troödos Sq; mains €12-15; ⏱9am-7pm; 🅿🛜) Located opposite the playground, this restaurant is geared towards tourists but still serves reasonable food, including local trout.

ℹ️ Information

The excellent **Troödos Visitor Centre** (☎2542 0144; ⊘10am-3pm Jun, to 4pm Jul-Aug, shorter hours rest of the year) includes a small museum (admission €1), and is surrounded by a 250m botanical and geological trail, which offers an easy introduction to the area's attractions. All maps, brochures and published information about the region, including hiking trails and vegetation, are available here.

Troödos Geopark Visitor Centre (☎2295 2043; www.troodos-geo.org; Archiepiskopou Makariou III 62, Amiantos Old Mine; adult/child €3/2; ⊘9am-4pm Tue-Sun) has informative displays of rocks and minerals, some history about the site's former incarnation as an asbestos mine, detailed descriptions about the geology of the area and a gift shop.

ℹ️ Getting There & Away

Central Troödos is best reached from Lemesos (via the B8) or Nicosia (via the B9). It can also be accessed from Pitsylia, in the east, and from Pafos in the west, via good but slow, winding roads. On Sunday evenings traffic can be very heavy on all the roads off the mountain, as weekend visitors head home to Nicosia and the coast.

From the square, the road north heads towards the Solea Valley and Nicosia. To the west is the road to Prodromos and the Marathasa Valley. The third approach (and most common) is from the south, which takes in Platres (some-

SKI CYPRUS

Cyprus is better known for beaches and sun, but remarkably, Troödos has four ski slopes, ranging in length from 150m to 500m. The two longer slopes are on the north face of the mountain; the Hera lift takes you to the 350m beginners' slope, and the Zeus lift takes you to the peak for the advanced 500m-long Jubilee run and the racing runs. The North Face Ski Centre (☎2542 0105; Dias Restaurant; ⊘9am-7pm Jan-Mar), which offers ski-equipment rental, is located here at the Dias Restaurant.

On the southern shoulder are the ski lifts to the shorter Aphrodite and Hermes runs, great for beginners and intermediates. The Sun Valley Centre (☎2542 0104; ⊘9am-6pm Jan-Mar) and a ski shop are located here.

Visit www.skicyprus.com for snow reports and the latest information on slope conditions and road access to Troödos in winter.

times Pano Platres on maps), and the *krasohoria* (wine villages) of the Commandaria region.

Emel (www.limassolbuses.com) buses run from Lemesos to Central Troödos at 9.30am and 6pm Monday to Friday and at 9.30am only on Saturday and Sunday (€1.50,1¼ hours). Buses return at 8.45am and 3.30pm Monday to Friday and 3.30pm only on Saturday and Sunday.

Osel (www.osel.com.cy) buses run twice daily from Constanza Bastion, Nicosia, to Central Troödos at 5.45am and noon weekdays and 8am and 2pm weekends (€1.50,1½ hours). There is the same frequency of return trips.

Service taxis don't operate out of Troödos. A standard taxi will take you there, but it can be expensive due to the time it takes to drive up the mountain.

PLATRES

POP 280

Platres (formerly Pano Platres) is the highest of the mountain communities, with an altitude of approximately 1200m.

A popular health retreat with British colonialists and personalities from the past, Platres has now merged its former charm with modernised restaurants and hotels, making it a delightful place to stay while visiting the surrounding mountains. It's a perfect retreat during summer with its dry climate, scenic surrounds and overall tranquillity; in winter it converts into the perfect ski resort, with cosy restaurants and roaring log fires. Modelled somewhat on the hill stations of colonial Asia, it has all the trappings of a cool mountain retreat: forest walks, bubbling streams, relief from the heat of the plains, and gin and tonics on the balconies of old-world hotels.

🏃 Activities

Platres has some good hikes, such as the downhill route to Foini, 9km to the west, the slightly easier 7km route to Perapedhi, and an excellent 3km uphill ramble to Pouziaris. Check out the www.platres.org website for more info on these hikes.

🍽 Eating

Enjoy local dishes accompanied by superb wines from the nearby *krasohoria* valley and Commandaria region. Most of the restaurants and bars are located on the lower road of the village.

★ Mimi's Restaurant   CYPRIOT €€

(☑ 2542 1449; Olympou; mains from €8, meze €15; ☉ 9am-10pm) This may not be the most atmospheric spot to eat in town, but ask any local where they like to dine and this is the place they will probably cite. You won't hear the dreaded ping of the microwave: everything here is freshly made. The meze is the menu highlight, and the complimentary dessert is an additional sweet touch.

It's located just past the police station on the main road through town.

Village Tavern   CYPRIOT €€

(☑ 9966 3772; Leoforos Archiepiskopou Makariou III 26; mains €8-10; ☉ 8am-9pm) Open views from the terrace, a cosy taverna-style interior and tasty traditional food served in good-sized portions make this a pleasant spot to recharge after a hike. Try the fresh Cypriot salads with the lightly browned moussaka. Owner Agis also has a few rooms to rent (€55 per night).

To Anoi   CYPRIOT €€

(Olympou 37; mains from €10; ☉ 10am-10pm; 🅿) Set in a large stone building, this family tavern serves such traditional dishes as *kleftiko* (oven-baked lamb) and *souvla* (skewered meat, usually lamb) cooked over hot coals.

Skylight Restaurant Bar & Pool   MEDITERRANEAN €€€

(☑ 2542 2244; www.skylight.com.cy; Leoforos Archiepiskopou Makariou III 524; mains €10-25; ☉ noon-10pm; 🅿 🐾) On a warm summer's day, especially with kids in tow, this is the best choice in town. Where else can you enjoy your meal in between taking a dip in the restaurant pool (admission per day €5)? The menu is a family pleaser too, with grills and seafood dishes, as well as a dozen salads, pastas and homemade chips.

Skylight also has a vast and sunny terrace, from where you can enjoy views over the rooftops to the mountains beyond.

Psilo Dendro Restaurant   CYPRIOT €€€

(☑ 2581 3131; Aidonion 13; trout €12-15; ☉ 11am-5pm) Close to the southern end of the Kaledonia Trail from Troödos, this restaurant receives many hungry hikers. It has an adjoining trout farm, from which it serves some of the freshest fish on the island.

🛍 Shopping

Platres Chocolate Workshop   CHOCOLATE

(☑ 9976 6446; Olympou 1; ☉ 9.30am-5.30pm) New premises, new owner, but the choco-

CHILDREN'S CYPRUS: HORSE RIDING

The small horse- and pony-riding outfit that operates from the south side of the village (near the public toilets) is ideal if you want to give your kids an introduction to riding. The beasts are very friendly and gentle, so don't expect any galloping chases. A 10-minute escorted ride around Troödos costs €6, 20 minutes will set you back €10 and half an hour costs €15.

lates are as delicious as ever (€2 each). Fillings are unusual, ranging from brandy sour to Cyprus royal jelly, which is promoted as being beneficial to health – as if we needed any persuading. Chocolate workshops also take place with prices according to the number of participants.

ℹ Information

The helpful **Cyprus Tourism Organisation** (CTO; ☑ 2542 1316; www.visitcyprus.com; Platres Sq; ☉ 9am-3.30pm Mon-Fri, to 2.30pm Sat) office can assist with accommodation and information on hiking trails in the area.

ℹ Getting There & Around

All public transport arrives at and departs from the area adjoining the **Cyprus Tourism Organisation** (p85) office. You'll definitely need a car or suitable alternative to explore the greater area.

Emel bus 64 (€1.50, 1¼ hours) runs to/from Lemesos three times daily Monday to Saturday, and once on Sunday.

Travel Express Taxis (☑ 2587 7666; www.travelexpress.com.cy) run from Lemesos to Platres for approximately €50 (about 50 minutes).

OMODOS & THE KRASOHORIA

POP 600

Omodos is a popular destination for day trippers from the coastal resorts. And for good reason: despite the proliferation of souvenir shops, the backstreets have a timeless cobbled charm and are home to an excellent restaurant and small hotel, plus a quirky museum and a collection of idiosyncratic shops.

The extensive vineyards of the *krasohoria* occupy the scenic slopes around Omodos;

there are more than 50 boutique wineries in the area. This is a traditional winemaking region where, up until around the 1960s, every house had its own winemaking tools. Many villages still sell a variety of traditional grape-based products, such as *soujoukkos, espuma* (grape honey) and *palouzes* (grape sweets).

⊙ Sights

Timiou Stavrou Monastery MONASTERY
(Holy Cross Monastery; Omodos; ⊙9.30am-1pm & 2-7pm Thu-Tue, 9.30am-12.30pm Wed) Fronted by the town's impressive, massive cobbled square, the monastery's entrance is guarded by a statue commemorating Dositheos, a former abbot murdered by Turkish troops during the Greek War of Independence in 1821. Now acting as the parish church, the monastery was originally built around 1150; it was extended and extensively remodelled in the 19th century. Several of the outbuildings now house small museums.

The harrowing **National Struggle Museum** is small and simple, but the memories evoked by the black-and-white photos of the men and women killed (some reputedly tortured) by British forces between 1955 and 1959 might linger in your mind long after you leave.

Another outbuilding houses the **Museum for the Preservation of Lace**, with delicate examples of the *pipilies* (needlepoint lacework) for which the village is famed.

Socrates Traditional House MUSEUM
(Linou, Omodos; ⊙9.30am-7pm) `FREE` Located in the backstreets but well signposted, this quirky museum in a traditional house has an eclectic assortment of exhibits and furnishings, including historic wine presses, wedding attire, old photos, looms, a corn mill, typical village furniture and objects from rural life.

🏃 Activities

Many of the region's wineries are open by appointment only. Check out www.wineriescyprus.com for profiles and seasonal opening times, and pick up the *Cyprus Wine Routes* booklet from local Cyprus Tourism Organisation (p85) offices.

Zenon WINE
(☑2542 3555; Dimitri Liperti, Omodos; ⊙11am-7pm Mon-Sat) Located just outside Omodos, this small family-run winery offers free tastings and has a small wine museum. Try its

award-winning reds, including the shiraz maratheftiko and cabernet sauvignon.

Revecca Winery WINE
(☑9946 1089; www.revecca.com; Amvrakikou 1, Agios Mamas; ⊙10am-5pm Mon, Tue, Thu & Fri, to 1pm Wed & Sat) This traditional winery is best known for its Commandaria sweet wine, though it also produces two dry red and white wines in small quantities. In addition to tastings, visitors can have a look around a small museum in the Revecca Christou family house (1925) dedicated to the history of winemaking in the *krasohoria*.

Call Eleni in advance to plan a tasting and tour.

Vlassides Winery WINE
(☑9944 1574; www.vlassideswinery.com; Koilani; ⊙11am-4pm Mon-Sat) This small winery in Koilani offers tours and tastings of its wines, including a particularly aromatic and full-bodied cabernet sauvignon. The vineyards are more than a century old and cover some 16 hectares surrounding the village.

Kilani is approximately 10km east of Omodos via Mandria.

Yiaskouris Winery WINE
(☑9963 3730; www.yiaskouriswines.net; Kyriakou Matsi 6, Pachna; ⊙11am-5pm) Located in Pachna village, this small winery has great shirazes and dry whites. A tasting room, opened in 2017, offers local cheeses to sample along with wines.

🍴 Eating

George's Bakery BAKERY €
(☑2542 2142; 1 Octovriou, Omodos; bread from €1.20; ⊙9am-6pm) This bakery and deli serves a vast range of breads, cakes, halva, nut brittle and the like, most happily available for tasting. Try the local *apkatena* bread with ingredients including chickpeas, cinnamon, nutmeg and citrus peel. Located adjacent to the town's main car park.

⭐ **Stou Kir Yianni** CYPRIOT €€
(☑2542 2100; www.omodosvillagecottage.com; Linou 15, Omodos; mains €10-17; ⊙10am-10pm) Head for the courtyard with its cool colour palette of limestone and whitewash and local art on the walls. The menu includes *fattoush* (salad with fried pitta) with pomegranate juice, *kleftiko*, vegetarian moussaka, kebabs and *karaolous me pnigouri* (snails with bulgur wheat), a traditional Cypriot dish.

There's live music, from blues to Greek, Thursdays to Saturdays, and an ouzo bar (tasting €5).

Taverna tou Themistokli   TAVERNA €€

(☎ 2542 2649; Panagia Halkidiki 39, Omodos; mains €8-12, meze €17; ☺ 10am-4pm) At this taverna, tucked up a side street away from the tourist clamour, head for the terrace shaded by a magnificent walnut tree. Dishes are made to order here, and you may have a bit of waiting time to work up an appetite. Choose one of the time-tested traditional dishes such as moussaka or *keftedes* (meatballs).

🛍 **Shopping**

Byzantine Icon Studio   GIFTS & SOUVENIRS

(maria.icon.painter@gmail.com; Linou, Omodos; ☺ 9.30am-6pm) Maria Aristou is an icon painter and sells her work at this small shop in the backstreets of Omodos. Prices range from €80 to €120.

ℹ️ **Getting There & Away**

From Lemesos, Emel runs four buses (bus 40) to/from Omodos on weekdays and two on Saturdays and Sundays (€1.50, 1¾ hours). Buses leave from the main car park at the entrance to the village.

MARATHASA VALLEY

This scenic valley situated on the north-western slopes of the Troödos Mountains cradles some of the region's most important and impressive sights, such as the splendid Kykkos Monastery, Pedoulas' beautifully frescoed church Archangelos Michail, and the humble Agios Ioannis Lambadistis Monastery. The Marathasa Valley is home to several picturesque villages which are slowly being discovered by more discerning visitors: Kalopanayiotis is an example of how agrotourism can transform the fortunes of a previously little-known mountain village. The area is also one of the best regions for hiking in the Troödos, with trails available to suit all levels of fitness.

The best times to visit the Marathasa Valley are spring and autumn when wildflowers display their dazzling rainbow of colours. Fruit trees also flourish in this mild climate; cherries are famously grown here, giving a vibrant cascade of brilliant pink blossoms in springtime.

ℹ️ **Getting There & Away**

Apart from buses running between Omodos and Lemesos, the Marathasa Valley is not well served by public transport; the ideal mode of transport is a car.

The valley can be reached from the north via the Nicosia–Evrychou–Troödos road and from the south along the Lemesos–Platres–Prodromos road.

Pedoulas

POP 195

Pedoulas is the main town and tourist centre in the Marathasa Valley. Set on the edge of the valley with a series of terraces tumbling down it, Pedoulas is most famous for its tiny painted church Archangelos Michail, which dates from the Byzantine period. Dominating the skyline is the far more recent (and huge) white Church of the Holy Cross. Located in the town centre, it's a good place to start your explorations and orientate yourself with Pedoulas' maze of streets.

Pedoulas has excellent facilities, including a small supermarket, banks and ATMs, a petrol station and reliable eating and sleeping options. Famous for its spring water (sold all over Cyprus), it's particularly cool and breezy in summer.

ANCIENT COMMANDARIA

Homer made mention of its amber colour and rich sweetness in his writings. The Knights Templar were so fond of it they named it after their Commanderie (Headquarters) in Lemesos (Limassol), exporting it to the royal courts of Europe. Upon Richard the Lionheart's marriage in Lemesos, he declared it 'the wine of kings' and 'the king of wines'. For over 4000 years it has been made at the vast vineyards in the Commandaria valley, exposed to the southerly sun. Made from dark and white grapes, Commandaria is as excellent as ever, with over a dozen villages still producing it. You can visit a number of local wineries and sample their produce: **Revecca Winery** (p86) in Agios Mamas, 20km east of Omodos, has a large selection.

◉ Sights

★ Archangelos Michail   CHURCH

(☑ 2295 2629; Holy Cross St; ⊘ 10am-6pm Tue-Sun) Most people visit Pedoulas to see this extraordinary Unesco-listed church. Dating from 1474, the gable-roofed building sits in the lower part of the village. Its evocative and brightly coloured frescos, restored in 1980, show a move towards the naturalism of the post-Byzantine revival. The works are credited to an artist known only as Adamos, who, unusually for that time, signed his work. If it's not open, the key is held at the Byzantine Museum across the street.

Also depicted are, of course, the Archangel Michael, looming above the faithful, as well as the denial of Christ, the sacrifice of Abraham, the Virgin and Christ, and a beautiful baptism scene where an unclothed Christ exits the River Jordan with fish swimming at his feet.

Be sure not to mistake the looming white Church of the Holy Cross just up the road for this far more famous and historic church.

★ Pedoulas Byzantine Museum   MUSEUM

(☑ 2295 3636; Pedoulas; ⊘ 10am-4.30pm Tue-Sun) FREE The museum's rich collection of 12th- to 15th-century icons come from six ancient Byzantine churches in the village and include the late-13th-century icon of the

---

CYPRUS WINE: 4000 YEARS IN THE MAKING

Archaeologists have traced the island's winemaking history back to around 4000 BC, with amphorae, wine jugs and even grape pips excavated in the Lemesos (Limassol) region suggesting Cyprus could be the oldest wine-producing country in the world. Dionysus is making his presence felt once more, as Cypriot wines grow in stature and popularity.

The fertile hills and valleys of the Troödos Mountains are where some of the island's finest grapes are cultivated. Indigenous mavro (dark red grapes) and xynisteri (white grapes) vines are cultivated here, along with 11 other varieties. They contribute to red wines including ofthalmo, maratheftiko, cabernet sauvignon, mataro, lefkada and shiraz, and to whites, such as sauvignon blanc and chardonnay.

Virgin Vorinis. Many pieces have featured in exhibitions worldwide.

Folk Art Museum   MUSEUM

(☑ 2295 2140; Pedoulas; ⊘ 10am-4pm Tue-Sun) FREE Near the village centre, this museum houses clothing, furniture and agricultural tools that provide a snapshot of the culture, customs and history of the Marathasa region. Housed in an attractive stone and timber house, it's a notch above many similar museums in these parts, with information in English as well as Greek.

✖ Eating

★ Elyssia   CYPRIOT €€

(☑ 9975 3573; www.elyssiahotel.com; Filoxenias 47; mains €10-12, meze €16; ⊘ 10am-11pm) The moussaka here is so good that it apparently attracts regulars from Pafos; the fresh trout is another winner. The meze – comprising 20 different small dishes – really showcases the cuisine. The congenial owner (who runs the hotel of the same name) also sells a tantalising range of homemade preserves and chutneys.

Platanos   TAVERNA €€

(Vasou Hadjiioannou; mains €9-12; ⊘ 8am-6pm) In the shade of the *platano* (plane tree), this restaurant serves such traditional dishes as *souvlakia* and *afelia* (slow-cooked pork with wine and herbs). Cypriot coffee here is a must, prepared the time-honoured way by using a tray of hot sand between the *brikki* (small saucepan) and the open flame. This allows the coffee to heat gradually, giving a richer taste.

❶ Getting There & Away

Osel buses go to/from Anigma Kolokasi, Nicosia four times daily on weekdays, three times on Saturday and twice on Sunday (€1.50, 1½ hours).

Kalopanayiotis

POP 350

Long famous for its monastery and Byzantine museum, Kalopanayiotis is today gaining renown as an agrotourism trailblazer. Established by a wealthy former resident, the massive Casale Panayiotis project has transformed the historic core of this small mountain village, turning almost 45 traditional dwellings into tasteful accommodation. A luxury spa based around Kalopanayiotis' natural sulphur springs, two top-tier restaurants and a sophisticated wine bar have further enhanced the village's agro-appeal.

The project has been a boon for residents: before Casale Panayiotis came along, the school had closed and most young people fled the village in favour of the coast or bigger cities. It remains to be seen whether this template for regenerating flagging villages will be repeated elsewhere in the region.

◉ Sights

Agios Ioannis
Lambadistis Monastery MONASTERY
(⊙ 9am-4pm Tue-Sun May-Sep, shorter hours rest of the year; P) FREE This Unesco-listed site is a complex of three churches in one, dating from the 11th century and built over 400 years. Now under one huge pitched wooden roof, they represent some of the region's most wonderfully preserved churches. The monastery also houses an icon-filled Byzantine Museum.

Get there by following the narrow, winding main street to the opposite side of the valley. Opening hours can fluctuate; you can generally find the priest (plus key) at the nearby coffee shop.

The main domed Orthodox church exhibits colourful, intricate 13th-century frescos dedicated to Agios Irakleidios. These include depictions of Jesus' entry to Jerusalem on a donkey, with children climbing date trees to get a better look. Other frescos include the *Raising of Lazarus*, the *Crucifixion* and the *Ascension*, with vivid colour schemes suggesting artistic influence from Constantinople.

The antechamber and Latin chapel have more frescos, dating from the 15th and 16th centuries. Those in the chapel are considered the most comprehensive series of Italo-Byzantine frescos in Cyprus. The scenes representing the Akathistos hymn (praising the Virgin Mary in 24 verses) are shown as 24 pictures, each carrying a letter of the Greek alphabet. The *Arrival of the Magi* depicts the Magi on horseback, wearing crusader armour and grandstanding red crescents (a Roman symbol for the Byzantines and later the Turks). Photographs of the iconography are not permitted.

The original Orthodox church has a double nave, to which a narthex and Latin chapel were later added.

The monastery's **Byzantine Museum** displays a collection of 15 icons discovered in 1998. Dating from the 16th century, the icons were hidden underground for many

---

WORTH A TRIP

PANAGIA TOU MOUTOULLA

The oldest of the 10 Unesco-listed painted churches in the Troödos Mountains, **Panagia tou Moutoulla** (Moutoullas; ⊙ dawn-dusk) is believed to have once been a private chapel. It has the steep aisle and pitched roof common to the region. The rare unrestored paintings include depictions of St Christopher, St George and the Virgin, and date back to AD 1280. You will need to seek out the key, held by Eleni at a nearby house; the village coffee shop will direct you.

The church is located in the small village of Moutoullas, on the road between Pedoulas and Kalopanayiotis. The village is well known for its traditional woodcarvings, as well as its bounty of apples and cherries from the vast surrounding orchards.

---

years by Orthodox priests escaping the invading Ottomans. The iconostasis is covered in carvings of local ferns found at the river in Kalopanayiotis, confirming its origins.

✕ Eating

★**Loutraki** CYPRIOT €€€
(☑ 2295 2444; www.casalepanayiotis.com; Upper Village Rd; mains €14-20; ⊙ noon-3pm & 6-11pm Wed-Mon; ☎) This fashionable spot, with its minimalist dining room and fabulous valley views, has a refreshingly short menu of primarily grilled choices, including trout with artichokes, spinach, and lemon pesto. Other innovative combinations include a goat and haloumi (hellim in Turkish) burger, and ravioli stuffed with roasted beetroot, anari cheese and white truffle. Popular with well-heeled Nicosians: don't turn up in flip-flops.

❶ Getting There & Away

Osel buses go from Anigma Kolokasi, Nicosia, to Kalopanayiotis six times daily on weekdays, three times on Saturday and twice on Sunday (€1.50, 1¼ hours).

Kykkos Monastery & Around

Heading west from Pedoulas, a mountain road snakes through peaceful pine forests to Kykkos, the island's most famous monastery, and the nearby tomb of Cyprus' first

THE FRESCOED BYZANTINE CHURCHES OF CYPRUS

Many visitors come to the Troödos region to see the remarkable Byzantine churches, built and decorated with stunning frescos between the 11th and 15th centuries. Ten of these churches are Unesco World Heritage Sites.

When the French Catholic Lusignan dynasty took control of Cyprus in 1197, work on a series of small churches in the mountains had already begun. But it was the repression and discrimination exercised by the Lusignans against the Orthodox Greek Cypriots that prompted the Orthodox clergy, along with artisans and builders, to retreat to the northern slopes of the Troödos Mountains. Here they built and embellished private ecclesiastical retreats where Orthodoxy flourished undisturbed for 300 years.

Many of the churches were built in a similar fashion. Most were little larger than small barns; some had domes, some did not. Because of the harsh winter weather, large, steeply inclined overhanging roofs were added to protect the churches from accumulated snow. Inside, skilled fresco painters went to work producing a series of vivid images.

Not all churches were lavishly painted, but the Unesco-designated churches represent the finest examples. The frescos are remarkable for their clarity of detail and the preservation of their colour. The later didactic-style frescos are unusual in that they are painted like a movie strip, ostensibly to teach illiterate villagers the rudiments of the gospels.

You will need at least two days to visit all the churches. A number of them are kept locked, so you'll have to track down their caretakers. Donations of €1 to €3 are appreciated. A car is the easiest way to visit most of the churches, as public transport is sporadic.

In viewing order, the Unesco churches are: Archangelos Michail (p88), Agios Ioannis Lambadistis Monastery (p89), Panagia tou Moutoulla (p89), Agios Nikolaos tis Stegis (p92), Panagia tis Podythou (p92), Panagia Forviotissa (p92), Stavros tou Agiasmati (p95), Panagia tou Araka (p95), and Timios Stavros (p95).

president. There are no buses running to Kykkos so you'll need your own transport, or you can join a tour from the coast.

◎ Sights

★ Kykkos Monastery   MONASTERY
(☏ 2294 2736; www.kykkos.org.cy; ☉ dawn-dusk)
The island's most prosperous and opulent Orthodox monastery was founded in the 11th century by Byzantine emperor Alexios I Komninos after a bizarre series of events. Over the centuries, a series of fires all but destroyed the original monastery. The surviving building, an imposing and well-maintained structure, dates from 1831.

The monastery is about 20km west of Pedoulas; try to visit early, as it can get busy from late morning onwards. Dress conservatively (though shawls and cover-up clothing are provided).

The story behind the monastery started with a hermit called Esaias (Isaiah), who lived in a cave close to the site. One day in the forest, Esaias crossed paths with a hunter from Nicosia, Manouil Voutomytis, who was also the Byzantine governor of Cyprus. Voutomytis was lost and asked directions from the recluse, only to be ig-

nored because of Esaias' ascetic vows. The self-important hunter became outraged at what he perceived to be the hermit's insolence, cursing at him and shoving him as a lesson.

Upon returning to Nicosia, Voutomytis began to suffer incurable lethargy. He recalled how he had mistreated Esaias and set out to beg forgiveness, in the hope of restoring his failing health. Meanwhile, a vision from God appeared to Esaias, telling him to charge Voutomytis with the task of bringing an icon of the Virgin Mary from Constantinople to Cyprus.

At the hermit's request, and after much soul-searching, Voutomytis was eventually able to bring the icon to Cyprus. He convinced the Byzantine emperor in Constantinople, whose daughter suffered the same lethargic affliction, that she would be saved if they did what the hermit (and therefore God) had asked.

The icon, said to be painted by St Luke, is one of only three that survive. For the last four centuries it has sat in a sealed, silver-encased box within the Kykkos Monastery.

Byzantine Museum   MUSEUM
(☑ 2294 2736; www.kykkos.org.cy; Kykkos Monastery; admission €5; ☺ 10am-6pm Jun-Sep, to 4pm Oct-May; P) This museum houses much of Kykkos Monastery's fabulous wealth, including Byzantine and ecclesiastical artefacts. On the left when you enter is an antiquities display. In the large ecclesiastical gallery are early Christian, Byzantine and post-Byzantine vestments, vessels and jewels. A small circular room houses old manuscripts, documents and books, and a rich display of icons, wall paintings and carvings can be found in the larger circular chamber.

Tomb of Archbishop Makarios III   TOMB
(Throni Hill) The tomb of the first president of Cyprus is located on Throni Hill, 2km past Kykkos Monastery. Makarios was buried here at his request, close to the place where he served as an apprentice monk in 1926. The simple stone sepulchre is overlaid with black marble and covered by a round, stone-inlaid dome. A huge bronze statue of the archbishop, moved from Nicosia's Archepiscopal Palace in 2008, now stands on the hill, adding to its grandeur.

Higher up on the path from the tomb is the **Throni Shrine** to the Virgin Mary. It has spectacular, endless views of the valleys and roads leading to Kykkos from the east. A **wishing tree** is located just near here, where the pious tie paper and cloth messages in the hope that the Virgin Mary will grant their requests.

Treis Elies

Southwest of Prodromos via the F10 and F811 is Treis Elies, a quiet hamlet perfect for relaxation. There's a small river and na-

ture trail around the village, and just outside is the **lamatikes sulphur spring** (signposted as 'Ιαματικές'), spurting through large rocks.

Its location is convenient for hikes to the Kelefos, Elies and Roudhias medieval bridges, which were built during Venetian rule in an effort to streamline the camel-caravan route near the village. The camels transported copper from Troödos to Polis and Pafos, where it was traded. Unfortunately, the original path is now all but lost.

The three bridges are connected by the European Long Distance Path E4.

Closest to Treis Elies is **Elies Bridge**, just after the village of Kaminaria. Set in dense forest, with an underground fresh stream, it was believed to be the easterly link of the caravan route.

Kelefos Bridge is the most elegant of the bridges, with a strong single-pointed arch stretching over a wide waterway. It takes about two hours to hike from Elies to Kelefos, where you'll find an excellent picnic spot. You can also reach Kelefos Bridge by car, following the signs towards Agios Nikolaos.

The third bridge, **Roudhias Bridge**, is impressive but far more remote. It's a long-distance four-hour hike away, along the trail past the Pera Vassas forestry station and picnic ground. The bridge can be difficult to find, so be sure to take a good map. If you choose to drive, the direct road is a narrow track with limited access. There is also a river crossing that requires a 4WD.

You'll need your own transport to reach Treis Elies.

EUROPEAN LONG DISTANCE PATH E4

Located in the southern Marathasa Valley, Treis Elies is a fantastic base from which to explore European Long Distance Path E4, a famous trail that starts at Gibraltar and passes through Spain, France, Switzerland, Germany, Austria, Hungary, Bulgaria, Greece and Cyprus. The E4 is linked to Cyprus by air and sea, starting at Larnaka and Pafos airports, and covering the Troödos Mountains. It continues on to the Akamas Peninsula and stretches across to the eastern regions of the Cypriot areas of Famagusta (Gazimağusa).

The path is a rambler's delight, and detailed maps are essential. You can download the mapped route via the www.wandermap.net website; the Cyprus Tourism Organisation (CTO) booklet *European Long Distance Path E4 & Other Cyprus Nature Trails* also gives an overview of the Cypriot walks, stating lengths, degrees of difficulty, starting and ending locations and points of interest.

Conquering the Cypriot portion is a soul-stirring start to being part of the greater project, so lace up those hiking boots and stride out.

SOLEA VALLEY

The Solea Valley, bisected by the Karyotis River, is home to significant frescoed churches built during the late Byzantine era, when the area was revered for its importance as a former crusader stronghold.

The valley's reputation as a strategic refuge was furthered in the 1950s, when it served as the prime hideout area for Ethniki Organosi tou Kypriakou Agona (EOKA; National Organisation for the Cypriot Struggle) revolutionists during their anti-British campaigns. With its concealed terrain and proximity to Nicosia, it was an ideal location.

Today, it's still perfect for accessing the mountains and beyond, with roads to both the east and west. The main village in the valley is Kakopetria, which is convenient for day trips and longer stays, with decent hotels and good facilities.

 Getting There & Away

Though there are regular buses between Nicosia and Kakopetria, there's no direct public transport to the Unesco-listed churches in the valley. The area, approximately 56km from Nicosia, is located along the main Nicosia–Troödos road, and is roughly the same distance from Lemesos via the B8 and B9 roads.

Kakopetria

POP 1200

Kakopetria, or *kaki petra* (meaning 'bad rock'), gets its name from the line of huge rocks along the ridge around the village that were clearly a hindrance to the first settlers. This village is situated across both banks of the Karyotis River, and visitors can expect steep roads, hanging trees and the sound of natural storm drains.

The area is very popular with wealthy Cypriots, who retire to their homes in the mountains for the summer months. The pedestrianised tangle of streets that comprise the historic quarter is heritage listed, and many of the houses have been restored accordingly, enabling it to retain its charm.

Kakopetria has good restaurants and accommodation. It's an ideal place to base yourself while exploring the region's frescoed churches and surrounds.

 Sights

While Kakopetria is peacefully picturesque, it's the frescoed churches in the surrounding countryside that everyone wants to see. Public transport is limited so the best option is to drive yourself, or walk.

Agios Nikolaos tis Stegis CHURCH
(⊙9am-6pm Tue-Sat, 11am-4pm Sun) This Unesco-listed church, known in English as St Nicholas of the Roof because of its large, heavy-pitched top, was founded in the 11th century and contains frescos which are a mix of images and styles, the best including the Crucifixion and the Nativity. The dome and narthex were added in the 15th century, along with the roof, to protect against the region's snowfall. The church was originally part of a monastery complex.

It's situated 5km north of Kakopetria.

Panagia tis Podythou CHURCH
(☑2292 2393; Galata; ⊙hours vary) Located in the village of Galata, on the Nicosia road, this 16th-century Unesco-listed church was established in 1502 by Dimitrios de Coron, a Greek military officer in the service of James II (king of Cyprus).

Its 17th-century frescos cover the pediment of both the east and west walls. The two striking frescos on the north and south walls appear uncompleted. They depict the apostles, Peter and Paul, in a Renaissance-influenced (Italo-Byzantine) style with vivid colours that provide a three-dimensional appearance.

Occupied by monks until the 1950s, the church is rectangular, with a semicircular apse at the eastern end and a portico (built later) that surrounds it on three sides. It also has a characteristic pitched roof.

If the church is closed, ask for the caretaker at the Galata village coffee shop.

Panagia Theotokou (Arhangelou) CHURCH
(Galata; ⊙hours vary) Dating from around 1514, this smaller chapel is just near Panagia tis Podythou. It's quite dark inside, so you may want to bring a torch. It has vivid didactic-style (teaching) panels with frescos depicting an interesting panoply of images from Jesus' life. Opening hours are sporadic; to access the church you'll need to ask for the caretaker at the Galata village coffee shop.

★**Panagia Forviotissa** CHURCH
(Panagia Asinou; ☑9983 0329; ⊙9.30am-1pm & 2-4pm Mon-Sat, 10am-1pm & 2-4pm Sun) This Unesco-listed church is in a stunning setting on the perimeter of the Adelfi Forest 4km southwest of Nikitari village. Dedicated to the Virgin of 'Phorbiottissa', it has arguably

the finest set of vibrant and colourful Byzantine frescos in the Troödos Mountains. They date from the 12th to the 17th centuries.

To view the church, you'll need to ask its priest and caretaker, Father Kyriakos, who can usually be found at Nikitari's coffee shop.

A 5.6km (roughly two-hour) forest hike to the village of Agios Theodoros begins from just before the church; other attractions include the shady, well-equipped Asinou picnic site and a good local taverna across the road.

Panagia Forviotissa can be reached by following the signs off the B9 from Nicosia, via Vyzakia.

✕ Eating

Village Pub   CYPRIOT €
(mains from €6; ⊙12.30-3.30pm & 6-10pm Tue-Sat) This place has a wooden terrace overlooking the village, and provides good and simple summer meals, such as fresh salads, *fassolia* (white beans) and *faggi* (lentils).

★ Mylos Restaurant   MEDITERRANEAN €€
(Mill Hotel; ☑2292 2536; www.cymillhotel.com; Mylou 8; mains €10-15; ⊙noon-4pm & 7-11pm; ⚫🍴) This excellent restaurant at the Mill Hotel is ideally situated next to the river, with a slow-turning mill wheel and a shady terrace offering superb views. The trout here is legendary and served either grilled or in a delicious garlic-spiked sauce. In winter the historic fireplace is lit. You'll need a reservation on weekends.

Linos Inn   CYPRIOT €€
(☑2292 3161; www.linosinn.com; Palea Kakopetria 34; meze per plate from €5; ⊙restaurant 10am-midnight year-round, cafe to 10pm May-Sep) An atmospheric restaurant (part of the same-name hotel with excellent meze and great local reds. Meze dishes are priced individually, which can equal a heftier bill than the fixed-price norm, but offers the advantage of being able to sample as little or as much as you want. There's also a relaxing terrace cafe-cum-bar (summer only) with essentially the same menu.

Tziellari   ARGENTINE €€
(☑2292 2522; Palias Kakopetrias 72; mains €10-15; ⊙noon-4pm & 7-10pm Tue-Sun) With gaucho-themed decor and an Argentinian chef and owner, Tziellari is authentic and unpretentious. If you like cowboy-sized quality steak, you will love this place. The meatballs

KAKOPETRIA'S HISTORIC QUARTER

To find the most picturesque and historic part of town, take the lane east of the **Village Pub** past a large boulder known as the *Stone of the Couple*, which has a plaque describing how it was thought to bring good luck to newlyweds...until it toppled over and crushed one very *unlucky* couple.

The houses here have traditional trussed roofs, covered with reeds and tiles and supported by beams with overhanging wooden balconies. Seek out the simple **Metamorposis Sotiros chapel**, as well as a small **wine museum**, tucked up a side street but well signposted.

smothered with a traditional *tuco* (rich tomato) sauce also receive rave reviews from diners.

❶ Getting There & Away

Osel buses run from Constanza Bastion, Nicosia, to the centre of Kakopetria about every hour from 5.45am to 8pm on weekdays and less frequently, from 8am, on weekends (€1.50, 1¼ hours). There are roughly the same number of buses doing the return trip.

PITSYLIA

This wide-reaching region stretches east from Mt Olympus and Troödos village, encompassing around 40 villages across to the Maheras Monastery (p170) due west. Its northern slopes are covered in tall, aromatic pines and its valleys are full of grapevines and nut and fruit trees. There are also a number of tucked-away, colourful Byzantine churches, as well as challenging walks for long-distance hikers, and some more gentle options for strollers. Historically, this region is associated with the struggle for independence, and memorials to EOKA fighters can be seen in several of the villages.

Agros is the hub of the region. Other villages with significant sites include Kyperounda, Platanistasa, Palaichori and Pelendri.

❶ Getting There & Away

Apart from buses servicing Agros, public transport to the Pitsylia region is limited. However,

HIKING AROUND PITSYLIA

Pitsylia has some well-marked hiking trails, including two short circular trails. Most take an out-and-back approach, unless you're hiking to the next village. Routes traverse forests, orchards, villages, valleys and mountain peaks, offering some of the best recreational hiking on the island.

The pamphlet *Cyprus: Nature Trails* by the Cyprus Tourism Organisation (CTO) provides good maps of these trails, but it's still advisable to take detailed maps of the greater region. You'll find self-guided walks and maps of the region at www.maps-and-walks.com/product-category/cyprus.

Doxasi o Theos to Madari Fire Station (3.75km, two hours) A panoramic ridge-top hike with excellent views. The trail starts 2km outside Kyperounda.

Teisia tis Madari (3km, 1½ hours, circular) A continuation of the first route, this involves a circular cliff-top hike around Mt Madari (Adelfi; 1613m) with first-rate views.

Panagia tou Araka (Lagoudera) to Agros (6km, 2½ hours) A longer hike through vineyards and orchards, with a great viewpoint from the Madari-Papoutsas ridge.

Panagia tou Araka to Stavros tou Agiasmati (7km, 3½ hours) Takes in two of the most important Byzantine churches and weaves through forests, vineyards and stone terraces. This is the longest hike.

Agros to Kato Mylos (5km, two hours, circular) A gentle hike through cherry and pear orchards past vineyards and rose gardens.

Petros Vanezis to Alona (1.5km, 30 minutes, circular) A shorter hike around the village of Alona, passing through hazelnut plantations.

Agia Irini to Spilies tou Digeni (3.2km, 1½ hours) A simple out-and-back hike to the concealed Digenis caves, where EOKA (Ethniki Organosi tou Kypriakou Agona; National Organisation for the Cypriot Struggle) members hid during the insurgency of 1955–59.

the roads are good and well signposted, especially from Lemesos where the best access is via the excellent B8. Note that at weekends, this road can get busy with locals returning back to the coast.

Agros

POP 1000

Situated at 1100m in a cool valley cradled by the surrounding mountains, Agros is an appealing village with its distinctive red roofs and feeling of remoteness. Well placed for hiking and driving forays into the surrounding hills, Agros is renowned in the region for its locally made rose products, including rose water and Cypriot delight; it also specialises in preserved fruit and traditional Cypriot meats, such as *loukanika* (spiced sausages) and *lountza* (smoked pork fillet). As such, most of the activity centres on its traditional warehouses and workshops. Agros makes an excellent base for exploring the surrounding region.

The village was named after the Monastery of Great Agros, which was built at the spot where the Church of Panayia of Agros is found today after the monastery was devastated by fire in 1894.

Eating

Pezema Tavern   CYPRIOT €

(☑9955 1381; www.pezematavern.weebly.com; E923; mains €6-8; ☺11am-3pm & 6-10pm) A reassuringly brief menu features traditional grilled dishes and Cypriot specialities, such as *keftedes* and *souvlakia*. The new chef-cum-owner obviously takes great pride in his dishes and uses seasonal produce whenever possible: stuffed local mushrooms, omelette with wild greens, and grilled fresh artichokes with herbs are delicious.

Shopping

Venus Rose   COSMETICS

(☑2552 1893; www.venus-rose.com; Triantafilou 12; ☺8am-5pm Mon-Fri, from 10am Sat & Sun) Check out this rose-product store's workshop for a glimpse of the many ways roses can be used. Great examples include flower water, skin cleanser, candles, rose liqueur and rose oil, one of the most sought-after beauty ingredients in the world. This is an excellent place for gifts.

If you visit in May, you can help them collect the rose petals.

Niki's Sweets FOOD
(☑ 2552 1400; www.nikisweets.com.cy; Triantafilou 5; preserves €3-5; ☺ 9am-6pm) Selling her products all over Cyprus, and exporting as far as Australia, Niki makes marmalades, fig preserves and walnut sweets. Many of her preserves offer soothing and healing properties. You can also purchase carob syrup here, purportedly a natural treatment for osteoporosis.

Kafkalia Sausages FOOD
(☑ 2552 1426; kafkalia@cytanet.com.cy; Kyriakou Apeitou; ☺ 8.30am-4pm Mon-Fri, 9am-3pm Sat) Some of the tastiest Cypriot meat products, including *lountza*, *hiromeri* (traditional smoked ham), *loukanika* and *pastourmas* (spicy smoked beef), are made fresh on the premises. Check out the smoke room next to the store.

ⓘ Getting There & Away

Emel operates bus 50 to/from Lemesos, five times daily from 5.25am to 2.40pm weekdays, three times on Saturday and twice on Sunday (€1.50, two hours). Osel buses run to Nicosia from Agros twice daily (€1.50, 1½ hours). The bus stop for both bus lines is outside the Rodon Mountain Hotel.

Around Agros

More Unesco-listed churches and traditional vineyards dot the hills around Agros. You'll need your own transport, or fit legs, to reach the following sights.

⊙ Sights

Timios Stavros CHURCH
(Pelendri; ☺ 10am-5pm) Built in the 12th century, this Unesco-listed church was originally dome-shaped with a single aisle. In the 13th and 14th centuries it was added to with a tiled roof and cupola-style adornment; only the frescoed apse is original.

The frescos (1178) include a rather oversized Jesus depicted in prayer from the waist up, with the Virgin Mary and John the Baptist, painted as miniatures, flanking him.

Other depictions include the altar and the grail near the small window in the apse and St Stephen on the north side. These latter frescos (painted by the same hand) are con-

sidered a preface to the great works found in other Troödos churches, with simple straight lines and shiny earth colours. The rest of the images are from the 14th century, when the church was completely repainted.

The church is at the southern end of the village of Pelendri. If the church is closed (which is likely), ask at any village coffee shop for the whereabouts of the priest.

Agia Sotira tou Soteros CHURCH
(☑ 9997 4230; Palaichori; ☺ 10am-1pm Tue & Wed) Perched on the slope overlooking Palaichori village, this Unesco-listed early-16th-century chapel contains one of the island's most complete groups of late Byzantine wall paintings. The work of an unknown master, the paintings depict vivid scenes, such as St Mamas upon the lion. The church also holds a series of iconostases painted by Mt Athos monk Mathaios. To see inside, you may have to call the custodian or ask in the village centre at the Byzantine Heritage Museum.

Stavros Tou Agiasmati CHURCH
(Orounda-Platanistasa; ☺ hours vary) This Unesco-listed Byzantine church is famous for its 15th-century murals by Orthodox Syrian painter Philippos Goul. In two tiers, the images decorate the ceilings and interior beams of the gabled roof, depicting such scenes as the discovery of the Holy Cross.

Opening hours are sporadic. If the priest cannot be found, ask for the key at the coffee shop in Platanistasa village centre. The church is 5km from the village, off the Orounda–Platanistasa route (E906). Follow the Unesco signposts.

Panagia tou Araka CHURCH
(Lagoudera; ☺ 9am-6pm; ℗) This 12th-century Unesco-listed church is on the outskirts of Lagoudera. From the outside, it appears enormous, the pitched roof and wooden trellis concealing the church within. Inside, it has some of the finest examples of late Comnenian style (1192) frescos in the Orthodox world. Its neoclassical works by artists from Constantinople display such images as the incredible Pantokrator featured in the *tholos* (beehive-shaped stone tomb). Other excellent frescos include the *Annunciation*, the *Four Evangelists*, the *Archangel Michael* and the *Panagia Arakiotissa*.

The unusual name of the church derives from *arakiotissa* (meaning 'of the wild pea') and owes its origins to the vegetable that grows profusely in the district. The church's priest can usually be found next door; check with him before you take any photos of the frescos.

Activities

★ Kyperounda Winery WINE

(☑ 2553 2043; www.photiadesgroup.com/kyperounda; Kyperounda; ⊙ 9am-3.30pm Mon-Fri) Surrounded by 12 hectares of vineyards, the Kyperounda Winery has won several national awards for its wines, including two gold medals in 2016 for its cabernet sauvignon and chardonnay. Complimentary tasting of several wines is offered by the charming owner, generally accompanied by the added treat of local olives and haloumi.

Tsiakkas Winery WINE

(☑ 2599 1080; www.tsiakkaswinery.com; George Sourris 2, Pelendri; ⊙ 9am-4pm Mon-Sat) Hidden in the woods – but well signposted – near the picturesque village of Pelendri, this welcoming winery produces around ten different wines, including an excellent cabernet and chardonnay. Tours and tastings are available, although it is wise to reserve in advance.

Spilia-Kourdali

POP 460

These two traditional villages, situated in the Adelfi Forest, were established in the 16th century near the monastery and church of Virgin Mary Chrysokourdaliotissa (Kourdali). Like many villages in the region, they grew as they became refuges from constant invasions by conquerors: the Francs and later the Turks.

Expansion came via the narrow valley of Kourdali towards the village of Spilia, which derived its name from the Roman graves (*spilioi* in Greek) found in the area. Local asbestos mining was the main proficiency of the villagers for many years; thereafter they became skilled tailors and cobblers. Today, the villages' cafes and craft shops are the main attraction.

◎ Sights

Olive Mill of Paphitaina HISTORIC SITE

(Spilia) FREE In operation until 1955, this well-preserved olive-stone mill and wooden press are now housed in a traditional building in Spilia's village centre.

The mill, originally privately owned, was usually turned by a donkey, with the broken olives later being crushed by the presser. Olive oil was then extracted into *tzares* (clay urns). Eventually the mill was superseded by modern presses in nearby villages.

You can obtain the key from the Friends of Spilia-Kourdali in the building next door.

Pafos & the West

Best Places to Eat

➡ Mandra Tavern (p108)

➡ Argo (p107)

➡ Kiniras Garden (p108)

➡ Imogen's Inn (p113)

➡ Kanalli Fish Restaurant (p118)

Best Places to Escape

➡ Lara Beach (p113)

➡ Kato Pyrgos (p118)

➡ Stavros tis Psokas (p119)

➡ Fyti (p120)

Why Go?

Pafos was nominated joint European Capital of Culture for 2017 in recognition of its extraordinary archaeological sights. Unsurprisingly, these have attracted tourists for decades – as have more hedonistic pursuits. If you find the beach strip at Kato Pafos (Lower Pafos) too developed, duck into the back streets or head up to Ktima (Upper Pafos) on the hillside, which has a more traditional feel. More beach resorts are strung out north along the coast towards Agios Georgios.

To seriously sidestep the crowds, consider renting a car and searching out traditional rural villages where some of the best tavernas are located. If you have sturdier wheels, check out the unspoilt Akamas Peninsula, where there are remote beaches and some of the best walks on the island. To the east, the vast Pafos Forest is equally enticing, melting almost imperceptibly into the sombre tracts of the Tyllirian wilderness.

When to Go

➡ Pafos is the island's top tourist destination and gets busy in summer, which is worth bearing in mind when planning your visit.

➡ The summer months of July and August are when you will find the most sunbeds on the sand, the most sunburned noses and the highest hotel prices.

➡ May, June, September and October are less crowded, with plenty of long sunny days.

➡ Spring and autumn are pleasantly warm, though evening temperatures cool down considerably.

➡ In winter some restaurants and hotels close down altogether; if you head to the Western Troödos, you may even see some snow.

y a traffic artery, Kato Pafos (Low-
os) and Ktima (Upper Pafos; 3km to
e northeast) form a contrasting whole.
Kato Pafos is geared towards tourists, with
bars and souvenir shops lining the palm-
fringed seafront. Dive into the backstreets
to discover historic gems such as medieval
baths, catacombs and a simple fishermen's
church. But the grand-slam sight is one of
the South's richest archaeological locales,
the Pafos Archaeological Site, just one reason the city was awarded joint European
Capital of Culture in 2017. Standing here,
surrounded by acres of history and fields
of wild flowers, feels a world away from the
busy resort just beyond the entrance.

Ktima, the old centre of Pafos, is overall a calmer place, where locals go about
their daily life as they have for decades. Its
neighbourhoods are culturally rich, with
handsome colonial buildings that house
government institutions and many of the
town's museums.

◉ Sights

◎ Kato Pafos

★ **Pafos
Archaeological Site**   ARCHAEOLOGICAL SITE
(Map p103; ☑ 2630 6217; adult/child €4.50/free;
⊙ 8.30am-7.30pm mid-Apr–mid-Sep, to 5pm mid-
Sep–mid-Apr; 🅿) Nea Pafos (New Pafos) is,
ironically, the name given to the sprawling
Pafos Archaeological Site, to the west of
Kato Pafos. Nea Pafos was the ancient city
of Pafos, founded in the late 4th century BC
and originally encircled by massive walls.
Despite being ceded to the Romans in 58
BC, it remained the centre of all political
and administrative life in Cyprus. It is most
famed today for its mesmerising collection
of intricate and colourful mosaics based on
ancient Greek myths.

Palea Pafos (Old Pafos) was in fact Kouklia, southeast of today's Pafos and the site
of the Sanctuary of Aphrodite (p104). At
the time of Nea Pafos, Cyprus was part of
the kingdom of the Ptolemies, the Greco-
Macedonian rulers of Egypt whose capital
was Alexandria. The city became an important strategic outpost for the Ptolemies, and
the settlement grew considerably over the
next seven centuries.

The city originally occupied an area of
about 950,000 sq metres and reached its
zenith during the 2nd or 3rd century AD.
It was during this time that the city's most
opulent public buildings were constructed,
including those that house the famous Pafos
mosaics.

Nea Pafos went into decline following an
earthquake in the 4th century that badly
damaged the city. Subsequently, Salamis in
the east became the new capital of Cyprus,
and Nea Pafos was relegated to the status
of a mere bishopric. Arab raids in the 7th
century set the seal on the city's demise and
neither Lusignan settlement (1192–1489) nor
Venetian and Ottoman colonisation revived
Nea Pafos' fortunes.

The archaeological site is still being excavated since it is widely believed that there are
many treasures still to be discovered. The following sections detail the major sights.

➡ **Pafos Mosaics**

This superb collection of mosaics is located
in the southern sector of the archaeological
site, immediately to the south of the Agora.
Discovered by accident in 1962 by a farmer
ploughing his field, these exquisite mosaics
decorated the extensive floor area of a large,
wealthy residence from the Roman period.
Subsequently named the House of Dionysus (because of the number of mosaics
featuring Dionysus, the god of wine), this
complex is the largest and best known of the
mosaic houses.

The most wonderful thing about the mosaics is that, apart from their artistic and
aesthetic merits, each tells a story, mostly
based on ancient Greek myths.

The first thing you'll see upon entering
is not a Roman mosaic at all but a Hellenistic monochrome pebble mosaic showing
the monster Scylla. Based on a Greek myth,
this mosaic was discovered in 1977, a metre
underground in the southwestern corner of
the atrium.

The famous tale of Narcissus is depicted in a mosaic in Room 2, while the Four
Seasons mosaic (Room 3) depicts Spring
crowned with flowers and holding a shepherd's stick; Summer holding a sickle and
wearing ears of corn; Autumn crowned with
leaves and wheat; and Winter as a bearded,
grey-haired man.

Phaedra and Hippolytos (Room 6) is
one of the most important mosaics in the
house. It depicts the tragic tale of a step-
mother's bizarre love for her stepson.

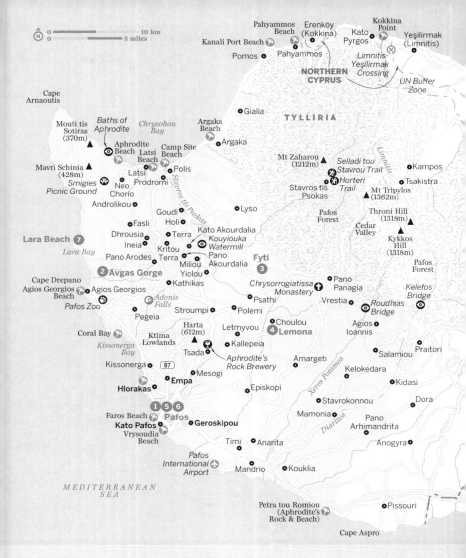

Pafos & the West Highlights

1 Tombs of the Kings (p102) Exploring Pafos' ancient past by visiting its Roman mosaics and the necropolis.

2 Avgas Gorge (p111) Keeping an eye out for tree frogs when hiking this scenic gorge in the Akamas Heights.

3 Folk Art Museum (p120) Watching the weavers in picturesque Fyti, a village famed for its craftwork.

4 Tsangarides Winery (p120) Sampling organic wines in pretty Lemona.

5 Argo (p107) Enjoying delicious *kleftiko* at this long-time favourite Pafos restaurant.

6 Cydive (p106) Diving in the crystal-clear waters around Pafos with this reputable, long-standing operator.

7 Lara Beach (p113) Visiting the wildest beach on this stretch of the coast along with its fascinating turtle hatchery.

ROAD TRIP > WINERIES, WEAVING & ABANDONED VILLAGES

The countryside around Pafos has it all: traditional crafts, village cuisine, ancient monasteries and even the birthplace of the first leader of independent Cyprus. This loop from Pafos takes in the whole range, with plenty of stops at local vineyards to sample the local vintages.

❶ Fyti

From Pafos, take the B7 north towards Polis. After around 9km, look for the sign for **Aphrodite's Rock Brewery** (p112), where you can taste (and buy) craft beers. After a further 3km head towards **Fyti** (p120) on the signposted E703; this pretty country road winds between vineyards and orchards. Pass through Polemi and Psathi, then take the

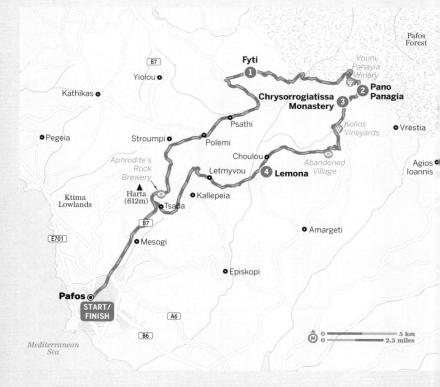

signposted left turn towards Fyti. Park by the church, stop at the **Phiti Pefkos Taverna** (p120) for a drink or snack, and duck into the **Folk Art Museum** (p120).

② Pano Panagia

Leave on the F725 towards Pano Panagia via Kritou Marottous and Asprogia. The scenery en route is lovely, with vineyards, citrus groves and distant mountains. Watch for the sign for the **Vouni Panayia Winery** (p120), a sophisticated stop for a wine tasting; the Barba Yiannis dry red comes particularly recommended. Continue on to Pano Panagia, the birthplace of Archbishop Makarios; have a quick nose around his **childhood house** (p119), a typical peasants' home with just two rooms.

③ Chrysorrogiatissa Monastery

Head south out of town on the F622, stopping at the well-signposted **Chrysorrogiatissa Monastery** (p120) for a simple cafe lunch on the terrace, accompanied by beautiful countryside views. Around 4km from here is another excellent winery, **Kolios Vineyards** (p120), which makes a highly regarded shiraz. Follow signs to the E702 and Choulou. After around 3km you will pass through an abandoned village, where a 1969 earthquake forced the vast majority of villagers to relocate; it is just starting to show some signs of life again.

④ Lemona

In Choulou have a look at the simple whitewashed mosque (this was a Turkish village before 1974) and enjoy a drink across the way at the traditional Antoyaneta coffee shop, with its shaded terrace. Make the last stop on your tour at the village of Lemona, home to microwinery **Tsangarides Winery** (p120), which produces organic wines and recently won a silver medal for its shiraz rosé at the annual Cyprus Wine Competition. Continue back to Pafos on the B7, via Letmyvou and Tsada.

Another stunning mosaic in the house is the **Rape of Ganymede** (Room 8). Ganymede was a beautiful young shepherd who became the cupbearer of the gods. The mosaicist had apparently miscalculated the space allowed to him, which is why the eagle's wings are cropped.

In the **Western Portico** (Room 16) is a mosaic based on a tale familiar to any lover of Shakespeare: the story of Pyramus and Thisbe, first narrated by Ovid in his *Metamorphosis*, and adapted in *Romeo and Juliet* (and *A Midsummer Night's Dream*).

A short walk away are the smaller **Villa of Theseus** and the **House of Aion**. The latter, a purpose-built structure made from stones found on the site, houses a 4th-century mosaic display made up of five separate panels. The house was named after the pagan god Aion, depicted in the mosaics. Although the image has been damaged somewhat, the name Aion and the face of the god can still be clearly seen.

The Villa of Theseus is thought to have been a 2nd-century private residence and is named after a representation of the hero Theseus fighting the Minotaur. The building occupies an area of 9600 sq metres and, so far, 1400 sq metres of mosaics have been uncovered. The round mosaic of Theseus and the Minotaur is particularly well preserved and can be seen in Room 36. Other mosaics to look out for are those of Poseidon in Room 76 and Achilles in Rooms 39 and 40.

Allow at least two hours to see the three houses properly.

➡ **Saranta Kolones Fortress**

Not far from the mosaics are the remains of the medieval Saranta Kolones Fortress, named for the '40 columns' that were once a feature of the now almost levelled structure. Little is known about the precise nature or history of the original fortress, other than it was built by the Lusignans in the 12th century

and was subsequently destroyed by an earthquake in 1222. A few desultory arches are the only visual evidence of its original grandeur.

➡ **Agora, Asklipieion & Odeion**

The Agora (or forum) and Asklipieion date back to the 2nd century AD. Today, the Agora consists mainly of the Odeion, a semicircular theatre restored in 1970 and not appearing particularly ancient. The rest of the Agora is discernible by the remains of marble columns that form a rectangle in the largely empty open space. What is left of the Asklipieion, the healing centre and altar of Asklepios, god of medicine, runs east to west on the southern side of the Odeion.

Be sure to stop by the Visitors' Centre at the top of the steps near the entrance. Interesting rotating exhibitions take place here and you can pick up a guidebook (€5.50), which explains the site in detail.

★ **Tombs of the Kings** ARCHAEOLOGICAL SITE
(☑ 2694 0295; admission €2.50; ☺ 8.30am-7.30pm; ℗; ◻ 615) Imagine yourself surrounded by ancient tombs in a desertlike landscape where the only sounds are waves crashing on rocks. The Tombs of the Kings, a Unesco World Heritage Site, contains a set of well-preserved underground tombs and chambers used by residents of Nea Pafos during the Hellenistic and Roman periods, from the 3rd century BC to the 3rd century AD. Despite the name, the tombs were not actually used by royalty; they earned the title from their grand appearance.

Located 2km north of Kato Pafos, the tombs are unique in Cyprus, being heavily influenced by ancient Egyptian tradition, when it was believed that tombs for the dead should resemble houses for the living.

The seven excavated tombs are scattered over a wide area; the most impressive is No 3, which has an open atrium below ground level, surrounded by columns. Other tombs have niches built into the walls where bodies were stored. Most of the tombs' treasures have long since been spirited away by grave robbers.

Pafos Buses (p110) 615 route to Coral Bay stops right outside the entrance (€1.50, 5 minutes), departing roughly every 15 minutes from the Harbour Bus Station (p110).

★ **Hrysopolitissa Basilica** ARCHAEOLOGICAL SITE
(Map p103; Stassándhrou) **FREE** This fascinating site was home to one of Pafos' largest religious structures. What remains are the foundations of a 4th-century Christian ba-

---

ℹ **TOMB TIPS**

➡ Allow at least two hours for the Tombs of the Kings site.

➡ Try to visit during the early morning as it can get very hot walking around the sprawling necropolis later in the day.

➡ Bring a hat and bottled water.

➡ Be very careful when descending into some of the tombs, as the stone steps are large and can be slippery.

Kato Pafos

Kato Pafos

silica, which aptly demonstrates the size and magnificence of the original church, destroyed during Arab raids in 653. Several magnificent marble columns remain from the colonnades, while others lie scattered around the site, and mosaics are still visible.

Further incarnations of the basilica were built over the years, leading to the present small Agia Kyriaki church, which is now used for Anglican, Lutheran and Greek Orthodox services.

A raised walkway provides excellent views of the extensive site and has explanatory plaques in English. Look also for the tomb of Eric Ejegod, the 12th-century king of Denmark who died suddenly in 1103 on his way to the Holy Land.

On the western side of the basilica is the so-called St Paul's Pillar, where St Paul was allegedly tied and scourged 39 times before he finally converted his tormentor, the Roman governor Sergius Paulus, to Christianity.

Pafos Castle   CASTLE
(Map p103; adult/child €2.50/free; ⊘ 8.30am-7pm) This small fort guards the harbour entrance and is entered by a small stone bridge over a moat. In 2017, to commemorate Pafos' stint as European Capital of Culture, the former dungeons used by the Ottomans were transformed into spaces for contemporary-art installations, an initiative that is set to continue. Visitors can also climb to the castle ramparts to enjoy the sweeping harbour views. The castle serves as an event venue during the Pafos Aphrodite Festival (p107).

Agia Solomoni &
the Christian Catacomb   ARCHAEOLOGICAL SITE
(Map p103; Leoforos Apostolou Pavlou, Kato Pafos) FREE This modest tomb complex is the burial site of the seven Machabee brothers, who were martyred around 174 BC. Their mother was Agia Solomoni, a Jewish woman who became a saint after the death of her sons. It is thought that the space was a synagogue in Roman times. The entrance to the catacomb is marked by a collection of votive rags tied to a large tree outside the tomb.

Agios Lambrianos
Rock-Cut Tomb   ARCHAEOLOGICAL SITE
(Map p103; Fabrica Hill, Kato Pafos) FREE North of the centre, on the side of Fabrica Hill, are a couple of enormous underground caverns dating from the early Hellenistic period. These are burial chambers associated with the saints Lambrianos and Misitikos. The interiors of the tombs bear frescos that indicate they were used as a Christian place of worship.

Roman Theatre   ARCHAEOLOGICAL SITE
(Fabrica Hill, Kato Pafos) FREE Located on the southern slope of Fabrica Hill and best seen from above (follow the dirt track from Leoforos Apostolou Pavlou just northeast of the Kings Avenue Mall), this Roman theatre, excavated over an 11-year period to 2016, is thought to be the oldest on the island, dating from 300 BC. A Roman road to the south of the theatre forms a crucial part of the excavations, providing historians with the presumed urban layout of the site, along with a nymphaeum (fountainhouse).

◉ Ktima & Around

★ Sanctuary of
Aphrodite   ARCHAEOLOGICAL SITE
(☑ 2643 2155; Kouklia; adult/child €4.50/free; ⊘ 8am-4pm Mon-Tue & Thu-Sun, to 5pm Wed; [P]) A World Heritage Site, the sanctuary is recognised as being one of the most important ancient sites related to Aphrodite in Cyprus and yet it is arguably the least known. The sprawling site includes the 12th-century conical stone that represented the goddess until Roman times, the ruins of a Roman temple, a second small sanctuary and ruins of a Roman house, set on a hillside in the village of Kouklia. The setting is lovely with panoramic views down to the sea.

The on-site museum has an extensive display of items discovered at the site, including some extraordinarily delicate white slip pottery dating from the late Bronze Age. For an additional €1 you can watch a 10-minute audiovisual presentation (in Greek and English), which provides a historical background to the site.

You will need your own wheels to get here. Kouklia is signposted off both the A6 and B6 highways, approximately 18km east of Geroskipou.

Ecclesiastical Museum   MUSEUM
(☑ 2627 1221; www.impaphou.org; Makariou III, Geroskipou Sq, Geroskipou; adult/child €4/free; ⊘ 9am-4pm Mon-Fri, to 1pm Sat; ⊟ 601, 606, 616) This noteworthy museum is worth visiting for its ecclesiastical vestments, vessels, copies of scripture and collection of impressive icons, including a 9th-century representation of Agia Marina, thought to be the oldest icon on the island, and an unusual double-sided icon from Filousa dating from the 13th century. Also of note are the elaborate frescos recovered from ruined churches in the region, as well as wood carvings, crucifixes and crosses.

The museum moved to its current location in 2017. From Pafos, catch bus 606 or 616 from the Harbour Bus Station (p110) and bus 601 from Karavella station (p110).

Ethnographical Museum   MUSEUM
(Map p106; ☑ 2693 2010; www.ethnographicalmuseum.com; Exo Vrysis 1, Ktima; €3; ⊘ 10am-6pm Mon-Sat, to 2pm Sun Apr-Oct, 10am-5pm Mon-Sat

Nov-Mar) Owned by the family of an eminent Pafos archaeologist, this museum houses a varied collection of coins, traditional costumes, kitchen utensils, Chalcolithic axe heads, amphorae and other assorted items. There's more of the same in the garden, including a Hellenistic rock-cut tomb. The €5 guidebook available at the entrance helps you sort out the seemingly jumbled collection.

Archaeological Museum MUSEUM
(Map p106; ☑ 2630 6215; Leoforos Georgiou Griva Digeni, Ktima; €2.50; ☺ 8am-4pm Mon-Fri) Essentially for admirers of archaeological minutiae, this small museum houses a varied and extensive collection of artefacts from the neolithic period to the 18th century. Displayed in four rooms, exhibits include jars, pottery and glassware, tools and coins. Note that at time of writing the museum was closed for refurbishment until November 2017.

Agia Paraskevi CHURCH
(Geroskipou; ☺ 8am-1pm & 2-5pm; ☑ 601, 606, 616) FREE One of the loveliest churches in the Pafos area is this six-domed Byzantine church in Geroskipou, 4.5km east of Pafos. Most of the surviving frescos date back to the 15th century AD. The first frescos visible when entering are the Last Supper, the Washing of Feet and the Betrayal. A primitive but interesting depiction of the Virgin Orans (the Virgin Mary with her arms raised) can be seen in the central cupola.

From Pafos, catch bus 606 or 616 from the Harbour Bus Station (p110) and bus 601 from Karavella (p110) station.

Pafos Zoo ZOO
(☑ 2681 3852; www.pafoszoo.com; Pegeia; adult/child €16/9; ☺ 9am-6pm; ℗ 🖐) A zoo and children's attraction rolled into one. Apart from birds (it started as a bird park), there are giraffes, antelopes, deer, gazelles, mouflon, reptiles, giant tortoises, emus, ostriches, small goats and so on. There is also a restaurant and snack bar, and a kiddies' playground. It's located in the Pegeia region near Coral Bay, approximately 3km from Pafos.

🏊 Beaches

Pafos' city beach is functional rather than beautiful. You'll find prettier sands north and south along the coast. Local buses run along the coastal strip.

Main Municipal Beach BEACH
(Bania; Map p103; Kato Pafos) In the centre of Kato Pafos, the main municipal beach is not your standard holiday-brochure-style sweep of sun-kissed sand: the beach area is paved and partly pedestrianised. Comprising a collection of wooden decks, rocks, sand and diving points, it's pleasant and the water is sparkling clean. Facilities include showers, toilets and a cafe-restaurant.

Alykes Beach BEACH
(Map p103; off Poseidonos, Kato Pafos) This is a perfect spot for families with paddling tots, featuring rock pools and shallow, clear water, as well as sufficient sand for sandcastles and that all-important lifeguard. It's located in front of the Annabelle Hotel.

Vrysoudia Beach BEACH
(Kato Pafos) Stretching some 400m, Vrysoudia is arguably the best municipal beach, where you can rent sunbeds and parasols (€5 for day). There is also a popular beach bar here.

Faros Beach BEACH
(Kato Pafos) You will need wheels to reach Faros Beach, an exposed, sandy beach with some sandstone rocks and a couple of on-site snack bars. Keep in mind that the open sea often develops a swell, which can be dangerous for swimming.

Kissonerga Bay BEACH
(℗; ☑ 615) Around 8km north of Kato Pafos, Kissonerga Bay is a long, sandy and undeveloped beach, where you can find banana plantations and solitude. There are almost no facilities. Be aware that this beach is notorious for riptides; enter the water with caution.

🏃 Activities

Aside from the organised tours offered by myriad companies (look for the flyers all over town), most activities here are centred on the sea. Check out the wide range of options from the kiosks at the harbour, including boat trips, pedalos and the ubiquitous banana ride.

Coastal Path WALKING
(Kato Pafos) Over recent years, the Kato Pafos promenade has been extended and it now stretches some 5km, from west of the Alexander the Great Hotel to the Louis Phaethon Beach Club, en route to Coral Bay. The most scenic stretch sets off from just east of the castle (p104) in Kato Pafos and curves around the coastal point.

Cyprus Yacht Charters CRUISE
(☑ 2691 0200; www.cyprusyachtcharters.com; Leoforos Apostolou Pavlou 54, Kato Pafos; yacht

PAFOS & THE WEST PAFOS

Ktima

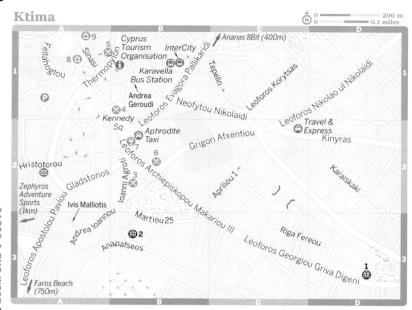

Ktima

hire from €685 (sunset cruise); ◐9am-7pm) Time to don the deck shoes? This reputable company offers several cruise options on its fleet of luxury yachts with captain and crew included in the price.

Mountain Bike Cyprus   CYCLING
(☑2643 2033; www.mountainbikecyprus.com; rental per day €20, bike tour €60) This company operates purely from its website but will deliver and pick up bikes free of charge from your accommodation in the Pafos area. It

also organises tours of the Troödos Mountains and Akamas Heights.

Pafos Watersports   WATER SPORTS
(Map p103; ☑9973 9344; www.pafoswatersportsandboattrips.com; Annabelle Hotel, Poseidonos, Kato Pafos; parasailing from €50; ◐9am-6pm) This reliable outfit is one of the most professional of the shoal of operators touting their boat trips, and similar, from the harbour. It offers just about any watery pursuit you can think of, including waterskiing and parasailing.

★ Cydive   DIVING
(Map p103; ☑2693 4271; www.cydive.com; Poseidonos 1, Myrra Complex 33, Kato Pafos; ◐9am-6pm; ⊕) The waters off Pafos are ideal for diving, with around 50 sites to explore. This is a professional, long-standing company with its own swimming pool and a large store selling diving kits, swimwear and similar. Single dives, including all equipment, cost €45; a package of four dives costs €155.

Paphos Sea Cruises   CRUISE
(Map p103; ☑8000 0011; www.paphosseacruises.com; Pafos Harbour, Kato Pafos; ◐9am-7pm; ⊕) A reputable choice; most cruises include extras such as an onboard barbecue, snorkelling gear, children's entertainment and

canoes. Day trips cost from around €35 per person. Children under 12 are free or pay half, depending on the cruise.

Aphrodite Waterpark WATER PARK
(2691 3638; www.aphroditewaterpark.com; Poseidonos, Kato Pafos; adult/child €30/17; 10am-5.30pm; ; 11, 611) A place for all-day entertainment – at a price to match – where the adults can have a massage while the kids battle the minivolcano. A wristband keeps track of your daily expenditure, which you pay at the end of the day. The water park is located off Poseidonos Ave, around 1.5km south of the centre.

Take bus 11 or 611 from the Harbour Bus Station (p110) in Kato Pafos.

👉 Tours

Micky's Tours SIGHTSEEING
(Map p103; 9908 9149; www.mickys-tours.com; Poseidonos, Kato Pafos; half/full day per person €24/32) Organises half- and full-day trips to the Akamas Peninsula and Troödos Mountains, among other tours, as well as car hire and even villa rentals.

🎉 Festivals & Events

Pafos Aphrodite Festival MUSIC
(Map p103; Sep) Enjoy opera under the stars every September, when a world-class operatic performance takes place in the suitably grandiose surroundings of Pafos Castle (p104). Recent operas include the classic *Cinderella* by Rossini.

🍴 Eating

Pafos' food scene varies considerably. Unfortunately, many of the restaurants along the seafront strip in Kato Pafos are looking increasingly dated and unimaginative with their menus of bland international cuisine; instead, wander back a street or two for more genuine local food. Ktima offers quality over quantity, with some excellent tavernas where you can taste authentic Cypriot cuisine.

🍴 Kato Pafos

Tea For Two BRITISH €
(Map p103; 2693 7702; www.facebook.com/TeaforTwoPaphos; Poseidonos 6; mains €6-8; 8am-11.30pm;) Just the ticket for nostalgic Brits hankering after yesteryear, with house-made classics such as lemon meringue pie and apple crumble, plus a classic ploughman's (cheese, bread and chutney), cottage pie and similar. Good for breakfast too and certainly superior to many of the Brit-geared restaurants in these parts. The service is exemplary and the decor, as you would expect, is classic tearoom chintz.

⭐ Argo CYPRIOT €€
(Map p103; 2693 3327; Pafias Afroditis 21; mains €10; 6-11pm) Located in a relatively quiet part of Kato Pafos, this place oozes rustic charm with its natural stone, original wooden shutters and walls washed in warm ochre. The specialities, such as moussaka, are reliably authentic, as is the twice-weekly (Tuesday and Saturday) *kleftiko* (slow-roasted lamb); on these days it's advisable to book as word is out and the place gets busy.

Hondros TAVERNA €€
(Map p103; 2693 4256; www.facebook.com/HondrosTaverna; Leoforos Apostolou Pavlou 96; mains €10-12; 11am-11pm;) This is the oldest traditional restaurant in Pafos, dating back to 1953, and still in the same family. Highlights include a succulent *souvla* (spit-roasted pork, chicken or lamb), and *kleftiko* cooked in a traditional clay oven, along with baked potatoes and bread. There is a delightful rambling terrace.

Christos Steak House CYPRIOT €€
(Map p103; 9916 5934; 7 Kostantias; mains from €7; 5-11pm) This no-frills, long-established place has bright lights, fake flowers and a menu illustrated with faded pics, but it is still well worth visiting for the homestyle

CAT LOVERS OF THE WORLD UNITE

Cat lovers won't want to miss the **Tala Monastery Cat Park** (9925 3430; www.facebook.com/talamonasterycats; Agios Neophytos Monastery, Tala; 10am-2pm;), where, at the latest count, some 700 kitties were being lovingly looked after by founder Dawn (who knows all their names!) and her team of volunteers. Donations (or cat food) gratefully received and it is not unheard of for tourists to volunteer here for a day (or more). It's that kind of place.

Tala is located between Pafos and Coral Bay.

traditional food. Steaks may be the speciality, but the typically Cypriot dishes and sides, such as pasta with grated haloumi (hellim in Turkish), are good choices as well. The owner is a delight.

Chloe's
CHINESE €€

(Map p103; ☑2693 4676; www.chloesrestaurants.com; Poseidonos 13; mains €10-12; ☺noon-11pm; ☑ ☼) The best Chinese restaurant in town, with a menu that reads like a book and includes all the standard dishes, including plenty of vegetarian choices. The decor is plushly oriental (but without the migraine-inducing moving pictures) and the service is top notch – if anything, a little *too* attentive.

★ Almond Tree
FUSION €€€

(Map p103; ☑2694 5529; www.facebook.com/almondtreepaphos; Konstantias 5; mains €14-19; ☺6.30-11pm; ☑) Almond Tree serves contemporary Asian-inspired flavours to titillate the palate. Try the crab cakes with Thai coconut curry, a speciality, or one of the Indian dishes, such as samosas in a yoghurt parsley sauce. The owner and chef spent a long time in Miami so classic US-style burgers are here too, along with steak and fries. Vegetarians are well catered for with stir-fries and similar.

PAFOS FOR KIDS

As a favourite holiday destination for British families, Pafos is well set up for children. As well as the myriad ruins and museums, the beaches and the zoo, several activity operators specialise in keeping teenaged holidaymakers entertained.

Zephyros Adventure Sports (☑2693 0037; www.enjoycyprus.com; The Royal Complex, Shop 7, Tafon Ton Vasileon, Kato Pafos; activities €36-59; ☼) serves up everything from mountain biking, kayaking, climbing and trekking to snorkelling, scuba diving and, in the winter months, skiing. Out in Pegeia, **George's Ranch** (☑9964 7790; www.georgesranchcyprus.com; Pegeia; 1hr trek €35; ☺9am-7pm; ☼; ☑615 & 616) offers pony treks to sea caves and taster sessions for younger riders.

★ Mandra Tavern
TAVERNA €€€

(Map p103; ☑2693 4129; www.mandratavern.com; Dionysou 4; main €12-15; ☺noon-11pm) Many Pafos restaurants claim to serve authentic Cypriot cuisine but sneak in some international dishes. Not here. The speciality is a glide-off-the-bone home-baked lamb *kleftiko* and the meat meze also comes recommended, as does the signature dessert, brandy pudding with dates and walnuts. Set in the owner's family home, dating from 1979, the courtyard setting is a leafy haven, especially on a balmy summer's evening.

✗ Ktima

★ Kiniras Garden
CYPRIOT €€

(Map p106; ☑2694 1604; www.kiniras.cy.net; Leoforos Archiepiskopou Makariou III 91; mains €8-15; ☺8am-midnight; � ☼) ☑ This family-run restaurant (for four generations) is a green oasis, with trees, statues and trickling waterfalls. Owner Georgios is passionate about his traditional cuisine; most of the recipes have been passed down from his grandmother and the produce comes from his own 60-hectare garden. There are homemade desserts and the wine list includes excellent vintages from family-owned local vineyards.

Laona
CYPRIOT €€

(Map p106; ☑2693 7121; Votis 4-6; mains €10, meze €10; ☺10am-3.30pm Mon, Wed, Thu & Sat, to 10pm Tue & Fri; ☼) Tucked up a side street, and with all the atmosphere of a village taverna, Laona has been a family-owned restaurant since the '80s. There's no microwave or deep-fat fryer in this kitchen – Cypriot owner Chris has a purposefully limited menu of freshly made Cypriot dishes, such as rabbit *stifado* stew, stuffed vegetables and reasonably priced meze.

Plato
JAPANESE €€

(Map p106; ☑7000 0785; www.plato.tbbagency.com; Grigori Afxentiou, Kennedy Sq; mains from €8.50, sushi €3-11; ☺9am-1.30am; ☎) This slick contemporary wine bar complements its tipple with a menu that concentrates on sushi and features all the classics, including sashimi, California rolls and *nigiri* (raw fish over rice). If chopsticks aren't your thing, there is a limited selection of alternatives, including pastas and salads, plus platters for sharing as well as a fine selection of wine – touted as being the most extensive in town.

Fetta's   CYPRIOT €€€

(Map p106; ☑ 2693 7822; Ioanni Agroti 33; mains €10-17, meze €18; ⊙ 7-10.30pm Tue-Sun) Fetta's specialises in classic regional fare made with salutary (and salivatory) attention to detail. The dining space is typical taverna style, only larger, with a small outside terrace overlooking the fountain and park. Dishes include a superb meze of grilled meats and *koupepia* (grilled meat or vegetables wrapped in young vine leaves). Reservations recommended.

 Drinking & Nightlife

The traditional street for clubs, Agiou Antoniou in Kato Pafos, is a sorry sight these days, with the majority of places shuttered up due to recent economic woes. A few places have survived, including a handful of English pubs with big-screen sports – as well as a lap-dancing club or two. Shisha bars are located around Agias Anastasias. Overall, the bars and cafes in Ktima are more sophisticated venues.

Kato Pafos

⭐ **Lighthouse Beach Bar**   BAR

(☑ 9968 3992; www.facebook.com/lighthouse. beachbar; Lighthouse Beach; ⊙ 7am-10pm; 🏄) The recommended route here is via the 1.7km coastal path from Pafos Castle (p104); by car it is trickier, but still possible via the Tombs of the Kings road. When you do arrive, you'll find this is what a beach bar should be: a Bob Marley soundtrack, seamless sea views and sand between your toes while you sip something long and cool.

Alea   BAR

(Map p103; ☑ 9952 4000; Poseidonos 5; ⊙ 8am-1am Mon-Sat, to 9pm Sun; 🏵) A thong's throw from the waves, this former restaurant has happily morphed into a fashionable cafe-cum-lounge bar, famed for its seven choices of daiquiri (€7). The music is suitably chilled with a nightly DJ in the summer. Sit on the sprawling terrace or duck into one of the more intimate spaces within, decorated with eclectic antiques and heavy wooden furniture.

Old Fishing Shack Pub   PUB

(Map p103; ☑ 9980 5390; Margarita Gardens, Tefkrou; ⊙ 6pm-midnight Mon-Sat, 1-11pm Sun; 🏵) Owner Athos loves good beer and good music (classic rock and blues), so come here for both. He also makes his own heavily recommended cider spiked with ginger, and is a craft-beer aficionado. Reserve in advance to arrange a private tasting of the latter (he stocks around 300 different brews!). Free black pudding and potatoes on Sundays (1pm to 3pm).

La Place Royale   BAR

(Map p103; ☑ 2693 3995; Poseidonos; ⊙ 8am-11pm; 🏵) This is one of Pafos' classiest cafe-bars, right on the busy pedestrian strip at the eastern end of Poseidonos. The little oasis of glass, cane, wrought iron and mini-waterfalls in a shaded paved patio is perfect for a preclubbing cocktail. Food is served but it's fairly forgettable.

Different Bar   BAR

(Map p103; ☑ 9945 3716; www.differentbar.com; Agias Napas; ⊙ 7.15pm-2.45am) A popular and welcoming gay bar, thanks to the gregarious owner, Panos, with an attractive dark-ochre colour scheme and tables on the terrace overlooking the street.

Ktima

Ananas 8Bit   CAFE

(☑ 2660 0126; www.facebook.com/ananas8bit coffee; Athinas 35, Ktima; ⊙ 10am-7pm Mon-Sat; 🏵) This place would fit in happily to any urban setting; an espresso bar–cum–hip hangout with contemporary decor, a cosy vibe and possibly the best coffee in town. It also serves sweet treats such as tahini carob pie and organises fun events including live gigs, old movie screenings and art exhibitions.

Noir   BAR

(Map p106; ☑ 2622 0737; Kennedy Sq, Ktima; ⊙ 8am-2am) This place is superbly poised right on the corner of the newly pedestrianised Kennedy Sq, coupling ace people-watching potential with upbeat modern decor. Tapas are available, including guacamole and mixed platters, and a regular line-up of live music equals a heaving venue, especially at weekends.

🛍 Shopping

The Place   ARTS & CRAFTS

(Map p106; ☑ 2610 1955; www.theplacecyprus. com; Kanari 56, Ktima; ⊙ 9am-6pm Mon, Tue, Thu & Fri, to 2pm Wed & Sat; 🏄) Opened in 2017, this multipurpose, multispace venue supports local craftspeople, plus small family producers, selling arts and crafts as well as spices, honey, preserves, olive oil, traditional sweets and more. The crafts include woodwork,

GOURMET GEROSKIPOU

The exceptional meze available at **Seven St George's Tavern** (☑ 2696 3176; www.facebook.com/7StGeorges; Anthipolochagou Georgiou Savva, Geroskipou; meze €25; ◷ noon-3pm & 7-11pm Tue-Sat; ☑ ☑; ☑ 601, 606, 616) 🍴 attracts a steady stream of diners. Owner George and his family have grown, dried or pickled (organically) everything you eat and drink in this place. Your meze only includes what is in season, so you might get hand-picked wild asparagus, wild mushrooms with fresh herbs, aubergines in tomato, or tender *kleftiko* (oven-baked lamb).

The restaurant is in an old house with a vine- and palm-leaf-covered terrace, near the centre of the pretty, traditional village of Geroskipou, located 4.5km east of Pafos.

From Pafos, catch bus 606 or 616 from the Harbour Bus Station or bus 601 from Karavella Bus Station..

ceramics and mosaics, and there is a daily demonstration by one of the artisans. It's also an inspiring space for kids, with a shadow theatre and craft corner.

Gappa   CERAMICS
(Map p103; ☑ 9670 9690; www.facebook.com/GabrielaGospodinova.pottery; Leoforos Apostolou Pavlou 92, Kato Pafos; ◷ 9am-9pm Mon-Sat) Colourful and highly original ceramics are on display here; you can watch the potters at work in the adjacent workshop.

Kings Avenue Mall   MALL
(www.kingsavenuemall.com; Leoforos Apostolou Pavlou, Kato Pafos; ◷ 9.30am-8pm Mon-Sat, 11am-7.30pm Sun; 🛜) The largest shopping mall in the Republic with around 125 stores, plus restaurants, coffee shops and a cineplex.

Municipal Market   MARKET
(Map p106; Agora St, Ktima; ◷ 8am-6pm Mon, Tue, Thu & Fri, to 2.30pm Wed & Sat) Recently renovated, this market lies at the centre of Ktima's pedestrian zone. As well as colourful fruit and veg, the market houses a large number of souvenir stalls, with the occasional more tasteful place selling locally produced embroidery and jewellery.

ℹ️ Information

Wi-fi is widely available in Pafos hotels, as well as in a number of cafes and bars, where you can generally connect free with a drink.

You can pick up stamps and weigh packages at the **Main Post Office** (Map p106; ☑ 2630 6221; Ikarou, Ktima; ◷ 7.30am-1.30pm & 3-5.30pm Mon-Fri) in Ktima.

Cyprus Tourism Organisation, with **Airport** (☑ 2642 3161; www.visitcyprus.org.cy; Pafos International Airport; ◷ 9.30am-11pm), **Kato Pafos** (Map p103; ☑ 2693 0521; www.visitcyprus.org.cy; Poseidonos, Kato Pafos; ◷ 8.15am-2.30pm & 3-5.30pm Mon, Tue, Thu & Fri, 8.15am-2.30pm Sat) and **Ktima** (Map p106; ☑ 2693 2841; www.visitcyprus.org.cy; Agoras 8, Ktima; ◷ 8.15am-2.30pm & 3-5.30pm Mon-Sat, closed Wed & Sat afternoons) offices, has decent maps, useful brochures and booklets on hiking, biking and agrotourism, as well as a hotel guide, transport information and other useful info about Cyprus. It organises free guided tours around Ktima every Thursday at 10am from the Ktima office. You need to book in advance.

ℹ️ Getting There & Away

AIR

Pafos International Airport (☑ 2624 0506; www.cyprusairports.com.cy) is 8km southeast of town. Both scheduled and budget airlines fly here and it is a hub for Ryanair, which serves seven destinations (at the time of research) from Pafos.

BUS

InterCity (Map p106; ☑ 8000 7789; www.intercity-buses.com; Karavella Bus Station, Leoforos Evagora Pallikaridi, Ktima) has nine daily buses weekdays to Nicosia (Lefkosia; €7, two hours) and 13 daily buses weekdays to Lemesos (Limassol; €4, one hour), departing from Karavella Bus Station in Ktima. There is a reduced service at weekends.

SERVICE TAXI

Travel & Express (Map p106; ☑ 2692 3800; www.travelexpress.com.cy; Kinyras 34, Ktima; ◷ 6am-6pm Mon-Fri, 7am-5pm Sat & Sun) runs service taxis to Lemesos (€9.50, one hour), to Larnaka (change at Lemesos; €19.50, 1½ hours) and to Nicosia (change at Lemesos; €23, 1½ hours).

ℹ️ Getting Around

Pafos Buses (Map p103; ☑ 8000 5588; www.pafosbuses.com; Harbour Bus Station) provides a city-wide and regional network of buses from its two stations: **Harbour Bus Station** (Map p103; Pafos Harbour, Kato Pafos;

⊙ 6am-midnight) in Kato Pafos and **Karavella Bus Station** (Map p106; Leoforos Evagora Pallikaridi, Ktima) in Ktima. A bus-schedule booklet is available at both stations. Fares cost €1.50 per journey, €5 per day or €15 per week within the district of Pafos, including rural villages. Note that from 9pm onwards a single fare increases to €2.50.

Frequent services from Kato Pafos (harbour) include the following:

Coral Bay Bus 615; 25 minutes.

Geroskipou Buses 601, 606; 25 minutes.

Kato Ktima (market) Bus 610; 15 minutes.

Polis Bus 626; one hour.

In Kato Pafos, there's a large free car park near the entrance to the Pafos Archaeological Site. In Ktima, there is a convenient free car park by Karavella Bus Station.

If you need a taxi, **Aphrodite Taxi** (Map p106; ☑ 2693 3301; www.aphrodite-taxi.com; Kennedy Sq, Ktima; ⊙ 24hr), Travel & Express (p110) and **Fytos Taxi** (☑ 9575 7575; www.paphosineedataxi.com; Kato Pafos) are reputable companies. You can also flag one down or head for one of the plentiful taxi stands across the city. Be aware that taxi drivers will charge an extortionate €8 for the 3km Kato Pafos–Ktima ride.

TO/FROM THE AIRPORT

Pafos Buses (p110) operates bus 613 to the airport from the Karavella Bus Station in Ktima at 7.25am and 6.30pm, while buses from the airport to Ktima run at 8am and 7pm. Bus 612 runs roughly hourly between the Harbour Bus Station in Kato Pafos and the airport from 7am to 12.30am, with stops or pick-up points including Coral Bay and Poseidonos in Kato Pafos. A single journey is €1.50.

A taxi between the airport and Pafos costs about €30.

AROUND PAFOS

Plenty of visitors rent a moped to zip up and down the coast from Pafos, but you'll need a hire car to explore the scenic wilds of the Western Troödos and the Akamas Peninsula.

Coral Bay & Agios Georgios

About 12km northwest of Pafos, Coral Bay is a popular family hang-out, with a string of busy beaches, dotted with beach umbrellas, water-sports centres and rather interchangeable snack bars and tourist res-

taurants. You'll find better nosh at Kissonerga, a few kilometres back towards Pafos, where Tweedie's (☑ 9912 6590; www.tweedies.com; Spyrou Kyprianou, Kissonerga; mains from €15; ⊙ 7-11pm Thu-Sun) serves an imaginative menu of modern European and fusion dishes (advance reservations are mandatory). Buses zip regularly between Kato Pafos harbour and Coral Bay.

Another 8km past Coral Bay is Agios Georgios Beach (Agios Georgios; P), a 100m stretch of shadeless sand and rock with a modest harbour; beach umbrellas and loungers are available for hire (€4.50). There is a small beach bar and, up on the bluff, one of the region's most popular seafood restaurants, Saint George's Fish Tavern (☑ 2662 1306; Agios Georgios; mains €14-17; ⊙ 9am-11pm). The beach can also be reached by road from Polis (via Pegeia).

Akamas Heights

If you're spending any time in the greater Pafos area – and have a car – make sure you check out the Akamas Heights region. A world away from the flop-and-drop coastal scene, the mainstay of the picturesque villages here is agriculture, which means goat herds, orchards and vegetable fields are the backdrop to those cobbled streets with their historic churches, tavernas and occasional donkey.

Avgas Gorge

★ Avgas Gorge   HIKING

(Avakas Gorge) This narrow split in the Akamas Heights escarpment is a popular and enjoyable hike of roughly 3.5km one way. The walk should take no longer than 40 minutes and starts from the gorge entrance, which becomes a defile with cliffs towering overhead. There is usually water in the gorge from November until at least May, hence the lush streamside vegetation (keep an eye out for tree frogs).

Some groups press on upwards, emerging on the escarpment ridge and heading for the nearby village of Ano Arodes. The gorge is reached by vehicle from its western end via Agios Georgios Beach. You can drive or ride more or less up to the gorge entrance, although low-slung conventional vehicles will have to take care.

PAFOS & THE WEST CORAL BAY & AGIOS GEORGIOS

WORTH A TRIP

REAL ALE ON THE MED

For a welcome break from insipid, metallic-tasting lagers, head inland from Pafos along the B7 highway. Just after the turn-off to Tsada, you'll reach **Aphrodite's Rock Brewery** (2610 1446; www.aphroditesrock.com.cy; Polis Rd, Tsada; 10am-4pm;), run by a cheerful family of Yorkshire brewers, committed to the production of hearty real ale, full-flavoured stouts, artisan lagers and fruity ciders. They offer a 200mL tasting of five beers for €6 and a range of brewery tours that include drinks, return transfers from hotels in Pafos and a pizza from the brewery's wood-fired oven. Reserve ahead at weekends.

Dhrousia, Kritou Terra & Around

Once you are up on the Akamas Heights escarpment, you will come across a series of centuries-old villages that enjoy a cool climate, grow fine wine grapes and are truly picturesque. These are villages of winding streets, moustached men sitting outside the *kafeneia* (coffee shop), lofty fig trees offering their fruit to passers-by, and an occasional donkey standing nonchalantly on the cobbles.

Particularly appealing are the villages of Dhrousia and Kritou Terra, with some splendid traditional houses. Dhrousia also has a small weaving museum, an attractive 18th-century church and one of the longest-standing and most popular tavernas in the region. In Kritou Terra, another charmer, don't miss the late-Byzantine church of Agia Ekaterini, at the southern end of the village and well worth a photo. Two other appealing villages, near Dhrousia and Kritou Terra, are unspoilt **Ineia** (population 350) and **Goudi** (population 160).

◉ Sights

Kouyiouka Watermill   HISTORIC BUILDING
(2663 2847; kouyiouka@cytanet.com.cy; B7, Goudi; museum €1; 7.30am-5pm;) FREE Located 7km south of Goudi on the B7, this 200-year-old listed renovated watermill houses a modest museum, a coffee shop and a traditional bakery. The museum displays the typical (and historical) equipment necessary for baking bread, while the bakery sells delicious haloumi rolls, which you can

enjoy with a coffee or beer by the stream, overlooking the orchards across the way.

✕ Eating

Erotokritos Tavern   TAVERNA €
(9965 0114; Kritou Terra; mains €7; 11am-3pm & 7-9pm Tue-Sun;) Easy to find, at the heart of the village, this traditional taverna has wonderful views from the courtyard (look for the giant hanging gourds). Expect honest homestyle cooking with a menu that is no-fuss traditional and depends on what is fresh in season. The playground across the way makes this a handy spot for families too.

Finikkas   CYPRIOT €€
(2633 2336; Dhrousia; mains €9-11, meze €13; noon-9pm Tue-Sat Apr-Sep; ; 641, 648) Located just off the crossroad in the centre of town, this is the village's most popular taverna, with a traditional dining room and a typical menu of meaty mains such as grilled souvlaki and lamb kebabs, as well as a girth-expanding 15-dish meze. It also serves *karaolia* (snails) prepared in a rich tomato sauce, a dish typical of the Akamas region.

❶ Getting There & Away

Pafos Buses (p110) runs bus 648 and bus 641 to Polis three times and two times daily respectively (€1.50, 45 minutes). Both routes have stops in Dhrousia and Ineia. However, to explore more than one of these villages at any given time, you will definitely need your own transport.

Kathikas & Around

Kathikas is the most easily accessible village from Pafos, midway between Pafos and Polis on the E709. A delightful village with honey-coloured stone buildings and traditional coffee shops, it is particularly famous for its vineyards and wine. Just outside the village, the Cypress tree of Agios Nikolaos is a lofty 14m high, with a pensionable age of more than 700 years.

From Kathikas you can detour onto the B7 (the direct road between Pafos and Polis) via the picturesque **Pano Akourdalia**, **Kato Akourdalia** and **Miliou** villages. Between them are a couple of excellent tavernas for a relaxing lunch.

✕ Eating & Drinking

Village Cafe   CYPRIOT €
(9622 4934; Kato Akourdalia; mains €5-7; 10am-11pm;) 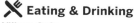 Maria and her partner

Zino, a talented artist, are committed to treating customers to produce from their vegetable patch, eggs from their chickens and keeping everything as organic as possible. Sit on the terrace enjoying the blissful valley views and dine on whatever is recommended, as it's sure to be delicious.

★ **Imogen's Inn** CYPRIOT €€
(☑ 2663 3269; Georgiou Kleanthous, Kathikas; mains €8-10, pizzas €6.50; ☺ 10am-3.30pm Thu-Tue; ☑ 648) For something different, head to Imogen's, located at the entrance to the village and resembling a French bistro, with the sounds of jazz and blues tinkling into the dining terrace–cum-garden shaded by a magnificent fig tree. Aside from Cypriot cuisine, there are some Middle Eastern dishes including *muhammara* (roasted red pepper dip), *tagines* (North African stews) and succulent lamb kebabs.

★ **To Stekki Tou Panai** CYPRIOT €€
(☑ 9977 1622; www.tostekkitoupanai.com; Kathikas; mains €8-10; ☺ noon-10pm May-Sep, noon-3pm Mon-Fri, to 10pm Sat & Sun Oct-Apr; ☑; ☑ 641) Despite its modern-looking exterior, this small taverna dates back over 200 years and is the family home of owner-cum-cook Maria; a lavishly embroidered dress belonging to her grandmother adorns one wall. Maria describes her cuisine as Cypriot with a touch of innovation, adding extra spices and herbs to such traditional dishes as moussaka. A small salad and dessert are provided free of charge.

Vasilikon WINE BAR
(☑ 2663 3999; www.vasilikon.com; B7; ☺ 8am-5pm; ☎; ☑ 641) This winery has won several prestigious international awards for its wines. The wine bar serves platters of cheese and cold cuts to share while enjoying sweeping vineyard views from the terrace. There is also complimentary wine tasting from 8am to 3pm daily. Vasilikon is signposted just after the turn-off to Kathikas on the B7 Pafos-to-Polis road.

❶ Getting There & Away

Pafos Buses (p110) runs bus 648 to Polis three times daily (€1.50, 45 minutes) with a stop in Kathikas. However, to really explore these villages in the Akamas Heights, you will need your own transport.

WORTH A TRIP

VIKLARI

If you haven't brought a picnic, excellent food is available near the entrance of Avgas Gorge at **Viklari** (Last Castle; ☑ 2699 6088; Avgas Gorge; mains €12; ☺ 1.30-4pm; ☑). For €12 you get delicious *kleftiko* (slow-roasted lamb), accompanied by salad and chunky homemade chips. You eat at heavy stone tables under grape-vines, surrounded by petrified-rock 'sculptures', lovingly nurtured pot plants and a pretty garden.

AKAMAS PENINSULA

At the far southwest of the Akamas Peninsula is Lara Beach, accessible by car and most famous for the green and loggerhead turtles that breed at its turtle hatchery. Beyond, this part of western Cyprus juts almost defiantly into the Mediterranean and is one of the island's last remaining wildernesses. Visitors can still traverse the peninsula as long as they're prepared to walk, ride a trail bike or bump along in a sturdy 4WD. If you are visiting the mythical Baths of Aphrodite, you can leave your car in the free car park and stride out from there.

The peninsula is home to abundant flora and fauna, including some 600 plant species, 35 of them unique to Cyprus. There are also 68 bird species, 12 types of mammal (including foxes and hedgehogs), 20 species of reptile and many butterflies, such as the native *Glaucopsyche pafos*, the symbol of the region.

❍ Sights

★ **Lara Beach** BEACH
(Akamas Peninsula; ℗) **FREE** This stunning unspoilt beach has clean, calm water and pristine sands for those who want to escape people and parasols. The beach is most famous, however, for being home to a **turtle hatchery**; this is one of the world's few remaining havens for green and logger-head turtles to nest. Volunteers monitor the female turtles and around June and July collect their eggs to place in the hatchery, to protect them from predators and inquisitive tots. Monk seals also dwell in the sea caves around the peninsula.

Note that the beach has been a protected area since 1971 and no sun loungers are permitted. Likewise, private vehicles are banned from coming to the beach during the egg-laying season; at other times you can approach, although the path is a dirt track. If you feel uneasy go for a 4WD rental vehicle or take a tour. Look for the signs to Lara Restaurant at the adjacent Lara Bay, where you can stop for a drink or snack on the vast terrace overlooking the beach.

Baths of Aphrodite   CAVE
(F713; ☺8am-7pm; P; ☐622) FREE These mythical baths attract a steady crowd, who possibly expect more than they find. Surrounded by fig trees and filled with the relaxing sound of running water, the grotto is a nice spot away from the heat, but it's far from the luxurious setting that may be associated with a goddess of such amorous prowess.

The surrounding botanical garden is pretty, however, with labelled plants and trees, including carob trees, red gum and the slightly less exotic dandelion.

The myth surrounding the cool cave that is the Baths of Aphrodite (Loutra tis Afroditis) is great advertising. Aphrodite, goddess of love and patron of Cyprus, came to the island in a shower of foam and nakedness, launching a cult that has remained to this day. Legend has it that she came to this secluded spot to bathe after entertaining her lovers.

The baths are 11km west of Polis, along a sealed road, on the edge of the Akamas Peninsula: a great spot to embark on a hike or just meander along one of the signposted nature trails. From the baths' car park, with its adjacent cafe and gift shop, follow the well-marked paved trail for 200m. You are not allowed to swim in the baths.

🏃 Activities

Easily the most popular way to get a taste of the Akamas Peninsula is to spend a few hours hiking one of the following trails, which run through the northeastern sector. All can start and end at one of two points: the Baths of Aphrodite, or Smigies picnic ground (www.visitpafos.org.cy; Akamas Peninsula), which is reached via an unsealed but driveable road 2.5km west of Neo Chorio.

The two most popular trails are those that start and end at the Baths of Aphrodite. They are both longer than the Smigies trails and offer better views. The first is the Aphrodite Trail (www.visitpafos.org.cy; Baths of Aphrodite; ☐ 622), a 7.5km, three- to four-hour loop. It heads inland and upwards to begin

with; as this can be tiring on a hot day, make an early start if you can. Halfway along the trail you can see the ruins of Pyrgos tis Rigainas (Queen's Tower), part of a Byzantine monastery. Look for the huge 100-year-old oak tree nearby before you head up to the summit of Mouti tis Sotiras (370m). Finally you head east and down towards the coastal track, which will eventually lead you back to the car park.

The second hike, the 3½-hour, 7.5km Adonis Trail (www.visitpafos.org.cy; Baths of Aphrodite; ☐ 622), shares the same path as the Aphrodite as far as Queen's Tower, but then turns left (south) before looping back to the car park. Note that, in order to complete its circular path, the trail follows the main road connecting the Baths of Aphrodite and Polis for about 400m. Alternatively, you can turn right (south) just after the village of Kefalovrysi and continue on to Smigies picnic ground if you have arranged a pick-up beforehand (approximately 5.5km).

Water is usually available at Queen's Tower and, on the Adonis Trail, at Kefalovrysi, but don't count on it in high summer. In any case, these trails are best attempted in spring or autumn; if you want to tackle one in Cyprus' extremely hot summer, stride out at sunrise.

The Cyprus Tourism Organisation (CTO) produces a description of these trails in a booklet entitled *Cyprus Nature Trails,* available from the main CTO offices. You can also download it from www justabout cyprus.com. Three other trails to consider commence from Smigies picnic ground: the circular 2.5km or 5km Smigies Trail and the circular 3km, 1½-hour Pissouromouttis Trail. Both afford splendid views of Chrysohou Bay to the northeast and the Akamas coastline to the west.

Polis

Known by locals as Polis Chrysochous, this appealing small town is mainly visited by Cypriots on their August holidays, although the number of coach tours from the coast has been increasing. There's a sand and shingle beach, a good campsite, and some decent hotels and restaurants, as well as an overall welcome lack of overdevelopment. Polis makes an ideal base for trips to the Akamas Peninsula.

Polis lies on wide Chrysohou Bay, where the north coast curves round towards the spur of the Akamas Peninsula. Buried beneath the streets are the ruins of ancient Marion and Arsinoe; treasures recovered from the sites are displayed in the town museum.

⊙ Sights

Agios Andronikos   CHURCH
(Iouliou; ⊙ 10am-6pm; **P**) This 16th-century church was latterly a mosque and the centre of local Turkish Cypriot religious life. Don't miss the fine Byzantine frescos that were hidden behind whitewash for decades. Sitting on the western side of town, the church can only be visited in groups of 10 or more. The key is held at the Archaeological Museum (p115).

**Archaeological Museum
of Marion-Arsinoe**   MUSEUM
(☑ 2632 2955; Leoforos Archiepiskopou Makariou III; €1; ⊙ 8am-2pm Mon-Wed & Fri, to 6pm Thu, 9am-5pm Sat) Housed in a handsome neoclassical building, the museum comprises two galleries: one spanning the history of the area from neolithic to medieval times, while the second includes the rich haul that was found at the graves at nearby Marion and Arsinoe, including some stunning statuettes and elaborate gold jewellery dating from Roman times.

🏝 Beaches

The best beaches in the area are west of Polis, towards the Baths of Aphrodite, but a short walk north from the centre will take you to **Camp Site Beach**, a pleasant spray of sand and shingle, backed by eucalyptus trees and the eponymous campsite.

With your own vehicle, or by bus, you can roam down the coast to **Latsi**, which offers a superior spread of sand and shingle and a gaggle of popular seafood restaurants. As well as enjoying the sand and surf, you can hire boats, don scuba gear and get involved in a variety of other watery activities at **Latsi Watersports Centre** (☑ 2632 2095; www.latchiwatersportscentre.com; Latsi Harbour; 🚑), based at the harbour, or take cruises to snorkelling spots along the Akamas Peninsula with **Cyprus Mini Cruises** (☑ 9930 2879; www.cyprusminicruises.com; Latsi Harbour; adult/child €25/15; ⊙ 10.30am & 4pm; 🚑).

Suitably sea-salted and sun-frazzled, you can recharge your batteries at the harbour-front **Yiangos & Peter Taverna** (☑ 2632

1411; Latsi; mains €12-16; ⊙ 8.30am-11pm), which has been serving locally caught seafood since 1939. Alternatively, head east past the harbour to **Psaropoulos Beach Tavern** (☑ 2632 1089; E713; fish meze €17.50; ⊙ 10am-11pm; 🚑), at the start of **Polis Municipal Beach**; the tavern is family run, packed with locals, and the seafood is so fresh it's virtually flapping.

A few kilometres west of Latsi, on the road to the Baths of Aphrodite, the appropriately named **Aphrodite Beach** is good for children, with its clear, swimmable waters and comfortably small pebbles.

🏃 Activities

Ride in Cyprus   HORSE RIDING
(☑ 9977 7624; www.rideincyprus.com; Lyso; rides from €30; ⊙ 9am-6pm; 🚑) For hour-long horse-riding treks, overnight safaris and picnic day rides, contact this company in Lyso (also known as Lysos), 12km southeast of town, on the road to Stavros tis Psokas.

Wheelie Cyprus   CYCLING
(☑ 9935 0898; www.wheeliecyprus.com; tours from €65; 🚑) Organises bike tours on little-known trails throughout the area. The price includes high-quality bike rental, all equipment and pick-up from your hotel. Book online.

✦ Festivals & Events

Summer Nights in Polis   MUSIC
(Town Hall Sq) In summer, Town Hall Sq is the venue for various free concerts, including traditional dancing, music, folkloric events, classical music and jazz performances.

✕ Eating

Polis Herb Garden & Restaurant   CYPRIOT €€
(☑ 9958 6354; www.polisherbgarden.com; Leoforos Archiepiskopou Makariou III 24; mains €8-12; ⊙ 10am-11pm; 🛜) Work up an appetite by having a stroll around this restaurant's

---

KOUPPAS STONE CASTLE

If you're exploring the interior of the Akamas Peninsula, a reliable lunchtime stop is **Kouppas Stone Castle** (☑ 2632 2526; Georgiou Paraskeva 49, Neo Chorio; meat meze €16; ⊙ 9am-11pm) in Neo Chorio, which pulls in a mainly local crowd with its hearty, meaty meze spread and nourishing homemade mousakka.

Polis

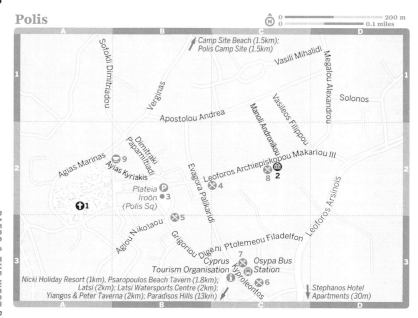

Polis

Sights
1 Agios Andronikos A2
2 Archaeological Museum of
   Marion-Arsinoe.................................. C2

Activities, Courses & Tours
3 Summer Nights in Polis..................... B2

Eating
4 Archontariki Restaurant-
   Tavern... C2
5 Arsinoe Fish Tavern B3
6 Mosfilo's Tavern C3
7 Old Town Restaurant.......................... C3
8 Polis Herb Garden &
   Restaurant C2

Drinking & Nightlife
9 Kivotis Art Cafe.................................. B2

delightful herb garden, lovingly planted and tended by owner Tasos, who also creates essential oils (to sell), along with herbal teas. The cuisine is also delicately seasoned with fresh herbs, which makes all the difference to such traditional dishes as *saganaki* (pan-seared haloumi with tomatoes and green peppers).

Mosfilo's Tavern CYPRIOT €€
(☏ 2632 2104; Kyproleontos; mains €8; ⊙noon-10pm Tue-Sat; 🚶) This place exudes a traditional ambience with its high ceilings, original tiles and columns, and gallery of historic pics of Polis. The menu includes classics like spinach and lamb, grilled chicken and a *stifado* that locals rate as being the best in town. The location is less sublime – across from the petrol station on the B7 main road to Pafos.

Arsinoe Fish Tavern SEAFOOD €€
(☏ 2632 1590; Grigoriou Digeni; fish meze €17.50; ⊙6-11pm Mon-Sat) Locals continue to rate this atmospheric, traditional family-owned place as one of the top spots in town for fresh fish. Try the succulent fish meze.

**Archontariki
Restaurant-Tavern** CYPRIOT €€€
(☏ 2632 1328; www.archontariki.com.cy; Leoforos Archiepiskopou Makariou III 14; mains €13-18; ⊙6-11pm Tue-Sun; 🚶) This tavern has a timeless, classic feel, set in an old stone house with original tiling and a garden with giant urns and shady trees. The menu reflects the chef's skill at combining traditional dishes with innovative flair. Try the chicken stuffed with haloumi and mushrooms or *kathisto* (octopus cooked in wine and oregano). Ostrich is also on the menu.

THE CULT OF APHRODITE

Cyprus is indelibly linked to the ancient worship of the goddess Aphrodite (known as Venus in Roman mythology). She is known primarily as the Greek goddess of sexual love and beauty, although she was also worshipped as a goddess of war – particularly in Sparta and Thebes. While prostitutes often considered her their patron, her public cult was usually solemn and even austere.

The name Aphrodite is thought to derive from the Greek word *afros*, meaning 'foam'. Cypriot legend has it that Aphrodite rose from the sea off the south coast of Cyprus. She was born out of the white foam produced by the severed genitals of Ouranos (Heaven), after they were thrown into the sea by his son Chronos (the father of Zeus, king of the Greek gods). The people of Kythira in Greece hold a similar view to that expressed in the legend; an enormous rock off the south-coast port of Kapsali is believed by Kytherians to be the place where Aphrodite really emerged.

Despite being a goddess, Aphrodite had a predilection for mortal lovers. The most famous of them were Anchises (by whom Aphrodite became mother to Aeneas) and Adonis (who was killed by a boar and whose death was lamented by women at the festival of Adonia).

The main centres of worship on Cyprus for the cult of Aphrodite were at Pafos and Amathous. Her symbols included the dove, the swan, pomegranates and myrtle.

Greek art represented her as a nude-goddess type. Ancient Greek sculptor Praxiteles carved a famous statue of Aphrodite, which later became the model for the Hellenistic statue known as *Venus de Milo*.

PAFOS & THE WEST POLIS

Old Town Restaurant CYPRIOT €€€
(☑9963 2781; www.theoldtownrestaurant.com; Kyproleontos 9; mains €20-28; ⊘7-11pm Tue-Sun) This is a discreet and relaxing place with a leafy, secluded garden and a stripped-back, stone-clad dining room with crisp white tablecloths, shelves of wine, and plants. The menu is seasonal, but you can expect dishes such as rabbit *stifado* with wild mushrooms and juniper berries, wood-roasted duck with white wine, and partridge ravioli. Reservations recommended.

🍷 Drinking & Nightlife

For harbour-front drinks head to Latsi, where most of the seafront restaurants double as popular terrace bars in the evening. In town, the cafes around Polis Sq open well into the evening in the summer and there's regular live music organised by the town hall. There are also several traditional coffee shops in town and an Irish pub on the Argaka coast road, 7km east of Polis.

 Kivotis Art Cafe CAFE
(☑9955 5183; Ayias Kyriakis; waffles €4.50, cakes €2.80; ⊘10am-6pm; 🖶) This shady oasis has a welcoming informality with its rambling terrace of mismatched furniture, quirky sculptures and shelves of board games and books. Homemade cakes, waffles and ice cream are the scrumptious specialities, plus light meals and drinks, ranging from excellent coffee to beer and wine.

ℹ Information

Cyprus Tourism Organisation (CTO; ☑2632 2468; www.visitcyprus.com; Vasileos Stasi-oikou 2; ⊘9am-1pm & 2.30-5.30pm Sun-Tue, Thu & Fri, 9am-1pm Sat) Central tourist office at the entrance to town by the large municipal car park.

ℹ Getting There & Away

Pafos Buses (☑8000 5588; www.pafosbuses. com) has daily services to/from Polis, leaving Pafos from the Karavella Bus Station in Ktima. Leaving Polis, all buses depart from the **Osypa Bus Station** (Kyproleontos).

Baths of Aphrodite Bus 622; €1.50, 30 minutes, hourly 6am to noon and 3pm to 6pm weekdays, seven daily on weekends.

Latsi Bus 623; €1.50, 20 minutes, two daily.

Pafos Bus 645; €1.50, one hour, up to 11 on weekdays, five on weekends.

Pomos Bus 643; €1.50, one hour, two daily.

TYLLIRIA

This is where you head for at the height of the summer season if you have grown weary of crowds, love untouched, tranquil nature, and long to discover a relatively undiscovered part of Cyprus. This is a sparsely populated, forested territory with a few very quiet beach resorts nestling between Chrysohou and Morfou Bays and some great scope for hiking. Tylliria has an interesting, if harrowing, history, having suffered considerably when it was partly isolated from the rest of Cyprus following the Turkish invasion in 1974.

Pomos

POP 570

The trip up the coastal road from Polis towards Tylliria becomes gradually more scenic, with the road flanked by oleander bushes and hugging the coastline. Aside from a couple of small communities en route, there is precious little development and the beaches are fairly empty. Don't expect golden sands in these parts, though; in the main, the beaches are shingle. Pomos is the first small town you come to (at 19km), its main street home to a handful of restaurants and coffee shops against a backdrop of lush agricultural land with olive trees, citrus groves and vines. Head for the harbour to look at the traditional fishing boats and take a dip in the shallow waters sheltered within a small cove.

Sights

The nearest beach is 5km east of town at Pahyammos.

Museum of Natural History   MUSEUM
(☏ 9921 0588; Charalambous Formides St; €1; ⊙ 7.30am-2.30pm Mon, Tue, Thu & Fri, to 4pm Wed, 8am-1pm Sat; P ⊕) Clearly signposted off the main street, this museum is an unexpected attraction to find here, with its two large galleries of animals and birds endemic to the island, as well as a modest display of rocks and minerals. While taxidermists may not be impressed with some of the mildly moth-eaten exhibits, the comprehensive display includes some surprises, such as pelicans, a mouflon, the loggerhead turtle and a prehistoric-looking *Gyps fulvos* vulture – all native to Cyprus.

Don't miss the photo of the skeleton of a hippopotamus found in caves in the Akrotiri area, along with skeletons of the pygmy elephant, both dating back to neolithic times.

Pahyammos   BEACH
Located along a lovely stretch of highway flanked by colourful oleander bushes, Pahyammos means 'broad sand'. Its beach is indeed broad and sweeps around a large bay up to the UN watchtowers that mark the beginning of Erenköy (Kokkina), a Turkish Cypriot enclave.

Eating

Paradise Place   CAFE €
(☏ 2634 2016; www.facebook.com/paradiseplace; E704; snacks €6; ⊙ 11am-midnight May-Sep; ☏) Look out for this place as you approach the centre; it gets particularly lively in August, when there is a jazz and reggae festival over two consecutive weekends. The rest of the time, it's a cool place to hang out and enjoy a brew on tap, together with a piled-high salad, vegie burger, omelette or similar.

★ **Kanalli Fish Restaurant**   SEAFOOD €€€
(☏ 9956 7056; www.kanalli.com; Pomos Harbour; mains from €12; ⊙ 10am-10pm; ☏ ⊕) Kanalli has as its main draw the stunning holiday-brochure view from its terrace: the turquoise bay and the small, upgraded harbour with forested mountains in the distance; romantics should head here at sunset. The kitchen specialises in fresh fish, namely sea bass, bream, red snapper and red mullet, served with freshly made (rather than frozen) chips.

Getting There & Away

Pafos Buses (p117) operates bus 643 from Polis to Pomos twice daily (€1.50, one hour).

Kato Pyrgos

POP 1135

Located in the northern Troödos foothills, the charm of this small resort lies in its remoteness. Kato Pyrgos is about as far out of the way as you can get in the Republic, yet attracts a regular summer clientele of Cypriots, who come to escape the commercialism that they feel has overwhelmed the more popular coastal resorts. Don't expect palm-fringed promenades and white sandy beaches; Kato Pyrgos has a mildly shabby, old-fashioned appeal.

Eating & Drinking

Pyrgiana Beach   SEAFOOD €
(☏ 2652 2306; www.pyrgianabeachhotel.com; Nikolaou Papageorgiou 34; mains €6-8; ⊙ 11am-

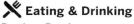

STAVROS TIS PSOKAS

If you are striking out south into the Tylliria hinterland from the north coast, make sure you visit the lovely forest reserve of **Stavros tis Psokas**, also accessible from Pafos (51km) via a picturesque road that is unsealed for a considerable distance. This vast picnic site is part of a forest station responsible for fire control in the Pafos Forest.

Nature-loving Cypriots come here to walk and enjoy the peace, and it can get quite crowded in summer. In a small enclosure, signposted from the main parking area, you can get a glimpse of the rare and endangered native Cypriot mouflon. Move quietly and slowly if you want to see them, as they get rather skittish at the approach of humans.

You can do some hiking from the Stavros tis Psokas forest station. The **Horteri Trail**, a 5km, three-hour circular hike, loops around the eastern flank of the Stavros Valley. The trail starts at the Platanoudkia Fountain, about halfway along the forest station's approach road, which turns off the main through-road at Selladi tou Stavrou (Stavros Saddle). The hike involves a fair bit of upward climbing and can get tiring in the heat of summer; tackle the walk early in the day if you can.

The second trail is the **Selladi tou Stavrou**, a 2.5km, 1½-hour circular loop of the northern flank of the Stavros Valley. The start is prominently marked from Stavros Saddle (at the junction of the forest station approach road and the main through-road). A longer option (7km, 2½ hours) is to follow the trail anticlockwise and then branch south to the heliport. From there you can walk along a forest road to the forest station proper.

The Cyprus Tourism Organisation (www.visitcyprus.com) should be able to provide you with more information on these trails. Alternatively, consult www.visitpafos.org.cy.

You will need your own car to get here. There's a small camp site at Stavros tis Psokas with capacity for 60 people.

3pm & 6-9pm) Overlooking the harbour, and part of an older hotel (desperately in need of an update!), this restaurant continues to dish up some of the freshest seafood you will find on this stretch of coastline. Ask for the fish dish of the day and don't forget to order an accompanying village salad; one of the better versions we have tasted in the Republic.

Grape by the Sea BAR
(☑ 9629 2959; Nicola Pylidis 2; ☺ 1-8pm Mon-Thu, from 11am Fri-Sun) This is the dreamy photo op that will be the envy of your pals back home, especially if you happen to be sipping a strawberry mojito at the time. Right on the sand with shaded sunbed gazebos, it also serves food, including tasty pork chops, salads and sandwiches.

❶ Getting There & Away

You will need your own transport to reach Kato Pyrgos; the easiest approach is via Pomos on the E704. Although the distance from Pomos is only 27km, the road is very windy so you should allow close to an hour for the journey.

The Kato Pyrgos crossing point to Northern Cyprus is signposted 4km to the east of town.

WESTERN TROÖDOS

The sparsely populated area flanking the western foothills of the Troödos Mountains is home to several delightful villages, where traditions hold fast and the local Cypriot dialect is just that bit more impenetrable. If you're looking for a route to central Troödos from the west coast, you can now easily follow a mixture of good sealed and unsealed roads into the mountains. The best route takes you to Kykkos Monastery (p90) via the village of **Pano Panagia**, the birthplace of the island's famous former archbishop-president Makarios III.

The Cedar Valley is the highlight of the Western Troödos hinterland, home to a large number of the unusual indigenous Cypriot cedar *(Cedrus brevifolia)*, a close cousin of the better-known Lebanese cedar. There is a picnic ground here and the opportunity to hike 2.5km to the summit of **Mt Tripylos**.

◉ Sights

**Childhood House
of Makarios** NOTABLE BUILDING
(Pano Panagia; ☺ 10am-1pm & 2-6pm) **FREE** The childhood house of Archbishop Makarios III, Cyprus' first president, contains photos

FYTI

Easily accessible from Pano Panagia or Pafos, the medieval village of Fyti is well worth a visit. Whatever your approach, the surroundings are a delight, with golden cornfields, undulating vineyards and lush woodland. Park near the imposing Greek Orthodox Agios Dimitris church (if it is open, take a look at the 19th-century altar screen with its vibrant, fresh colours); the friendly priest can often be found sitting at the adjacent coffee shop. At the centre of the village square is a fountain with a backdrop of colourful weaving fronting the Folk Art Museum (☺8am-1pm & 2-5pm) FREE and the adjacent souvenir shop. Known as *fytiotika*, the tapestries produced here with their traditional patterns and rich colours are a world away from the embroidery sold at tourist shops in places such as Omodos (usually machine-made or imported from China). After a wander around this picturesque village, its winding cobbles flanked by simple stone dwellings, stop by the Phiti Pefkos Taverna (☎2673 2342; mains €6.50, meze €13; ☺9am-10pm) for a drink or meal accompanied by a soundtrack of birdsong.

and memorabilia from his younger years. It's a considerable sized building, considering his family's peasant status (then again, the livestock would have lived in one of the rooms!). If the house is locked, you can obtain the key from the nearby cultural centre.

Makarios Cultural Centre   MUSEUM
(Pano Panagia; €0.50; ☺9am-1pm & 2-5pm) This museum is a place for hard-core fans only, containing memorabilia from Archbishop Makarios III's life as a priest and Cyprus' first president. The collection includes plenty of photos and his overcoat, slippers and dressing gown (from the famous London department store Selfridges).

Chrysorrogiatissa Monastery   MONASTERY
(F622, Pano Panagia; ☺9.30am-6.30pm May-Sep, reduced hours Oct-Apr; P) FREE Located just 1.5km south of Pano Panagia in a beautiful setting 850m above sea level, this peaceful monastery dates from 1152 and features an unusual triangular cloister, built of red stone, and some fine frescos. There is also a small gift shop and museum with a display of icons. The shaded terrace is a delightful place to enjoy a light snack from the adjacent cafe.

🏃 Activities

There are traditional wineries in several of the villages surrounding Pano Panagia, where the dramatic mountain views are as much an attraction as the local vintages.

Kolios Vineyards   WINE
(☎2672 4090; www.facebook.com/kolioswinery; Statos; meze €20; ☺10am-5pm) This winery

is widely lauded for its meat meze accompanied by its own wines and including a wine tour and tasting. Reservations are essential. Drop-by visitors are also made very welcome and can enjoy tasting the Kolios wines along with the glorious valley and mountain views. This is the highest winery in the Pafos region.

★Tsangarides Winery   WINE
(☎2672 2777; www.tsangarideswinery.com; Lemona; ☺9am-5pm Mon-Sat) FREE This popular winery, which is well signposted in the centre of the village, produces organic wines and is open for free tours and tastings. Try its award-winning shiraz rosé if available.

Vouni Panayia Winery   WINE
(☎2672 2770; www.vounipanayiawinery.com; Leoforos Archiepiskopou III 60, Pano Panagia; ☺9am-4.30pm) FREE Enjoy breathtaking scenery from the tasting room of this modern winery, where you can enjoy a free tour and wine tasting; its classic Barba Yiannis comes highly recommended. It also has an excellent restaurant.

❶ Getting There & Away

You'll need a vehicle to see these places, as public transport is patchy or nonexistent. Alternatively, you could join a tour from Polis or Pafos.

The Cedar Valley is approached via a winding, unsealed forest road from Pano Panagia on the Pafos side of the Troödos Mountains, or along a signposted unsealed road from the Kykkos Monastery side of the Troödos.

Larnaka & the East

Best Places to Eat

➡ Voreas (p130)
➡ Militzis (p130)
➡ Zephyros (p130)
➡ En Yevo (p138)
➡ Art Cafe 1900 (p130)

Best Beaches

➡ Makenzy Beach (p127)
➡ Kermia Beach (p137)
➡ Nissi Beach (p137)
➡ Fig Tree Bay (p143)

Why Go?

Those golden strips of sand along the coast are what beckon most travellers here, but Cyprus' east coast has more to offer than sunbathing and sandcastles. Hike Cape Greco's coastal path for glorious scenery and weird rock formations, then follow the winding roads inland to wander snoozy villages that hug hillsides speckled with wild fennel. Delve into the very beginning of this island's human habitation at the neolithic site of Choirokoitia or whizz through more recent history with a fresco-infused church-hop of the region's Byzantine relics. Larnaka is an easygoing seaside town, with a handful of excellent historic sites. It's an ideal base for further exploration.

Hedonist-fuelled Agia Napa and family-friendly Protaras may be as different as chalk and cheese but both resorts owe their success to the region's beach-sloth reputation. Pick a beach. Any beach. You're pretty much guaranteed to come up trumps.

When to Go

➡ Between February and March pink clouds of flamingos, waterfowl and many other migratory birds check in at Larnaka's salt lake for their annual spring break, turning the serene waters into birdwatcher central.

➡ June's Kataklysmos Festival in Larnaka is a great opportunity to witness how traditional ties still play an important role in modern Cypriot life.

➡ From May to September the hot switch is turned on and everyone makes for the beach. With excellent visibility and peak sea conditions, this is the best time to head underwater and check out the famed *Zenobia* wreck dive.

➡ In July and August Agia Napa's party scene reaches full throttle and all-night clubbing is the name of the game.

Larnaka & the East Highlights

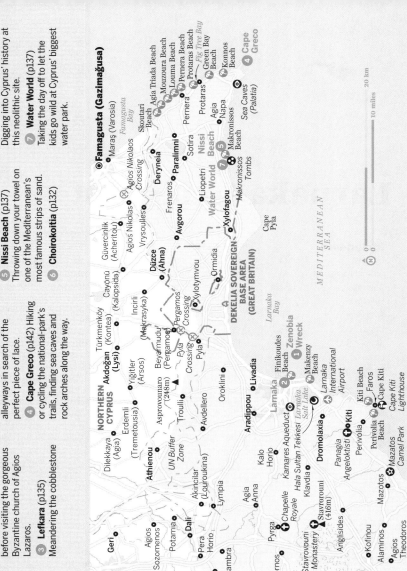

1 Zenobia wreck (p127)
Diving into the eerie innards of one of the world's most famous wreck dives.

2 Larnaka (p123)
Checking out the beach life before visiting the gorgeous Byzantine church of Agios Lazaros.

3 Lefkara (p135)
Meandering the cobblestone alleyways in search of the perfect piece of lace.

4 Cape Greco (p142) Hiking or cycling the national-park's trails, finding sea caves and rock arches along the way.

5 Nissi Beach (p137)
Throwing down your towel on one of the Mediterranean's most famous strips of sand.

6 Choirokoitia (p132)
Digging into Cyprus' history at this neolithic site.

7 Water World (p137)
Taking the day off to let the kids go wild at Cyprus' biggest water park.

LARNAKA

POP 51,470

Larnaka revolves around its seaside position. The coastal promenade – known universally as the Finikoudes – is where locals and visitors alike come for a morning coffee or an evening beer, to flop out on the beach during the day and to stroll at sunset. It's the hub of the scene, with restaurants, cafes and bars galore, and during summer it fully revs up for the annual flood of holidaymakers.

Take a few steps inland, though, and a less tourism-centred side of Larnaka unfolds. The modern downtown district has stayed determinedly low-rise and has a proper community feel and working-town atmosphere, while the old Turkish quarter of Skala is a slice of days-gone-by Cyprus, with plenty of quaintly dilapidated shutter-windowed and whitewashed houses. Between the two you'll find the Byzantine church of Agios Lazaros and Larnaka's little fort, both of which – in their own ways – have kept an eye on the town for centuries.

History

Larnaka, originally known as Kition, was established during the Mycenaean expansion in the 14th century BC. An influential Greek city-kingdom of the late Bronze Age, Kition prospered as a trading port through the export of copper. Withstanding rule by the Phoenicians and then the Persians, the city flourished into the Hellenistic period, even adopting the Phoenician fertility goddess Astarte, who was perhaps a precursor to Cypriot patron goddess Aphrodite.

During the Greek–Persian wars, Athenian general Kimon attempted to liberate the city from Persian rule in 450 BC. He died during the siege, urging his captains to conceal his fate from both enemies and allies. The episode is famously told as *'Kai Nekros enika'* (Even in death he is victorious!). His bust now stands on the Finikoudes as a tribute.

Under Ottoman rule between the 16th and early 19th centuries, Larnaka attracted merchants, dignitaries and foreign consuls. Many of these participated in amateur archaeology, prevalent at the time, and spirited away many of Larnaka's artefacts. The city's importance slowly decreased during Britain's 88-year rule as trade moved through the port at Lemesos (Limassol).

In 1974 the Turkish invasion of Northern Cyprus forced thousands of Greek Cypriots south, dramatically increasing Larnaka's population. Today Larnaka is home to Armenian, Lebanese, Pontian Greek and Palestinian settlers living alongside Cypriots and Europeans with mixed backgrounds of their own. Tourism is now the town's primary industry.

◉ Sights

★ Agios Lazaros   CHURCH

(www.ayioslazaros.org; Agiou Lazarou; ◷8am-6.30pm Mon-Sat, 6.30am-12.30pm & 3.30-6.30pm Sun Mar-Oct, 8am-12.30pm & 2.30-5.30pm Mon-Sat, 6.30am-12.30pm & 3.30-5.30pm Sun Nov-Feb) This 9th-century church is dedicated to Lazarus of Bethany, whom Jesus is said to have resurrected four days after his death. The church itself is an astounding example of Byzantine architecture, and further restoration in the 17th century saw Latinate and Orthodox influences added to the building, most prominently in the bell tower, which was replaced after being destroyed by the Ottomans. The beautiful interior is a showcase of unique Catholic woodcarvings and skilled gold-plated Orthodox icon artistry.

Lazarus has a close association with Larnaka. Shortly after he rose from the dead, thanks to Christ's miraculous intervention, Lazarus was forced to flee Bethany. His boat landed here in Kition, where he was ordained as a bishop and canonised by Apostles Barnabas and Paul. He remained a bishop for a further 30 years, and when he died for the second time he was buried in a hidden tomb.

In 890 the tomb was discovered; it bore the inscription 'Lazarus Friend of Christ'. Byzantine emperor Leo VI had Lazarus' remains sent to Constantinople and built the current church over the vault to appease local Christians. The remains were moved again, to Marseille, in 1204.

The **Tomb of Lazarus** is under the apse of the Agios Lazaros. Several sarcophagi were supposedly found in this catacomb when it was first discovered but only the empty tomb remains. In 1972 human remains were uncovered under the church altar; some believe they are those of St Lazarus, possibly hidden here by priests in anticipation of theft.

Byzantine Museum   MUSEUM

(Agiou Lazarou; €1; ◷8.15am-12.30pm & 3-5.30pm Mon, Tue, Thu, Fri & Sun, 8.15am-12.30pm Wed & Sat) Located in the courtyard of the Agios Lazaros complex, this museum originally contained many priceless relics and arte-

ROAD TRIP > CRAFTWORK OF TRADITIONAL VILLAGES

The villages dotted around Larnaka have been famous since ancient times for their handicrafts, passed down through the generations from father to son and mother to daughter. This drive links some of the most charming, starting in Kiti and finishing back in Larnaka.

① Maroni

From Kiti, start your drive from the church of **Panagia Angeloktisti** (p135), taking the 403 road west towards the agricultural village of Mazotos. Kids will love its camel park. From here take the old coastal road west through fields and sparse terrain. You'll travel about 17km, with a view of the sea on your left, before reaching attractive Maroni

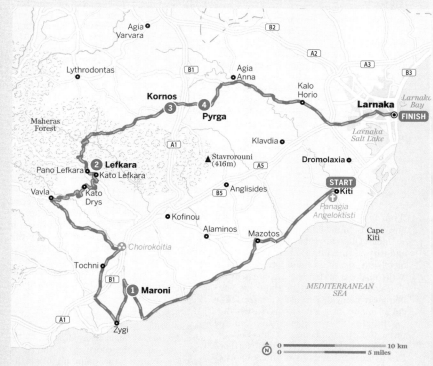

village, where you can buy some local cucumbers and have a Greek coffee. Then take the short road southwest to Zygi, a diminutive fishing village known for some of the island's best fish taverns. After you've had a bite to eat, it's back on track westward for 1km. Head inland and turn right onto the B1 underpass (crossing the A1 motorway) for about 6km, then head left towards the valley and the scenic village of Tochni.

➋ Lefkara

The north road out of the village takes you 4km to the impressive prehistoric settlement of **Choirokoitia** (p132). From this neolithic site take a long stretch of climbing road inland northwest to Vavla, which has some wonderfully restored homes. Next is the pretty, well-signposted stone village of Kato Drys, full of quaint balconies. A mere 4km more of winding road brings you to the town of **Lefkara** (p135), which combines the lace- and silverwork villages of Kato Lefkara and Pano Lefkara. You can wander the precipitous old town or get your shopping fix here.

➌ Kornos

From Pano Lefkara travel north for 7km on a good stretch of road until you see Lefkara dam on your left. Follow the road right over an incline for 16km to the pottery village of Kornos.

➍ Pyrga

After some clay hunting, follow the signs and road east, through the underpass (recrossing the motorway), to the town of Pyrga, home of the 14th-century Lusignan Chapelle Royale (signposted as 'Medieval Chapel'). This church is dedicated to St Catherine and houses some fine frescos. About 4km north of the village you can turn right (east) onto the 104 road, stop in Agia Anna for meze, then ease your way into Larnaka.

facts. Unfortunately, much of the collection was on loan to Lemesos' Archaeological Museum in the 1960s when sectarian violence broke out and the museum was looted. All that remains is the original catalogue of items, now on display.

The museum has worked hard to rebuild its collection, and exhibits ecclesiastical artefacts, icons and utensils, with many items donated by Orthodox Russian clergy.

★ **Pierides**
Archaeological Foundation   MUSEUM
(Zinonos Kitieos 4; adult/child €3/1; ⊘ 9am-4pm Mon-Thu, to 1pm Fri & Sat) This museum was established in 1839 by Demetrios Pierides as a protective answer to the region's notorious tomb raiders and the illegal selling of the area's precious artefacts.

The collection, expanded by Pierides' descendants, is housed in the family mansion, built in 1825. It features artefacts from all over the island, with detailed explanations in English. Although the museum is small, it has some stunning pieces; exhibits are well curated and arranged chronologically to present a comprehensive history of Cyprus.

The most famous piece in the collection is the neolithic ceramic howling man, dating to c 5500 BC. If water is poured into the seated figure's mouth it will drain from his phallus. No other piece like it has ever been found on the island. Archaeologists have debated whether the figure had a religious or a secular function, but no consensus has ever been reached.

The exhibits then wander through the Mycenaean and Achaean periods, the Iron Age, the Roman occupation, and Byzantine, Crusader, Lusignan, Venetian and Ottoman periods.

The collection also showcases intricate Greek and Roman glassware and offers fine examples of weaving, embroidery, woodcarvings and traditional costumes associated with Cypriot folk art.

Larnaka Fort   HISTORIC SITE
(Leoforos Athinon; €2.50; ⊘ 9am-7pm Mon-Fri) Built in the Lusignan era, the fort stands at the water's edge and separates the Finikoudes promenade from the old Turkish quarter. Its present form is a result of remodelling by the Ottomans around 1605.

The courtyard is home to some medieval tombstone exhibits and old cannons, and you can climb up onto part of the ramparts. The room on your right as you enter was where the British carried out executions during their rule over Cyprus.

Grand Mosque   MOSQUE
(Büyük Camii; Agias Faneromenis) Located at the beginning of Larnaka's Turkish quarter, with its maze of sleepy whitewashed streets, the Grand Mosque is the spiritual home of Larnaka's Muslim community. Left untouched when the Turkish community dispersed in 1974, it now predominantly serves Muslims from North Africa.

Originally built in the 16th century as the Latin Holy Cross Church, it was converted into a mosque during the Ottoman

---

THE WIDELY TRAVELLED LAZAROS

As with so many stories in the Bible, the legend of Saint Lazarus of Bethany – Agios Lazaros in the Greek Orthodox tradition – is a tantalising mixture of myths and elements of historical truth. The miraculous reincarnation described in the Gospel of John is impossible to verify, but a man called Lazaros did travel from Judea to become the bishop of Kition, on the site of modern-day Larnaka, in the early years of the Christian church.

When Bishop Lazarus departed this life, perhaps for the second time, his grave was forgotten for centuries, before being rediscovered by Cypriot priests in AD 890. To protect the saint's bones from invaders, the contents of the grave were moved to Constantinople, before being carted off to Marseilles by rampaging knights during the Fourth Crusade.

Over the following centuries, the chapel raised over the grave of Lazaros was used as a Catholic Church under the Franks, and a mosque under the Ottomans, before finally returning to its Orthodox roots in the 16th century. In a curious epilogue, more human bones (thought by some to be those of Lazaros) were discovered in the church in 1972, and a portion of the skeleton was sent to Russia in 2012 as a gift to the Russian Orthodox church. Cypriot pilgrims venerate the remaining bones of Lazaros on display in the church of **Agios Lazaros** (p123) in Larnaka.

era. The current construction is the result of 19th-century restoration. There is a small graveyard at the front, with Gothic-style tombstones.

Ancient Kition
ARCHAEOLOGICAL SITE
(Leoforos Archiepiskopou Kyprianos; €2.50; ☉9.30am-5pm Mon-Fri) Much of the original city-kingdom of Kition is covered by present-day Larnaka. The sparse remains that have been unearthed, referred to as Area II, lie about 1km northwest of the central city. A raised runway takes you over the remains of Cyclopean walls. Most remarkable are the remnants of five temples (from the 13th century BC) and the ship depictions etched into the walls of the nearby ancient port. The latter confirmed that the city was founded by sea-trading Mycenaeans.

Larnaka Archaeological Museum
MUSEUM
(Plateia Kalogreon; €2.50; ☉8am-4pm Mon-Fri, 9am-4pm Sat) Larnaka's one-room archaeological museum is sparse on information but houses a wide collection of ceramics from nearby sites. The collection's highlights are its skeletons unearthed at Choirokoitia, and its terracotta votive figures from Ancient Kition.

Municipal Art Gallery
GALLERY
(Plateia Evropis; ☉9am-1pm & 4-7pm Mon-Fri, 10am-1pm Sat) FREE This small gallery is made up of five adjoining colonial-style stone warehouses built by the British in 1881. Three of them show contemporary artworks by local artists. The buildings are also used to host occasional international exhibitions.

Natural History Museum
MUSEUM
(Municipal Gardens, Leoforos Grigoriou Afxentiou; €1.70; ☉9am-5pm Mon-Fri) This museum presents an excellent introduction to the natural history of the island, with exhibits dedicated to fauna, flora, geology, insects and marine life. Situated in the Municipal Gardens, it is regularly visited by school groups and is a fun place for children, who can see pelicans, flamingos, peacocks and macaws in cages outside the museum. There is also a little playground in the gardens.

🏖 Beaches

★ Makenzy Beach
BEACH
(off Piyale Pasha) Larnaka's most popular beach has all the facilities needed for a day

SKALA: THE TURKISH QUARTER

Strolling the streets of the old Turkish neighbourhood of Skala is a glimpse into the Cyprus of old. This quaint district is a watercolour-worthy scene of squat cottages with peeling whitewash, coloured window shutters and flowerpot-studded doorways. Road signs here still carry their Turkish names, a reminder of Larnaka's mixed community before 1974. Today the quarter is being revived by a clutch of ceramic workshops that have made Skala their home, giving the area a distinct bohemian edge.

in the sun, including plenty of cafes and restaurants rimming the promenade. It's about 2km south of the central city, straight down Piyale Pasha.

Seaside snoozes on your sunbed can be somewhat interrupted by the planes taking off and coming into land at the neighbouring airport.

Finikoudes Beach
BEACH
This clean, shallow beach is highly popular despite not being particularly pretty. Sunbeds and umbrellas can be hired for between €2 and €3, and there are kiosks and cafes galore all along the strip.

🏃 Activities

For divers, the one reason to come to Larnaka is to explore the Zenobia, a Swedish-built cargo ship that sank just off the coast of Larnaka in 1980. Classed as one of the top five wreck dives in the world, the *Zenobia* and its cargo of trucks lie scattered across the sea floor like a bizarre underwater scrapyard. Various routes through the ship's decks and halls can be explored, according to your level of dive experience.

Several local dive operators run trips to the wreck, which acts like an artificial reef, attracting plentiful sealife.

Alpha Divers
DIVING
(✉2464 7519; www.alpha-divers.com; Dhekalia Rd; 2 boat-dive package €80; ☉9am-6pm) This five-star Professional Association of Diving Instructors (PADI) centre offers PADI dive courses from beginner to advanced and both technical and recreational dives to the *Zenobia* wreck. It's 10km north of central

Larnaka

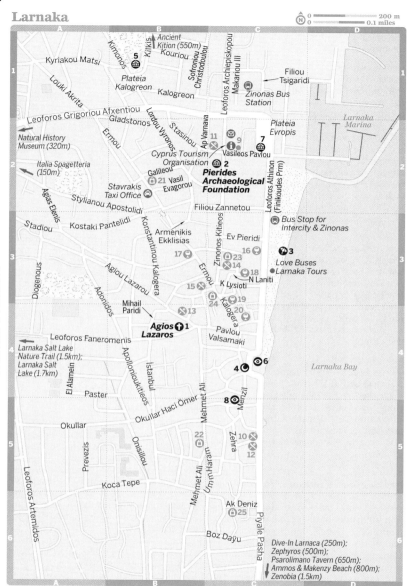

Larnaka along Dhekalia Rd, and opposite the large Lordos Beach Hotel complex.

Dive-In Larnaka　　　　　　　　　DIVING
(📞 2462 7469; www.dive-in.com.cy; Piyale Pasha 132; 1/2 dives €42/84; ⊙9am-6pm) This five-star PADI dive centre has a whole range of technical and recreational dive safaris and learn-to-dive courses, with the *Zenobia* wreck as its star attraction.

Larnaka

Anemos Water Sports   WATER SPORTS
(☑9953 5258; www.anemoswatersportscyprus.
com; Dhekelia Rd) If you want to get out on
Larnaka Bay in a kayak, board boat or jet
ski, head to this outfit based in front of the
Golden Bay hotel.

🧭 Tours

★ **CTO Guided Tours**   WALKING
The Cyprus Tourist Organisation (CTO) runs
two free guided walks that offer a great introduction to the layout of Larnaka and its
rich history. The 'Larnaka: Its Past & Present' walk starts at 10am every Wednesday
outside the CTO office. 'Skala: Its Craftsmen'
leaves at 10am every Friday from Larnaka
Fort. Walks take around two hours with
breaks.

Love Buses Larnaka Tours   TOURS
(☑9776 1761; adult/child €15/10; ◎11.15am &
5.15pm Jun-Sep, 11.15am & 3.15pm Feb-May & Oct-
Nov) If you are short on time, this 2½-hour
double-decker bus tour whizzes around
Larnaka's most important sights. Starting
from the seafront, the bus passes by Agios
Lazaros, then heads out to Kiti, with stops
at Panagia Angeloktisti, Hala Sultan Tekkesi
and Larnaka Salt Lake, before heading back
to the seafront via the Kamares Aqueduct.

🎉 Festivals & Events

Musical Sundays   MUSIC
(◎from 11am Sun Jan-May, Nov & Dec) On the
seafront stage at the Finikoudes, Musical
Sundays features a variety of rock, jazz, traditional music and dancing events. Line-ups
are listed in free brochure *Larnaka This
Month,* available at all bookshops.

Kataklysmos Festival   RELIGIOUS
(www.larnaka.org.cy; ◎Jun) Held each year 50
days after Orthodox Easter, this festival has
special significance for Larnaka as a coastal town. Kataklysmos, meaning 'Deluge' or
'Cataclysm' in Greek, is a traditional celebration of Noah and his salvation from the
Flood.

During the day there are all kinds of fun
water-based activities such as windsurfing,
kayak races and swimming competitions.

Larnaka Summer Festival   CULTURAL
(www.larnaka.com; ◎Jul) Larnaka's fort and
the municipal theatre are the venues for an
eclectic mix of music, dance and theatre performances throughout July.

Fengaros   MUSIC
(www.louvanarecords.com/festivals; Katro Drys;
◎Aug) A line-up of rock, pop, dance, blues,
folk and more, from both local and international bands and DJs, takes over the village
of Kato Drys in the hills above Larnaka for
three days during August.

Eating

Larnaka has plenty of variety in its eating
scene. Most places directly on the Finikoudes promenade dish up decent but bland international fare, so it's generally a better idea

to head to the taverns hidden in the back-streets a few steps off the main drag. Dinner dining usually begins after 7pm. Good restaurants often aren't full until 10pm.

Alasia
GREEK €

(Piyale Pasha 38; pastries €2.20-6, mains €7-10; ⊙10.30am-11pm; 🐾) When we're in town we always pull into Alasia for a quick lunch of *koupes* (mince-meat stuffed pastries) or a sneaky afternoon *loukoumades* (Cypriot honey balls) pit stop. This family-run cafe rustles up some of the best *koupes* we've had on the island.

Secret Garden
CAFE €

(☑2410 3078; Agiou Lazarou 26; sandwiches €5-7, sharing platters €16-17; ⊙11am-11.45pm; 🐾🚗) The low-key and friendly vine-draped back garden, complete with kooky angel statues and a trickling water feature, is where we head for an easy lunch of tasty sandwiches stuffed with fillings. We like the 'Greedy Vegie' and 'Cyprus Sub'. Secret Garden also does good coffee and is a great venue for a relaxed evening over a couple of wines.

To Kafe Tis Chrysanthis
INTERNATIONAL €

(☑2425 6262; Ifaistiou 1; mains €6-12; ⊙8am-11pm; 🐾🚗) This cute little cafe, tucked away just off the main coastal drag, has colourful ceramic plates decorating the walls inside and seating that spills out into the narrow alleyway. Service is friendly, and the simple menu deals in excellent sandwiches, crispy salads and a mighty fine piece of cake.

★Art Cafe 1900
CYPRIOT €€

(☑2465 3027; Stasinou 6; mains €9-14; ⊙6pm-late Wed-Mon; 🐾🚗) With art prints and photos covering the walls, and shelves weighed down with bric-a-brac, Art Cafe 1900 is by far Larnaka's most atmospheric dining choice. Dine on stuffed cabbage leaves or *stifado* (stew made with beef or rabbit and onions, simmered in vinegar and wine) then head downstairs to the cosy bar for a few beers.

★Militzis
CYPRIOT €€

(☑2465 5867; Piyale Pasha 42; mains €9-13, meze per person €14; ⊙11am-11pm; 🐾) This tavern serves up Cypriot soul food at its best, with soft, succulent lamb baked in the domed *fourno* (traditional ovens). As well as all the usual favourites, why not give specialities such as *kefalaki* (lamb's head) and *kokoretsi* (lamb's intestines) a try? Meze minimum two people.

Stou Rousia
CYPRIOT €€

(off Zinonos Kitieos; mains €7.50-12; ⊙noon-11pm) Despite indifferent service, we recommend this little taverna because it's one of few places in central Larnaca that dishes up proper home cooking. Daily specials feature hearty green beans and chicken, or chickpea and spinach stew, while the small main menu bursts with rustic flavours, including tangy, stick-to-your-ribs beef *stifado*.

★Voreas
CYPRIOT €€

(☑2464 7177; Agiou Demetriou 3, Oroklini; meze per person €12; ⊙noon-midnight Wed-Mon; 🐾) Ten minutes north of Larnaca in Oroklini village, this house with a courtyard offers traditional foods, surrounds and hospitality. The aroma of herbs, the succulent variety of meat and the wild vegetable meze dishes will have you scrambling for space at the table as you eat until you are full.

★Zephyros
SEAFOOD €€€

(Piyale Pasha 37; mains €12-15, meze per person €20; ⊙11am-11pm; 🐾) It's been around for more than 40 years, and although the big dining-hall-style surroundings lack any inspiration whatsoever, Zephyros' high-quality fish meze (two people minimum) with eight different kinds of seafood still consistently gets the thumbs-up from locals. If you like seafood, this is one of the top choices in town; just don't expect ambience – it's all about the food.

Psarolimano Tavern
SEAFOOD €€€

(☑2465 5408; www.psarolimano.com; Piyale Pasha 118; mains €12-30, meze per person €20; ⊙11am-11pm; 🅿️🐾) This seafood tavern is known for its fish meze (two people minimum, and well worth splashing out for), but we also like the fisherman's kebab and the grilled octopus. The view across the traditional fishing harbour complements the food perfectly, and service is friendly and efficient.

🍷 Drinking & Nightlife

The Finikoudes offers bars and cafes of every style. More intimate pubs and *kafeneio* (cafes) can be found in the side streets leading away from the coast. During summer Makenzy Beach, just west along the coast, is the favoured spot to hang out. In July and August the beach bars on the sand here host regular beach parties.

★ Heads & Tails
BAR

(Nicolaou Laniti; ☺ 6pm-2am; 🛜) Tucked away just off the waterfront (look for the lampshades swinging from electricity wires over the alley), this kooky little place is all colourful mismatched chairs and cupboard drawers reworked as tables. It's our new number-one cocktail spot in town, thanks to friendly staff, good music and some seriously inventive and delicious drinks using spice-infused syrups and herbs.

Old Market Street
BAR

(Kleanthi Kalogera 54; ☺ 5pm-2am; 🛜) This cool kid on the block makes a mean cocktail and has a chilled-out, friendly ambience. The signature cocktail menu includes plenty of creative and quirky twists. On a balmy summer evening, we're usually sipping the Indian Route, made with spiced gin, cardamom and lime.

Ammos
BAR

(www.ammos.eu; Makenzy Beach; ☺ 9am-late; 🛜) Right at the end of the Makenzy Beach promenade, Ammos (Greek for 'sand') is a splendidly bright, white venue that pumps out urban house and lazy funk until the wee hours. During the day it's good for coffee and lunch; in the evening it's all about cocktails under the cloud-free starry sky.

Savino's Rock Bar
BAR

(9 Ouotkins, Laiki Geitonia; ☺ 7pm-late; 🛜) Savino's has been around for years and is still one of the best spots to pull up a stool and enjoy a few beers. With a hardwood bar and pictures of rock gods on the wall, this diminutive place is hidden just off the main promenade, and plays classic rock, jazz and blues.

Geometry
CLUB

(www.facebook.com/Geometry-Club; Karaoli & Demetriou 8; ☺ 10pm-late Fri-Sun) The entrance is a floor-lit mirrored ramp that looks like a cross between a retro spaceship and Michael Jackson's 'Billy Jean' film clip. Inside is a decadent club kitted out with geometric light patterns and prisms. Aimed at a posh crowd, it plays a good selection of dance, club and Greek tracks. Dress well, so you'll feel at home with the locals.

Club Deep
CLUB

(www.facebook.com/clubdeep.larnacaofficial; Leoforos Athinon 76; ☺ 11pm-late) Two floors of all-night clubbing right on the seafront. The lower club plays mostly chilled trance and progressive house. The main club (Deep) houses a huge dance floor that melts with old-school, R & B and mainstream dance. It gets busy after midnight, with a young, easygoing crowd.

☆ Entertainment

Savino Live
LIVE MUSIC

(9 Ouotkins, Laiki Geitonia; ☺ 8pm-late Wed-Fri & Sat) This live rock venue fits up to 300 people – and it needs to. Its well-amplified stage and open dance floor mean a great night of vivacious dancing. Bands from all over Cyprus come to play classic blues, jazz and rock till late.

K Cineplex
CINEMA

(Kmax bowling alley 7777 8373, box office 2436 2167; www.kcineplex.com; Peloponisou 1; adult/child €9/7) A cineplex with six screens, wide reclining seats and all the usual Hollywood blockbusters on show. All films are subtitled in Greek, except animated features, which have Greek or English alternatives. The site also houses the 20-lane **Kmax bowling alley** and Finnegan's Irish pub-restaurant. The complex is 10 minutes' drive west of the city centre, near the Kamares Aqueduct.

🛍 Shopping

Pottery is Larnaka's signature collectable. There are some excellent ceramic workshops where you can pick up a piece of original Cypriot art.

★ Academic & General
BOOKS

(2462 8401; Ermou 41; ☺ 9am-7pm) Probably the best bookshop on the island. This friendly shop has a huge range of both English- and Greek-language titles, ranging from best-selling novels to classics and philosophy, along with plenty of books on Cyprus. There's also a big secondhand fiction section, ideal for beach reads. Feel free to make a coffee and lounge upstairs on the couches.

Municipal Market
MARKET

(Kalogera; ☺ 8am-2pm) This central market is great for self-caterers, with plenty of stalls piled high with fresh fruit and seasonal vegetables.

Flamma Art Gallery
CERAMICS

(2462 5530; www.stavrosceramics.com.cy; Zinonos Kitieos 113; ☺ 9.30am-1.30pm & 4-7pm Mon, Tue, Thu & Fri, 9.30am-1.30pm Wed & Sat) The unique, colourful and quirky pieces here are the work of local ceramic artist Stavros Stavrou, whose creativity has a slightly

LARNAKA & THE EAST LARNAKA

whimsical edge. Truly original and beautiful ceramic art.

Emira Pottery
CERAMICS

(9940 4414; www.emirapottery.com.cy; Mehmet Ali 13; ☺9am-1.30pm & 3-6pm Mon-Sat) Delicately patterned plates and traditional Cypriot cooking pots are some of the many pieces on offer. You can even try your hand at your own creation.

Studio Ceramics
CERAMICS

(☑2465 0338; www.studioceramicscyprus.com; Ak Deniz 18; ☺9am-1pm & 3-6pm Mon-Sat) The pottery here is inspired by ancient and medieval Cypriot art. The Pierides Archaeological Foundation museum replicas are a standout.

❶ Information

EMERGENCY

Police station (☑2480 4040; Leoforos Archiepiskopou Makariou III; ☺8am-6pm Mon-Fri) Near the Finikoudes promenade.

INTERNET ACCESS

Wi-fi is available all along the Finikoudes. Get online at **Amalfi Café** (Lordou Vyronos 35; per hour €2; ☺10am-1am) in the centre of town.

MEDICAL SERVICES

Larnaka Hospital (☑2480 0500; Leoforos Grigoriou Afxentiou; ☺24hr)
Night pharmacy assistance Call ☑1414.

MONEY

There are plenty of ATMs in the centre of town.
Hellenic Bank (☑2414 4141; Stasinou; ☺8.30am-2.30pm Mon-Fri) Opposite the CTO.

POST

Post office (Plateia; ☺8am-3pm Mon-Fri) Near the CTO office.

TOURIST INFORMATION

Cyprus Tourism Organisation (CTO; ☑2465 4322; www.visitcyprus.com; Plateia; ☺8.15am-2.30pm & 3-6.15pm Mon, Tue, Thu & Fri, 8.15am-1.30pm Sat) Has good maps of the city and plenty of brochures. Up-to-date information on local events.

❶ Getting There & Away

AIR

Larnaka International Airport (☑flight info 2464 3000; www.hermesairports.com;) is 7km southwest of the city centre. This is the busiest airport on the island and has decent facilities, including ATMs, cafes and restaurants in both Arrivals and Departure

halls. Frequent, direct flights connect to all major European cities, plus destinations in the Middle East and North Africa, operated by low-cost and charter carriers as well as national airlines. The airport is the hub for Cyprus Airways (www.cyprusairways.com), which relaunched in mid-2017.

BOAT

Larnaka Marina (☑2465 3110; ctolar@cytanet.com.cy) is an official port of entry into Cyprus for yachties, offering a complete range of berthing facilities. It requires advance reservations.

BUS

InterCity buses (☑8000 7789; www.intercity-buses.com) leave from the Finikoudes bus stop, on the beach side in the middle of the coastal promenade.

Agia Napa and Paralimni €4, 1¼ hours, 13 services from 6am to 8.30pm Monday to Friday, 10 services 6.30am to 8.30pm weekends.

Lemesos €4, 1½ hours, 10 services from 6am to 8.30pm Monday to Friday, six services 7.30am to 7pm weekends.

Nicosia €4, 1¼ hours, 16 services from 5.50am to 7.30pm Monday to Friday, nine services 6.30am to 8.30pm weekends.

Pafos €7, 2¾ hours, four services from 6.30am to 6.30pm Monday to Friday, one service 8.45am weekends.

SERVICE TAXI

Travel & Express (☑2466 1010; www.travel-express.com.cy; cnr Papakyriakou & Markelou; ☺6am-6pm Mon-Fri, 7am-5pm Sat & Sun) operates service (shared) taxis that will pick you up from any location; call to prebook. Taxis run to the following destinations:

Agia Napa, Paralimni and Protaras €8.50 Monday to Saturday, €10 Sunday, 45 minutes.

Lemesos €10 Monday to Saturday, €12 Sunday, one hour.

Nicosia €8.50 Monday to Saturday, €10 Sunday, 40 minutes.

Pafos €19.50 Monday to Saturday, €23 Sunday, 1¾ hours.

TAXI

There are several taxi stands along the Finikoudes. **Stavrakis Taxi Office** (☑2465 5988; Ermou 64) is in the centre of town. Sample journey fares and times:

Agia Napa €35, 30 minutes.
Lemesos €50 to €60, one hour.
Nicosia €45, 35 minutes.
Pafos €105, one hour 40 minutes.
Troödos €80 to €90, one hour.

ⓘ Getting Around

TO/FROM THE AIRPORT

The cheapest way between the airport and central Larnaka is by **Zinonas** (p133) public bus. Bus 425 picks up and drops off at the central **Finikoudes bus stop** (p132) as well as the bus station, and has frequent services (€1.50, 25 minutes, every 30 minutes between 5.55am and 11.25pm).

A taxi stand operates 24/7 at the Arrivals gate of Larnaka airport. The 10-minute ride costs approximately €15.

BUS

Larnaka's urban and regional bus network is run by **Zinonas Buses** (📞 2466 5531; www. zinonasbuses.com; Filiou Tsigaridi); its central bus station is opposite Larnaka Marina. One-way tickets cost €1.50 and all-day tickets €5.

Due to roundabout routes and irregular schedules, the bus network isn't used much by visitors except to go to the airport (p133). The website has route information and timetables in English.

CAR & MOTORCYCLE

All the big international car-hire firms are represented at Larnaka Airport.

Andreas Petsas Rent-a-car (📞 2464 3350; www.petsas.com.cy; Larnaka International Airport; 3-day hire per day from €34; ⊙ 24hr) One of Cyprus' largest car-hire companies.

Anemayia Car & Motorbike Rentals (📞 9962 4726; www.anemayiacarsbikes.com; 19 Leoforos Archiepiskopou Makariou III; 3-day car hire per day in low/high season from €15/25, 2-day scooter hire per day from €12; ⊙ 9am-5pm Mon-Sat) Also rents cruisers, mopeds and buggies.

Thames Car Rentals (www.thames.com.cy; 2-day car hire per day from €21) Branches in the **city centre** (📞 2465 6333, 8004 1044; Vasileos Pavlou 13; ⊙ 8.30am-5pm Mon-Fri) and at the **airport** (📞 2400 8700; www.thames. com.cy; Larnaka International Airport; ⊙ 24hr).

AROUND LARNAKA

The hills to the west of Larnaka hide teensy hamlets of cobblestone alleys and sturdy stone houses that feel like a different world to the modern made-for-tourism coast. Spending a day or two meandering the countryside lanes gives a refreshing dose of laid-back rural life. Closer to Larnaka, the vast salt lake of the same name sits right on the doorstep to the city, with the Hala Sultan Tekkesi mosque at its tail and the impressive arches of the Kamares Aqueduct at its tip.

Further west, roll back time at Choirokoitia, the island's most important neolithic site.

ⓘ Getting There & Away

The best, and easiest, way to see the greater Larnaka area is with your own wheels. If you're really strapped for time, the **Love Buses** (p129) sightseeing tour gives you a snapshot of the countryside, passing by a few of the most important historic sights.

⊙ Sights

Larnaka Salt Lake   LAKE

During winter this protected reserve fills with rainwater, creating an important migratory habitat for flamingos, wild ducks and water fowl. As summer approaches the waters slowly dry up and the birds leave. They are replaced by a crusty layer of salt, and heat waves bounce and shimmer off its white surface.

A nature trail that threads along the eastern bank is great for birdwatching in spring.

Archaeologists have determined that in prehistoric times the central lake (known to locals as Aliki) was a natural port that facilitated important trade to the island. It serviced a sizeable late–Bronze Age town that stood near where the Hala Sultan Tekkesi mosque stands now. In 1050 BC the town's population abandoned the site, and shortly after the waterway dried up, thus creating the salt lake. For centuries afterwards salt was harvested from the lake and became a valuable export for Cyprus. Temporary harvest houses were set up and donkeys were used to cart salt in large woven baskets. By the 1980s, rising costs and slowed production halted salt harvesting altogether.

Kamares Aqueduct   AQUEDUCT

Sanctioned in 1746 by Ottoman governor Bekir Pasha, and built in classical Roman style – some historians believe it is actually a Roman creation that was simply refurbished by the Ottomans – this aqueduct was constructed to solve Larnaka's freshwater problems. It originally ferried water from a source 10km south using underground tunnels, hundreds of air wells and a series of overland arches known as 'the Kamares' that survive today.

The aqueduct remained in use until the 1950s. Today the Larnaka municipality holds occasional open-air concerts on the lawns in front of the aqueduct, which is wonderfully

STAVROVOUNI

Perched 668m high at the peak of Stavrovouni (literally 'Mountain of the Cross'), the **Stavrovouni Monastery** (☺8am-noon & 3-6pm Apr-Aug, 8am-noon & 2-5pm Sep-Mar) is revered as the oldest on the island and is said to hold a piece of the Holy Cross, brought here by St Helena, mother of Emperor Constantine the Great, upon her return from Jerusalem in AD 327. Today this fragment from the Holy Land is preserved in an ornate 1.2m solid silver cross inside the church.

Ironically, nowadays St Helena herself could not view the cross, as the monastery grounds are closed to women. The site is still well worth the trip, though, for its uninterrupted views of the Mesaoria (Mesarya) plain. On a clear day you can see Famagusta to the east, Troödos Mountains to the northwest, all the way around to Larnaka and the salt lake, and as far as the clear blue Mediterranean.

Once inside the monastery you can take a seat in the sun-filled courtyard entrance to the church, admire the bell tower and ponder monastic life. While male visitors are freely exploring the many icons and arched hallways, female travellers can spend their time at the smaller **Church of All Saints** just outside the monastery. All can meet in the souvenir and bookshop, with a grand array of Bibles, hymn books and icons for sale. There are also handmade prayer bracelets (€4), which make wonderful souvenirs.

Stavrovouni is a working religious community with a score of monks dedicated to life-long ascetic principles. Pilgrims and visitors are welcome, and can take confession by request, but should arrive during visiting hours only. Photography is prohibited inside the monastery, so leave your camera behind. If you are a dedicated pilgrim (and male) you may be invited, by the monks, to sleep the night, meditate and dine with them on organically grown produce.

The monastery is located 17km from Larnaka, off the Nicosia–Lemesos motorway (A1).

illuminated at night. It is close to the K Cineplex on the old road to Lemesos.

Hala Sultan Tekkesi MOSQUE
(Hala Sultan Tekke; ☺9am-7.30pm May-Sep, to 5pm Oct-Apr) Surrounded by date palms, cypress and olive trees, this late-18th-century mosque and *tekke* (shrine) sits wistfully on the edge of Larnaka's salt lake. According to Muslim lore, during the Arab raids on Cyprus in 674, Umm Haram, the revered aunt of the Prophet Mohammed, fell from her mule and died at this exact spot. Her mausoleum and shrine are in the small room attached to the main mosque prayer hall.

The mosque itself is still used and is a place of great reverence and major religious significance to Muslims. If you wish to enter, dress modestly and remove your shoes before entering the prayer hall. The interior is very simple and modest, with little decoration except for the floor, layered with prayer mats.

The excavated tomb and sarcophagus of Hala Sultan (Umm Haram), meaning 'Great Mother' in Arabic, is found left of the entrance, in what feels like a cave.

It's 1km from the main road between Larnaka and the airport.

Beaches

Larnaka's beaches can be bland compared to those in Agia Napa and the east coast. Most have hard-packed, greyish sand and occasional pebbles. The waters, though, are generally very shallow and great for kids.

CTO Municipal Beach BEACH
(Dhekelia Rd) East of Larnaka, this beach is very popular with locals and is backed by dozens of taverns, restaurants and hotels.

Cape Kiti & Perivolia BEACH
Southwest of Larnaka, these two adjoining narrow beaches have large, white stones and shallow waters. The Perivolia side of the cape is often exposed to tremendous winds, ideal for kite- and windsurfing. You'll need to have your own equipment, though.

Choirokoitia

Occupying a well-defended hillside with a large perimeter wall, this small but well-preserved **neolithic site** (€2.50; ☺8.30am-

5.30pm) is the earliest permanent human settlement found in Cyprus, dating back to 7000 BC. A walkway guides you around the settlement, starting at the foot of the hill where reconstructions of huts, built by archaeologists, help you visualise how Choirokoitia's people would have lived. The best remains are on the hilltop, where you can also see sparse remnants of the settlement's walls.

Choirokoitia is believed to have been established by peoples from Anatolia and Asia Minor. The remains of more than 50 cylindrical stone and mud dwellings have been discovered, along with prehistoric utensils, indicating that the Choirokoitians practised a sophisticated lifestyle that included well-developed hunting and farming. They also appear to have buried their dead under the floors of their dwellings, as is indicated by the remains of more than 20 skeletons, including those of infants.

The site's significance in our understanding of neolithic culture was recognised in 1998 when it was added to the Unesco World Heritage list.

Choirokoitia is 32km from Larnaka, just off the main Larnaka–Lemesos highway. If you continue a further 10km towards Lemesos, you can see the neolithic site at Tenta (Kalavasos), easily recognisable by the huge cone-shaped tent shielding it from the elements. It is a simpler version of Choirokoitia but just as important archaeologically.

Lefkara

POP 900

It may be hard to imagine now, but during the Renaissance this mountain village combining Pano and Kato Lefkara was one of the island's largest and most influential towns, with an affluent population of nearly 5000. Surrounded by a steep valley of pines and wild carob trees, Lefkara has been famous since medieval times for its exquisite lace produced by village women, and for fine silverwork, incorporating lacing techniques, produced by its smiths. This craft industry boomed right up to the 1930s when the bottom fell out of the market and people emigrated en masse for work.

Today Lefkara may be a shadow of its former self but the narrow cobbled streets are still lined with fine Venetian-style merchant houses and, thanks to tourism, the lace-making and silverwork traditions continue. After some lace shopping, it's an atmospheric place to ramble, with hidden courtyards, dead-end alleys and finely carved traditional doorways to explore.

◉ Sights

Lefkara Folk Art Museum   MUSEUM
(Patsolos House; €2; ⊙9.30am-4pm Mon-Thu, 10am-4pm Fri & Sat) Formerly the home of one of Lefkara's wealthiest families, this restored building is set around a large courtyard complete with outdoor oven and pomegranate and citrus trees. The ground floor has information boards on Lefkara's history and a typical 19th-century dining area. Upstairs there are examples of original lace and silverwork as well as traditionally styled bedrooms, complete with antique dressers, mirrors and beds.

**Timiou Stavrou
Church**   CHURCH
(Timiou Stavrou; ⊙8am-2.30pm & 4-6pm) Although the building you see today was greatly remodelled in the 19th and early 20th centuries, the Timiou Stavrou (Holy Cross) Church dates back to the 14th century. The iconostasis holds some lovely 18th-century icons, and the wooden cross kept in the crypt is said to contain a piece of the true cross.

WORTH A TRIP

KITI

This village 9km southwest of Larnaka is home to the 11th-century domed cruciform church of **Panagia Angeloktisti** (⊙9.30am-noon & 2-4pm Mon-Sat). Literally meaning 'Built by Angels', the church is home to the extraordinary 6th-century **Mosaic of the Virgin Mary**. The mosaic was discovered in 1952 amid the remains of the original 5th-century apse, which has been incorporated into the current building. Brilliantly preserved, the mosaic portrays Mary standing on a jewelled pedestal with baby Jesus in her arms, bordered by the archangels Gabriel and Michael. The church is a working place of worship, with regular services.

Eating

Tasties Cafe CAFE €€
(Timou Stavrou 38; mains €10-13; ☺10.30am-6pm Wed-Sun; 🐾) With its blue shuttered windows and a gorgeously restored blue-and-white old-world interior, including original ornate lintels and cornice detailing, this may just be the cutest cafe in all of Cyprus. There's always a couple of scrummy home-made cakes available, and the small menu features international favourites (think lasagne and English-style curries) along with the odd Cypriot speciality such as *kleftiko* (oven-baked lamb).

🛍 Shopping

In 1481 Leonardo da Vinci is said to have visited Lefkara and to have obtained a fine piece of lace for the altar of Milan's cathedral. Lace and silver lovers the world over still visit for these crafts and are not disappointed. Shop owners sit outside in the streets, weaving lace and calling for you to come and watch their work or to look inside their stores with 'no obligation'. They can be overzealous but are genuinely pleasant about it. The lace is of exceptional quality, but it can be very pricey, so it's best to pick your favourite from the hundreds on offer and bargain about the cost. You will find the best quality and variety in the village itself. Keep in mind that the finest pieces are always found inside the stores and not displayed outside.

ⓘ Getting There & Away

By car, you can reach Lefkara from the Lefkosia–Lemesos motorway (A1) or by the scenic road from Choirokoitia via Vavla.

TO PATRIKON

It's meze, but with a twist. **To Patrikon** (☎2442 4831; Tersefanou; meze per person €18; ☺6pm-midnight Fri & Sat, noon-5pm Sun; 🐾) infuses a modern-Med approach to classic Cypriot meze (minimum two people), adding touches of creative flair. Grilled meats get lashed with Commandaria (sweet wine); the haloumi (hellim in Turkish) is home-made; and the salads are inventive, fresh and full of herbs. Service is stellar, and the bright, modern interior cosy and welcoming. It's on the main street in Tersefanou.

By bus, take the 402 from Larnaka to Kofinou (€1.50, four services daily Monday to Friday, three on weekends) and then bus 405 from Kofinou to Lefkara (€1.50, five services daily Monday to Friday, three on weekends). Buses are run by Zinonas (p133), which has up-to-date timetables on its website.

AGIA NAPA
POP 3210

Endless blue-sky days and a coastline riddled with sandy pockets helped transform this village into the Mediterranean's summer clubbing capital in the 1990s. Hundreds of clubs and bars set up shop to cater for hedonist-seeking crowds flocking here between June and August and, a couple of decades on, for young Europeans from London to Moscow, Napa (as many visitors refer to it) is still where the party is at its hardest.

Let's get one thing straight; Agia Napa isn't everyone's cup of tea. Its brashly tacky themed clubs have as many detractors as devotees, and the usual problems that come with rife alcohol and drug consumption rear up every summer. In recent years the municipality has pushed towards increasing family-oriented tourism. Despite this, if you're not into the nightlife scene and just want to experience the region's beaches, you could be more comfortable in nearby beach resort Protaras (p143).

◉ Sights

Agia Napa Monastery MONASTERY
(Plateia Seferi; ☺9am-6pm) **FREE** Surreally surrounded by modern temples to partying, this beautiful monastery is a serene reminder of the great history of Agia Napa. Built in 1500 by the Venetians, it protects a cave in which an icon of the Virgin Mary was hidden during the iconoclasm of the 7th and 8th centuries. Surviving Ottoman rule undamaged, it served as both a convent and a monastery during different periods until it was abandoned in 1758.

The structure is remarkably well preserved. Stout protective walls open up onto a peaceful arcaded courtyard, with a marble fountain dating from 1530, covered by a domed stone roof. Also of interest is the enormous 600-year-old sycamore tree just outside the southern gate, which has modern steel props designed to help hold its giant branches.

The modest church has steps down into the cave alcove where the Virgin Mary icon was hidden.

Thalassa Municipal Museum of the Sea

MUSEUM

(Leoforos Kryou Nerou 14; adult/child €4/1.50; ☺9am-5pm Tue-Sat, to 3pm Mon year-round, 3-7pm Sun Jun-Sep) Dedicated to all things relating to the sea, this contemporary museum shows the enormous impact the ocean has had on Cypriot life and culture.

The museum covers more than 700 years of maritime history, and is home to an exact replica of the famed 3rd-century BC Kyrenia shipwreck, the remains of which are on display in Kyrenia Castle (p188). Dubbed *Kyrenia II,* the replica of the Ancient Greek merchant ship was reconstructed using traditional methods and materials.

Makronissos Tombs

ARCHAEOLOGICAL SITE

(Macronissos Beach; ☺dawn-dusk) Overlooking the sea, this ancient necropolis of 19 tombs cut into the rock is attributed to the Hellenistic and Roman periods. The chambers are practically identical, with wide steps leading down into the simple tombs, which have stone benches originally designed to hold sarcophagi. The site was heavily looted during the 1870s.

Further excavations have found remnants of a quarry and evidence of ancient Greek interments. The site is well signposted off the main road west of Agia Napa.

🏖 Beaches

★Nissi Beach

BEACH

(off Leoforos Nisiou) Agia Napa's main attraction, Nissi Beach boasts shallow crystal-clear water, soft white sand and a picturesque rock island about 60m from its shore. It's widely regarded as one of the prettiest stretches of sand on the island, but do be aware that its fame means in summer it gets jam-packed. Everything you need for a day of sand and sea (bars, water sports and shower amenities) is at your fingertips here.

It's 3km west of town; Osea buses 102 and 201 pass right by. You can also easily get here on public transport from Larnaka; Intercity buses to Agia Napa stop here.

★Kermia Beach

BEACH

(off Leoforos Protara-Kavo Greko) Ideal for those who prefer a quiet spot where they can find a sunbed, Kermia Beach is about 2km east of Agia Napa towards Cape Greco. This is a wonderfully secluded beach with golden sands and a rock break. A great choice for families.

Pantahou Beach

BEACH

Starting from Agia Napa's fishing harbour, this strip of sand swings east for 1km. It has loads of eating and snacking options, and bundles of activities on offer. Be aware that it gets extremely crowded in July and August.

🏄 Activities

A variety of big boats, glass-bottom boats and speedboats operate out of Agia Napa's harbour. Most do return trips taking in the coastline around Cape Greco.

The waters from Nissi Bay to Cape Greco provide exceptional diving conditions, with calm seas that are both warm and clear, and have a multitude of inlets and natural caves to explore.

★Water World

WATER PARK

(www.waterworldwaterpark.com; Agias Theklis 18; adult/child €35/20; ☺10am-6pm Apr-Oct) Based around a Greek-mythology theme, this water park 5km west of central Agia Napa is easily the best of its kind in Cyprus. It's home to more than 18 rides, with whirlpools, slides bringing varying levels of thrills and spills, a wave pool and a rafting river. There are rides specifically for younger children too. Fun for kids of all ages.

Sunfish Divers

DIVING

(🖂2372 1300; www.sunfishdivers.com; Leoforos Archiepiskopou Makariou III 26; discover scuba try-dives €60, 2-dive packages €90) This trusted operator caters for both novices and professionals, and covers more than 10 diving spots, including the sea caves around Cape Greco and the famous *Zenobia* wreck. Certification programs are offered, ranging from Discover Scuba diving all the way through to master certification. Snorkelling to a depth of 2m is available and is suitable for kids as young as eight.

Black Pearl Pirate Boat

BOATING

(🖂9940 8132; www.blackpearlayianapa.com; Agia Napa Harbour; adult/child €35/15; ☺departs 11am-3pm May-Sep) This pirate-themed cruise on a large buccaneer ship is great fun for kids, with live pirates and treasure hunts. It stops at two picturesque swimming spots in the bays around Cape Greco. A full roast lunch, including Greek salad, is served afterwards on deck. There is also a bar on board (with rum, of course!), but drinks cost extra.

Fantasy Boat Party
BOATING

(📞 9940 8132; www.fantasyboatparty.com; Agia Napa Harbour; adult excl drinks €55; ⊙ departs 5.30-9pm daily Jun-Aug, Tue, Fri & Sat Sep, Sat Apr, May & Oct) DJs pump music while the crowd dances and drinks away their time on the sea. It's basically a floating nightclub, but there are some swimming stops where diving games and screaming are encouraged. These cruises are not for the faint-hearted, and hard-core revellers are always expected. Drinks cost extra.

Parko Paliatso
AMUSEMENT PARK

(www.parkopaliatsocy.com; Leoforos Nisiou; entry package incl some rides €15-25; ⊙ 6pm-midnight) The highlight of Parko Paliatso (also known as Luna Park) for most thrills-and-spills fans is the Slingshot – the highest ejection-seat ride in Europe. It shoots you 90m skyward in a caged ball in 1.5 seconds. It's all caught on camera too, so you'll have a keepsake of your contorted, petrified face.

Napa Bungee
BUNGEE JUMPING

(www.facebook.com/NapaBungee; off Leoforos Nisiou; jump incl photo, DVD & 1 drink €70-80; ⊙ 10am-6pm May-Sep) Perfect for adrenalin junkies, Napa Bungee has an excellent safety record and a great set-up, with a jump more than 60m high. Offers solo jumps and tandems for those in need of some support. Wedding jumps and naked jumps have also been performed. This team has seen it all before.

CAMEL RIDES FOR KIDS AT MAZOTOS

If the kids have had enough of archaeological sites and church icons, the **Mazotos Camel Park** (📞 2499 1243; www.camel-park.com; Mazotos; adult/child €4/3, incl camel ride €10/7; ⊙ 9am-7pm May-Sep, to 5pm Oct-Apr) makes a great family day out. Camels were once a mainstay of transport in Cyprus but this is the last place on the island where they can still be seen. Camel rides are the big attraction, but there's also a swimming pool, a play area and a petting zoo.

Mazotos Camel Park is 20 minutes from Larnaka by car (€20 by taxi).

Tours

CTO Guided Walks
WALKING

(www.visitcyprus.com; Leoforos Kryou Nerou 12; ⊙ 10am Wed Nov-Mar) 🚶 **FREE** The CTO runs free Agia Napa and the Sea walking tours every Wednesday between November and March. Tours start at 10am at the CTO office.

✕ Eating

While most eating options in Agia Napa offer generic international fare, there are some decent places hidden among the weirdly themed restaurants and fast-food chains. Prices, though not exorbitant, tend to reflect the high tourism in the area.

Some of the better restaurants close for winter, only opening their doors again at the start of the tourism season in April or May.

★ En Yevo
CYPRIOT €€

(📞 9938 8555; Dionysiou Solomou; mains €8-14; ⊙ noon-11pm; 🛜 🍴) Typical Cypriot favourites get cooked up in the blue-and-white interior of this traditional taverna, where the ceiling is hung with creeping vines. Everything is fresh and tasty, and the staff is wonderfully friendly. One of the best places in town to head to if you want to get stuck into the meze or try out *sheftalia* (grilled sausages wrapped in caul fat) or *kleftiko*.

★ Limelight
CYPRIOT €€

(📞 2372 1650; D Liperti; mains €11-25; ⊙ 11am-11pm; 🛜) This well-established and family-run traditional restaurant excels at what it does best: chargrilled dishes. It also serves pasta and steak, lobster and seafood, but it's the yielding beef, lamb and *stifado* that really bring folk flocking to the tables. There's a proper children's menu here, too.

Quadro
ITALIAN €€

(Leoforos Kryou Nerou 7; mains €10.50-16; ⊙ 10am-midnight; 🛜 🍴) Agia Napa's best bet for Italian offers great pizza (we're a tad partial to the not-entirely-authentic Pizza al Greco, served with feta, olives, oregano and tomato) and a huge array of pasta. There are plenty of vegetarian dishes, such as *ravioli pomodori* (with sun-dried tomatoes and cream) and *pasta pesto e rucola* (with pesto, tomatoes and pine nuts), and even some gluten-free options.

Sage
INTERNATIONAL €€€

(📞 2381 6110; www.sagerest.com; Leoforos Kryou Nerou 10; mains €8.50-29; ⊙ 11am-11pm Mar-Nov; 🛜) The menu riffs on modern European din-

Agia Napa

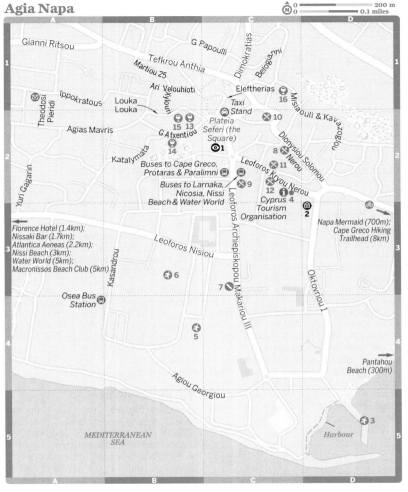

Agia Napa

◎ Sights
1 Agia Napa Monastery............................C2
2 Thalassa Municipal Museum of
   the Sea D3

⊕ Activities, Courses & Tours
3 Black Pearl Pirate Boat..........................D5
4 CTO Guided Walks.................................C2
   Fantasy Boat Party..........................(see 3)
5 Napa Bungee..B4
6 Parko Paliatso B3
7 Sunfish Divers C3

⊗ Eating
8 En Yevo C2
9 Fiji C2
10 Limelight...C2
11 Quadro C2
12 Sage C2

⊜ Drinking & Nightlife
13 Black & White...B2
14 Castle Club...B2
15 Club Ice...B2
16 River Reggae Club.................................C1

ing, with dishes such as baked halibut with tomato and lemon pesto, and herb-crusted racks of lamb with red-wine sauce, while the slate walls and concatenate doors imbue the interior with elegance. The food has a high price tag, but deservedly so, and the outdoor courtyard is a very relaxing spot on summer evenings.

Fiji ASIAN €€€
(Leoforos Archiepiskopou Makariou III 23; mains €13-25; ☺6pm-midnight May-Nov; 🛜🅿️) A Polynesian-themed restaurant complete with banana trees and oversized flowers that serves Asian-inspired food. You don't get more Agia Napa than this. The Thai-style menu is tasty, though, and it's a fun and friendly place for a bite.

🍷 Drinking & Nightlife

From May to September Agia Napa morphs into a party town. It all begins in Plateia Seferi (The Square), where there are shoulder-to-shoulder bars and clubs. The sight of thousands of tourists heaving together in this locale in the heat of a July night is mind-boggling.

Revellers drink and dance in the bars between 10pm and 2am. Then it's time to hit the clubs, of which there is a whole host to choose from. Most venues open after 1am and don't reach capacity until 3am. A cover charge of €10 to €15 is normal – the best deals are found from ticket sellers in the Square.

By mid-autumn it's all over, and many places close completely for winter, not opening again until mid-April.

Club Ice CLUB
(www.facebook.com/AyiaNapaClubIce; Louka Louka 14; ☺midnight-late) A long-time player on the Agia Napa clubbing scene, Club Ice is known for its regular theme nights – foam parties, UV-paint parties, popcorn parties... you name it, they probably do it – and for hosting some of the top current names on the British urban-music scene. The attached Igloo Bar opens earlier in the evening.

Macronissos Beach Club BAR
(Macronissos Beach; ☺noon-late; 🛜) Out of town on the beach opposite Water World water park, Macronissos Beach Club is one of Agia Napa's premier drinking spots. It morphs from cruisy lounge-style bar-restaurant to club as the night wears on.

It's known for being one of the venues for the weekly Kandi Beach Party (p140) from May through to September, which hosts big-name UK urban-music acts.

Castle Club CLUB
(www.thecastleclub.com; Grigoriou Afxentiou; ☺10pm-5am Apr-Oct) The Castle is hard to miss. It holds more than 2000 people in three separate music rooms (each hosting separate sounds, from commercial dance to R & B), and plays host to some of the world's best DJs during summer. If you're here to party, it continues to be Agia Napa's top venue.

River Reggae Club CLUB
(Misiaouli & Kavazoglou; ☺2am-sunrise Apr-Oct; 🛜) An outdoor club with palm trees, a wooden dance floor, a winding pool, and reggae and R & B music, this is one of the town's most popular late-night venues. It's usually best after 4am, when things can get crazy as revellers skinny-dip and dance. So, if you're up for it...

Black & White CLUB
(www.facebook.com/ClubBlackNWhite; Louka Louka 6; ☺1am-5am) A staple of the urban-music scene since the 1990s, this dark little venue pumps out grime, R&B, garage and hip-hop across its multiple bars, chill-out room and intimate dance floor. It gets full quickly and draws a big crowd.

☆ Entertainment

Kandi Beach Party LIVE MUSIC
(www.kandibeachparty.com; entry £59; ☺from 5.30pm Fri May-Sep) Billed as 'Europe's biggest beach party', this weekly bash is one of Agia Napa's hugest draws for young hedonists and clubbers. Ticket-holders (prebooking necessary) party hard first at Macronissos Beach, where international acts such as Tinie Tempah, Chris Brown and Ms Dynamite have all topped the billing, and then continue into town for the after-party at Club Ice.

ℹ️ Information

EMERGENCY

Police station (📞 2472 1553; Leoforos Rethymnou) North of central Agia Napa, at the big roundabout.

INTERNET ACCESS

Wi-fi is available in most hotels, cafes and restaurants.

3W Internet Café (☑2372 3032; Leoforos Nisiou 27; per hour €3; ☺10am-midnight) Internet, printing, photo downloads.

Backstage Internet Centre (☑2381 6097; Ari Velouchioti 7; per hour €3; ☺10am-midnight) Internet access, with games and pool table.

MEDICAL SERVICES

After-Hours Pharmacy Assistance (☑192)

Ammochostos General Hospital (☑2320 0000; Christou Kkeli 25; ☺24hr) The main public hospital for the entire region is in Deryneia, 15 minutes' drive from Agia Napa.

Napa Olympic Private Hospital (☑2372 3222; Chavares 24; ☺24hr) Located near Nissi Beach.

Saveco Health Centre (☑2381 6512; https:// savecohealthcentre.com; Giourin Gkagkarin 29; ☺24hr) Offers a doctor call-out service to hotels.

MONEY

There are ATMs along the main streets.

Hellenic Bank (☑2372 1588; Leoforos Archiepiskopou Makariou III 18; ☺8am-2pm) Just south of Agia Napa main square.

POST

Post office (☑2472 2141; Odyssea Elyti; ☺8am-3pm Mon-Fri)

TOURIST INFORMATION

Cyprus Tourism Organisation (CTO; ☑2372 1796; Leoforos Kryou Nerou 12; ☺8.20am-2.30pm Mon, Wed & Fri, to 3.30pm Tue & Thu) Helpful, friendly staff and good maps of town.

ⓘ Getting There & Away

AIR

Larnaka International Airport (p132), 48km away, is the closest airport to Agia Napa.

BUS

Intercity Buses (☑8000 7789; www.inter-city-buses.com) pick up and drop off passengers at the **bus stop** (Leoforos Archiepiskopou Makariou III) opposite Agia Napa Monastery, right in the centre of town. Services include the following:

Larnaka Twelve services (€4, one hour) between 6.10am and 8.40pm Monday to Friday, nine between 7.55am and 8.10pm weekends, via Nissi Beach. Will stop at Water World on request.

Nicosia Nine services (€5, two hours) between 6am and 6.40pm Monday to Friday, eight between 6.40am and 8.40pm weekends.

Pafos One daily at 7.40am (€9, three hours).

SERVICE TAXI

Travel & Express (☑2382 6066; www.travel express.com.cy; Griva Digeni 105, Paralimni; ☺6am-6pm Mon-Fri, 7am-5pm Sat & Sun) runs prebooked service-taxi (shared-taxi) routes between any pick-up point in Agia Napa and the following:

Larnaka €8.50, daily, 45 minutes.

Lemesos €18.50 Monday to Saturday, €22 Sunday, 1½ hours.

Nicosia €17 Monday to Saturday, €20 Sunday, 1¼ hours.

Pafos (change Lemesos) €28 Monday to Saturday, €33 Sunday, two hours.

TAXI

Standard taxis can be found at the edge of Plateia Seferi (The Square). Journey fares and times from Agia Napa:

Larnaka €35 to €43, 30 minutes.

Lemesos €60 to €70, one hour.

Nicosia €60 to €70, one hour.

Pafos €150, 1¾ hours.

Troödos €90 to €100, one hour.'

ⓘ Getting Around

Central Agia Napa is compact enough to walk around. The urban bus network is pretty good, or join the masses and hire a scooter, motorbike or buggy.

TO/FROM THE AIRPORT

Travel & Express (p141) offers a shared taxi service from the airport to Agia Napa at 9am, 1pm, 3pm and 5pm (€11.50). This must be prebooked.

A cheaper option from the airport is to take a public bus into central Larnaka and then catch an **Intercity** (p141) bus to Agia Napa.

A metered taxi from the airport costs around €60. Prebooking is usually cheaper; around €40.

BUS

Agia Napa's local and regional bus network is run by **Osea** (☑2381 9090; www.osea.com.cy; tickets one way €1.50, daily €5), which has a number of routes useful for visitors. All the following buses pick up and drop off at the central **bus stop** (Leoforos Archiepiskopou Makariou III) opposite Agia Napa Monastery.

Bus 101 Runs from Water World, through Agia Napa, to Cape Greco, Protaras, Pernera and Paralimni (approximately every 20 minutes from 7am to 9pm, less frequent from 9pm to 4am).

Bus 102 Runs bus 101's route in reverse starting from Paralimni (approximately every 20 minutes from 7am to 9pm, less frequent from 9pm to 4am).

Bus 201 The Agia Napa Circle Line route, usually operational only in summer, runs from Osea's bus station to Nissi Beach, then loops through the centre of town before returning to the bus station (hourly from 8.15am to 4.15pm).

Bus 501 From Agia Thekla beach via Water World to Agia Napa, then direct to Paralimni and Deryneia (eight services daily, approximately hourly from 7.45am to 11.45am, then less frequent).

Bus 502 Runs bus 501's route in reverse starting from Deryneia (eight services daily, approximately every 45 minutes from 6.15am to 10.30am, then less frequent).

CAR & MOTORCYCLE

Easyriders (☑ 2372 2438; www.easyriders. com.cy; Gianni Ritsou 1; low/high season motorbikes & mopeds from €20/35, ATVs & buggies from €30/50; ☺ 9am-9pm) Rents mopeds, all-terrain vehicles (ATVs), buggies (UTVs), and Kawasaki or Suzuki 800cc heavies. Has a second outlet at Dimokratias 17.

V&L Tsokkos (☑ 2372 5710; www.facebook. com/VLTsokkos; Leoforos Nisiou 58; ☺ 9am-7pm) Rents cars, quad bikes, buggies and scooters at competitive prices.

AMMOCHOSTOS REGION

The coastal Ammochostos (Famagusta) region east of Agia Napa delivers up sun, sand and sea by the bucketful. The area's smaller resort towns of Protaras and Pernera are completely devoted to the summer tourist crowds, and become chock-a-block with families and older visitors looking for a holiday that involves nothing more demanding than kicking back on the sand.

The region has more to offer than just beach, though. The peninsula of Cape Greco has easy walking and cycling trails across limestone cliffs to rock formations and sea caves, and the potato-growing countryside around the Kokkinohoria villages, just inland from Paralimni, allows a peek at a more rural side of life.

Palaces & Sea Caves

Five kilometres east of Agia Napa, located at the inlet between Limnara Beach and Cape Greco, are unique rock formations known as the Palaces. Carved into the cliff face by centuries of waves buffering the coast, they look like spy holes, framing the clear blue sea. The natural architecture plays host to

divers, who can approach the rocks here only by boat.

Further east are spectacular sea caves cut into the face of the rocky coastline. From look-out seats above you can hear the echoing created by the sea as it funnels back and forth. When the sea is calm you can access some of the caves on foot, but on rough and windy days the spray reaches your face some 10m above, leaving you with tight cheeks and the taste of salt in your mouth.

The best views are had from the sea, so consider one of the many charters that run from Agia Napa's harbour.

Cape Greco

This national park has sweeping views of the sea and coast, and is excellent for leisurely day hikes and cycling. Although much of the park is accessible by road, there are also 14km of nature trails rimmed by interesting local flora, such as sea squill, wild orchids and sand lilies, which have managed to prosper in high-salinity soil. At various points in the park you can scamper down staircases to sea caves, or onto rock platforms from where you can swim.

Within the park, trail heads for the various walks are signposted at points off the road. The two most popular are the circular Aphrodite Trail, which has great overall views of the area, and the linear Agia Anargyroi Trail, which leads past Cape Greco's landmark Kamara tou Koraka natural rock bridge formation, onto the small white-and-blue chapel of Agia Anargyroi where there are sea caves to explore, and then along the cliff to Konnos Beach.

Osea buses 101 and 102 between Agia Napa and Paralimni regularly pass by the park entrance throughout the day.

Konnos Beach

This little swath of sheltered sand (Leoforos Protaras-Kavo Greko), bordered by a high cliff behind, is one of the nicest beaches in the area. The excellent Konnos Bay Bar (Konnos Bay; sandwiches & snacks €5-6; ☺ 10am-late; ☻🍴🐾) is on the hill bordering the sand. You can lunch with great views of the water below, while shaded by pine trees. The menu offers good sandwiches, salads and snacks, and there's a well-stocked bar. It's possible to walk all the way along the cliff path here from Cape Greco. Osea bus 101 (from Agia Napa) and 102 (from Paralimni) can drop you at the Konnos Beach turn-off.

Protaras

POP 14,960 (INCL PARALIMNI & PERNERA)

For an easygoing beach break, family favourite Protaras ticks a lot of boxes. Fig Tree Bay is the centre of all the beach action, but the entire shore front has been beautifully manicured with a wide seaside pedestrian promenade that wriggles its way up the coast, past hotel lawns and patches of golden sand, all the way to Pernera. The town unashamedly caters to the tourist crowd, so you're more likely to find all-day full English breakfasts on menus here than Cypriot flavours, and many of the bars tout faux-British pub names. During summer the beaches pack out and the promenade bustles with strollers and joggers. In early November many hotels and restaurants shut up shop and Protaras presses snooze, rolls over and goes back to sleep until April.

◉ Sights

Agios Elias   CHURCH
(Profitilia; ⊙ 9am-6pm) Rebuilt in 1980, this church is situated on a rocky peak just off the Protaras–Pernera road. A long set of stairs leads to the top, where you can enjoy magnificent views of Protaras and the bay. Follow the signs to get here.

Magic Dancing Waters   WATER SHOW
(www.magicdancingwaters.com; Leoforos Protara-Kavo Greko; adult/child €23/15; ⊙ 9pm daily May-Sep, Mon & Thu Apr, Oct & Nov) If a bit of jazz-hands dazzle helps get your young kids to bed easier, this one-hour show where water seems to dance and spin, followed by a dramatic erupting volcano experience, should wear them out. It's all accompanied by music with laser lights, holograms and various other special effects. Keep your expectations in check, though; despite the price tag, this isn't Las Vegas.

Protaras Beach   BEACH
(Protaras Seaside Promenade) The patches of golden sand that stretch north from Fig Tree Bay up to the pier are collectively known as Protaras Beach, Vrisi Beach or Sunshine Beach (just to confuse things). Water-sports kiosks and cafes are dotted along the seaside promenade here, between the green

lawns of the resort hotels. If Fig Tree Bay is crammed with sunbathers, it's well worth a meander north to try to find a slightly less busy slice of sand.

★ **Fig Tree Bay**   BEACH
(Protaras Seaside Promenade, off Leoforos Protara) The most popular, and best, of Protaras' sandy strips, Fig Tree Bay lies at the southern end of the Protaras seaside promenade. It has a small sand island just off the coast, which is great for snorkelling, with lots of fish to be seen, and the promenade behind it is shoulder-to-shoulder bars, cafes and restaurants.

🏃 Activities

Moonshine Ranch   HORSE RIDING
(☑ 9960 5042; Cape Greco; 1hr rides €40; ⊙ 8am-8pm) This ranch has a glorious position with sweeping views of Cape Greco. It offers accompanied rides that take in Konnos Bay, the cape and the surrounding mountainous valley. All skill levels are happily catered for. The ranch is just off the coastal road between Agia Napa and Protaras.

XS Watersports   WATER SPORTS
(☑ 9963 7453; www.xswatersports.com; Protaras Beach; ⊙ 9am-6pm) Your one-stop water-sports stop in the Protaras area, with highly qualified staff and instructors. The full gamut of activities is on offer, from parasailing and waterskiing to pedalo and kayak rentals.

🍴 Eating

Kyklos Restaurant   GREEK €€
(Leoforos Protara; mains €10-15; ⊙ 5-11pm; 🛜) Offers authentic and flavourful Mediterranean dishes. The stand-out item is the lamb *souvla* (large chunks of meat cooked on long skewers over a charcoal barbecue) tenderised with garlic and lemon. It's located at the southern end of Protaras' main street.

Nicolas Tavern   CYPRIOT €€
(Leoforos Protara; mains €9-15; ⊙ 11.30am-11pm; 🛜) Well-priced, consistently good Cypriot favourites, with friendly service to boot. *Kleftiko* (oven-baked lamb) is the speciality, but Nicolas is also good for *afelia* (pork cooked in red wine) and *tava* (lamb and beef casserole cooked with tomatoes, onions, potatoes and cumin). There's a fine selection of local wines here, too.

WORTH A TRIP

KOKKINHORIA

The Kokkinohoria (The Red Villages) are so named because of the deep-red, mineral-rich earth found in the area. The area comprises the inland rural villages of **Xylofagou**, **Avgorou**, **Frenaros**, **Liopetri** and **Sotira**. Most of these villages rely heavily on agriculture and are famous for their potato and *kolokasi* (a root vegetable similar to taro) produce. Wind-powered water pumps dot the landscape, and prosperous crops are cultivated three to four times annually. When tootling about with your own wheels in this area, take a good map, as signposting is limited.

With all this agriculture it's not surprising that you can find some excellent country taverns serving up simple dishes and fresh local produce. For a meze feast, which conjures up rural Cyprus on a plate, head to **Mousikos Tavern** (2382 8833; Kyriakou Matsi 6, Sotira; meze per person €18; ☉ 6.30-11.30pm; ☎).

⊙ Getting There & Away

Protaras is well connected by the Osea Agia Napa–Paralimni bus route. Osea bus 101 to Paralimni (€1.50, 20 minutes) and bus 102 to Agia Napa (€1.50, 15 to 20 minutes) trundle through central Protaras every 20 minutes during the day.

Paralimni

Just inland from the coastal tourism bustle, Paralimni has a more local, lived-in feel than the seaside resorts and is the unofficial capital of the Ammochostos (Famagusta) district. The town sprawls beside a seasonal lake – from which it derives its name – while its core is centred on a large main square home to two fine churches. Anyone with an interest in frescos will appreciate a quick stop off here to view the churches on a drive through the region.

⊙ Sights

Agios Georgios CHURCH
(St George's Church; Agiou Georgiou; ☉ 9am-1pm & 3-6pm Mon-Fri, 9am-1pm Sat) Paralimni's town square is dominated by two churches both, dedicated to St George. The older church (tucked behind the modern church) was built in the 19th century and is home to a large, beautiful fresco of St George. The larger, modern Agios Georgios was constructed in the 1960s and has an interior covered in colourful frescoes, including Christ Pantocrator on the dome.

Traditional House MUSEUM
(Ayia Marina 5; ☉ 9am-2pm & 4-6pm Mon-Fri) **FREE** Although small, this local folk museum is well worth a stop if you're passing through Paralimni – if only for the exceptional enthusiasm of host Andreas, who guides visitors through the rooms, explaining the uses and history of the exhibits. The household implements, farming tools and furniture on display come from the local Paralimni area and combine to create a snapshot of traditional life.

✖ Eating & Drinking

Express Coffee CAFE €
(Leoforos Protara; sandwiches & cakes €3.50-5.50; ☉ 10am-6pm; ☎) This small family-run place on the edge of the main square rustles up a mighty fine piece of cake and some good sandwiches, accompanied with chatty, friendly service.

Senso Cafe CAFE
(Agiou Georgiou 11; ☉ 10am-11pm; ☎) There's a reason this cafe-bar is always full of young locals: this may just be the best coffee in the area. With a prime view of the main square and plenty of people-watching appeal, Senso is a relaxed place for a coffee, a beer or a few wines. It also has a menu of contemporary European-style dishes.

⊙ Getting There & Away

All buses leave from Paralimni's main square.
Intercity (www.intercity-buses.com; Agiou Georgiou) Buses run to Nicosia (€5, two hours, nine daily weekdays, eight daily weekends), Larnaka (€4, 1¼ hours, 12 daily weekdays, nine daily weekends) and Pafos (€9, three hours, daily at 7.30am).

Osea (8000 5200; www.osea.com.cy; Agiou Georgiou, Paralimni) Bus 102 runs to Agia Napa via Protaras and Pernera (€1.50, 30 minutes, every 20 minutes). Bus 501 runs to Deryneia (€1.50, 15 minutes, hourly).

Travel & Express (p141) Runs shared taxis to Larnaka, Larnaka International Airport, Nicosia (Lefkosia), Lemesos and Pafos.

Deryneia

The small town of Deryneia spreads across the coastal plain just a few hops north of Paralimni. It has a clutch of Byzantine churches dating from the 12th century and a folk art museum (Demetris Lipertis 2; €2.50; ◷9am-1pm & 4-6pm Mon-Sat) worth visiting, but primarily it's known for its location at the eastern rise of the Green Line that separates the Republic of Cyprus from the North. Most people come to visit the Famagusta Cultural Centre (Ammochostos; ◷7.30am-6pm Mon-Fri, 9.30am-4.30pm Sat) FREE, which offers views across the UN Buffer Zone to the eerie, empty and derelict ghost town of Varosia (p215), which before 1974 was Famagusta's modern district and the island's high-rolling seaside resort. For anyone interested in Cyprus' modern history, it's well worth stopping in.

Dekelia Sovereign Base

During independence negotiations between the nascent Republic of Cyprus and the British administration in 1960, the rights to two major British Sovereign Base Areas (SBAs) were brokered. Dekelia SBA is the one of these.

The area comprises a large part of eastern Cyprus, running from Larnaka Bay to the border with the North. You can pass through the base, and even stop and enjoy fish and chips in the civilian area. It has a small beach populated with a few British-styled shops and a playground for kids.

The military site itself is off limits. While Dekelia SBA remains a critical centre for intelligence gathering and monitoring of the Middle East, the British government has stated that it is prepared to cede back some of the area if Cyprus becomes reunified.

Pernera

Pernera's rocky shoreline is dotted with pocket-sized bays of golden sand where Europeans, escaping the grey clouds to the north, soak up the sun during the summer months. Although the town is officially separate from neighbouring Protaras, in reality the two resorts have merged with no clear definition of where one ends and the other begins. Despite this, Pernera has a quieter ambience than its sibling a couple of strides to the south. This is mainly due to its abundance of holiday villas, which have attracted a stable of older visitors who live all or at least part of the year here.

◉ Sights & Activities

Louma Beach BEACH
(Vrysoudion) A small, curving strip of beach that drops away gently and is protected by an artificial bay. The sand is fine and the water clear. Sunbathing comes with a rather picturesque view of the blue-and-white, domed Agios Nikolaos Church, which sits at the northern end of the beach.

Pernera BEACH
(off Leoforos Peneras) Tiny Pernera beach is a curvy sliver of good, soft sand with shallow waters and a beach restaurant. It's highly popular with families.

Agia Triada BEACH
(Agias Triadas) This cute little beach with low water levels and coarse sand is an excellent boat-launching site.

Skoutari BEACH
(off Leoforos Protaras-Kavo Greko) An isolated cove encircled by a cliff, with hard-packed sand and rocks. Ideal for snorkelling.

THE LAST MIXED CYPRIOT VILLAGE

Located in the UN Buffer Zone, Pyla (Pıle) is the only village in the South where Greek Cypriots and Turkish Cypriots still live side by side. There's a token UN peacekeeping contingent in the village, but it's the inhabitants themselves who have made it work. In the village square, a red-and-white Turkish Cypriot coffee shop stands opposite a blue-and-white Greek Cypriot *kafeneio* (cafe) in peaceful harmony.

Almost the only differences that arise relate to local taxes and utility costs. These are paid by the Greek Cypriots only; as the Turks are citizens of the North, they pay nothing. Politics, though, come second here. The neighbourhood contains a mix of Cypriots simply going about their daily lives.

There are nearby vehicle crossings to Northern Cyprus at the town of Pergamos.

LARNAKA & THE EAST DERYNEIA

Under Sea Adventures WATER SPORTS
(☑9956 3506; www.underseawalkers.com; Agia Triada beach, Agias Triadas; helmet walking adult/child €47/37, BOB €57) Get a taster of what scuba diving is like by shallow-water helmet walking (for ages six and up) or riding on a 'Breathing Observation Bubble' (BOB; 13 years and up). Both are a fun and safe way to experience underwater life.

✖ Eating

Blue Spice INTERNATIONAL €€
(☑2383 2088; Leoforos Pernera; mains €6.50-19; ☺9am-midnight; 🔊🍴) A vast menu that covers all the bases, from jacket potatoes to grilled seafood platters and kebabs, along with one of the best vegetarian dish selections we've seen in all our Cypriot travels. There's also a pool; it's no wonder Blue Spice continues to be consistently popular among Pernera diners.

It also has holiday apartments next door (from €60).

★**La Cultura del Gusto** MEDITERRANEAN €€€
(Ifaistou Skarou Markou 9; mains €14-28; ☺6-11pm; 🔊) This fashionable and highly popular restaurant is known for its steaks and a menu that's more innovative than others in the area. Dishes such as monkfish served with a spicy mango sauce and organic Black Angus rib-eye steak keep diners coming back during their stay. There's also a good kids' menu.

❶ Getting There & Away

Osea bus 101 trundles through central Pernera en route to Paralimni (€1.50, 15 minutes) roughly every 20 minutes throughout the day. Bus 102 heads in the opposite direction, towards Agia Napa (€1.50, 25 minutes) and operates on the same time schedule.

Nicosia (Lefkosia)

Best Places to Eat

➡ Shiantris (p159)

➡ Piatsa Gourounaki (p159)

➡ Syrian Arab Friendship Club (p160)

➡ Zanettos Taverna (p160)

➡ D.O.T (p159)

Best Museums & Galleries

➡ Leventis Municipal Museum (p148)

➡ AG Leventis Gallery (p155)

➡ CVAR (p151)

➡ Nicosia Municipal Arts Centre (p151)

➡ Cyprus Museum (p155)

Why Go?

The capital of the Republic of Cyprus is also its cultural heartbeat. Overlooked by most visitors, reduced to a day-tour jaunt from beach resorts, Nicosia (or Lefkosia, as it's officially known) is a curious and fascinating mix of vibrant street life, confronting division and rich history.

Nearly everything of interest lies within the snowflake-shaped Venetian walls. Inside the Old City, the lively, contemporary cafe and bar scene punches well above its weight for a city so small, while a bundle of museums and a series of looping lanes lined with colonial-era buildings, churches and mosques reveal an evocative history. Meanwhile, if you brush up against the sandbag and oil-barrel barriers of the Green Line (the UN Buffer Zone) you'll get a sense of the surreal and sad present-day state of limbo for the world's last divided capital.

When to Go

➡ The best time of year to visit is during spring and autumn, when the weather is pleasantly warm, interrupted by only an occasional outbreak of rain.

➡ Easter can be an extra special time here, with traditional parades and a generally festive atmosphere.

➡ July and August are hot, hot, hot, with temperatures hovering around 36°C. This is low season in the capital and hotels drop their prices.

➡ Many restaurants and hotels close their shutters in August to allow employees to leave the hot, dusty capital for the relative cool of the coastal resorts.

➡ December and January can be colder than you think – particularly in the evenings. Pack an umbrella and bring warm clothing.

NICOSIA (LEFKOSIA)

POP 55,010

History

Nicosia was first inhabited in the early Bronze Age and grew to become the city-kingdom of Ledra. Unlike the island's other city-kingdoms, however, which exploited their coastal positions to grow rich from trade, Ledra remained insignificant politically. It wasn't until the Arab raids of the 6th century AD that this small town, now known as Lefkousia, began to grow in stature. With the defences of the coastal cities so weak and prone to attack, Lefkousia's inland position upon the Mesaoria plain provided at least some protection against marauding invaders. By around the 9th century AD, it had become the island's capital.

Nicosia flourished during the Byzantine period. The Byzantines were followed by the Venetians, who took command of the city in 1489 but failed dismally in repelling the Ottomans, who took control in 1570. The city stagnated until the British arrived in 1878, which also marked the time that development started to spread beyond the city walls.

In the 1950s violence against the British instigated by the Ethniki Organosi tou Kypriakou Agona (EOKA; National Organisation for the Cypriot Struggle) saw considerable carnage on the streets of the capital.

Further violence in the form of intercommunal disturbances between Greek Cypriots and Turkish Cypriots in 1963 brought a de facto partition of the city. The so-called 'Green Line' came into being at this time when the British army defined the Greek and Turkish areas by using a simple green pen on a military map. The name has stuck to this day.

The Turkish invasion of 1974 cemented the division of the city, which has remained bisected ever since, chaperoned by the watchful, but increasingly weary, eyes of UN peacekeeping forces. In 2003 crossing the Green Line was made possible for ordinary citizens while the opening of the Ledra St pedestrian-only crossing in April 2008 facilitated easier access in both directions. Meanwhile, the Nicosia Master Plan continues to work with both sides of the Green Line in the generally agreed assumption that one day the city will be unified once again.

◉ Sights

Nicosia's most interesting district is the Old City, lying within the 16th-century Venetian walls. **Ledra Street** is the Old City's hub, where locals can be found cafe-hopping, shopping or simply strolling with ice creams in hand, from morning to night. East and west of Ledra, the alleyways spool out, with museums and other sights scattered within.

◉ Inside the Old City

★**Leventis Municipal Museum** MUSEUM
(www.leventismuseum.org.cy; Ippokratous 17; ⊙10am-4.30pm Tue-Sat) FREE The best place in town to get to grips with Nicosia's rich and convoluted history. The permanent collection inside this handsome neoclassical mansion includes a wealth of ceramic pieces from the Bronze Age to the medieval era; a fine collection of maps dating back to the 16th century; photos, posters and artefacts from the early 20th century, through Cyprus' independence and then division; and so much more. Everything is accompanied by detailed and clear information boards that help shed light on the exhibits.

Shacolas Tower Observatory OBSERVATORY
(11th fl, Shacolas Tower, cnr Ledra St & Arsinois; €2.50; ⊙10am-6pm Mon-Sat, 11am-6pm Sun) Shacolas Tower Observatory provides a superb vantage point across the city and the mountain range beyond. Boards below each window point out and provide explanations (in English, French and German) of various buildings and neighbourhoods, and trace the Green Line along its length as it bisects the city.

Laïki Yitonia AREA
Meaning 'Popular Neighbourhood', Laïki Yitonia was restored after serving for many years as an area for painted ladies and dodgy merchants. This tiny southern part of the Old City is Nicosia's only tourist area. That means it's full of unremarkable restaurants with tacky water features where waiters try to lure you in with cheesy greetings to eat food that is often overpriced. However, it's still pretty and pleasant enough for a short stroll.

Church of Archangelos Michail CHURCH
(Solonos 8; ⊙6.30am-noon & 4-6pm) This domed church was built in 1695 and is thought to have replaced an earlier Gothic church on the same site. The exterior is

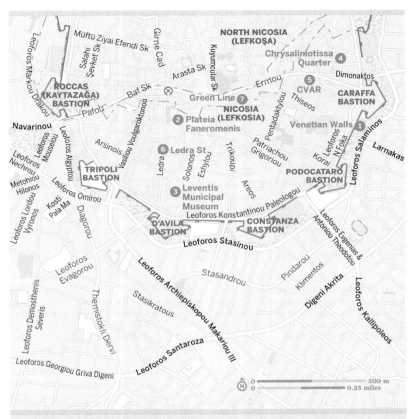

Nicosia (Lefkosia) Highlights

1 Venetian Walls (p153) Viewing the emblematic and superbly preserved walls snaking around the Old City.

2 Plateia Faneromenis (p163) Idling away an afternoon the local way, with a freddo cappuccino at a pavement cafe.

3 Leventis Municipal Museum (p148) Discovering the long and complicated history of Nicosia within this Old City mansion.

4 Chrysaliniotissa Quarter (p153) Wandering this slowly revitalising neighbourhood of cottage terraces and traditional architecture.

5 CVAR (p151) Untangling Cyprus' complex modern era among the fascinating exhibits in this museum.

6 Ledra Street (p148) Joining everyone else, ice cream in hand, to promenade down the Old City's main drag.

7 Green Line (p160) Exploring the issues of Europe's last divided capital by walking the UN Buffer Zone's sandbagged barriers.

built in Franco-Byzantine style; it's a synthesis of Byzantine, traditionally used by the Greek Orthodox Church, and Gothic devices, resulting from the influence of Lusignan and Venetian rule. The interior is home to an elaborate glinting gold iconostasis that holds some lovely icons, the oldest of which date back to the 15th century.

Church of Panagia Faneromeni CHURCH
(Plateia Faneromenis) Built in 1872 on the site of an ancient Orthodox nunnery, this is the largest church within the city walls and is a mixture of neoclassical, Byzantine and Latin

NICOSIA (LEFKOSIA) IN...

One Day

Nicosia's old city was made for walking, so pull on your comfy shoes and hit the cobblestones. Head to the **Leventis Municipal Museum** (p148) first for the low-down on the city's history, then to the **Makarios Cultural Foundation** (p150) to view the wealth of Byzantine icons before soaking up the colourful frescos of **Agios Ioannis Church** (p151). Afterwards, head up to **Chrysaliniotissa Quarter** (p153) to stroll lanes rimmed by terraced cottages and visit the **Panagia Chrysaliniotissa** (p153). Stop for a late lunch at **Shiantris** (p159), then follow the **Venetian walls** (p153) out of the city to get your head around the island's mind-boggling history at the **Cyprus Museum** (p155) and to see the art collection at the **AG Leventis Gallery** (p155).

Two Days

Begin day two at the **House of Hatzigeorgakis Kornesios** (p150) to discover the finery of Ottoman architecture. Then head far further back in time with the stunning ceramic collection at the the **Bank of Cyprus Cultural Foundation** (p150). While in the Faneromenis (p163) area, do like the locals do and grab a seat at a pavement cafe for coffee and people-watching. Fully revitalised, spend the afternoon exploring the alleyways that rub up against the **Green Line** (p160) then finish up at **CVAR** (p151), which does an amazing job of explaining the story of modern Cyprus.

styles. The **Marble Mausoleum** on the eastern side of the church was built in memory of four clerics executed by the Ottoman governor in 1821 during the newly declared Greek War of Independence.

Bank of Cyprus
Cultural Foundation   MUSEUM

(www.boccf.org; Faneromenis 86-90; ⊙10am-7pm) **FREE** The highlight here is the beautifully curated **Museum of George and Nefeli Giabra Pierides Collection** on the mezzanine floor, which contains more than 600 (mostly ceramic) items dating from the Bronze Age through to the 16th century. In particular, exhibits include some incredibly rare Mycenaean pottery examples. Don't overlook the small **Museum of the History of Cypriot Coinage** on the ground floor which, thanks to excellent historical information panels, is much more interesting than it sounds.

Omeriye Mosque   MOSQUE

(cnr Trikoupi & Plateia Tyllirias; ⊙closed during prayer times) Originally the Augustinian Church of St Mary, the Omeriye Mosque dates from the 14th century, with its tall minarets added after its conversion in 1571. This is a working mosque that serves Nicosia's diverse Arab and Asian Muslim population. Non-Muslims may visit as long as you observe the general etiquette required: dress conservatively, leave shoes at the door and avoid official prayer times.

House of
Hatzigeorgakis Kornesios   HISTORIC BUILDING

(Patriarchou Grigoriou 20; €2; ⊙8am-3.30pm Tue-Fri, 9.30am-4.30pm Sat) From 1779 to 1809 the House of Hatzigeorgakis Kornesios belonged to Kornesios, the Great Dragoman of Cyprus, who accumulated his vast wealth through various estates and tax exemptions, and became the most powerful man in Cyprus. The house itself is more interesting and beautiful than the exhibits within. Upstairs, a couple of rooms have been set up in typical Ottoman style while other rooms hold a few displays of antiques and Ottoman memorabilia.

Makarios Cultural Foundation
Byzantine Museum & Art Gallery   MUSEUM

(Plateia Archiepiskopou Kyprianou; €4, audio guides €2; ⊙museum 9am-4.30pm Mon-Fri, to 1pm Sat, gallery 9am-1pm & 2-4pm Mon-Fri) This foundation next door to the Archbishop's Palace is home to the magnificent Byzantine Museum, which holds a collection of more than 300 icons and frescos dating from the 9th to 19th centuries. Don't miss the many beautiful artworks looted after the 1974 Turkish invasion from churches now situated in Northern Cyprus, and only returned after lengthy court battles. In particular, look for the frescoed dome from **St Eufemianus** and the six fragments of the superb **Kanakaria mosaics** from the Panagia Kanakaria.

Among the more interesting other exhibits are the icons of Christ and the Virgin Mary (12th century) from the Church of the Virgin Mary of Arakas at Lagoudera, and the Resurrection (13th century) from the Church of St John Lambadistis Monastery at Kalopanayiotis.

The foundation's adjoining Art Gallery displays European paintings from the late Renaissance up to the 20th century. Most space is given over to Hellenic artworks from the 19th century onwards, with some contemporary Cypriot art represented.

Agios Ioannis Church
CHURCH

(Cathedral of St John the Evangelist; Plateia Archiepiskopou Kyprianou; ⊙9am-3pm Mon-Fri, 9am-noon Sat) Located in the courtyard of the Makarios Cultural Foundation (p150), this 17th-century church has an interior covered in lively and intricate frescos dating from the 18th century.

Archbishop's Palace
PALACE

(Plateia Archiepiskopou Kyprianou) This rather grand building is the residence of the current archbishop and also houses the offices and administration of the archdiocese. It was built in the late 1950s, in neo-Byzantine style, to replace the old palace, which now houses the Folk Art Museum. There is no public access.

National Struggle Museum
MUSEUM

(Plateia Archiepiskopou Kyprianou; €2; ⊙8am-2pm Mon-Wed & Fri, 8am-2pm & 3.30-7.30pm Thu) This display is really for die-hard history buffs and perhaps bloodthirsty children. The National Struggle Museum exhibits documents, photos and other memorabilia from the often bloody 1955–59 National Liberation Struggle against the British. Exhibits include a harrowing copy of the gallows.

Pancyprian Gymnasium Museums
MUSEUM

(cnr Agiou Ioannou & Thiseos; ⊙9am-3.30pm Mon, Tue, Thu & Fri, to 5pm Wed, to 1pm Sat) FREE The extensive museum collection belonging to the Pancyprian Gymnasium (Plateia Archiepiskopou Kyprianou) lies just to the north of the school, housed in a line of restored houses. The gymnasium dates back to 1812 and is the oldest school still operating in Cyprus. Its collection includes items and artefacts from student life, artworks and an extensive natural-history collection, but the highlight is the archaeological and old map exhibits on the 2nd floor, including the

1885 land-survey map made by Lord Horatio Kitchener.

Folk Art Museum
MUSEUM

(Plateia Archiepiskopou Kyprianou; €2; ⊙10am-2pm Mon, 9.30am-4pm Tue-Fri, 9am-1pm Sat) This museum houses the largest collection of popular art and ethnography in the Republic. The building dates back to the 15th century and was used as the archbishop's palace until the current palace across the plaza was built in the 1960s. Today the rooms hold a diverse collection including exquisite examples of embroidery and lace, costumes, pottery, metalwork, basketry, folk painting, engraved gourds and woodwork, the latter of which include beautiful, intricately carved wooden dowry chests.

★ Nicosia Municipal Arts Centre
MUSEUM

(Pierides Foundation; www.nimac.org.cy; Palias Ilektrikis 19; ⊙10am-9pm Tue-Sat) FREE This contemporary-art museum is housed in a former power station, and is the city's equivalent to London's Tate Modern. The former industrial setting is suitably dramatic, with looming pitched ceilings and some original equipment (pulleys etc) that blend well with the cutting-edge installations. The permanent collection includes paintings, photography, video, sculptures and other works from the Dimitris Pierides Museum of Contemporary Art in Greece. Exhibitions vary monthly and often focus on edgy political and cultural themes.

To get here, duck into the small arcade to the right of the National Struggle Museum and head straight up the road for one block. The centre also has a sophisticated restaurant, gift shop and comprehensive art library for visitors.

★ CVAR
MUSEUM

(Centre of Visual Arts & Research; www.severis.org/cvar; Ermou 285; adult/student €5/free; ⊙10am-6pm Mon-Sat, closed Mon in winter) Opened in 2014, CVAR's collection of art and archival material showcases the story of modern Cyprus. Galleries full of paintings and other artworks display Cyprus as seen by its visitors, dating from the 1400s up to the mid-20th century, while exhibits of photographs, books, artefacts and primary documents from the island's colonial period give an engrossing look into the era of British rule. There's also a library containing a vast collection of books about Cyprus and the eastern Mediterranean.

NICOSIA (LEFKOSIA) SIGHTS

Nicosia (Lefkosia)

NICOSIA (LEFKOSIA) SIGHTS

200 m
0.1 miles

Loukia & Michael Zampelas Art Museum (830m)

Leoforos Salaminos

CARAFA BASTION

13

Leoforos Athinas

Leoforos Salaminos

Larnakas

Digeni Akrita

5 Venetian Walls

Venetian Walls

Leoforos N Foka

PODOCATARO BASTION

67 9
76
36
31
23

Dimonaktos
Ermou
Minoos

Othellou

Korai

Travel & Express

Leoforos Evgenias & Antoniou Theodotou

Theokritou

39
73

2 CVAR

Thiseos

Thiseos

25
20
14
6
24

Archiepiskopou Kyprianou

plateia Archiepiskopou Varnava

18
17
16

Patriarchou Grigoriou

35

Alkeou

Leoforos Stasinou

CONSTANZA BASTION

27

83

65

NORTH NICOSIA (LEFKOŞA)

Kuyumcular Sk

Ermou

Lidinis

43 21
53

Dionysou Apostolou Varnava

Pentadaktilou

51

Plateia Tylirias

22

Areos

Annis Komninis

Iras

Afroditis

Soutsou

Trikoupi

29
47
30

Trikoupi

Aristidou

Eshylou

Ippokratous Cyprus Tourism Organisation

Leoforos Konstantinou Paleologou

Bouboulinas

Liperti

69
79
40
61
75

Evripidou

Solonos

NICOSIA (LEFKOSIA)

15

Leoforos
Girne Cad
Arasta Sk

48
11
56
8

Faneromenis

55

81
52
33
32

Solonos

10
62

71
28
78
84

D'AVILA BASTION

64

Arnaldas
Trailas

63
57
74
80
49
59
70
77
37

Ledra St

Onasagorou

Arsinois

26

60
38
72
42

Leventis Municipal Museum

4
17

Pygnhalionos

Granikou

12

Megalou Alexandrou

Vasiliou Voulgaroktonou

Paleon Patron Germanou

45

Ethniko Apollonos

Taxi Stand

InterCity Plateia Buses

Plateia Eleftherias

Apostrati

Plateia Theodoton

Theofamous Theodoton

Leoforos Evagorou

Holy Cross Catholic Church

Salahi Sevket Sk

68

Pafou

Leoforos Konstantinou Paleologou

TRIPOLI BASTION

Ouzounian

Regenis
34

Solomou

Urban Bus Station

AG Leventis Gallery

1

Diagorou

Sofouli

82

Leoforos Vyronos
Lordou Vyronos

ROCCAS (KAYTAZAĞA) BASTION

Leoforos Markou Drakou

Leoforos Aigyptou

Navarinou

19

Cyprus Museum

3

Leoforos Mouseiou

Leoforos Nechrou

Leoforos Omirou

Metohiou Hilonos

Syrian Arab Friendship Club (700m); Eleon Swimming Pool (1.3km); Kykko Bowling Centre (3.4km)

Municipal Swimming Pool (450m); Averof (900m)

Home for Cooperation (160m); Ledra Palace Hotel Crossing (250m)

66

The ground-floor courtyard is home to the lively, modern restaurant Balthazar (☎ 2230 0992; Ermou 285; mains €10-14; ⏰ 9.30am-midnight Tue-Sat, to 6pm Mon Apr-Oct, closed Mon Nov-Mar; ❄ ⑧). It's a good place to put your feet up with a coffee after viewing the galleries.

★ **Chrysaliniotissa Quarter**　　AREA
Centred around the Panagia Chrysaliniotissa church, this residential neighbourhood on the edge of the Old City rubs right up against the Green Line, and so was left for years to decay. Today its narrow streets have been revitalised with some lovely restored facades of early 20th-century town houses and alleyways of cottage terrace rows, fringed by pot plants. Its lanes are a charming and peaceful place for a stroll.

Panagia Chrysaliniotissa　　CHURCH
(Chrysaliniotissa; ⏰ 8.30am-12.30pm & 2-4pm) The church of Panagia Chrysaliniotissa is dedicated to the Virgin Mary and its name means 'Our Lady of the Golden Flax' in Greek. It's considered to be the oldest Byzantine church in Nicosia and was built in 1450 by Queen Helena Paleologos. It is renowned for its rich collection of old and rare icons.

**Cyprus Classic
Motorcycle Museum**　　MUSEUM
(☎ 2268 0222; www.agrino.org/motormuseum; Granikou 44; ⏰ 9am-1pm & 3-6pm Mon-Fri, 9am-1pm Sat) FREE The owner of this private museum is more than happy to chat extensively about his 150-plus bike collection. It may just bring out your inner Hell's Angel (bring a bandanna, just in case).

Around the City Walls

★ **Venetian Walls**　　HISTORIC SITE
The Venetian walls form a border around the Old City and are so unusual that, once seen on a map, you'll never forget the odd snowflake-like shape.

Dating from 1567, the circular defence wall was erected by the Venetian rulers to ward off Ottoman invaders. Unfortunately it failed. In July 1570 the Ottomans landed in Larnaka and three months later stormed the fortifications, killing some 50,000 inhabitants. The walls have remained in place ever since.

Five of the bastions, Tripoli, D'Avila, Constanza, Podocataro and Caraffa, are in the southern sector of Nicosia. The Flatro (Zeytilni) Bastion on the eastern side of the Old City is occupied by Turkish, Greek

NICOSIA (LEFKOSIA) SIGHTS

Nicosia (Lefkosia)

Cypriot and UN military forces. The remaining bastions, **Loredano** (Cevizli), **Barbaro** (Musalla), **Quirini** (Cephane), **Mula** (Zahra) and **Roccas** (Kaytazağa), are in North Nicosia (Lefkoşa).

The Venetian walls and moat around Nicosia are in excellent condition. They are used to provide car-parking spaces and venues for outdoor concerts, as well as space for strolling and relaxing. In North

Nicosia, the walls are in poorer shape and have become overgrown and dilapidated in parts.

Vehicle access points around the walls allow regular traffic access to the Old City.

Famagusta Gate HISTORIC SITE
(Caraffa Bastion; ☉10am-1pm & 4-9pm Mon-Fri) Easternmost city gate Famagusta is the most photographed and best-preserved of the three original gates that led into the Old City of Nicosia. Its impressive wooden door and sloping facade open out into a tunnel that leads through the rampart wall. Beyond the tunnel to the right is a small open-air arena, where concerts are held during the summer months.

State Gallery of Cypriot Contemporary Art MUSEUM
(cnr Leoforos Stasinou & Kritis; ☉10am-4.45pm Mon-Fri, to 12.45pm Sat) FREE Housed in a historic colonial-style building, this museum comprises a vast collection of quality Cypriot art, ranging over the 19th and 20th centuries, including some fine sculpture and multimedia artworks.

★**AG Leventis Gallery** GALLERY
(www.leventisgallery.org; Leonidou; adult/student €5/3, audio guides €2; ☉10am-5pm Thu-Mon, to 10pm Wed; P) Located just outside the Old City, this art museum features three collections displaying European paintings and sculpture from the 16th to the 20th centuries. The Paris Collection features masters such as Chagall, Monet and Renoir, while the Greek Collection includes significant works by 19th- and 20th-century Greek artists. The highlight of the Cyprus Collection, located on the ground floor, is a magnificent and thought-provoking 17m-long painting entitled *The World of Cyprus* by renowned Cypriot artist Adamantios Diamantis.

The artwork on display is from the private collection of the late Anastosios G Leventis, a wealthy Cypriot businessman and philanthropist, and from the AG Leventis Foundation. The foundation was created after Leventis' death in 1978, and was also fundamental in the establishment of the Leventis Municipal Museum (p148). The Paris Collection is named after the home of Leventis, where the paintings used to be displayed away from public view. The Greek Collection is the result of a private purchase he made in 1973, while the Cyprus Collec-

tion was amassed more recently by the foundation.

★**Cyprus Museum** MUSEUM
(☎2286 5888; www.mcw.gov.cy/da; Leoforos Mouseiou 1; €4.50; ☉8am-6pm Tue-Fri, 9am-5pm Sat, 10am-1pm Sun) Just outside the Old City walls, this excellent museum houses the island's most important collection of archaeological finds. Highlights include Hall 11's haul of riches from the Royal Tomb excavations at Salamis, including a huge, intricately decorated bronze pot and a bed frame bedecked in ivory and glass. Hall 4's remarkable display of 2000 terracotta votive statues and figurines, dating back to the 7th and 6th centuries BC, were unearthed during the 1929 excavation of the Sanctuary of Agia Irini.

While in Hall 4, don't miss the interesting video on the Agia Irini discovery.

A further highlight is the collection of three limestone lions and two sphinxes found in the Tamassos necropolis south of Nicosia. Also look out for the famous Aphrodite of Soli statue in Hall 5, widely marketed as the 'goddess of Cyprus' on tourist posters. An enormous bronze statue of Emperor Septimus Severus, found at Değirmenlik (Kythrea) in 1928, is the magnificent main exhibit in Hall 6. A couple of lovely mosaics, such as Leda & the Swan from Palea Pafos, are exhibited in Room 7B, alongside various displays of gold objects excavated from tombs.

To further understanding of the exhibits and their historical context, the Cyprus Tourism Organisation (p166) runs a free archaeological museum tour every Tuesday and Friday at 10am and noon, and again on Wednesday at 4pm. The tour takes 90 minutes and the starting point is the museum entrance.

Loukia & Michael Zampelas Art Museum GALLERY
(http://zampelasart.com; Leoforos Archiepiskopou Makariou III, Kaimakli; adult/child €6/2; ☉10am-1pm & 3-6pm Tue, Thu-Sat, 11am-1pm & 3-7pm Wed) This small private gallery, dedicated to promoting contemporary Cypriot art, houses the Zampelas family's permanent art collection. A range of Cypriot and Greek modern artists are represented, but also on show are etchings by Picasso and Dalí, and two standout paintings by Welsh artist Glyn Hughes, who spent much of his life in Cyprus.

NICOSIA (LEFKOSIA) SIGHTS

CHILDREN'S CYPRUS: NICOSIA

Unlike Cyprus' seaside towns and resorts, Nicosia is not immediately appealing to children, although its residents are child-friendly, as are most Cypriots. There are no professional baby-sitting services in the city, as many families seem to have their own live-in nannies.

High chairs are available at most restaurants, and nappies and baby food are easily sourced. **Green Tea Supermarket** (p165) is the best-stocked supermarket within the Old City.

Many of the smaller lanes in the Old City have pavements too narrow for pushchairs (strollers), so be extra vigilant with traffic.

Cyprus Tourism Organisation (p166) Has a list of child-friendly events taking place throughout the year.

Eleon Swimming Pool (☑ 2245 1444; www.eleonpark.com; Ploutarhou, Egkomi; adult €7-8, child €4; ☺ 9am-6pm mid-May–mid-Sep; ⊞) Family-friendly swimming pool out in the suburbs, with added bouncy castle and playground.

Extreme Park (☑ 2242 4681; www.extremepark.com.cy; 149 Strovolos Ave, Strovolos; adult free, child €3-6; ☺ 5-10pm Tue-Fri, 5.30-10.30pm Sat & Sun; ⊞) This playground with inflatable slides, trampolines and aeroboards is where to head when the kids need to blow off some steam.

Municipal Swimming Pool (p156) Because sometimes on a furnace-hot summer's day visiting a museum just ain't going to cut it.

🏃 Activities

Hamam Omerye   HAMMAM
(Turkish Bath; ☑ 2246 0006; www.hamamomerye.com; Plateia Tyllirias; hammam €30, hammam & massage from €75; ☺ 10.30am-12.30pm & 1-9.30pm Tue-Sun) The stunning 16th-century Hamam Omerye has been tastefully restored and sports a luxurious Ottoman-inspired design. Facilities include hot and cold rooms, and there is a range of massages, body scrubs and treatments available.

Municipal Swimming Pool   SWIMMING
(Agiou Pavlou; €6; ☺ 10am-7pm May-Sep) A central-city oasis perfect for a stinking-hot summer's day, this well-maintained pool has on-duty lifeguards and is surrounded by big shady palms and tended gardens.

🧭 Tours

CTO Guided Tours   WALKING
(Aristokyprou 11) The Cyprus Tourism Organisation (CTO) runs three guided tours. On Mondays there's a 'Chrysaliniotissa and Kaimakli: the Past Restored' combined bus and walking tour; on Wednesdays 'Nicosia outside the Venetian walls' explores the area near Pafos Gate; and on Thursdays the 'Discover Old Nicosia' walk takes in the walled city. Tours last 2¾ hours (including a break) and depart 10am from the CTO office (p166).

Segway Station Cyprus   SEGWAY
(☑ 2276 3736; www.segwaystationcyprus.com; Aischylou 77a; 2/3hr tours €32/44; ☺ tours 10.30am, 3.30pm & 7pm Mon-Sat, times vary in winter) Run by enthusiastic and knowledgable guides, these Segway tours are a great way to orientate yourself in Nicosia's walled city. The routes weave through the back alleys of the Old City, exploring lesser-known nooks and crannies, as well as well-known sights. Booking 48 hours in advance is recommended.

🎭 Festivals & Events

Medieval Nicosia Festival   CULTURAL
(www.visitnicosia.com.cy; ☺ Apr) Nicosia hosts a bundle of free events over four days that focus on its medieval past. For visitors to the city at this time there are free guided tours, concerts and talks, all with medieval themes.

International Pharos
Chamber Music Festival   MUSIC
(www.pharosartsfoundation.org; ☺ May) This long-running festival brings a wealth of internationally acclaimed classical musicians to the island. The opening and closing concerts are usually held at the Shoe Factory in Nicosia, while a series of chamber-music concerts take place in the village of Kouklia,

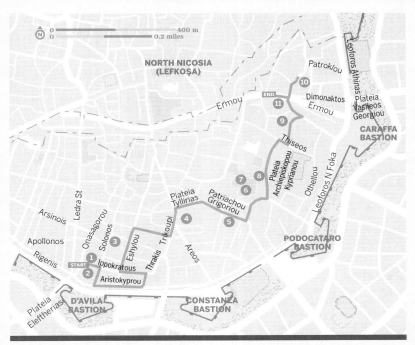

Walking Tour
Museums & Memories

START LEVENTIS MUNICIPAL MUSEUM
END CVAR
LENGTH 2KM; THREE HOURS

Begin at the ❶ **Leventis Municipal Museum** (p148) to give yourself a solid picture of Nicosia's history. Then corkscrew your way through the pipsqueak-sized ❷ **Laïki Yitonia** (p148) quarter, before heading north on Eshylou. As you walk up the road you'll pass the late 17th-century ❸ **Church of Archangelos Michail** (p148), a good example of the Franco-Byzantine architectural style.

Swing right on Liasadou and then left onto Trikoupi, strolling north for a block, to arrive at the ❹ **Omeriye Mosque** (p150). If you're suitably dressed you can enter to view its stark, soaring interior. Afterwards, turn right onto Plateia Tyllirias and right again on Patriarchou Grigoriou. About 125m along this street on the right is the ❺ **House of Hatzigeorgakis Kornesios** (p150), an imposing example of a private Ottoman mansion, once home to the island's famed dragoman.

The next left leads you to Plateia Archiepiskopou Kyprianou, dominated by the ❻ **Archbishop's Palace** (p151). Right beside the palace you'll find the Makarios Cultural Foundation, with its not-to-be-missed ❼ **Byzantine Museum** (p150), while the courtyard out the front is home to the ❽ **Agios Ioannis Church** (p151), with frescos dating from 1736.

Continue north, crossing over Thiseos and heading up Antigonou, to arrive at the doll's-house-sized ❾ **Tahtakale Mosque**. The lanes of pretty cottages around the mosque were a lively Turkish Cypriot neighbourhood before 1963, when intercommunal violence led to the Turkish Cypriots fleeing to safety behind the newly created Green Line. Keep on northward, crossing over Ermou, up to the ❿ **Panagia Chrysaliniotissa** (p153), thought to be the city's oldest surviving Byzantine church. Then scoot south back onto Ermou to finish up at ⓫ **CVAR** (p151), where exhibits trace the modern story of Cyprus.

in Pafos district. Tickets for individual concerts can be bought on the website.

Pharos Contemporary
Music Festival
MUSIC

(www.pharosartsfoundation.org; ⊙ Oct) A 10-day series of concerts, recitals, music-themed lectures and documentary screenings dedicated to highlighting talented new composers and classical musicians. Most events take place at the Shoe Factory in Nicosia. Tickets for individual events can be bought on the website.

Buffer Fringe Festival
PERFORMING ARTS

(www.home4cooperation.info; ⊙ Nov) Since 2014 the Buffer Fringe has brought three days of cutting-edge and experimental performing arts, and a kicker of a closing party, to Nicosia. Events are organised by and held at the Home for Cooperation in the UN Buffer Zone.

Eating

Nicosia's dining scene is booming. You'll find everything from simple canteens dishing up traditional stews to contemporary bistros concentrating on modern Med cuisine.

The Old City is the dining hub but the New City also offers some foodie treats, and burgeoning western and southern suburbs such as Engomi and Strovolos have their own culinary enclaves; a drive to either of the latter may turn up surprising finds.

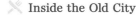

Inside the Old City

Restaurants are scattered throughout the Old City. The most buzzing dining strip is around Ledra St and Onasagorou. Just to the east there are plenty of small taverns speckling Laïki Yitonia, mainly popular with the lunchtime crowds of day trippers. Around Famagusta Gate several bistros and restaurants are frequented at night by locals in the know.

For cheap eats head to Areos or along Rigenis where there are plenty of little Middle Eastern fast-food joints.

Mattheos
CYPRIOT €

(Plateia 28 Oktovriou 6; mains from €6-8; ⊙ 10am-4pm Mon-Sat) As simple as it gets, this little canteen squeezed up next to the Arablar Mosque dishes up homestyle Cypriot cooking to lunching nine-to-fivers. There's nearly always gutsy *kleftiko* (oven-baked lamb), *afelia* (pork cooked in red wine) and stuffed vegetables on the small menu. This is rustic, hearty village-kitchen fare, and locals love it.

Christakis
CYPRIOT €

(✆ 2266 8537; Leoforos Kostaki Pantelidi 28; mains €7; ⊙ 8am-10pm Mon-Sat) This rough-and-ready canteen across from the bus station

---

PREPARING A NEW SQUARE

Head to the southern end of Ledra St and you'll find yourself face to face with a marching line of corrugated-iron fencing that you have to zigzag around to head out of the Old City. No, you haven't hit a strange looping veer in the Green Line (the UN Buffer Zone). It's the building site of Nicosia's most controversial rejuvenation project.

Since 2008 the massive reconstruction of Nicosia's Plateia Eleftherias – the main square leading into the Old City – has been obstructing direct access to this major artery. The architect of the square's new design was the late Zaha Hadid, who was renowned for her socially aware projects. Together with her Cypriot associate, Christos Passos, Hadid planned a green belt along the moat that surrounds the Venetian walls, turning the area within into Nicosia's central park, encircled by a palm-tree-lined pedestrian walkway. In the midst of the green belt would be a (concrete) square, where pedestrians would stroll and congregate, giving the area a new town centre. Hadid called the design an 'urban intervention'.

From the start the project has been mired by numerous delays and economic woes. And it has attracted its fair share of opposition, with some locals complaining of too little public consultation on the project, concerns about the impact of a large concrete structure on the ancient walls, and the reduction of access to the Old City. But what's a grand architectural work without controversy?

The light at the end of the tunnel may just be in sight. After a decade in the making, word is that Plateia Eleftherias may soon be finished. Fingers crossed then that the ugly fencing has been rolled away to reveal Nicosia's new park by the time you get there.

buzzes with locals tucking into cheap and cheerful souvlaki, grilled to perfection. A mixed grill with three skewers of meat, *sheftalia* (grilled sausages wrapped in caul fat), salad and pitta sets you back €7. Extra sides of griddled haloumi (hellim in Turkish) and olive-doused artichokes start from €1.

Lahmajoun Avo   ARMENIAN €
(☑ 2266 1172; Onasagorou 22; pastries & lahmajoun €1-1.30, souvlakis & grills €3-6; ☺ 8am-midnight; ☑) The *khachapuri* (bread stuffed with haloumi and eggs) and *spanakopita* (spinach, feta cheese and eggs wrapped in filo pastry) are both good, and the souvlakis are great value, but seriously, you're here for the Armenian-style *lahmajoun* (thin-based pizza topped with minced lamb and parsley).

Alaadin   MIDDLE EASTERN €
(☑ 9924 7313; Onasagorou; pastries €1-1.50, felafel, souvlakis & pizzas €3-11; ☺ 8am-midnight; ☎ ☑) Hands up fellow Levantine cuisine fans. We've found you the best *muhammara* (hot red-pepper paste) flatbreads in town. The felafel sandwiches make for a quick, tasty lunch, and there's decent pizza and *lahmajoun* (thin-based pizza topped with minced lamb and parsley), too.

★ Shiantris   CYPRIOT €€
(Pericleous 38; mains €8-10; ☺ 8.30am-9pm Mon-Sat) Soul food at its best, Shiantris serves traditional dishes just like a Cypriot mama makes. It's named after its ebullient owner, who cooks up a fantastic array of seasonal beans with lemon, parsley and olive oil, as well as other simple classics, including stuffed vine leaves and *afelia* (pork cooked in red wine). The menu changes daily according to what's fresh and in season.

★ Piatsa Gourounaki   GREEK €€
(☑ 7000 7670; Faneromenis; dishes €1-7, 2-person platters €12-16; ☺ 12.30-4pm & 7-11pm; ✳ ☎ ☑) Incredibly popular, and for good reason: this contemporary-style *souvlakeri* dishes up some of the freshest Greek tastes in town, with charming service to boot. Pick the number of perfectly grilled meat skewers you'd like and then choose from the long list of tasty meze and sides, from *bouyiourdi* (oven-baked feta and vegetables) and pickled peppers to *tirokefteri* (spicy cheese dip).

There's a no-reservations policy, so get here earlyish or expect to wait for a table.

There's a second 'express' **restaurant** (☑ 7778 7777; Leoforos Kostaki Pantelidi; dishes €1-6.50, platters €6-7; ☺ 12.30-4pm & 7-11pm; ✳ ☎) near the southern end of Ledra St.

D.O.T   MEDITERRANEAN €€
(☑ 2210 1228; Leoforos Athinas 6a; mains €11-14; ☺ noon-4pm & 7-11.30pm Mon-Fri, 11am-2.30pm & 7-11.30pm Sat & Sun; ✳ ☎ ☑) From salmon marinated in maple syrup to pumpkin risotto tweaked with lavender and macadamias, D.O.T takes the sunshiny tastes of the Mediterranean and adds modern flair. It serves inventive burger options, too, and at weekends locals crowd in for a lazy long brunch. Service is haphazard when busy, so don't come expecting to eat and run.

Kathodon   GREEK €€
(☑ 2266 1656; Ledra St 62; mains €7-10, meze per person €15-17; ☺ 9am-1am; ☎) Large, noisy and touristy...but known for its authentic Greek cuisine, with fall-off-the-bone *kleftiko* (oven-baked lamb), crunchy salads and a range of seafood. Head inside to check out the wall full of photos showing contented customers, including Bill Clinton, but sit on the sprawling outside terrace for views of the border bustle. Live Greek music nightly.

Da Paolo   ITALIAN €€
(☑ 2243 8538; Leoforos Konstantinou Paleologou 52; mains €7.50-14; ☺ 7.15-11.30pm; ✳ ☎) During summer this small Italian restaurant has an outdoor terrace right on the Venetian walls. There's proper wood-fired pizza and plenty of pasta on offer. Go for the *cipriota pizza* with feta, haloumi, mozzarella, olives, salami and tomatoes for a real local take on Italian food.

Inga's Veggie Heaven   VEGETARIAN €€
(☑ 2234 4674; Chrysaliniotissa Crafts Centre, Dimonaktos 2; mains €10.50-12; ☺ 9.30am-5.30pm Tue-Sat; ☑) Inga is a friendly Icelandic chef who prepares several homely vegan and vegetarian dishes of the day, such as stuffed peppers; eggplant and feta lasagne; and roast beetroot and chickpea felafel – always served with salad and homemade bread. The lovingly created cakes are a calorific high point. Check out the surrounding arts and crafts studios afterwards.

Aegeon   GREEK €€
(☑ 2243 3297; Ektoros 40; meze from €18; ☺ 7-11pm Tue-Sat; ☎) Aegeon continues to draw in a faithful following of fashionable local devotees, who come here to feast on meze and drink ouzo in the vine-draped courtyard long into the night. During colder months

NICOSIA (LEFKOSIA) EATING

the action moves into the attached atmospheric old house. Reservations essential.

★ **Zanettos Taverna** CYPRIOT €€€
(📞2276 5501; Trikoupi 65; meze spread per person €21; ⏱6.30pm-midnight) When you've been in business since 1938 you must be doing something right. This is the real-deal meze experience and locals lap it up. We recommend you join them. There's no menu, just a parade of meze, usually including pork belly, calf liver, *sheftalia* (grilled sausages wrapped in caul fat) and snails. Come hungry and pace yourself. Bookings recommended at weekends.

Power House INTERNATIONAL €€€
(Apostolou Varnava 19; mains from €12; ⏱10am-11pm Tue-Sat; 🐾) Part of the Nicosia Municipal Arts Centre, this sophisticated restaurant is suitably decorated with striking paintings and sculptures. The menu includes steaks, kebabs, pasta and salads, and desserts are in the innovative mode of chocolate mousse infused with Earl Grey tea. There is live jazz most Saturdays in summer.

Atelier FRENCH €€€
(📞2226 2369; http://ateliernicosia.com; Archangelou Michail 3; mains €16-42; ⏱7pm-1am Mon-Sat; ✳🐾) This intimate restaurant serves modern French cooking with what must be the best selection of French wines in Nicosia The small menu focuses on fresh, seasonal produce, and so changes throughout the year, but expect meaty choices such as bone marrow for starters and succulent, falling-off-the-bone lamb shoulder for mains. Save room for dessert because they do sweets proud here.

New City

The New City's restaurants are spread across town but there are a couple of eating-out hot spots. In particular, the leafy and affluent residential street of Klimentos has some top dining choices, while Stasandrou, Pindarou and Themistokli Dervi are home to several contemporary cafes.

★ **Syrian Arab Friendship Club** MIDDLE EASTERN €€
(SAFC; Vassilisa Amalia 17; meze dishes €2-7, meze spread per person €17; ⏱noon-midnight; 🐾✏) The meze spread (minimum two people) gives your taste buds a tour of Levantine cuisine's greatest hits, but if you know your Arabic dishes, you can go à la carte and cherry-pick your own feast. We recommend

WALKING THE GREEN LINE

Start your walk of the Green Line on the eastern side of the Old City at the northern end of Leoforos Athinas, where a metal gate and UN bunker signal the end of the road. Turn left into Antasias Toufexi, rimmed by terraced cottages, some restored and others with their adobe-brick innards exposed, and then right onto Axotheas, which ends abruptly with a cement-bunker barricade. Then take a hard left onto the lane of Aftokrateiras Theodoras; residents here have the Buffer Zone's abandoned building shells right across the alleyway from their front door, and so have prettified this depressing scene with pot plants and colourful flowers.

Scoot through the courtyard of the small Agios Kasianos Church onto Minoös, where the road ends with a couple of banged-up old cars (including a Morris Minor van) abandoned right next to the metal fence. There's a good view of the empty streets inside the Buffer Zone behind. Next head southwest onto Pentadaktylou and then west onto Tritonos and Lidinis where, in some of the dead-end lanes running off these streets, the oil-barrel barricades have been planted with geraniums. From here, stroll down Dionysou and Alexandrou Ypsilanti, home to the evocative sight of once-grand, now-withered, town houses with ornate upper-storey balconies stacked with sandbags and windows smashed. Loop around Asklipiou, which turns into Lefkonos, and follow this as it runs up to Ledra St.

On Ledra Street, walk straight up to the crossing checkpoint, and take the first left turn down the Stoa Tarsi arcade. This brings you out onto Ious, where a park bench sits incongruously in front of a tall oil-barrel barricade. Keep heading west, onto Artimidos with its staffed soldier bunker, and then zigzag your way to Pafou, where the Roman Catholic Holy Cross Church sits beside the barricaded-off stub of the street with the wire fencing dividing off the Roccas Bastion right behind.

the *batinjan makle* (aubergines soaked in yoghurt and pomegranate molasses), *kibbeh nayeh* (Levantine version of lamb tartare) and *fattoush* (salad with fried pita).

Silver Pot   CAFE €€
(☑ 2210 1722; www.silverpot.com.cy; Themistokli Dervi 3; mains €7-10; ⊙ 8am-8pm Tue-Fri, 10am-5pm Sat & Sun, 8am-5pm Mon; 🗑🍴) Tight on space but big on boho-urban atmosphere, Silver Pot has a menu featuring locally sourced produce which is, as far as possible, organic. Dishes change daily, but typical mains include Thai curry, oven-baked pork chops marinated in lemon juice and thyme, and inventive salads with ingredients such as blue cheese, figs, pecans and cranberries. The Saturday brunch is justifiably popular.

Pinakkothiki   INTERNATIONAL €€
(AG Leventis Gallery, Leonidou; mains €10-14; ⊙ 10am-5pm Thu-Mon, to 10pm Wed; ❋🗑) This contemporary space features glossy black and soothing cream decor, and a long bar with stools, perfect for sipping predinner cocktails. Dishes are light and appetising, including oven-baked salmon, duck pancakes in ginger-spiked soy sauce, and six different salads. There's an ample children's menu.

Sawa   MIDDLE EASTERN €€
(☑ 2276 6777; Klimentos 31; meze from €15; ⊙ noon-11.30pm; 🅿🗑🍴) Known throughout town for its superb Syrian dishes and a fabulous sultan's-palace-style setting, Sawa has an elaborate carved-stone exterior, bubbling fountains and an elegant dining room. The meze feasts are recommended, ideally accompanied by a bottle of Lebanese Chateau Ksara riesling. Reservations essential.

Limoncello Deli-Bar   DELI €€
(☑ 7000 9787; Ayios Antonios Municipal Market, Digeni Akrita; mains €6.50-20; ⊙ 12.45-3pm & 7.45-11.15pm Tue-Sat; 🗑) Deli by day, casual bar-restaurant by night, Limoncello is all about fresh, locally sourced ingredients. Its main suppliers – the grocers and butchers of Ayios Antonios Municipal Market (p165) – are just a stone's throw away. The small menu features *piadina* (Italian pizza-style flatbread), steaks, fish and meat dishes (the oven-roasted duck is delicious), as well as quirky artisan burgers.

🍷 Drinking & Nightlife

From cafe culture to chichi cocktail bars, this is a city that revels in a night on the town.

🏆 Inside the Old City

★ Patio Cocktail Bar   COCKTAIL BAR
(☑ 2266 4488; www.patiococktailbar.com; Megalou Alexandrou 55-56; ⊙ 6pm-2am; 🗑) Step inside the show-stopping leafy courtyard with its dazzling wall of shutters painted in primary colours. Inside the main bar, exposed brickwork, chic furnishings and plenty of glass and light have an equally punchy effect for enjoying that pre- (or post-) dinner cocktail. Great mood music as well.

★ Pivo Microbrewery   CRAFT BEER
(Asklipiou 36; ⊙ 7pm-12.30am Tue-Thu, to 1.30am Fri & Sat; 🗑) The craft-beer movement finally hits Nicosia, and it's not just beer-geeks who'll love this place. The setting – inside a restored 1910 house – is chic but casual, and the beer is handcrafted, unfiltered and brewed on-site in the city's first microbrewery. Try the half-

NICOSIA (LEFKOSIA) DRINKING & NIGHTLIFE

NICOSIA MASTER PLAN

In an effort to preserve the historic fabric of the Old City, combat the urban decay creeping into neighbourhoods within the Venetian walls and foster trust between the capital's two divided communities, the Nicosia Master Plan was founded in 1979. The project was initially conceived to help solve the Old City's serious infrastructure problems, which had been further magnified by division. City leaders from both the Greek Cypriot and Turkish Cypriot sides committed to working together to improve life for all residents of the capital and to helping conserve the city's historic core.

Under the plan, churches and mosques, hammams (Turkish baths) and tombs, mansions and monuments, museums and cultural centres have all been restored, along with neglected neighbourhoods such as Chrysaliniotissa (Nicosia) and Arabahmet (North Nicosia), both of which abut the Green Line UN Buffer Zone, being rejuvenated. Efforts have even been made to renovate some of the crumbling buildings inside the Buffer Zone itself, ignored for more than 40 years. The aim of this important work is to preserve and promote the shared history of both communities inside the city.

For more information, check the UNDP in Cyprus website (www.cy.undp.org).

pint sampler of four beers for a good taste of what these guys are about.

Haratsi
CAFE

(Lidinis; ⊙4pm-midnight) The joy of this traditional coffee shop dating from the 1930s is that little has changed. There's no chill-out background music, no cutting-edge decor and, somehow, it's not the sort of place where you feel tempted to whip out your iPad.

Kalakathou
CAFE

(Nikokleous 21; ⊙10am-1am; 🛜) Kalakathou is one of a clutch of cafes that share a laid-back alternative vibe. Come for board games, buskers and to sip a frappé under the vines. This evocative building formerly belonged to the Church of Panagia Faneromeni across the way. Light snacks and homemade cakes are also available.

Kafeneio Mousiko
CAFE

(☎2266 0123; Onasagorou 78; ⊙10am-late) If you're looking for us during the evening in Nicosia, we're usually here, people-watching and listening to the *rebetiko* (urban Greek folk music) musicians who jam here with their friends. Drinks-wise, there's a full list of beer, spirits and wines, but some nights everyone seems to be drinking ouzo. Mousiko also does a mean toasted sandwich.

Plato's
BAR

(Platonas 8; ⊙8pm-2am) Atmospheric bars are spread over several rooms at this early 20th-century building complete with original tiles, arches and a courtyard. Expect rock and blues on the soundtrack and a convivial local crowd.

Gym
BAR

(☎2200 2001; Onasagorou 85-89; ⊙10am-late; 🛜) This corner venue is always heaving. Food is served, but stick to drinks – you should find something to suit from the 20-plus cocktails. The space is cavernous and contemporary, with a small art gallery out the back, and a DJ playing at weekends.

Ithaki
BAR

(www.facebook.com/Ithaki33; Leoforos Nikiforou Foka 33; ⊙7pm-3am Mon-Sat summer, from 9pm winter) This decidedly unflashy bar-club is one of the granddaddies of the Old City scene, having been in the business of providing a fun night out since 1998. Monday is R & B night and Friday is a 'Thinking Outside the Box' gay-friendly party. Some nights there's a small admission fee (usu-

ally around €3). Happy hour (two-for-one drinks) is between 10pm and 11pm.

Berlin Wall 2
BAR

(Faneromenis; ⊙noon-1am) Yep. It's a shack, complete with corrugated-iron roof and plastic windows (during chillier months). And yep. It's rubbing up against the UN Buffer Zone and smack-bang next door to an army guard station. The name starts making sense now, doesn't it. Definitely one of the oddest locations to sink a few beers in town.

Kafeneio Xalara
CAFE

(Faneromenis; ⊙11am-midnight; 🛜) You could pretty much pick any of the boho-vibe pavement cafes along Faneromenis and come up trumps for a beer or coffee break, but we reckon Xalara does the best latte.

Pieto
CAFE

(Ledra St 207; ⊙8am-2am) All mismatched vintage chairs, leafy pot plants and fairy lights strung from the ceiling, Pieto is the kind of quirky-comfy place we love. The cool-kid interior comes at a cost: drink prices are higher here than elsewhere. But if you want character, it can't be beaten. It's on the Ledra St side of the Stoa Klokkari arcade.

Yiayia Biktupia
CAFE

(☎2277 7252; Liperti 80-82, off Ledra St; ⊙10.30am-10pm) Head straight up to the Ledra St crossing and turn right. This cafe is tucked in a corner, with tables spilling out right up to the sandbagged wall of the UN Buffer Zone, and it's always buzzing with young locals. Yes, you can get a latte or cappuccino, but take a cue from the locals and order a Cypriot coffee.

Brew Fellas
BAR

(☎2226 4007; Pygmalionos 7; ⊙6pm-late; 🛜) Beer connoisseurs, you have found your Nicosia nirvana. Just off Ledra St, this chilled-out bar is home to what must be the best range of beers from across the world, with plenty of draught options too, and clued-up bar staff to boot. A great option for a relaxed, casual night on the town.

O, Ti Na' Nai
BAR

(Sokratous 17; ⊙noon-late) We love sitting in the graffiti-covered and pot-plant-filled alleyway in front of this narrow, laid-back bar-cafe, with a Cypriot coffee mid-afternoon or a cold Keo later, while the bar's cat patrols the area. Happy hour (5pm to 9pm) brings beer, wine and shots for €2.

Erodós
BAR

(☑2275 2250; Patriarchou Grigoriou 1; ⊙11am-late) A handsome colonial-style building is home to an atmospheric bar, with dark burgundy walls, warm woodwork and several moodily lit rooms. There's live music on Thursdays at 10.30pm, ranging from jazz to blues.

🍴 New City

If you're about to hit the streets of the New City for a night out, be aware that jeans and trainers just won't cut it; this is a much more dressy scene. For cafe life, head to Stasikratous.

Brew Lab
CAFE

(www.brewlab.com.cy; Stasikratous 3; ⊙7am-8pm Mon-Sat; 🛜) Follow the rich aroma of roasted fair-trade Costa Rican coffee, proudly served here along with freshly made bagels, brownies and similar baked goodies. There's a small courtyard out the back, as well as pavement seating.

Zoo
CLUB

(Leoforos Stasinou 15; ⊙7pm-late Thu-Sun) Zoo is the embodiment of style and sophistication on Nicosia's club scene, with music that ranges from international to Greek pop. The summer-only Zoo Lounge on the top floor is a great place for a little locked-eyes-over-cocktails time with chill-out soundtracks and laid-back live music.

☆ Entertainment

Nicosia is home to a thriving local theatre scene; however, plays performed are almost always in Greek. If this doesn't deter you, check at the tourist office for any performances that may be taking place.

For traditional music, many of the restaurants and cafes in Laïki Yitonia and around Ledra St in the Old City often offer live Greek music. In summer, keep your eyes peeled for posters advertising visiting musicians from Greece.

Cyprus National Theatre
THEATRE

(☑box office 7777 2717; www.thoc.org.cy; Grigori Afxentiou 9) Purpose-built for the Cyprus Theatre Organisation (THOC), this contemporary theatre is the main venue for the national theatre company's productions. Plays are usually in Greek but there are also occasional visiting theatre productions from the UK and other nations. Check the website to see what's on while you're in town.

Granazi Art Space
LIVE MUSIC

(Agion Omologiton 14; ⊙5.30pm-midnght) Mellow bar, art space and live-music venue: intimate Granazi manages to roll all three into one. Thursdays and Fridays usually host live music, and each month sees a different local artist exhibiting their work on the walls. The cocktails here are a bit knock-your-socks-off as well.

Pallas Theatre
CONCERT VENUE

(☑2241 0181; www.cyso.org.cy; cnr Rigenis & Arsinois) Home of the Cyprus Symphony Orchestra (CYSO), this theatre has a regular program of recitals and concerts. Check the website to see if anything is on while you're in town.

Ennalax Live
LIVE MUSIC

(www.facebook.com/pg/enallax; Leoforos Athinas 16-17; ⊙5pm-3am Mon-Sat) This long-running live-music venue showcases everything from reggae and rock to traditional folk. The crowd here is always up for fun. The venue's Facebook page usually announces upcoming gigs.

DownTown Live
LIVE MUSIC

(www.facebook.com/downtownlivenicosia; Emanuel Roidi 2; ⊙9pm-3am Wed-Sat; 🛜) Nicosia's biggest live-music venue has a regular line-up of rock bands and musicians, both local and international. Check the Facebook page for upcoming concerts.

Weaving Mill
CULTURAL CENTRE

(☑2276 2275; Lefkonos 69; ⊙2-10pm Mon-Sat, 10am-10pm Sun; 🛜) Owner Leontios started this nonprofit educational and cultural association as a teaching base for the children

---

FANEROMENIS CAFE CULTURE

The square and pedestrian zone surrounding the Church of Panagia Faneromeni in the Old City is Nicosia's most buzzing cafe scene. Around a dozen independently owned teensy cafes with tables and chairs sprawl across the Plateia Faneromenis within confessional distance of the picturesque church. Nicosia's alternative set were first to set up shop here, and although the arty-edgy vibe survives in the graffitied walls and small craft shops tucked between the coffee shops, pretty much everyone now heads here for a latte, a freddo cappuccino or a beer.

PROMOTING COOPERATION

Inside the Buffer Zone between Nicosia (Lefkosia) and North Nicosia (Lefkoşa), the **Home for Cooperation** (Map p176; www.home4cooperation.info; Markou Drakou, Buffer Zone; ⊘9am-6pm) is a community centre that's home base for many NGO projects focused on peace-building and dialogue between the Greek Cypriot and Turkish Cypriot communities. For visitors to the city, it rents bikes (€5 per day), organises city walking tours (€10 per person, minimum eight people), and runs both Greek- and Turkish-language courses.

The on-site **Home Cafe** (Map p176; www.home4cooperation.info; Home for Cooperation, Markou Drakou, Buffer Zone; ⊘9am-9pm Mon-Sat, to 5pm Sun; 🛜) has a small library and is a relaxed spot for coffee and cake. On Tuesdays and Thursdays between noon and 4pm it also serves vegetarian meals.

of immigrants. These days the Mill has a multicultural purpose, showing films, staging the occasional concert and providing a large, comfortable space for wi-fi use, board games, reading (there is an extensive library) or just socialising. There is a modest bar for light snacks and drinks.

Academy 32   LIVE MUSIC
(Leoforos Konstantino Paleologou 32; ⊘7pm-2am Tue-Sun; 🛜) Housed in the basement of the Cyprus Academy of Music (the owner is the Academy's artistic director) this is, unsurprisingly, one of the best places in town to hear live music. The emphasis is on jazz, classical and world music. There is also an art gallery, and fine wines and light eats are served.

K-Cineplex   CINEMA
(www.kcineplex.com; Makedonitissis 8, Strovolos; adult/child €9/7; 🛜) Located 2.5km out of the city in Strovolos, K-Cineplex shows all the latest movie releases on six screens, and offers ample parking, a cafeteria and high-tech sight-and-sound systems.

Skali Aglantzias   LIVE MUSIC
(www.facebook.com/skali.cavebar; Agiou Georgiou 15, Aglantzia; ⊘10.45pm-2am) This bar and arts centre often hosts live-music nights.

☆ Sport

Football (soccer) is the main spectator sport in Nicosia. The football season is from September to May. Nicosia's Apoel FC (www.apoelfc.com.cy), 25-times champions, are the Republic's most popular team. The city is also home to clubs Omonia and Olympiakos. Match tickets can be bought through Apoel FC's website and also at the gate on the day.

The **GSP Stadium** (☑2287 4050; www.gsp.org.cy; Pangyprion) is the main and largest stadium in Cyprus, with a capacity for 22,850 people. It is mostly used for football matches (as well as major concerts). The stadium is located in Strovolos, southeast Nicosia, approximately 6.5km from the city centre.

Shopping

Ledra St has plenty of familiar big-name European brands and is the city's main shopping street. More interesting are the tiny boutiques run by artisans and designers, found strewn through the surrounding alleyways. Souvenir-style stores (selling plenty of tat as well as lacework and backgammon boards) are centred in Laïki Yitonia. In the New City, Stasikratous is the central shopping hub.

★Diachroniki Gallery   ART
(☑2268 0145; www.diachroniki.com; Aristokyprou; ⊘10am-7pm Mon-Sat) This collection of paintings, sculpture, etchings, antique maps and prints has been lovingly collected by owner Chris Kikas, who used to run a gallery in London's King's Rd. Art collectors come from far and wide to peruse the artwork here. Don't miss it.

Workshop Kalliroi   JEWELLERY
(Aristokyprou 21; ⊘9am-4pm Mon-Sat) This tiny shop sells quirky, individual handcrafted pendant necklaces, earrings, chunky stone rings and funky bracelets.

Etsi Ki Allios   CERAMICS
(☑2275 3900; www.etsikiallios.com; Lefkonos 33; ⊘9am-6pm Mon-Fri, to 3pm Sat) Geometric Moroccan-style wall tiles and colourful, abstract teapots and homewares, all hand-made and hand-painted.

Ochi Market   MARKET
(Leoforos Konstantinou Paleologou; ⊘7.30am-4pm Wed) Get your five-plus a day here on Wednesdays when local farmers set up their fruit and vegetable stalls on Constanza Bastion.

Collective FASHION & ACCESSORIES
(https://thecollectiveconcept.com; Palaion Patron Germanou 4-6; ⊘ 11am-7pm Mon-Sat) Second-hand bliss. This is the number-one stop in Nicosia for lovers of vintage fashion, accessories and homewares. From funky industrial lighting and delicately hand-painted Worcester bone china from the 1950s to colourful Turkmenistan robe coats, the collection here is always fun, fresh and surprising.

Bakali FOOD
(☑ 2266 5503; Nikokleous 4; ⊘ 11am-7pm) Foodie treats ahoy. Head here for homemade and locally produced preserves, honey, olive oil, sweets, nougat, carob products and so much more, sourced from villages around Cyprus.

Bomba DESIGN
(www.bomba-design.com; Mouson 4; ⊘ 10am-1pm Mon-Thu & Sat, 10am-1pm & 4-7pm Fri) Funky screen-printed clothes, homewares and accessories, plus some quirky and cute T-shirts and gifts for kids.

Ayios Antonios Municipal Market MARKET
(Leoforos Evgenias & Antoniou Theodotou; ⊘ 7am-4pm Thu-Sat, Mon & Tue, to 2pm Wed) This municipal market in the New City sports a small but select array of stalls selling fruit, veg, spices, bakery goods, cheeses and similar. There's also a good cafe on-site and the excellent restaurant-cum-deli Limoncello (p161).

Gatapou ARTS & CRAFTS
(Stoa Papadopoulou 25; ⊘ 9am-7pm Mon, Tue, Thu & Fri, to 2pm Wed & Sat) With one of the more colourful shop windows you'll find anywhere, Gatapou sells accessories, handmade kids' toys and decorations, including slippers, mobiles, knitted dolls and jazzy cushions.

Phaneromenis 70 ARTS & CRAFTS
(www.kyriakicosta.net; Faneromenis 70; ⊘ 11am-6pm Mon-Fri, to 1pm Sat) The owner of this fascinating shop, Kyriaki, is an artist – and it shows in the quirky and quality crafts, textiles and artwork on sale here, including handmade children's clothes and toys, jewellery, bags, fashion and fanciful ornaments, and decor items.

Atelier D'Art CERAMICS
(Aristotelous 14; ⊘ 9.30am-6.30pm Mon-Sat) Prepare to be impressed by the highly original pottery, including homewares, colourful mobiles and jewellery, created by master ceramicist Stavros. He studied his craft in Italy, France and London.

Antiques ANTIQUES
(Palaion Patron Germanou; ⊘ 10am-6pm Mon, Tue & Fri, to 2pm Wed & Sat) There's no actual name for this store crammed with retro tin trays, old vinyl, funky 1970s ceramics and ornaments, and more. If you love nothing more than a good rummage, you'll be in heaven.

Chrysaliniotissa Crafts Centre ARTS & CRAFTS
(Dimonaktos 2; ⊘ 10am-1pm & 3-6pm Mon-Fri, 10am-1pm Sat) This small arts centre is worth dropping into for its display of Cypriot arts and crafts. Several workshops surround a central courtyard in a building designed along the lines of a traditional inn.

Moufflon Bookshop BOOKS
(☑ 2266 5155; www.moufflon.com.cy; Sofouli 38; ⊘ 9.30am-7pm Mon-Fri, to 5pm Sat) Dating back to 1967, this bookshop has the largest selection of English-language books in Cyprus. There are loads of secondhand books, as well as hard-to-find nonfiction titles on Cyprus.

Green Tea Supermarket FOOD & DRINKS
(Onasagorou 1; ⊘ 7.30am-8pm Mon-Sat, 9am-8pm Sun) The best-stocked supermarket in the Old City area, with two floors of stock that includes both local and international brands.

Astor SHOES
(Ippocratous 16b; ⊘ 10am-4.30pm Tue-Sun) Locally produced handmade sandals and boots with simple designs and quality leather are the standout items here, with prices starting from just €25. The bags are imported from Greece.

Cyprus Handicrafts Centre ARTS & CRAFTS
(☑ 2230 5024; Leoforos Athalassis 186, Strovolos; ⊘ 8am-2pm & 4.30-7pm Mon, Tue, Thu & Fri, 8am-2pm Wed, 8.30am-1pm Sat) Get your Cypriot lace and embroidery at decent prices, as well as leatherwear, mosaics, ceramics and pottery. Even better, watch these products being made in various workshops at a government-sponsored foundation committed to preserving Cypriot handicrafts. It's just off the main Nicosia–Lemesos highway.

ℹ️ Information

EMERGENCY
Police station (☑ 2247 7434; Rigenis) By Pafos Gate.

INTERNET ACCESS

Free wi-fi is standard at nearly all hotels and is available in most cafes, bars and restaurants.

MEDICAL SERVICES

If you need a private doctor or pharmacy, call 9090 1432. Visiting hours for doctors are normally from 9am to 1pm and 4pm to 7pm. Local newspapers list pharmacies that are open during the night, and on weekends and holidays, as well as the names of doctors who are on call outside normal hours. You can also check www. cytayellowpages.com.cy for details of doctors and dentists.

Nicosia General Hospital (☑ 2260 3000; www.moh.gov.cy; Nicosia-Lemesos Hwy 205; ⊙ 24hr) West of the Old City.

POST

Central Post Office (Leoforos Konstantinou Paleologou; ⊙ 8am-3pm Mon-Fri)

TOURIST INFORMATION

Cyprus Tourism Organisation (CTO; ☑ 2267 4264; www.visitcyprus.com; Aristokyprou 11; ⊙ 8am-4pm Mon-Fri, to 2pm Sat) Good free maps of the city, loads of pamphlets and helpful, friendly staff.

ⓘ Getting There & Away

AIR

Larnaka International Airport (p132) is the nearest airport in the Republic to the capital. Most airlines have offices or representatives in Nicosia.

Nicosia's international airport is in the UN Buffer Zone and has been out of service since 1974.

BUS

The conveniently located **Urban Bus Station** (Plateia Solomos) abuts the Tripoli Bastion in the Old City.

InterCity Buses (☑ 7000 7789, free call 8000 7789; www.intercity-buses.com; Plateia Solomos) runs regular services to the main cities and resorts.

Agia Napa and Paralimni €5, two hours, nine services from 6am to 9pm Monday to Friday, eight from 8am to 7.30pm weekends.

Larnaka €4, 1¼ hours, 16 services from 6am to 9pm Monday to Friday, nine from 8am to 8.30pm weekends.

Lemesos €5, 1¾ hours, 17 services from 6am to 9pm Monday to Friday, eight from 7am to 7.30pm weekends.

Pafos €7, two hours, nine services from 5am to 7pm Monday to Friday, five from 7am to 7pm weekends.

CAR & MOTORCYCLE

Traffic approaching Nicosia tends to come from either the Troödos Mountains to the west or Larnaka and Lemesos in the South. The Larnaka–Lemesos motorway ends fairly abruptly on the outskirts of Nicosia, about 6km south of the Old City. By following the extension of the motorway into the city centre, you will eventually reach Leoforos Archiepiskopou Makariou III, the main thoroughfare in the New City. Traffic from Troödos enters the city along Leoforos Georgiou Griva Digeni.

Getting out of Nicosia is made easy by the prominent signs all along Leoforos Stasinou. Be wary, however, of the many one-way streets and numerous on-street parking restrictions. Avoid the peak period of 11am to 1pm on weekdays when traffic can be very slow.

NICOSIA (LEFKOSIA) GETTING THERE & AWAY

ⓘ CROSSING TO NORTH NICOSIA

The Ledra Street and Ledra Palace Hotel (Map p176) crossings are the only places on the island reserved exclusively for pedestrian and bicycle crossings between the Republic and Northern Cyprus. Both operate 24 hours daily, with masses of tourists and locals crossing from one side to the other, mostly via Ledra St, for shopping, work, business or a late night out. Don't forget to take your passport or you will not be allowed through the checkpoint.

At the Ledra St crossing, your passport will be checked by police officials staffing the Republic of Cyprus checkpoint, and then you'll walk through the UN Buffer Zone (no photographs allowed) to the Northern Cyprus checkpoint, where your passport will be stamped. If you have luggage, you will most likely be stopped on your return for a bag search by the Republic of Cyprus customs officials. They are generally friendly and are checking for smuggled cigarettes and alcohol (only 40 cigarettes and 1L of alcohol are allowed to be brought into the South from the North).

The process is exactly the same at the Ledra Palace Hotel crossing but it's a good 400m walk across the UN Buffer Zone between the two passport checkpoints, so most people prefer the shorter Ledra St crossing.

ℹ DRIVING TO NORTHERN CYPRUS

There is no vehicle crossing point across the Green Line (UN Buffer Zone) between central Nicosia (Lefkosia) and central North Nicosia (Lefkoşa). The nearest passport checkpoint if you are driving is Agios Dometios/Metehan, roughly 4km west of the centre.

Although some people do take rental cars across the Buffer Zone into Northern Cyprus, be aware that you will have to purchase additional car insurance at the passport checkpoint. It's much cheaper, and easier, to walk between Nicosia and North Nicosia using one of the two pedestrian crossings (p166) in the central city and rent a car on the other side.

Many taxi drivers in Nicosia can drop you at destinations anywhere in the North – if a driver refuses, try another. Again, however, it's much less expensive to cross via one of the two pedestrian checkpoints and hire a taxi within North Nicosia.

Parking is most easily found at the large car parks abutting the Old City bastions – to the right of Leoforos Archiepiskopou Makariou III if you're driving in from Larnaka, or to your left if you approach from Troödos and are heading into the centre along Georgiou Griva Digeni. The most convenient for new arrivals is the large lot between the D'Avila and Constanza Bastions on Leoforos Stasinou. Parking per day should cost no more than €10.

SERVICE TAXI

Travel & Express (☑2273 0888, 7777 7474; www.travelexpress.com.cy; Municipal Parking Place, Leoforos Salaminos, Podocataro Bastion; ☺6am-6pm Mon-Fri, 7am-5pm Sat & Sun) runs routes between Nicosia and Agia Napa, Protaras and Paralimni (€17 Monday to Saturday, €20 Sunday, 1¼ hour); Larnaka (€8.50 Monday to Saturday, €10 Sunday, one hour); Lemesos (€11 Monday to Saturday, €12 Sunday, 1½ hours); and Pafos (€20.50 Monday to Saturday, €23 Sunday, 1½ hours) with a change at Lemesos.

Although Travel & Express will pick you up at an appointed time from anywhere in urban Nicosia, delays of up to 30 minutes are the norm; similarly, passengers boarding at the station at Podocataro Bastion will usually spend up to 30 minutes picking up other passengers before actually departing Nicosia. Be prepared and allow for at least an extra hour.

ℹ Getting Around

TO/FROM THE AIRPORT

Kapnos Airport Shuttle (☑2400 8718; www.kapnosairportshuttle.com; Kyrenias, off Leoforos Lemesou; adult/child Larnaka Airport-Nicosia €8/5, Pafos Airport-Nicosia €15/5) has regular, direct services between Nicosia and Larnaka International Airport (40 minutes) and Pafos International Airport on the west coast (1½ hours). The pick-up/drop-off point in Nicosia is quite a hike from the Old City, but both OSEL buses 158 and 160 run

along Leoforos Lemesou, near to the Kapnos station, down to the **Urban Bus Station** (p166) at the edge of the Old City.

Service taxis run by **Travel & Express** (p167) also link Nicosia to Larnaka airport (€11 Monday to Saturday, €13 Sunday) and Pafos airport (€23.40 Monday to Saturday, €25 Sunday).

A taxi will cost €40.50/47.50 (day/night) to Larnaka airport and €106.50/124.50 to Pafos Airport.

BUS

Nicosia's urban bus company, **Osel** (www.osel.com.cy), has a network of routes covering the city and suburbs. The website has route and timetable information in English. One-way tickets cost €1.50.

CAR & MOTORCYCLE

Most of the big international companies have offices in Strovolos, outside of the centre. Beware that some companies charge a drop-off fee if you rent a car in Nicosia and leave it in another city.

A Petsas & Sons (☑2246 2650; www.petsas.com.cy; Leoforos Kostaki Pentelidi 24; 6 days per day from €47; ☺8am-4pm Mon-Fri) Local company located near Plateia Solomos. Short-term day rates (one or two days) are much higher than weekly rates.

Hertz (☑2220 8888; www.hertz.com.cy; 16 Aikaterinis Kornaro, off Leoforos Athalassis; per day from €34.50; ☺8.30am-5pm Mon-Fri)

Sixt Car Rental (☑2531 2345; www.sixt.global/car-rental/cyprus; Chrysanthou Mylona 1, Strovolos; per day from €24; ☺8am-1pm & 3-6pm Mon-Fri, 8am-1pm Sat & Sun)

TAXI

There are **taxi stands** (☑2266 3358; Plateia Eleftherias) by the walls of the Old City, including a convenient **taxi stand** (☑2266 0880; Plateia Solomos) right beside the bus station on Plateia Solomos.

In the New City, **Elpis Taxi** (☑2276 4966; Leoforos Archiepiskopou Makariou III 63c) is a decent choice.

NICOSIA (LEFKOSIA) GETTING AROUND

THE MESAORIA PLAIN

The plain of the Mesaoria (meaning 'Between Two Mountains') is a sprawling, parched landscape during the summer months, when the land is totally exposed to the relentless sun. But come spring, it erupts into a green, fertile plain, with the patchwork quilt of cereal fields peppered with rainbow-shots of wildflowers.

This area of slow-paced villages and just a handful of historic sites is prime road-trip territory. Doodling through the region, which is squeezed between the Kyrenia Range to the north and the Troödos Mountains to the west and southwest, allows you to capture a glimpse of the agricultural heartbeat of the island.

⊙ Sights

Agios Mamas Church   CHURCH
The somewhat forgotten site of the 16th-century Gothic church of Agios Mamas is like an exercise in nonstarters: it was never finished in the first place, and today the roofless walls and arches built in retrograde Lusignan style have a heady sense of nostalgia about them. The isolated ruins are in the deserted village of Agios Sozomenos, a once-thriving village that was abandoned due to intercommunal conflict in 1964. Now, the slumping remains of the mudbrick houses are a poignant reminder of a lost era.

The church and village can be reached from Nicosia on the A1, taking exit 6 (for Potamia) and going on to a minor, paved road about 2km before Potamia, following the sign for Agios Sozomenos.

Ancient Tamassos   HISTORIC SITE
(Politiko; €2.50; ⊙9.30am-5pm Mon-Fri Jun-Sep, 8.30am-4pm Mon-Fri Oct-May) Tamassos' main

DRESS CODE FOR MOSQUES & MONASTERIES

If planning to visit a mosque or monastery on the island, be aware that modest dress is obligatory. Neither men nor women should wear shorts or short-sleeved shirts and women, in particular, should cover up as much as possible. The good news is that, increasingly, mosques and monasteries are supplying expansive capes, or similar, for visitors to borrow free of charge – a brilliant solution if it's a hot day.

claim to fame was its once seemingly endless supply of copper – the mineral from which the name of Cyprus (Kypros in Greek; Kıbrıs in Turkish) is derived. A copper-producing settlement here dates from at least the 7th century BC, and production ran well into the Hellenistic period. Excavations of the remains of the citadel began in 1889 and, around this time, two tombs dating back to the 6th century BC were discovered, which today comprise the site's major attraction.

Ancient Greek poet Homer apparently mentioned Ancient Tamassos in *The Odyssey,* where it is referred to as Temese. The goddess Athena says to Odysseus' son, Telemachus: 'We are bound for the foreign port of Temese with a cargo of gleaming iron, which we intend to trade for copper.' The site of this otherwise obscure and little-known city-kingdom is on a small hillside about 17km southwest of Nicosia next to the village of Politiko.

It is thought that the tombs probably contained the remains of the citadel's kings. Looters have long since spirited away the rich burial treasures that may once have been buried here. You can even see a hole in the roof of the larger tomb showing where grave robbers broke in. The walls are unusually carved in such a way as to imitate wood – a feature that some archaeologists have linked to a possible Anatolian influence at the time of the citadel's zenith. Some theorists suggest that Tamassos was even part of the Hittite empire.

Among the discoveries unearthed by archaeologists on the larger site are three limestone lions and two sphinxes, which are on display at Nicosia's Cyprus Museum (p155) and a magnificent bronze head of Apollo, now in London's British Museum.

Monastery of Agios Irakleidios   MONASTERY
(⊙8.30am-noon & 2.30-5pm Mon-Fri, 8am-5pm Sat & Sun) A visit to this historic monastery – a nun's convent since the 1960s – is easily combined with an excursion to the nearby archaeological site of Ancient Tamassos (p168). The original church was built in the 5th century AD, but the current monastic buildings date from the late 18th century. The church today boasts the usual panoply of frescos and icons. On a table to the eastern side of the church you can spot a jewelled reliquary containing the skull of St Irakleidios.

St Irakleidios was born in Tamassos and guided St Paul and St Barnabas around

Mesaoria Villages

VILLAGES OF THE MESAORIA

One of the more popular villages in the area is Pera (population 1020), situated a couple of kilometres from Ancient Tamassos (p168). While there are no specific sights here, Pera is nonetheless pretty. Head for the signposted Arghaggelou Michail church, where you can park and wander around the surrounding cobbled backstreets. Photographers will find some particularly evocative scenes: old houses covered in bougainvillea, ancient stone jars, pretty doors, and cats atop walls. Visitors stop for refreshments at the *kafeneio* (coffee shop), where the locals, and often the village priest, enjoy coffee and gossip in a world where time means little.

The villages of Orounda (population 660) and Peristerona (population 2100), west of Nicosia, have interesting and photogenic churches. The village of Lythrodontas (population 2620), 25km south of Nicosia, has a lovely large central square with a couple of atmospheric traditional cafes.

The postcard-pretty village of Fikardou (population 16) is close by the sprawling Maheras Monastery (p170); visits to both are easily combined. Fikardou is the 'official' village in a clutch of well-preserved villages in the eastern Troödos Mountains. Its Otto-man-period houses with wooden balconies are gradually being restored and are a visual relief after the cement structures of many modern Troödos Mountain villages. That said, there's not a lot to Fikardou, and only a handful of people live here permanently. The main street is no more than a few hundred metres long, dominated by the Church of Apostles St Peter and Paul. Most visitors passing through are content to simply meander the alleys, soaking up the traditional atmosphere of the village.

Cyprus. He was later made one of the first bishops in Cyprus by Barnabas. The bishop has been subsequently credited with the performance of a number of miracles, including exorcisms.

Maheras Monastery MONASTERY
(⊙8am-6pm) It's a fair hike out to this sprawling monastery perched in the foothills of the eastern spur of the Troödos Mountains and under the all-seeing radar installation on Mt Kionia (1423m) to the south. The Maheras Monastery was founded in 1148 by a hermit named Neophytos, who found an icon (supposedly painted by St Luke) guarded by a sword (*maheras* means 'knife' or 'sword' in Greek) in a cave near the site of the present monastery.

The monastery developed around the icon and flourished over time, but due to a fire in 1892 nothing remains of the original structures. The current building dates from around 1900. The monastery has become a popular outing for Cypriots, who possibly come as much for the cooler climate as for spiritual enlightenment. There is a small cafeteria in the grounds and pilgrims may stay overnight.

Visits should be conducted with reverence and solemnity. Maheras Monastery is best approached via Klirou and Fikardou, since the alternate route via Pera and the E902, while very pretty, is winding and very slow.

Eating

Katoï CYPRIOT €€
(☑2285 2576; Avgousti Ieremia 13, Agia Marina Xyliatou; mains from €8; ⊙noon-3pm & 7pm-midnight Tue-Sat, noon-midnight Sun) Katoï is advertised widely around Agia Marina and overlooks the village itself. The restaurant's lights are visible from some distance away at night, and it commands a great view over the Troödos foothills and the Mesaoria. It serves solid Cypriot staples, with a penchant for game dishes, and a decent selection of meze.

To Koultouriariko CYPRIOT €€€
(☑9962 5695; Grigori Afxentiou 40, Gouri village; meze per person €18; ⊙noon-midnight) We can think of no better place we'd like to stop for lunch while exploring the Mesaoria than this local meze tavern. From snails and fried zucchini flowers to comforting *pastitsio* (the Greek version of lasagne), the meze feast is a tour through Cyprus' rustic flavours. The fried potatoes alone are worth the drive from Nicosia.

❶ Getting There & Around

To fully explore, you'll need to hire a car. Public buses, run by Nicosia's Osel Buses connect many of the Mesaoria villages, but be aware that timetables are scheduled to service workers and school children and so are often limited in their scope.

Cycling in the area is easy as most gradients are gentle, but bear in mind the weather gets very hot in summer and traffic on the main highways can be heavy and dangerous.

North Nicosia (Lefkoşa)

POP 61,400

Best Places to Eat

➡ Saraba (p177)

➡ Rüstem Kitabevi (p177)

➡ El Sabor (p179)

➡ Sham Food (p177)

➡ Asmaalti Bereket Fırını (p177)

Best Historic Sights

➡ Selimiye Mosque (p173)

➡ Büyük Han (p173)

➡ Arabahmet Quarter (p175)

➡ Mevlevi Tekke Museum (p174)

➡ Haydarpaşa Mosque (p174)

Why Go?

Strolling the back streets of the Old City in North Nicosia (Lefkoşa in Turkish) feels like dropping into an earlier era. Its wiggling alleys are home to half-derelict town houses, washing lines strung between window shutters with peeling paint, and the occasional strutting rooster.

The scent of yesteryear is further evoked towards the centre, which is watched over by the Gothic pile of the Selimiye Mosque and the Ottoman bulk of the Büyük Han. The main thoroughfare to the sights, Arasta Sokak, is a brushed-up modern-day bazaar catering to day-trippers, with its glut of stalls selling tacky trinkets. Skate your way through the crowds, though, and you'll find pockets of contemporary cafe-cool breaking out, slowly awakening the Old City from its slumber.

Sit down with a latte as the call to prayer echoes and soak up the merging of old and new that permeates this side of the walled city.

When to Go

➡ North Nicosia can be uncomfortably hot and dusty in July and August, which is also when many locals escape to the coast.

➡ Take note of when Ramadan (Ramazan in Turkish) falls. Although the Muslim month of fasting is not strictly observed here, more-religious people and some older people will fast during daylight hours.

➡ Eid el-Fitr (Şeker Bayram; the end of Ramadan holiday) can be up to a four-day public holiday depending on which day of the week it begins; ATMs generally run out of cash by the end of it.

➡ December and January see the most rainfall and night-time temperatures regularly plummet to 7°C. You will need to pack warm clothing.

North Nicosia (Lefkoşa) Highlights

1 Selimiye Mosque (p173) Craning your neck to take in the soaring Gothic arches within this stunning cathedral-turned-mosque.

2 Arabahmet Quarter (p175) Falling into a time-warp amid this quiet neighbourhood's lanes, fringed by preserved Ottoman-era town-house architecture.

3 Büyük Han (p173) Reliving the long-gone days of travelling merchants within this grand old caravanserai.

4 Armenian Church & Nunnery (p174) Viewing the stately and austere church interior, one of the city's finest restoration jobs of recent years.

5 Cafe culture (p180) Joining the locals and watching the world go by from a pavement seat at one of a clutch of funky new cafes.

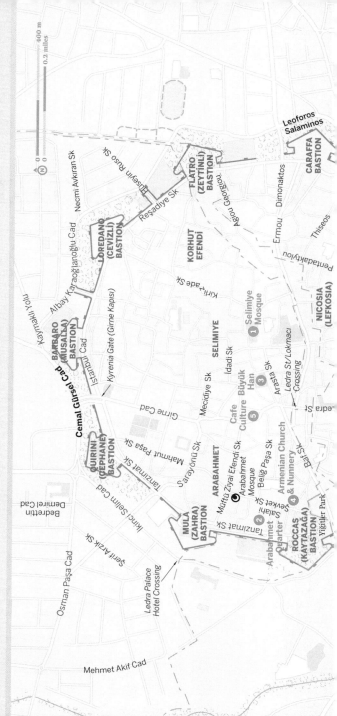

400 m
0.2 miles

Leoforos Salaminos

CARAFFA BASTION

FLATRO (ZEYTİNLİ) BASTION

Necmi Avkıran Sk

Reşadiye Sk

Hüseyin Ruso Sk

LOREDANO (CEVİZLİ) BASTION

Albay Karaoğlanoğlu Cad

Kaykaklı Yolu

KORHUT EFENDİ

Agiou Georgiou

Ermou

Dimonaktos

Thiseos

Pentadaktylou

Kirlizade Sk

BARBARO (MUSALLA) BASTION

Istanbul Cad

Kyrenia Gate (Girne Kapısı)

SELİMİYE

Selimiye Mosque **1**

İdadi Sk

NICOSIA (LEFKOŞIA)

Cemal Gürsel Cad

Mecidiye Sk

Girne Cad

Cafe Culture **5**

Büyük Han **3**

Arasta Sk

Ledra St/Lokmacı Crossing

Ledra St

QUIRINI (CEPHANE) BASTION

Mahmut Paşa Sk

Sarayönü Sk

Tanzimat Sk

Bedrettin Demirel Cad

MULA (ZAHRA) BASTION

İkinci Selim Cad

Müftü Ziyai Efendi Sk

Arabahmet Mosque

ARABAHMET

Beliğ Paşa Sk

Salahi Şevket Sk

Tanzimat Sk

Armenian Church & Nunnery **4**

Baf Sk

ROCCAS (KAYTAZAĞA) BASTION

Yiğitler Park

Arabahmet Quarter

Şerif Arzık Sk

Osman Paşa Cad

Ledra Palace Hotel Crossing

Mehmet Akif Cad

History

Until 1963 North Nicosia (Lefkoşa), not surprisingly, shared much of the same history as its dismembered southern sector, Nicosia (Lefkosia). In this year, however, the capital was effectively divided into Greek and Turkish sectors, when violence against Turkish Cypriots by insurgents from the Ethniki Organosi tou Kypriakou Agona (EOKA; National Organisation for the Cypriot Struggle) forced them to retreat into safe enclaves or ghettos. The UN Buffer Zone, or Green Line as it has become known, was established when a British military commander divided up the city on a map with a green pen. The name has remained ever since.

The Turkish military invasion of 1974, which most Turkish Cypriots saw as a rescue operation, formalised the division between the two halves of the city. A wary truce was brokered by the blue-bereted members of the UN peacekeeping forces, who had been guarding the Green Line since sectarian troubles broke out in 1963.

It is now easy for Turkish Cypriots and most visiting tourists (p182) to cross into the South but, despite this, the city remains both physically and symbolically divided, and many of the older generation (both Greek and Turkish Cypriots) continue to bear grudges and refuse to cross the divide.

◉ Sights

North Nicosia's main sights are all within the Venetian walled Old City and easily explored on foot. There is good signposting of sights through most of the Old City to help aid navigation within the alleyways.

★ Selimiye Mosque   MOSQUE

(St Sophia Cathedral; Kuyumcular Sokak; ⊘ closed to non-Muslims during prayers) **FREE** North Nicosia's most prominent landmark (also clearly visible from the southern half of the city), the Selimiye Mosque is a beautiful mongrel of a building. A cross between a French Gothic church and a mosque, its fascinating history stretches back to the 13th century. Although it's a working place of worship, non-Muslims may visit, except during prayer time. For the most atmosphere, time your visit either just before or after one of the five daily prayer sessions.

Work started on the church in 1209 and progressed slowly. Louis IX of France, on his way to the Crusades, stopped by in 1248 and gave the building process a much-needed shot in the arm by offering the services of his retinue of artisans and builders. The church took another 78 years to complete, however, and was finally consecrated in 1326 as the Church of Agia Sofia.

Until 1570 the church suffered depredation at the hands of the Genoese and the Mamelukes, and severe shakings from two earthquakes in 1491 and 1547. When the Ottomans arrived in 1571, they stripped the building of its Christian contents and added two minarets, between which the Turkish Cypriot and Turkish flags now flutter. The Gothic structure of the interior is still apparent despite Islamic overlays, such as the whitewashed walls and columns, and the reorientation of the layout to align it with Mecca. Note the ornate west front with its three decorated doorways, each in a different style. Also look out for four marble columns relocated from Ancient Salamis and now placed in the apse off the main aisles.

Bedestan   CHURCH

(St Nicholas Church; Kuyumcular Sokak; ⊘ 10am-5pm Mon-Sat) Renovated as part of the Nicosia Master Plan (p161), the imposing Bedestan dates from the 6th century, when it was built as a small Byzantine chapel. It was grandly embellished in the 14th century and reborn as St Nicholas Church.

Today it's used primarily as the venue for whirling dervish performances (p180). Unfortunately, this means the beauty of the building's swooping Gothic arches is somewhat curtailed by rows of garish orange plastic chairs and other additions. The Bedstan is only open to ticket-holders during performances.

★ Büyük Han   HISTORIC BUILDING

(Great Inn; Asmaaltı Sokak; ⊘ 8am-7pm) **FREE** The Büyük Han is Cyprus' best-preserved example of Ottoman caravanserai architecture. Built in 1572 by the first Ottoman governor of Cyprus, Lala Mustafa Pasha, it was renovated in the early 1990s, and has once again become the hub of North Nicosia's Old City bustle. The courtyard is home to a couple of cafes, including the ever-popular Sedirhan, and traditional craft workshops are housed in the small cells leading off the 1st-floor balcony that originally served as the inn's sleeping areas.

During the Ottoman period, *hans* (inns) like this one were used as hotels for travellers and traders. The ground-floor rooms rimming the courtyard functioned as stables for horses, storage areas and shops where traders could carry out their business.

The central courtyard has a *mescit* (Islamic prayer room) in the centre, which is balanced on six pillars over a *şadırvan* (ablutions fountain). This design is rare; it's found only in this *han* and two others in Turkey.

Kumarcılar Han   HISTORIC BUILDING
(Asmaaltı Sokak; ⊘8am-7pm) This caravanserai is a smaller version of the neighbouring Büyük Han and was built in the early 18th century. Today its courtyard hosts cafes, and the surrounding cells where merchant goods were once stored are home to local craft shops.

Bandabulya   MARKET
(Municipal Market; Kuyumcular Sokak; ⊘6am-3pm Mon-Sat) Dating back to the early 20th century, this covered market has a mix of produce stalls piled high with fruit and vegetables for local shoppers, craft shops aimed squarely at visitors, and a couple of cafes.

★**Haydarpaşa Mosque**   MOSQUE
(Church of St Catherine; Haydarpaşa Sokak; ⊘9am-1pm & 2.30-5pm Mon-Fri, 9am-1pm Sat) FREE The second-most important Gothic structure in North Nicosia after the Selimiye Mosque, this building began life as the 14th-century Church of St Catherine. Annoyingly, despite the mosque being open officially, in practice it rarely is. Even if it's shut when you stroll by, take the time to admire its chunky facade, and also the ornate carving at the top of the entrance gates, which sprout dragon

and rose motifs. The southern and western entrances have the Lusignan coat of arms.

Eaved House   HISTORIC BUILDING
(Kütüphane Sokak; ⊘8am-3.30pm Mon-Wed & Fri, 8am-1pm & 2-6pm Thu) FREE Unique for its wide eaves, this house is a combination of Lusignan and Ottoman architecture and now functions as an art and culture centre hosting occasional exhibitions. The main reason to visit is for the view of the Selimiye Mosque from the upper balcony.

Lapidary Museum   MUSEUM
(Taş Eserler Müzesi; Züfdüzade Sokak; adult/student 7/5TL; ⊘8am-3.30pm Mon-Wed & Fri, 8am-1pm & 2-6pm Thu) Housed in a lovely 15th-century building, exhibits of the medieval-era stonework here include a varied collection of column capitals, stelae, and a Gothic window rescued from a Lusignan palace that once stood near Atatürk Meydanı.

★**Armenian Church & Nunnery**   CHURCH
(Sourp Asdvadzadzin; Şehit Mehmet Hüseyin Sokak; ⊘8am-3.30pm Mon-Wed & Fri, 8am-1pm & 2-6pm Thu) This church and nunnery is first thought to have been established in the 13th century as the Abbey of Our Lady of Tyre, and was handed over to the island's Armenian community in the 15th century, when it became a principle place of worship. With the displacement of the city's Armenian community after the Green Line divided the city in 1963, the building fell into disrepair, but an eight-year project has restored the golden-stoned church to its former glory.

Dervish Pasha Mansion   MUSEUM
(Derviş Paşa Konağı; Beliğ Paşa Sokak; adult/student 7/5TL; ⊘8am-3.30pm Mon-Wed & Fri, 8am-1pm & 2-6pm Thu) This small ethnographic museum is housed in a 19th-century mansion. Built in 1807, it belonged to wealthy a Turkish Cypriot, Derviş Paşa, who published Cyprus' first Turkish-language newspaper. The house became an ethnographic museum in 1988. Household goods, including an old loom, glassware and ceramics, are displayed in former servants' quarters on the ground floor, while upstairs is a rich display of embroidered Turkish costumes.

The building was being restored on our last visit and was closed to visitors; we were assured that it would be opening again soon.

★**Mevlevi Tekke Museum**   MUSEUM
(Mevlevi Müzesi; Girne Caddesi; adult/student 7/5TL; ⊘8am-3.30pm Mon-Wed & Fri, 8am-1pm &

DON'T MISS

ARABAHMET QUARTER

The Arabahmet Quarter rubbing up against the Green Line is home to well-preserved examples of Ottoman-era town-house architecture. The narrow alleyways are rimmed by tall whitewashed houses – some recently restored, others sinking into genteel dilapidation – with painted shutters and upper-storey overhanging *cumbas* (bay windows). Note the skinny balconies (not a common feature in Ottoman architecture) and carved crosses across front-door lintels on some houses; Arabahmet was the Armenian quarter of Nicosia (Lefkosia) until 1963 when the Green Line was drawn through the city.

The entire area is imbued with a heady sense of yesteryear and is one of North Nicosia's most interesting neighbourhoods to stroll through.

2-6pm Thu) This 17th-century former *tekke* (dervish house) was once Cyprus' central meeting place for the island's followers of the Mevlevi Order. Made famous by the whirling dervishes, the Mevlevis are a Sufi (the mystical branch of Islam) sect that began in Konya (Turkey) during the 13th century under the spiritual leadership of mystic, poet and theologian Mevlana Rumi. Inside, the rooms contain exhibits on dervish life as well as the tombs of the island's 16 sheiks of the Mevlevi Order.

Today, only the *semahane* (room where the dervishes performed their whirling prayer ritual), the kitchen and the tomb room survive of what was once a much larger structure. The adjoining courtyard is home to a collection of Muslim tombstones.

Samanbahçe Quarter AREA
(Girne Caddesi) This neighbourhood of whitewashed terraced cottages, tucked off Girne Caddesi, was Cyprus' first social housing project. Built in the early 20th century, the 70 houses were all constructed using local materials and with careful consideration given to the island's climatic conditions, resulting in traditional mudbrick walls and *hasır* (thatched reed) ceilings. Today, with the narrow alleyways festooned with pots of geraniums, gerberas and creeping vines, it's a rather charming place for a peaceful stroll.

Ethnographic Museum of Cyprus MUSEUM
(☑0392 227 1785; Şehit Ecvet Yusuf Caddesi 56; adult/student €5/3; ☺9am-5pm Tue-Sun) This eclectic museum in the New City is the work of Ergün Pektaş, who scoured Northern Cyprus to salvage and preserve local craftwork, day-to-day objects, woodwork and furniture. The result is a cornucopia of Cypriot popular arts and design dating back more than 150 years. The collection spreads over three vast galleried floors, and ranges from agricultural implements and traditional costumes to beautiful wood beams with carved capitals that were once typical of village house architecture on the Karpas Peninsula.

Museum of Barbarism MUSEUM
(Barbarlık Müzesi; Irhan Sokak 2; ☺8am-3.30pm Fri-Wed, 8am-1pm & 2-5pm Thu) **FREE** Set in the house where the family of Dr Nihat İlhan was murdered during 1963's intercommunal attacks, this museum is a gruesome reminder of the brutal and violent years following the island's independence. As well as harrowing exhibits about the family's murder, there are similarly confronting photo displays of Turkish Cypriots murdered in the villages of Agios Sozomenos and Agios Vasilios.

The Museum of Barbarism is quite a hike from the Old City, around 3km straight up Mehmet Akif Caddesi in the New City.

🏃 Activities

Büyük Hamam HAMMAM
(Grand Turkish Bath; Irfan Bey Sokak 9; treatments 60-100TL; ☺men only 9am-3pm Wed & Sat, 9am-4pm Sun, women only 9am-3pm Tue, mixed & touristic services 3.30-9pm Tue, Wed, Thu & Fri, 4.30-9pm Sat & Sun) Originally part of the 14th-century Church of St George of the Latins, the Büyük Hamam is entered via a low, ornate door, sunk 2m below street level, and today provides a typical Turkish bathhouse soak-and-scrub experience. For the full deal, including a scrub-down with traditional black soap and a pounding massage, come in the hours reserved for 'touristic services'.

Inside is a nail that marks the height reached by the waters of the Pedieos River (Kanlı Dere), which drowned about 3000 Lefkosians in 1330.

🍴 Eating

Due to the hordes of day-trip group tours that cross over from the South, the Old City

North Nicosia (Lefkoşa)

200 m
0.1 miles

CARAFFA BASTION

FLATRO (ZEYTİNLİ) BASTION

Leoforos Athinas

KORHUT EFENDİ

OREDANO (CEVIZLİ) BASTION

BARBARO (MUSALLA) BASTION

SELİMİYE

NORTH NICOSIA (LEFKOŞA)

NICOSIA (LEFKOŞA)

Selimiye Mosque

North Cyprus Tourism Organisation

QUIRINI (CEPHANE) BASTION

Kyrenia Gate (Girne Kapısı)

Cemal Gürsel Cad

Atatürk Meydanı

MULA (ZAHRA) BASTION

ARABAHMET

Arabahmet Quarter

ROCCAS (KAYTAZAĞA) BASTION

Yiğitler Park

Ledra Palace Hotel Crossing

Muzaffer Ersu Sk

Leoforos Markou Drakou

Ledra St/
Lokmacı Crossing

North Cyprus Tourism Organisation

Ledra St

Girne Cad

İrfan Bey Sk

Kurtbaba Sk

Büyük Han

Yeşil Gazino Sk

Liperti

Artemidos

Patoiu

Pentadaktylou

Thiseos

Ermou

Dimonaktos

Patroklou

Agiou Georgiou

Minoos

Haydarpaşa Sk

Zülfüzade Sk

Uray Sk

Kuyumcular Sk

Selimiye Sk

Arasta Sk

İdadi Sk

Asmaaltı Sk

Cumhuriyet Sk

Med!iye Sk

Tabak Hilmi Sk

Abdi Çavuş Sk

Celaliye Sk

Eski Saray Sk

Yeni Cami Sk

Kirlizade Sk

Karababa Sk

Atilla Sk

Marmara Sk

Reşadiye Sk

Saraçoğlu Meydanı

Albay Karaoğlanoğlu Cad

İstanbul Cad

Nato Taxi

Özner

North Nicosia Minibuses

İkinci Selim Cad

Şehit Arzık Sk

Server Sk

Somunoğlu Sk

Osman Paşa Cad

Müftü Ziyai Efendi Sk

Salahi Şevket Sk

Tanzimat Sk

Zahra Sk

Sarayönü Sk

Mahmut Paşa Sk

Posta Sk

Ankara Sk

Koroylu Sk

Beliğ Paşa Sk

Bat Sk

Service Taxis to Kyrenia (Girne)

Necmi Avkıran Sk

İzmir Sk

Defne Sk

Yenice Sk

Yüksel Sk

Satak Sk

Hüseyin Ruso Sk

Reşadiye Sk

İtimat Bus Station (180m);
City Royal (600m); Bus Station;
Kıbhas Airport Shuttle (800m)

Minibuses to Kyrenia (Girne)

Ethnographic Museum of Cyprus (700m)

Street Corner Pub (80m);
Cafe Biyer;
Californian Gold (450m);
Avenue Cinemax (900m);
Museum of Barbarism (1km)

North Nicosia (Lefkoşa)

buzzes at lunchtime. Post sunset, eating options are fewer on the ground.

✖ Old City

Nearly all restaurants in North Nicosia's Old City accept euros as well as Turkish lira.

★**Sham Food**　　　　　　MIDDLE EASTERN €
(Arasta Sokak; shawarma 16-18TL; ⊘11am-10pm)
There are plenty of *shawarma* (meat sliced from a rotating spit) sandwich joints on the island, but this may just be the best one. Have the mixed (chicken and lamb) with all the fillings and we think you'll agree.

★**Asmaaltı Bereket Fırını**　　　TURKISH €
(Asmaaltı Sokak; lahmacun/pide 5/18TL; ⊘8am-3pm Mon-Sat) This rough-and-ready kiosk, run by İlker, is the place to go for pide and *lahmacun* (thin-based pizza topped with minced lamb and parsley) served up from the stone oven. Pull up a plastic seat streetside or munch on the go.

★**Saraba**　　　　　　　　　CYPRIOT €€
(☑0392 228 9345; Selimiye Meydanı 35; mains 22TL, meze dishes 4-10TL; ⊘11am-3pm; ☑)
The kind of hearty village food that's kept farmers tilling fields for centuries is served at this modest restaurant half-

hidden at the side of the Selimiye Mosque. Mains such as *molohiya* (a viscid meat and jute-leaves stew) and *karnıyarık* (stuffed aubergines) keep the courtyard tables buzzing with lunching locals. Don't forget to order the hummus, which has a distinct lemony kick.

★**Rüstem Kitabevi**　　　　CYPRIOT €€
(Girne Caddesi 22; mains 25TL; ⊘11am-2pm Mon-Sat) Traditional Cypriot home cooking is served in the upstairs salon of North Nicosia's most famous bookshop, with a daily changing menu of simple classic dishes such as stuffed vine leaves and *köfte* (grilled meatballs).

Old Mosaic Bar & Restaurant　　TURKISH €€
(☑0392 227 9551; Selimiye Meydanı 4-5; mains 18-26TL; ⊘10am-late; ☑) Old-school tunes pump out the front, but if you head through the ramshackle house you can dine in a courtyard amid tumbling bougainvillea to a soundtrack of chirping canaries. The best choices are the meze dishes, so order hummus, *patlıcan salata* (eggplant in garlic), *pastırma* (spicy sausage) and *barbunya* (barlotti beans in olive oil) for a tasty lunch.

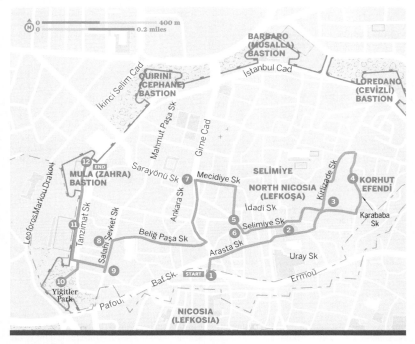

🏃 Walking Tour
Stepping Back in Time

START LEDRA ST/LOKMACI CROSSING
END MULA BASTION
LENGTH 4KM; TWO HOURS

Begin at the ❶ **Ledra St/Lokmacı crossing** (p174) and work your way up Arasta Sokak to the splendid ❷ **Selimiye Mosque** (p173). Leave your shoes at the door and don a headscarf (if female) to view the interior, where soaring Gothic splendour meets the meditative minimalism of Islam.

Head behind the Selimiye Mosque and up to the ❸ **Haydarpaşa Mosque** (p174) and its ornate facade. Turning east from here brings you onto the alleyways that abut the UN Buffer Zone. ❹ **Karababa Sokak**, and the narrow lanes leading off it, are rimmed with town houses teetering into decay right beside the Buffer Zone's makeshift walls.

Loop back southwest via Kirlizade Sokak and Selimiye Sokak to admire the bulky Ottoman finery of the ❺ **Kumarcılar Han** (p174) and ❻ **Büyük Han** (p173). Afterwards, head to ❼ **Atatürk Meydanı**, which is centred

around a column that once stood in Ancient Salamis.

From here, stroll south to reach the ❽ **Arabahmet Quarter** (p175). The main street, Salahi Şevket Sokak, ends abruptly with a fence marking the Buffer Zone. The ❾ **Armenian Church** (p174) here has been recently restored and is well worth a visit.

Zigzag through the lanes, then surface on Zahra Sokak and enter scruffy Yiğitler Park sitting atop the ❿ **Roccas Bastion**. From the top of the bastion you to can peer down onto the avenue of Markou Drakou in Nicosia (Lefkosia) below. Up until 2004, this was the only point along the entire Green Line where Turkish and Greek Cypriots could see each other up close.

Afterwards, wander up ⓫ **Zahra Sokak** to the Mula Bastion, fringed by the vast moat on its west side and home to some of Arabahmet's most stunning town-house architecture. At the ⓬ **Mula Bastion** you can either turn east to head back into the Old City centre, or head out of the Old City to the Ledra Palace Hotel Crossing to enter Nicosia (Lefkosia).

Sedirhan　　　　　　　　TURKISH €€
(Büyük Han; mains 17-25TL; ⊙8am-7pm; 🛜🍴)
Enjoying prime position within the Büyük Han, Sedirhan is the lunchtime hub for day-tripping tour groups. Don't let that put you off, though. Despite the easy foot traffic, the kitchen turns out solid, typical Turkish and Cypriot dishes. The *sheftalia* (Cypriot sausage, *şeftalı kebap* in Turkish) is moist and well spiced and there are good, lighter meal options such as *mantı* (Turkish ravioli).

Boghjalian　　　　　　　TURKISH €€
(🖉0392 228 0700; Salahi Şevket Sokak; meze dishes 10TL; ⊙noon-3.30pm & 7-11pm Mon-Sat) Reservations are recommended to dine on the meze in this former mansion of a wealthy Armenian, where meals are served in a leafy courtyard or in a choice of two elegant dining rooms. During our last visit, the restaurant was closed for restoration, but we're assured it should be back open soon.

★**El Sabor**　　　　　INTERNATIONAL €€€
(🖉0392 228 8322; Selimiye Meydanı 29; mains 16-55TL; ⊙11am-midnight Mon-Sat; 🟦🛜🍴) Tired of kebabs? El Sabor mixes things up with generous dishes of pasta, Asian noodles and plenty of steaks. There's a kid's menu, a decent wine selection, and you can't beat eating outside with a view of the bulky Selimiye Mosque. The resident cat population adds entertainment and unbearable cuteness to the dining experience.

Bibliotheque　　　　INTERNATIONAL €€€
(Mihat Paşa Sokak 7; mains 25-50TL; ⊙11am-11pm; 🟦🛜🍴) Bibliotheque's huge, beautifully renovated interior (with a great bar area) and alleyway seating, shaded by colourful upturned umbrellas, make it a highly atmospheric lunch or dinner stop. The extensive menu leapfrogs from fajitas to noodles to kebabs; the food doesn't always hit the mark but the great location keeps this place popular.

✗ New City

The main restaurant street in the new part of town is Mehmet Akif Caddesi. It's home to a line of restaurants and cafe-bars that are nearly always packed with young locals munching on international-style dishes.

Califorian Gold　　　INTERNATIONAL €€
(🖉0392 444 7070; Mehmet Akif Caddesi 74; mains 17-36TL; ⊙8am-11.30pm; 🅿🛜) The sprawling

---

THE WHIRLING DERVISHES OF THE MEVLEVI ORDER

The founder of the Mevlevi Order was the poet Jelaluddin Mevlana, known in the West as Rumi, and born in the 13th century. Mevlana's most famous work is *Mathnawi*, a long poem that details his teachings and understanding of the world, and emphasises the belief that an individual's soul is separated from the divine during one's earthly life; only God's love has the power to draw it back to its source. Rumi's teachings were also based on the belief that everything was created by God, so every creature was to be loved and respected. The order paid special attention to patience, modesty, unlimited tolerance, charity and positive reasoning.

But most importantly, and shockingly to orthodox Muslims at that time, Rumi claimed that music was the way to transcend the mundane worries of life, and that one could connect with the divine through dancing or, indeed, whirling.

The slow, whirling, trancelike dance of the dervishes is called *sema,* and it is accompanied by the sound of the *ney* (reed flute), an instrument central to Rumi's idea of yearning for the divine. The sound of the *ney,* whose tonal range is equal to that of a human voice, is supposed to symbolise the soul's cry for God. The *oud* (Levantine lute) and *kudum* (paired drums) are the other instruments that accompany *sema.* During their dance, the dervishes hold one palm upwards and the other downwards to symbolise humanity's position as a bridge between heaven and earth. The *sema* was originally performed exclusively as a spiritual exercise, and it was considered blasphemy to perform for money or show.

The Mevlevi Order flourished for 700 years in Turkish life and spread from Konya in Turkey to the Balkans and southeastern Europe, until they were banned in Turkey by Atatürk in 1925. Today the dervishes perform in theatres all over the world, and it's possible to see their beautiful dance in most Western countries.

ⓘ DAYLIGHT SAVING IN NORTH CYPRUS

In 2016 Turkey decided to scrap daylight savings time. Northern Cyprus followed suit. This means that from late October to March Northern Cyprus is one hour ahead of the Republic, and North Nicosia (Lefkoşa) one hour ahead of Nicosia (Lefkosia).

terrace here is nearly always packed with a youthful, well-heeled crowd tucking into dishes from fajitas to Asian noodles to Turkish kebab plates. It's a big ask for one kitchen to be able to prepare so many different cuisines, and it shows. Nevertheless, the sandwiches make a nice change from kebabs for lunch.

Note that, amusingly, the name is intentionally spelt this way to avoid any potential copyright infringements from the US sunshine state.

🍷 Drinking & Nightlife

Cafe culture is currently stoking a revival of the Old City, with a handful of cafe-bars at the forefront of creating a new nightlife scene within North Nicosia's Venetian walls. In saying that, North Nicosia can in no way compete with the buzzing cafe and bar scene of Nicosia. If you're looking for more vigour and choice, head over the Green Line into the South.

Cafe No:3 CAFE

(Girne Caddesi 3; ⊘8am-midnight) A serious statement of the revival of North Nicosia's Old City, Cafe No:3 is a contemporary, light-filled space of sleek Scandi styling that attracts everyone from groups of hip 20-somethings to suited businesspeople. It rustles up some of the best lattes in town and is a relaxed venue for a few beers during the evening.

Hoi Polloi BAR

(off Arasta Sokak; ⊘11am-3am; 🛜) This bar-cafe packs a whole load of personality into a very tiny space. By day it's a chilled-out cafe, with tables claiming the alleyway at the back of the Büyük Han. By night it's a hip but welcoming hang-out, which often hosts live music and jam sessions, and attracts an arty, slightly boho crowd.

Tezgah Cafe CAFE

(Asmaaltı Sokak; ⊘9am-11pm) This quirky little cafe does a whole swag of different teas and coffees, including – we never thought we'd see the day – flat whites. There's a cheerful budgie chirping away by the door, and some pretty tempting-looking cakes. It's directly opposite the Kumarcılar Han.

Luna Cafe CAFE

(Uray Sokak; ⊘11am-11pm) This arty, alternative hang-out, with comfy couches inside and Antoine de Saint-Exupéry quotes on the courtyard walls out the back, is a cosy, casual place for a quiet drink.

Özerlat CAFE

(Arasta Sokak 73; ⊘8.30am-7pm Mon-Sat) This cafe and shop has been around since 1935 and is famous for its own brand of coffee, which is even exported to the US. Unsurprisingly, the coffee here is excellent, and the friendly owner makes her own delicious cakes each day.

Cafe Biyer BAR

(Mehmet Akif Caddesi 61; ⊘11am-midnight; 🛜) A cosmopolitan-style bar with live music Fridays and Saturdays, and an impressive range of 14 speciality cocktails and eight brands of tequila. Bar snacks, including cheese platters and wraps, are available, or you can head to the swankier Biyer restaurant next door.

Street Corner Pub BAR

(Osman Paşa Caddesi; ⊘noon-2am) Look for the pink Cadillac poised precariously on the roof at this popular Irish pub. There's frothy ale on tap and live music on Wednesdays.

☆ Entertainment

There isn't a huge amount of entertainment choice in North Nicosia. Both Hoi Polloi and Cafe No:3 often host live music on weekend nights.

Avenue Cinemax CINEMA

(✆0392 444 2400; www.avenuecinemax.com; Mehmet Akif Caddesi; adult/student 17/14TL) Shows all the latest film offerings from Hollywood as well as Turkey. English-language films are generally shown in their original language with Turkish subtitles.

Whirling Dervish Performance LIVE PERFORMANCE

(✆0542 881 0303; www.danceofcyprus.com; Bedestan; €7; ⊘noon, 2pm, 3pm & 5pm Mon-Sat) Performances of the mesmerising whirling dervishes are held in the Bedestan (p173) from April to September. Performances last approximately 30 minutes.

🛍 Shopping

The Büyük Han (p173) is the best place to pick up some memorable souvenirs; arts and crafts stalls congregate on the upper balcony.

Hippo VINTAGE
(Uray Sokak; ⊙10am-6pm Mon-Sat) Lovers of kitsch and vintage would do well to have a rummage in this tiny shop; it has a vinyl collection, mid-20th-century ornaments and signage, and some serious geek paraphernalia.

Senay Erkut ARTS & CRAFTS
(Büyük Han, Asmaaltı Sokak; ⊙10am-7pm) Beautiful handmade ceramic jewellery with a floral theme, which make fabulous, inexpensive and unusual gifts.

Rüstem Kitabevi BOOKS
(☑0392 228 3506; Girne Caddesi 22; ⊙9am-5pm Mon-Sat) This historic bookshop, crammed to the rafters with books, has plenty of secondhand and some new titles (as well as many English-language reads). It also does lunches (p177) of traditional Cypriot home-cooking in the upstairs salon.

The ground floor also has a branch of Gloria Jean's Coffee and a shady outside patio.

Koza ARTS & CRAFTS
(Büyük Han, Asmaaltı Sokak; ⊙10am-7pm) Cyprus' heritage of producing silk from silkworms and the once-ubiquitous mulberry tree comes alive in this shop, where owner Munise and her elderly mother hand-weave the silk patterns. The patterns were traditionally used for picture frames, or simply as framed wall decorations themselves.

Shiffa Home FOOD, COSMETICS
(Büyük Han, Asmaaltı Sokak; ⊙10am-7pm) Shiffa's owner makes some of the funkiest handmade soaps we've ever seen, as well as jams, preserves and yummy marmalade. She also sells and advises on local herbal and aromatherapy remedies.

Yağcıoğlu ARTS & CRAFTS
(Yeşil Gazino Sokak 46; ⊙9am-7pm Mon, Tue, Thu & Fri, to 1pm Wed & Sat) Hidden away among the endless stalls of lycra leggings and similar is this shop that has been selling buttons since the 1950s. The choice is wonderfully diverse,

---

ⓘ BUYER BEWARE

A word of warning: if you're visiting from the South and decide to go on a shopping spree in the North, or vice versa, beware the Greek Cypriot customs regulations. You can't take more than 40 cigarettes and 1L of alcohol or wine, plus €100 worth of other goods through the North–South passport checkpoint. So don't go indulging in expensive carpets!

---

including translucent and delicate, big and brassy and enticingly retro. Local crafts are also sold.

ⓘ Information

EMERGENCY
The emergency number for the police in North Cyprus is ☑155.

Police station (☑0392 228 3311; Girne Caddesi; ⊙8.30am-5pm Mon-Fri)

INTERNET ACCESS
Most hotels, cafes and restaurants in North Nicosia have wi-fi. You can also get online at busy and cental **Orbit Internet Cafe** (Girne Caddesi 180; per hr 5TL; ⊙24hr).

MEDICAL SERVICES
Near East University Hospital (Yakın Doğu Üniversite Hastanesi; ☑0392 444 0535; www.neareasthospital.com; Yakın Doğu Bulvarı; ⊙polyclinics 8am-5pm Mon-Fri, emergency 24hr) Northern Cyprus' leading private hospital has a centre for international patients with English-speaking doctors. Translators are available for other languages. It's on the Near East University campus, north of the centre.

MONEY
You can change your money into Turkish lira (TL) at the exchange office just past the passport-control booth at the Ledra St crossing. Within the Old City, though, most shops, restaurants and cafes quote their prices in both euro and lira, and plenty of day trippers from the Republic find it unnecessary to change money.

There are ATMs along Girne Caddesi. Both **Ziraat Bankası** (Girne Caddesi; ⊙8.30am-12.30pm & 1.30-4.30pm Mon-Fri) and **Kıbrıs Vakıflar Bankası** (Sarayönü Sokak 22; ⊙9am-5pm Mon-Fri) have ATMs and change foreign currency.

POST
Post office (Sarayönü Caddesi; ⊙8am-12.30pm & 1.30-4.15pm Mon-Fri)

ℹ️ SAFETY IN NORTH NICOSIA

North Nicosia (Lefkoşa) is a safe city and you shouldn't feel concern about walking the streets. At night, though, some parts of the Old City can be uncomfortably quiet and visitors may feel intimidated walking alone along dimly lit and often-narrow streets.

Some areas abutting the UN Buffer Zone have large black-and-red signs that clearly forbid photography. It's best to heed these, as watchful soldiers, not obviously stationed, may confront you and confiscate your camera if caught taking a snap.

TOURIST INFORMATION

North Cyprus Tourism Organisation (NCTO; ☑ 0392 227 299; www.northcyprus.org; Kyrenia Gate, Girne Caddesi; ⊙ 8am-5pm) is packed full of brochures, has an excellent free town map and usually has clued-up English-speaking staff in attendance. This is the best tourist info office to go to.

There are other offices just after the **Lokmacı/ Ledra St passport checkpoint** (⊙ 9am-5pm) and inside the **Bandabulya** (Uray Sokak; ⊙ 9am-5pm Mon-Sat, to 2pm Sun).

ℹ️ ARRIVING BY AIR VIA THE REPUBLIC

Many travellers to Northern Cyprus use **Larnaka International Airport** (p130) which, due to the number of airlines flying direct from European destinations, generally has a better choice of flights at lower cost than Ercan Airport.

Non-EU citizens wanting to visit all of the island would be wise to fly into either Larnaka or Pafos rather than Ercan. The Republic of Cyprus regards Ercan – and the ferry ports of Kyrenia (Girne) and Famagusta (Gazimağusa) – as an illegal point of entry and reserves the right to refuse entry into the South to anyone who has arrived at these points. EU citizens are not affected by this. In practice, officials at the passport checkpoints rarely enforce it, but we hear of a couple of cases each year where travellers have been refused entry.

ℹ️ Getting There & Away

AIR

Ercan Airport (Ercan Havalimanı; ☑ 0392 600 5000; www.ercanhavalimani.com; Ercan Havalimanı Yolu) is 24km east of North Nicosia. The only direct flights to or from Ercan are to Turkey. All flights from other destinations transit through Turkey (even if there's no change of plane) before heading on to Ercan. Note that this means flights from Ercan to the UK are affected by the current ban on laptop and electronic devices, which must be stowed in checked baggage.

The airport has a couple of good cafes and a huge duty-free shop in the Departure hall, and ATMs and car-hire kiosks in the Arrivals hall.

The main airlines operating out of Ercan are Turkish Airlines and its subsidiary Anadolu Jet (www.turkishairlines.com), and Pegasus Airlines (www.flypgs.com).

BUS

Dolmuşes (minibuses) and buses to Famagusta (Gazimağusa; 11TL, one hour) and Kyrenia (Girne; 5TL, 25 minutes) leave every 15 minutes from the main **bus station** (Otobüs Terminalı; Cemal Gürsel Caddesi) in the New City. There are also *dolmuşes* to Morfou (Güzelyurt; 8TL, 45 minutes), and Lefke (Lefka) and Gemikonağı (Karavostasi; 11TL, one hour) from here every 30 minutes, as well as to a few other destinations.

Buses to Famagusta begin at the separate **İtimat bus station** (Kaymaklı Yolu) nearer to the Old City, before making a stop at the main bus station. Dolmuşes to Kyrenia all make a stop to pick up passengers at a bus stop just outside the Old City walls near Kyrenia Gate (Girne Kapısı).

CAR & MOTORCYCLE

Drivers and riders enter North Nicosia via one of two main roads leading directly to the Old City. From Famagusta or Ercan Airport you will enter North Nicosia via Mustafa Ahmet Ruso Caddesi, which turns into Cemal Gürsel Caddesi. This road leads directly to Kyrenia Gate. Arriving from Kyrenia, you will enter North Nicosia via Tekin Yurdabay Caddesi and eventually Bedrettin Demirel Caddesi, which also leads towards Kyrenia Gate.

If you are entering North Nicosia from the Republic of Cyprus, the car crossing point is at Agios Dometios, west of the city. The easiest way into the Old City is to turn off Osman Paşa Caddesi onto Memduh Asaf Sokak and follow that down to the moat. Turn left onto Tanzimat Sokak as soon as you cross the moat and you will reach Kyrenia Gate after about 200m.

Finding a place to park in the Old City can get tricky if you arrive late in the morning on a working day. If you arrive early, you can easily park on Girne Caddesi.

SERVICE TAXI

The quickest and most comfortable public transport to Kyrenia is by *kombos* (shared taxis). These leave from the *kombo* office just south of the Mevlevi Tekke Museum every 10 to 15 minutes (8TL, 20 minutes).

❶ Getting Around

TO/FROM THE AIRPORT

Kibhas airport shuttle (☎ 0392 228 8590; www.kibhas.org; Cemal Gürsel Caddesi; per person 13TL) has 12 services between Ercan and the bus station on Cemal Gürsel Caddesi daily (35 minutes).

A taxi from the airport to North Nicosia Old City costs around 70TL.

BUS

There are plentiful *dolmuşes* zipping between the Old City and the New City suburbs. These leave from just outside Kyrenia Gate.

CAR

Sun Rent a Car (☎ 0392 227 2303; www.sunrentacar.com; Abdi Ipekçi Caddesi 10; per day from £20; ☉ 8am-5pm Mon-Fri, to 4pm Sat) If you're coming from the South, you can call ahead and see if this outfit can pick you up from Kyrenia Gate. It also arranges pick-ups from Larnaka International Airport for clients. Minimum hire period three days.

TAXI

There are plenty of taxi ranks in the Old City; the most convenient and easiest to find are **Nato Taxi** (☎ 0392 227 1556; İstanbul Caddesi) and **Özner Taxi** (☎ 0392 227 4012; Tanzımat Sokak), both at Kyrenia Gate. A ride within town should cost between 10TL and 15TL, and drivers are usually good about turning on the meter.

Kyrenia (Girne) & the North

Best Places to Eat

➡ İkimiz (p190)

➡ Tervetuloa Restaurant (p196)

➡ Corner Restaurant (p190)

➡ Bella Moon (p198)

➡ Niazi's Restaurant & Bar (p190)

Best Views

➡ Kyrenia Castle (p185)

➡ Panagia Absinthiotissa Monastery (p194)

➡ St Hilarion Castle (p192)

➡ Buffavento Castle (p193)

Why Go?

Castles cling to craggy hilltops. Lonely churches peek out amid wild-flowered slopes. Fields of gnarled olive trees march across the coastline where the harbour town of Kyrenia (Girne), backed by the imposing silhouette of jagged mountain ranges, looks out towards the sea. This bite-sized region combines the best of Cyprus' natural charm with oodles of history.

Most visit for sun and sea holidays, which has led to a flurry of less-than-pretty developments being flung up along the shore. Ignore the concrete-block oddities and you'll find there's plenty left to explore. From Bellapais Abbey to the fairy-tale-fluff of St Hilarion Castle, there are ruins with million-dollar views galore.

This region is famed for its outdoor potential, with hiking, turtle-spotting, orchid-hunting and bird-watching on the agenda. The trails are underpromoted and gloriously quiet; a perfect incentive to get your walking shoes on and discover them before everyone else does.

When to Go

➡ A vibrant palette of wildflowers and rare orchids blooms across Kyrenia's coastline from February to April, splashing the rolling fields with a paintbox of colours.

➡ April is also the prime hiking period, with gloriously clear and warm weather nearly guaranteed.

➡ Musicians and singers serenade crowds amid the Gothic arcades where Augustinian monks once trod at the Bellapais Music Festival in May.

➡ Turtle-nesting season begins in June and continues through August.

➡ The fierce humidity in July and August makes this the perfect time to take to the water. Hop on a gület (traditional wooden ship with raised bow) and sail out of Kyrenia's harbour to catch a sea breeze.

Ancient Soli (p201)
Gaz[...]
Esentepe
Yenierenköy (Yialousa) (58km)

Koruçam Burnu (Cape Kormakitis)

MEDITERRANEAN SEA (AKDENIZ)

Sadrazamköy (Livera)

Koruçam (Kormakitis) Peninsula
Koruçam (Kormakitis)
Church of Agios Georgios
Koruçam (Kormakitis)

Paliocastro

Horseshoe Beach
Geçitköy (Panagra)
Güzelyalı
Karşıyaka (Vasileia)

Alsancak Beach
Lapta (Lapithos)
Çamlıbel (1024m)

Escape (Yavuz Çıkarma) Beach
Alsancak (Karavas)
Kyparissovouno (1024m)

Karakum (Karakoumi) Vrysi (Acapulco) Beach
Alagadi (Turtle) Beach

Bellapais (Beylerbeyi)
Kyrenia (Girne)

KYRENIA RANGE

Antifonitis Monastery
Karaağaç (Harkia)
Troulli

Vrysi
Shayna Beach
Çatalköy (Agios Epiktitos)

Besparmak (Pentadaktylos) (740m)
Sourp Magar Monastery
Yialias (2km)
Alevkaya (935m) Forest Station

Karaoğlanoğlu (Agios Georgios)
Karaman (Karmi)
St Hilarion Castle
Profitis Ilias (888m)

Ozanköy (Kazafani)

Ağırdağ (Agirda)
Alonagra (935m)

Besparmak Pass

Değirmenlik (Kythrea)
Demirhan (Trahoni)
Balıkesir (Palaikythro)

Mavi Köşk
Tepebaşı (Diorios)
Hisarköy (Kampyli)
Akçiçek (Syskilpos)
Pınarbaşı (Krini)
Yukarı Dikmen (Pano Dikomo)

Aşağı Dikmen (Kato Dikomo)
Panagia Absinthiostissa Monastery

Taşkent (Vouno)

Buffavento Castle

Güngör (Koutsoventis)
Minareliköy (Neo Horio)

Ercan Airport

Akdeniz (Ayia Irini)
Kalkanlı (Kalo Horio)
Özhan (Asomatos)
İkidere (Duo Potami)

Kılıçaslan (Kontemenos)
Yılmazköy (Skylloura)
Türkeli

Gönyeli (Kioneli)
Haspolat (Mia Milia)
Kızılay (Trachonas)

NORTH NICOSIA (LEFKOŞA)
NICOSIA (LEFKOSIA)

Ozanya
Atsos
Olive Tree Orchard

Şahinler (Masari)
Gayretköy (Avlona)

Alayköy (Gerolakkos)
Agios Dometios Crossing
Kokkinotrimithia

UN Buffer Zone

Engomi (Egkomi)
Strovolos (Strovolos)

Taşkent
Aglantzia (Agianga)

MESAORIA
Geri

MESARYA
Gazimağusa (Agia)
Dilekkaya (Agia)

Kato Lakatamia
Pano Lakatamia

Morfou (Güzelyurt)
Akçay (Argaki)
Zümrütköy (Kato Kopia)

Yeşilırmak (Pentageia)
Güneşköy (Nikitas)
Aşağı Bostancı (Kato Zodeia)
Yukarıbostancı (Pano Zodeia)

Akaki
Peristerona
Paleometoho

Astromeritis
Zodhia Crossing

REPUBLIC OF CYPRUS

Kokkinitrimithia
Agioi Trimithias
Meniko

Agios Mamas Church
Tourmba tou Skourou

Yayla (Syrianochori)
Aydınköy (Prasto)
Gemikonağı (Karavostasi)
Piri Osman Paşa Mosque
Lefke (Lefka)

Yedidalga Belediyesi Plaji

Ancient Soli
UN Buffer Zone

Ancient Vouni

Yeşilyurt (Pentageia)
Taşpınar (Angolemi)
Taşköy (Petra)
Elatia

Morfou Bay (Güzelyurt Körfezi)

Gemikonağı (Karavostasi)

N
0
0
10 miles
20 km

Kyrenia (Girne) & the North Highlights

① Kyrenia (p185) Climbing up onto the Byzantine castle's ramparts before sitting back in the Old Harbour area to watch sunset.

② St Hilarion Castle (p192) Reliving the golden days of hermit monks and shining-armoured knights amid the towers of a castle fit for a fairy tale.

③ Bellapais Abbey (p197) Getting your literary-pilgrimage fix exploring this medieval abbey and wandering the quiet lanes of Bellapais (Beylerbeyi) village.

④ Buffavento Castle (p193) Savouring bird's-eye views of the coast from the crumbled remnants of this castle.

⑤ Agios Mamas Orthodox Church (p202) Filling up on fresco-frippery at Northern Cyprus' best-preserved church.

ROAD TRIP > COMBING THE NORTHEASTERN RIDGE & COAST

Inland from Kyernia (Girne), the land bucks up into great ridges and the limestone massifs of the Beşparmak (Pentadaktylos) mountains soar into view. This scenic drive loops around the outcrops, passing monasteries, castles and ruins from Cyprus' multilayered past.

① Antifonitis Church

The drive to Antifonitis traces the coastline east of Kyrenia, passing scattered villages and beaches. Little Ozanköy is noted for its olive oil and carob *pekmez* (molasses) and medieval church, while nearby Çatalköy (Agios Epiktitos) is famous locally for the caves that provided sanctuary to the hermit Epiktitos in the 13th century. There'll be

time for a quick dip at **Alagadı Beach** (p195) before you reach the turn-off for Bahçeli (Kalograia) and head inland to the Byzantine **Antifonitis Church** (p194) with its beautiful dome and frescos.

② Alevkaya Herbarium

After visiting the church take the scenic ridge road for 17km west, parallel to the mountains, until you come to Alevkaya (Halevga) Forest Station, where nature lovers can check out the **Alevkaya Herbarium** (p194). After a recuperative stroll, drive on for 2.5km until you spy the battered ruins of the 11th-century Coptic Armenian Sourp Magar Monastery nestled in pine trees below. The road to the monastery isn't open to cars, so park at the picnic site and follow the forestry track that winds down to the monastery on foot.

③ Buffavento Castle

Backtrack onto the main road and head west for 9km onto the Beşparmak Pass until you get to the **Buffavento Restaurant** (p197).

Turn left here and take the winding road for 6km up to **Buffavento Castle** (p193) for some of the best views in Northern Cyprus. When you've finished scrambling around the ruins, exit the castle car park and continue along the tarmac road for 3km until you see the domed roof of the lonely Byzantine **Panagia Absinthiotissa Monastery** (p194) below. Take the left-hand turn-off to the picnic ground to arrive at the monastery.

④ Bellapais

From Panagia Absinthiotissa, drive down into the tidy village of Taşkent (Vouno), taking the second left-hand turn on the ridge road above the village and continuing on this road as it heads northwest out of the village. From here it's 10km onto Bellapais (Beylerbeyi) and the beautiful Gothic architecture of **Bellapais Abbey** (p197), made famous by Lawrence Durrell.

KYRENIA (GIRNE)

POP 33,207

Kyrenia (Girne) has always been governed by the sea. Its natural harbour, once coveted by anyone with dreams of empire and bustling with traders and exporters, is today just as popular with visitors whose only desire is to stroll the seaside strand and hop on a boat cruise around the bay.

Catch a whiff of the days long gone by strolling the narrow twisty lanes of the Old Town. Then climb up the honey-coloured fortifications of the Byzantine castle, lording it up over the horseshoe-shaped inlet, and stare down at the fishing boats bobbing in the water. Afterwards, join the flocks of day trippers and travellers taking up residence outside the former carob warehouses that now house harbourside restaurants. Here on the waterfront is the ideal spot to ponder this ancient port's mammoth history while staring out to sea.

History

Once one of the ancient city kingdoms of Cyprus, Kyrenia (Girne) was founded by Mycenaean Greeks around 1200 BC. From this point Kyrenia's history is, in essence, the history of its castle. Little more is known about the town until the castle's construction by the Byzantines in the 7th century to ward off continuing Arab raids.

In 1191 the castle was captured by Richard the Lionheart of England, on his way to Jerusalem and a third crusade. The castle was then used as both a residence and prison. It was sold to the Knights Templar and then gifted to Guy de Lusignan when he became king of Cyprus.

In the 14th century the Venetians extended the castle and built the bulbous seafacing fortifications still seen today. During Ottoman rule, changes to the castle were again made, while Kyrenia itself functioned primarily as the island's only northern port.

Kyrenia has long since given up this port role, as the Old Harbour's size and depth only allow it to service tourist crafts, fishing boats and the small yachts commonly found in its cluttered quays. Two kilometres to the east of Kyrenia, there is now a large purpose-built harbour created to receive commercial and passenger ships from Turkey.

During British rule, the town became a favourite with retiring (ex-colonial) British civil servants. When Turkey invaded Cyprus in 1974, it used the beaches to the west of Kyrenia as the prime location for landing its army. Almost all Greek Cypriots and many British retirees fled.

Now, 40 years later, Kyrenia supports a large and growing tourist industry, mainly from Britain, Germany and Turkey.

◉ Sights

The compact Old Harbour and Old Town (p189) district just behind the bay are home to Kyrenia's major sights.

★ Kyrenia Castle
HISTORIC SITE

(Girne Kalesi; Old Harbour; adult/student 14/5TL; ⊙8am-6pm Jun-Sep, to 4pm Oct-May) If the grand fortifications of Kyrenia Castle could talk, they could sure tell some tales. The castle was first built by the Byzantines – possibly over the remains of an earlier Roman fort – and every era of conquerors from Richard the Lionheart to the Ottomans has added its own touch to the castle's bulk.

A large rectangular structure, the castle contains a cistern, dungeon, chapel and two small museums, though the real highlight is walking along the ramparts high above the harbour.

You enter the castle via the stone bridge over the former moat, which leads to the small 12th-century Byzantine Chapel of St George. Its broken mosaics and Corinthian columns, originally outside the walls, were incorporated into the larger structure by the Venetians.

The western side of the inner castle is home to the infamous dungeon where King Peter I's pregnant mistress, Joanna L'Aleman, was tortured by order of the king's jealous wife, Queen Eleanor. You can peer down into the deep hole where a hilariously bad mannequin representing the unfortunate Joanna is displayed.

Across the courtyard, the northeast Lusignan bastion tower features mannequins dressed in armour. The Venetian bastion tower is in the southeast corner. Between the towers are two small museums. The Gallery of Tomb Finds holds a small collection of finds from surrounding archaeological sites, including the Neolithic site of Vrysi (near Çatalköy) and the Kirni Bronze Age tombs (in Pınarbaşı). There's also an exhibit of Hellenistic-period ceramics unearthed at Akdeniz (Ayia Irini).

Next door, the Kyrenia Shipwreck Museum contains the remains of the oldest shipwreck recovered from Cypriot waters. This wooden-hulled (Aleppo pine) Greek merchant ship sank off the Kyrenia coast around 300 BC, and was discovered by a local diver in 1967. Its cargo consisted of amphorae, almonds, grain, wine and millstones from the Greek islands of Samos, Rhodes and Kos. Its crew most likely traded along the coast of Anatolia and as far as the islands of the Dodecanese in Greece.

Evidence suggests that the boat, 80 years old at the time, sank because of piracy. Much of its cargo seems to have been plundered, and it has what appear to be spear marks in its hull. A curse tablet – displayed among the exhibits – was also found with the wreck. At the time, pirates believed that placing these tablets on a sinking ship would conceal its fate, by keeping the wreck forever at the bottom of the sea. Upstairs from the main gallery, a small separate chamber exhibits the preserved hull of the boat.

You can walk between the castle's four towers via the handrailed ramparts, but follow the marked routes as some sections can be quite dangerous. Keep younger children close by at all times. Views of the Old Harbour are fantastic from here, especially in the morning light.

Cyprus House MUSEUM
(Old Harbour; 7TL; ☉9am-6pm Mon-Sat) This lovingly restored old carob warehouse on the harbour contains interesting ethnographic exhibits of traditional clothing, furniture and Cypriot textile craftwork. There are also displays on the harbour's history as a major trading port exporting carob to Europe.

Archangelos Michael Icon Museum MUSEUM
(Canbulat Sokak; 7TL; ☉8am-3.30pm Mon-Wed & Fri-Sat, to 5pm Thu) The 19th-century Archangelos Michael Church, with its white bell tower rising up above the surrounding harbourside buildings, displays icons dating from the 18th and 19th centuries. The collection is made up of icons salvaged from Orthodox churches throughout Northern Cyprus. Notable depictions include Saint George and the Dragon, the beheading of John the Baptist, and the Virgin and Child.

Chysopolitissa Church CHURCH
(Erdal Akça Sokak) FREE This small roofless ruin is Kyrenia's oldest church, dating back to the 1500s. It's usually kept open so you can check out the two intricately carved wood beams inside.

Greco-Roman Tombs TOMB
(Canbulat Sokak) FREE These ancient tombs, carved into the rock face, and usually partially obscured by parked vehicles, are thought to have been used in the Hellenistic and Roman eras.

🏃 Activities

During summer the Old Harbour is lined with stands, where boat-cruise operators tout their trips. There's a plethora of options but in reality they're all selling the same thing. For 50TL to 60TL you can expect to get a day cruise on a gület with two swimming/snorkelling stops, usually finishing with an on-board barbecue lunch (drinks are extra). The boats typically leave at 10.30am and return at 5pm, taking up to 20 passengers.

Ladyboss Fishing FISHING
(☑0542 855 5672; www.fishingnorthcyprus.com; Old Harbour; per person €60) The same team behind Highline paragliding (p186) also operates these great fishing trips which set out to sea for some angling action on the 34ft *Ladyboss*. Trips are usually five hours long and your catch of the day can be cooked for you afterwards.

Aphrodite Boat Charters & Fishing BOATING
(☑0533 868 0943; www.kyreniaboattrips.com; Old Harbour; cruises/fishing trips per person €45/90; ☉Mar-Oct) This gület offers cruises around the bay and fishing excursions. Captain Musa Aksoy was the first to start sport-fishing tours in Northern Cyprus, so if you're after hooking the big catch, you're in safe hands.

Leisure cruises (for up to 12 passengers) include snorkelling and swimming in isolated bays that bigger boats don't visit.

Highline Tandem PARAGLIDING
(☑0542 855 5672; www.highlineparagliding.com; Old Harbour; tandem flight incl transport & insurance €95) Run by a New Zealander–Cypriot couple, Highline helped a 100-year-old Scottish woman paraglide her way into the *Guinness Book of Records* as the oldest woman ever to take up the adventure sport. Weather permitting, tandem flights run throughout the year from an altitude of 750m, allowing incredible panoramas across the countryside.

KYRENIA (GIRNE) & THE NORTH KYRENIA (GIRNE)

Kyrenia (Girne)

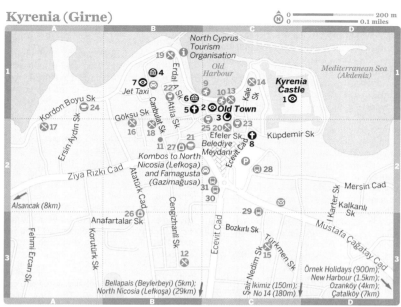

Kyrenia (Girne)

Tours

Side Tour TOURS
(☎0392 815 3008; www.side-tour.com; Canbulat
Sokak 7a; day trips per person €29-45; ◷9am-

6pm) This excellent travel operator runs a
range of good-value day trips, focused on exploring the historic sites and natural beauty
of this region, including tours to the Karpas

KYRENIA'S OLD TOWN

Wrapping around the Old Harbour, the diminutive Old Town is an atmospheric area for a wander. Its winding alleyways hold a jumble of abandoned stone buildings slowly slipping into disrepair, mixed with newer concrete additions.

Modest remnants of Kyrenia's long history are speckled throughout the lanes. Two of the major monuments are the Ottoman-era Ağa Cafer Paşa Mosque (Ağa Cafer Paşa Sokak; ⊙ open outside prayer hours) FREE and the dilapidated remains of 16th-century Chysopolitissa Church (p186). There are also ancient Greco-Roman tombs (p186) on the road leading to Archangelos Michael Church (p186).

During the Lusignan era, the town was protected by fortifications which, over the years, were dismantled and reused for other building works. The Round Tower on Ziya Rızkı Caddesi next to one of the entrance ways into the neighbourhood is one of the few still-standing pieces of wall. At the eastern edge of the Old Town, leading down to the castle, is bijoux St Andrew's Anglican Church (Ecevit Caddesi; ⊙ 9am-6pm) FREE, built in 1913 and still serving Kyrenia's Christian foreign resident community today.

Peninsula (€45); Famagusta (Gazimağusa; €45); a 'Wild West' tour (€45) taking in the Koruçam (Kormakitis) Peninsula and the ancient cities of Vouni (p205) and Soloi (p204); and a half-day tour to St Hilarion (p192) and Bellapais (Beylerbeyi; €29).

Cyprus Active Jeep Safaris　　OUTDOORS
(✆ 0533 881 8993; www.cyprusactive.com; per person €45) Discover the Kyrenia Range's lesser-seen sights on these fun jeep safaris. The full-day tour winds up the mountainside, taking in an abandoned village and a Turkish tank memorial site, with spectacular views of the coast all the way, before heading to the Koruçam Peninsula and Horseshoe Beach (p204) with a visit to the Agios Panteleimon Monastery (p203) en route.

Price includes lunch and pick-up from hotel.

Eating

The most atmospheric place to dine in Kyrenia is the Old Harbour. Although many of the restaurants depend on their setting rather than their menus to get you in the door, there are a couple of gems among the more mundane places. There are also some excellent restaurants in Kyrenia's old Turkish Quarter.

Mantı Sofrası　　TURKISH €
(Göksu Sokak; dishes 15-20TL; ⊙ 11am-10pm; ✆) Nothing fancy, just plates of the wholesome and simple Anatolian village food that Turkish mamas have been dishing up to their families for centuries. Mantı (Turkish ravioli, drenched in a yoghurt and tomato sauce), kuru fasulye (white-bean stew) and mene-

men (Turkish-style scrambled eggs) are the stars of the small menu here.

Özgulen Restaurant　　KEBAB €
(Öztep Kebap; ✆ 0392 868 6872; Canbulat Sokak 13b; lahmacun 5TL, dürüm meal-deal 12TL, kebab plates from 20TL; ⊙ 11am-10.30pm) This cheerful canteen is the place to come for tasty, filling Turkish staples of lentil soup, lahmacun (thin-based pizza topped with minced lamb and parsley) and dürüm (kebab wraps), which come with a side of crispy salad and a pot of ayran (salty yoghurt drink). Filling, tasty and great value. Kebab plates also available.

Kıbrıs Evi　　CYPRIOT €€
(Kale Sokak, Old Harbour; mains 21-25TL; ⊙ 10.30am-11pm; ✆) Traditional Cypriot cooking is dished up with unbeatable harbourside views at this restaurant beside the castle. Grab a table on the rooftop, or – even better – on one of the teensy balconies for panoramic dining at its best. Try the bumbar (sausages) and tuck into the stuffed artichokes.

Beyti Restaurant　　KEBAB €€
(✆ 0392 815 2573; Cengizhanli Sokak; mains 23-30TL; ⊙ 24hr) When local workers clock off for the night, they head here, away from the harbour hullabaloo. This kebap (kebab) house has the full caboodle of grilled meats, from its namesake beyti kebap (mincemeat wrapped in lavash bread and served with yoghurt and tomato sauce) to seriously succulent izgara köfte (grilled meatballs). For the adventurous, there's işkembe çorbası (tripe soup) too.

KYRENIA: CITY OF CAROB

The Old Harbour in Kyrenia (Girne) may be chock-a-block full of restaurants and cafes today, but the beautiful stone buildings that line the waterfront once played an important role as warehouses for the carob industry.

Carob has been cultivated in Cyprus since the 1st century AD and was one of the island's major exports from the medieval era right up to the end of the British mandate period. As the Kyrenia region harvested nearly 30% of Cyprus' carob-tree pods, Kyrenia port became the centre for the trade.

The harbour-front buildings were used as warehouses to store the carob (as well as other exports such as olive oil and cotton) before being shipped out to Europe. Although the international carob trade collapsed in the 1960s, carob continues to be harvested in Northern Cyprus to be made into the beloved *pekmez* (molasses) condiment.

Interestingly, the carat – the unit of measurement for the size of diamonds and other gemstones – is based on the weight of a carob bean, which is remarkably consistent from pod to pod and tree to tree. There are records of carob beans being used to weigh gems as early as the Roman period.

Six Brothers Restaurant TURKISH €€
(Kordon Boyu Sokak; mains 20-50TL; ◷10.30am-midnight) A harbourside staple, Six Brothers has a large menu of simple kebabs and seafood. Portions are on the small side but the restaurant remains popular for its extensive terrace seating, stretching right up to the entry to the harbour breakwater path.

★ **Corner Restaurant** SEAFOOD €€€
(Old Harbour; mains 28-45TL, meze per person 50-60TL, min 2 people; ◷10.30am-11pm; ⧉) The seafood menu here is a cut above other offerings on the harbour, in quality as well as quantity. Succulent grilled king prawns, octopus and a bundle of different fish dishes are on the menu with generous salad included. If you're truly hungry, the meze menus are a real showcase of seafood cookery, and are near-impossible to finish.

Grab a seat waterside for the full harbour dining experience.

★ **İkimiz** CYPRIOT €€€
(⧉0392 815 1589; http://ikimiz-kyrenia.com; Meşeli Sokak 22, Turkish Quarter; small dishes 12 TL, large dishes 25-33TL; ◷noon-3pm & 7pm-late Mon-Fri, 7pm-late Sat; ⧉⧉) The mother-and-daughter duo behind this cute-as-a-button restaurant dish up Cypriot soul food. The small menu (which changes regularly) features hearty and wholesome specialities such as *molohiya* (a viscid stew made from jute leaves) and *pirohu* (Cypriot ravioli), as well as fall-off-the-bone lamb.

To find İkimiz, walk up Ecevit Caddesi from Belediye Meydanı, turn left onto Bozkırlı Sokak and then right onto Şair Nedim Sokak. Walk up this street and take the second left-hand turn.

★ **Niazi's Restaurant & Bar** KEBAB €€€
(⧉0392 815 2160; www.niazis.com; Kordon Boyu Sokak; mains 32-50TL; ◷11am-11pm; ⧉⧉⧉) A carnivore's heaven, Niazi's is the inventor of the 'full kebab' – don't even think about ordering one unless you're seriously hungry. Luckily, if you're not up for multiple grilled meats and a bundle of meze all in one sitting, there's a good selection of alternatives ranging from king prawns in garlic butter to chicken in plum sauce.

Amazingly, in this temple devoted to meat, there's even a small menu section for vegetarians.

Kyrenia Tavern CYPRIOT €€€
(⧉0392 815 2799; Türkmen Sokak, Turkish Quarter; meals 50TL; ◷6.30-11pm) If you like your dining experiences authentic and eccentric, this garden restaurant serving Cypriot favourites is the spot for you. There's no menu, just a choice of two mains with meze to start. Don't expect to eat and run; this is a full-evening affair, giving you time to admire the bizarre surroundings including beat-up cars and bikes, and kind-of-creepy mannequins.

Coming from Belediye Meydanı on Mustafa Çağatay Caddesi, turn right onto Şair Nedim Sokak and the Kyrenia Tavern is on the first left-hand corner, after the small fire station. Booking is essential.

Stone Arch INTERNATIONAL €€€
(⧉0392 815 4753; Efeler Sokak 13, Old Harbour; mains 24-55TL; ◷6.30-11pm; ⧉) Stone Arch is all starched white tablecloths and roman-

tic lighting. The small menu offers seafood (king prawns and salmon feature in a few dishes) and steaks, there's a decent wine list and the service is unobtrusive. In summer you dine in the outdoor stone-walled courtyard.

No 14 INTERNATIONAL €€€
(☑0392 859 2072; Yazıcızade Sokak 14, Turkish Quarter; mains 28-45TL; ⊙6.30pm-midnight Mon-Sat; 🔊) This poolside garden restaurant offers home-cooked delights such as pork with peppercorn, and stuffed calamari. Its simple menu is accompanied by excellent service. Follow the signs from Namik Kemal Sokak and turn left at the mosque.

🍷 Drinking & Nightlife

The harbour area is where most travellers congregate for a drink. The outdoor tables spread across the waterfront are just the ticket for a coffee break or beer. If you're looking for clubbing-style nightlife, some of the bigger resorts along the coast have attached clubs. Most are quite cheesy.

Grand Akpınar CAFE
(Kordon Boyu Sokak; ⊙11am-11pm; 🔊) Despite its terrace opening up onto the main road which rims the waterfront down to the Old Harbour, this quaint cafe has a rather tranquil feel. Decent lattes and other European-style coffee drinks (served with rather tasty shortbread-style biscuits) and efficient service make this a good choice for mid-afternoon caffeine pick-me-ups.

Casablanca BAR
(Atila Sokak; ⊙8pm-late Thu-Sat) This quirky little bar in the Old Town has decently priced drinks and attracts a good mix of locals, foreign residents and travellers.

Ego Bar BAR
(Doğan Türk Sokak; ⊙6pm-2am; 🔊) With its chilled-out atmosphere, this is a great spot in the Old Town for an evening drink within the stone walls of an open-air courtyard. In summer the Ego Bar showcases live bands, playing a mix of jazz, rock, blues and soul.

Whiskey Joes BAR
(Ağa Cafer Paşa Sokak; ⊙4pm-midnight Tue-Sun) This British-run bar in the Old Town has a relaxed atmosphere, and also offers a menu of exceedingly English dishes.

Ali's Special Cafe CAFE
(Ziya Rızkı Caddesi; ⊙10am-7pm) Take a break with a syrupy Cypriot coffee, or freshly squeezed orange juice, at this cute little place under a shady tree and watch the world go by.

Shopping

Ziya Rızkı Caddesi is the main shopping street.

Round Tower ARTS & CRAFTS
(Ziya Rızkı Caddesi; ⊙10am-6pm Mon-Sat) Inside the restored Lusignan-era Round Tower, this small art-and-crafts shop has a range of interesting souvenirs, including books, local art, old photographs and ceramics. There's also a section of secondhand English-language books for 5TL each.

Ordu Pazarı FOOD & DRINKS
(Atatürk Caddesi; ⊙8am-9pm) The most central decently stocked supermarket in Kyrenia.

ℹ Information

INTERNET ACCESS

Cafe Net (Mustafa Çağatay Caddesi; per hour 3TL; ⊙10am-midnight) The best place for checking your email. English-speaking owner Mehmet Çavuş serves hot and cold drinks and jacket potatoes. He also runs a small book exchange. Located southeast of the town centre.

City.Net Internet Cafe (off Ziya Rızkı Caddesi; per hour 2TL; ⊙10am-midnight) In the shopping arcade between Ziya Rızkı Caddesi and Ecevit Caddesi. Fast internet and friendly service.

MEDICAL SERVICES

Akçiçek Hastahanesi (☑0392 815 2256; Mustafa Çağatay Caddesi; ⊙24hr) Kyrenia's public hospital is 300m southeast of the post office.

Kyrenia Medical Centre (Kamiloğlu Hastahanesi; ☑0392 815 3282; www.kyreniamedicalcenter.com; Işıl Sokak 4-6; ⊙24hr) Private hospital, just west of the centre.

MONEY

Banks and ATMs are clustered along Ziya Rızkı Caddesi.

Gesfi Money Exchange (Kordon Boyu Sokak 40; ⊙8.30am-8pm) Opposite the Dome Hotel.

Türk Bankası (Ziya Rızkı Caddesi; ⊙8am-noon & 2-5pm Mon-Sat) Near Belediye Meydanı.

POST

Post office (Mustafa Çağatay Caddesi; ⊙8am-3.30pm Mon-Fri) Southeast 150m from Belediye Meydanı.

TOURIST INFORMATION

North Cyprus Tourism Organisation (NCTO; Old Harbour; ⊙8am-6pm May-Sep, to 4pm Oct-Apr) Free maps and bundles of glossy pamphlets. Actual help from staff can be hit-or-miss depending on who is working the desk.

ℹ️ Getting There & Away

AIR

Ercan Airport (p182), 40km southeast of Kyrenia, is the main airport in North Cyprus, served by flights only from mainland Turkey.

Cyprus XP Travel (☑ 392 815 4631; Atatürk Caddesi; ⊙9am-5pm Mon-Sat) represents Pegasus Airlines in Northern Cyprus.

BOAT

Two Turkish ferry companies run regular boats from the New Harbour, east of town, to Taşucu in Turkey.

Akgünler (www.akgunlerbilet.com) Runs three boats every week with sailings at 6pm on Monday and Friday and at 11.30pm on Thursday (adult/child/car 105/40/181TL including all port departure taxes).

Filo Shipping (www.filoshipping.com) Runs three car ferries per week on Monday, Wednesday and Friday at midnight (adult/child/car 105/40/206TL including all port departure taxes).

Tickets for both can be purchased on the company websites or from travel agencies around town.

BUS & MINIBUS

Buses to Famagusta (12TL, 1¼ hours, hourly from 7am to 6pm) and North Nicosia (Lefkoşa; 5TL, 30 minutes, every 30 minutes between 7.50am and 7pm) leave from the **Virgo Transport Office** (☑ 0392 815 7248; Ecevit Caddesi; ⊙7am-9pm).

Dolmuşes (minibuses) to North Nicosia (5TL to 7TL, 35 minutes, every 30 minutes from 7am to 6.30pm); Lapta (Lapithos; 5TL to 5.50TL, 20 minutes, roughly every 30 minutes from 7am to 8pm); Çatalköy (Agios Epiktitos; 5TL, 20 minutes, roughly every 20 minutes from 7am to 8pm); and Çamlıbel (Myrtou) and Tepebaşı (Diorios; both 7.50TL, one hour, hourly between 7am and 6pm) leave from a minibus stand just east of the central car park.

Dolmuşes to Morfou (Güzelyurt; 10TL, 1¼ hours, hourly) depart from a stand on Mustafa Çağatay Caddesi.

SERVICE TAXI

Kombos (service taxis) are the quickest, and often most comfortable, way to travel between Kyrenia and North Nicosia (8TL, 20 minutes, roughly every 15 minutes from 7am to 8pm) and Famagusta (13TL, 45 minutes, hourly between

7am and 6pm). They leave from the Kombo office on Belediye Meydanı.

ℹ️ Getting Around

TO/FROM THE AIRPORT

Kibhas (☑ Ercan Airport 0533 870 7848, Kyrenia 0533 870 7846; www.kibhas.org; ticket 17.50TL) runs airport shuttle buses between Kyrenia and the airport (1¼ hours) with regular departures throughout the day. The pick-up and drop-off point, and ticket office, is the Virgo Transport Office (p192) in the centre of town.

A taxi to/from the airport costs around 120TL.

CAR

There are plenty of car-hire outlets, including **Oscar Car Rentals** (☑ 0392 815 1068; www. oscarrentacars.com; Kordon Boyu Sokak 49/A; per day (3-day min) from €30; ⊙9am-6pm).

TAXI

Private taxis such as those run by **Jet Taxi** (☑ 0392 815 4943; Canbulat Sokak) are useful for going to Bellapais (25TL one way) and St Hilarion Castle (p192) (100TL return), both of which aren't serviced by public transport. To North Nicosia it can cost anywhere between 70TL to 100TL, depending on the driver. Polite bargaining doesn't go amiss.

AROUND KYRENIA & THE RANGES

The craggy peaks of the Kyrenia Range loom large over this region. The furrowed mountainsides are a nature-filled flip side to the built-up buzz of the narrow coastal plain. Follow winding roads into the hills to hidden monasteries, churches and medieval-castle remnants or hike out, across the countryside on old shepherding trails, for some of the best views this island has up its sleeve. Then dawdle your way back down to the shore where life during the summer is all about the beach.

👁 Sights

⭐ **St Hilarion Castle** CASTLE
(Hilarion Kalesi; adult/student 9/5TL; ⊙9am-6.30pm Apr-Oct, to 3.30pm Nov-Mar) The full fairy-tale outline of St Hilarion Castle only becomes apparent once you're directly beneath it. The stone walls and half-ruined buildings blend into the rocky landscape, creating a dreamscape castle plucked from a child's imagination, complete with hidden rooms, tunnels and crumbling towers.

The site has three main parts: the lower enceinte (fortified defensive enclosure), the upper enceinte and Prince John's Tower, all linked by steep staircases. The stunning views are well worth the arduous climb to the top.

Rumour has it that Walt Disney drew inspiration from the jagged contours of St Hilarion when he created the animated film *Snow White*. And a local folk legend tells that the castle once boasted 101 rooms, the last of which led to a secret internal garden that belonged to a fairy queen. This enchantress was known for seducing hunters, shepherds and travellers who stumbled into her lair and robbing them after placing them into a deep slumber.

The castle's real history is a bit less fantastic. The lofty fort is named after the monk Hilarion, who fled persecution in the Holy Land. He lived (and died) in a mountain cave that overlooked the Kyrenia plain, protecting the pass between the coast and Nicosia.

In the 10th century the Byzantines built a church and monastery over Hilarion's tomb. Due to the site's strategic position, it was used as a watchtower and beacon during the Arab raids of the 7th and 8th centuries and was an important link in the communication chain between Buffavento and Kantara Castles further east.

In 1191 Guy de Lusignan seized control of St Hilarion, defeating the self-proclaimed Byzantine emperor of Cyprus, Isaak Komninos. The castle was then extensively expanded and used as both a military outpost and a summer residence of the Lusignan court. Later, during Venetian rule, the castle was neglected and fell into disrepair.

In 1964 the Türk Mukavemet Teşkilatı (TMT), an underground Turkish nationalist group, took control of the castle, again for its strategic position. It has been in Turkish Cypriot hands ever since, with a sheltered Turkish military base located on the ridge below.

You enter by the barbican main gate into the lower enceinte, once used as the main garrison and stabling area. Then follow the meandering path up to the middle enceinte, originally protected and sealed by a drawbridge. Here you'll find remains of the church, barrack rooms, four-level royal apartments and a large cistern, vital to the storage of water.

Access to the upper enceinte is via a paved winding track, which leads to the Lusignan Gate. Guarded by the Byzantine tower, it opens on to the central courtyard, adorned with more royal apartments, kitchens and ancillary chambers.

One last climb takes you to Prince John's Tower. Legend has it that Prince John of Antioch became convinced his two Bulgarian bodyguards were plotting to assassinate him and had them thrown from the cliff, to their deaths.

From the tower on clear days you can see the Taurus Mountains, 100km away in Turkey.

In summer it's best to arrive early and avoid climbing in the heat of the day.

★ **Buffavento Castle** CASTLE
(Buffavento Kalesi; adult/student 7/5TL; ☉ dawn-dusk) Buffavento perches precariously at 940m, overlooking the Mesaoria plain. The constant pummelling it endures from high winds is how it derived its Italian name, 'Challenger of the Winds'.

The castle is divided into two sections: the lower enceinte (fortified defensive enclosure) and the upper enceinte, which occupies a smaller area on the rocky peak. Built in such a way that no fortifications other than its outer walls were needed, the castle's naturally guarded location has only one entrance approach.

Little is known about the castle's early history. In medieval times, it was known as the Castle of the Lion, when Richard the Lionheart took it from the daughter of Byzantine emperor Isaak Komninos in 1191. The Lusignans later used it as a prison and a beacon tower, connecting both Kantara Castle to the east and St Hilarion Castle to the west.

Although it has deteriorated more than the other castles – and some of its buildings have been sadly defaced by graffiti – Buffavento's surviving towers and walls have an ambience of lingering grandeur topped off by the dizzying views sweeping downwards over the forested slopes.

Prominently signposted (as Buffavento Kalesi) off the Beşparmak (Pentadaktylos) Pass, it's a 15-minute drive along the uphill road to the parking area below the castle. From here it's a steep but gradual walk that takes about 20 minutes. Closed footwear is advised. Note that there is rarely anyone manning the ticket booth.

Panagia Absinthiotissa Monastery   MONASTERY

FREE Located on the flank of the Beşparmak Range, this monastery sits idyllically among juniper trees, taking in the views over the Mesaoria plain.

Built in the late-Byzantine era, with its colossal 12-windowed drum and dome, the monastery was inhabited by Latin monks during the 15th century who added Gothic vaulting and an unusual narthex with double apses at its end. Across the courtyard, to the north, is the refectory with its shallow ceiling, vaulting and distinctive lancet windows.

Fastidiously restored during the 1960s, the monastery was unfortunately badly vandalised after 1974, with its many frescos either stolen or defaced. The plastered interior, now completely covered with graffiti, and the floor, covered with goat droppings, make a bizarre and slightly eerie contrast with the still-beautiful and soaring architecture.

The monastery is approximately 10 minutes' drive from Buffavento Castle, sitting just above the village of Taşkent (Vouno). To make this your next stop, simply exit the car park and follow the tarmac road heading down the western flank of the mountain. The monastery is signposted from Taşkent's municipality park.

Antifonitis Church   CHURCH

(adult/student 7/5TL; ☺9am-4pm) This beautiful secluded church is well worth the drive up a twisty mountain road to get to it. Dating from the 12th century (though substantially added on to and rebuilt in the 1400s and 1800s), the church's architecture is notable for its surviving eight-pillared central dome and for its beautiful, though extensively damaged, frescos. The Christ Pantocrator on the central dome and St George on the narthex are the best-preserved frescos.

Alevkaya Herbarium   PARK

(Alevkaya Forest Station; ☺8am-4pm) **FREE** One for the botany fans, the herbarium here is home to a vast pressed-plant collection of endemic Cypriot flora, including some 1250 native plant species. The collection was originally created by English botanist Deryck Viney, whose book *Illustrated Flora of North Cyprus* documents the country's diverse botanical treasures. The herbarium is in Alevkaya (Halevga) Forest Station, on the back road in the Beşparmak Range.

To get here, take the signposted forest road off the southern side of the Beşparmak Pass. Alternatively, from the northern coastal road, take the road signposted as Karaağaç (Harkia) or Esentepe.

Beaches

Northern Cyprus has separated many of its beaches into paid and public beaches, the latter called *halk plajları*. The paid beaches are designed to be tourist-friendly and entry usually costs around 10TL.

Escape Beach   BEACH

(Yavuz Çıkarma Plajı; www.escapebeachclub.com; Alsancak; 10TL) This is one of Kyrenia's best swimming beaches. It's hugely popular and during summer you should get here early to find space. Swimmers should be mindful of the strong wind that can come in off the open water, which also makes it great for water sports (parasailing, kayaking and pedalos are all available here). Facilities offered by Escape Beach Club include a restaurant, bar, showers and, of course, plentiful sunloungers. It's roughly 10km west of Kyrenia.

Shayna Beach   BEACH

(Çatalköy; adult/child 10/5TL) This sheltered cove is home to a nice, narrow strip of sand, run by the Shayna Beach Club. For an easygoing and family-friendly day at the beach with full facilities, you usually can't go wrong; the sand is kept clean, there's plentiful shaded sunloungers, lifeguards patrol from 9am to 6pm during summer and all your dining needs are taken care of by Shayna's restaurant (Shayna Beach; mains 20-40TL, seafood meze per person 55TL; ☺10am-midnight April-Oct; ☎). It gets absolutely packed to the rafters during summer, though, so don't expect tranquillity.

Vrysi (Acapulco) Beach   BEACH

(Çatalköy; 25TL) Now commonly called Acapulco Beach, thanks to the megaresort of Acapulco Holiday Village which manages it, Vrysi caters mainly to package tourists. Day visitors are welcome as well though and the (rather expensive) admission fee includes access to all the hotel facilities such as pools, changing rooms, sunloungers and umbrellas. The beach itself is lovely and clean, though it can get extremely crowded.

★ Alagadı Beach   BEACH

(Turtle Beach; Alagadı) **FREE** Alagadı (Turtle) Beach, approximately 19km east of Kyrenia,

KARMI

The quaint village of Karmi (officially called Karaman, but still known as Karmi by everyone) is all traditional stone villas, whitewashed cottages, tumbling bougainvillea and narrow streets wriggling up the hillside. If its brushed-up facade seems at odds with other Northern Cyprus villages, that's because it is. Karmi is a pastiche of a Mediterranean village. All the houses are owned by Europeans on long leases from the Ministry of Tourism and have to comply with strict building codes to retain 'authenticity'.

After the Greek Cypriot villagers fled Karmi in 1974, Turkish Cypriot refugees from the South refused to settle here due to its secluded hillside location. To revive the village, the Ministry of Tourism hatched a plan in the 1980s to give foreigners long-leases on the crumbling houses as long as they paid the restoration costs. Today, Karmi is probably the prettiest village in the North and it's fun to wander the skinny alleys checking out the houses and their immaculately kept gardens. Just below the village is a small Bronze Age tomb site, while for walkers there is an excellent hike starting from here to St Hilarion Castle (p192; signposted from the main square). To take a break on your village rambles, cute Cafe Corner (main street, Karmi; cakes 6TL, sandwiches & breakfasts 15-25TL; ⏰10am-6pm; 🛜✏️) has a shady front terrace, excellent cake and decent coffee.

is where the Society for the Protection of Turtles (SPOT) has its small sea-turtle conservation and research centre (open 9am to 8.30pm May to September), where you can find out about turtle conservation. This is not really used as a swimming beach, but visitors can enjoy the scenery. Alagadı's twin sandy beaches are intentionally undeveloped, as they are considered turtle territory, and the beach is closed from 8pm to 8am from May to October.

If you get hungry, family-run St Kathleen's Restaurant (✏️0533 861 7640; Alagadı; mains 25TL; ⏰11am-10pm) is nearby. The grilled fish and meat dishes, served with a mountain of meze, are excellent and good value.

🏃 Activities

Walking

The Kyrenia Mountain Trail is an excellent hiking option. It covers 240km in total as it traverses Northern Cyprus west to east, from Koruçam Burnu (Cape Kormakitis) to Zafer Burnu (Cape Apostolos Andreas). You can choose a section that appeals to you, or for serious ramblers, it can constitute one long, amazing trek.

Spring is the best season for hiking, as you'll get to see a large number of the impressive 1600 plant, 350 bird and 26 reptile species that live in Northern Cyprus. This is prime orchid-spotting time too. Autumn is also ideal for walking.

Unfortunately the North Cyprus Tourism Organisation (p192) has stopped producing

its brochure on the Kyrenia Mountain Trail and decent maps of hiking trails can be difficult to come by. Check out www.kyrenia mountaintrail.org for route-planning information and to buy maps. All sections of the Kyrenia Mountain Trail are marked with green-and-white trail blazes.

Buffavento Castle Walk   HIKING

Starting from the Buffavento Restaurant on the Beşparmak Pass road, you can hike up the mountain road to where the remnants of Buffavento Castle (p193) cling to the clifftop. Two and a half kilometres uphill, a walking track – marked by red trail blazes – verges off to the right, winding its way to the castle car park at the top.

This is a great day walk for those who don't have their own transport as the Kyrenia–Famagusta (Gazimağusa) bus passes right beside the Buffavento Restaurant.

Karmi (Karaman) to St Hilarion Walk   HIKING

A good day-hike choice for experienced walkers. Starting from the village main square in Karmi (p195), next to the church, a signpost points to the trailhead of this circular hike which winds up the mountainside to St Hilarion Castle (p192) with excellent views on the ascent. Coming back, be aware that part of the descent is exceedingly steep.

Ağırdağ to Geçitköy Trek   HIKING

The trek from Ağırdağ (Agirda) to Geçitköy (Panagra) is a good hike for experienced walkers. Best tackled in sections over a few days, it runs west along the southern flank of the Kyrenia Range. It starts at Ağırdağ village on the Kyrenia–North Nicosia road and finishes at Geçitköy on the Kyrenia–Morfou road.

Alevkaya to Kantara Trek HIKING
Alevkaya to Kantara is a long easterly trail, with over 40km of hiking, connecting the Alevkaya Herbarium (p194) Forest Station to Kantara Castle.

Beşparmak Range Trek HIKING
The ultimate trek for mountain-view fans is this hike along the spine of the Beşparmak Range, taking in forest trails and villages along the way. As with the Ağırdağ to Geçitköy trek (p196), this route is best walked in sections, staying in local villages. The section starting from Buffavento Castle (p193) and ending at Bellapais is among the most beautiful.

Diving

Amphora Diving DIVING
(☑ 0542 851 4924; www.amphoradiving.com; Kervansaray Beach, Karaoğlanoğlu; Discover Dcuba €30, Zenobia Wreck day excursion €130) As well as offering all the usual Professional Association of Diving Instructors (PADI) courses, Amphora Diving operates regular dive safaris to the *Zenobia,* one of the world's top-five wreck dives, off the coast of Larnaka in the Republic of Cyprus. Amphora is based approximately 6km west of Kyrenia.

Scuba Cyprus DIVING
(☑ 0533 865 2317; www.scubacyprus.com; Hacı Ali Sokak, Alsancak; 1 dive €22, 5-dive package €100; ☺ 9am-5pm) Offers regular PADI and Scuba Schools International (SSI) diving courses as well as good-value dive packages and dive cruises. The company's boat is often moored in Kyrenia's Old Harbour while its main office is located 12km west of Kyrenia.

Tours

Cyprus Wildlife Ecology BIRDWATCHING
(☑ 0392 224 0850, 0548 886 8684; www.cypruswildlifeecology.com; day trips for 1-4 people €220) 🕊 These excellent birdwatching trips are led by conservation-biologist duo Robin Snape and Damla Beton. Hugely involved with the North Cyprus Society for Protection of Birds and Nature, they design tailored trips to spot the incredible wealth of bird life in both the Kyrenia and Famagusta areas.

Highly recommended for anyone interested in discovering Northern Cyprus' wealth of wildlife.

SPOT Turtle Watching Tours OUTDOORS
(☑ 0548 886 8684; www.cyprusturtles.org; Alagadı Beach; suggested donation per person €10; ☺ late May-late Sep) 🕊 The Society for the Protection of Turtles (SPOT) runs regular night tours between late May and August at Alagadı Beach (p195), where visitors can watch female turtles covering up their nests (tours are occasionally run on the Karpas Peninsula as well). From late July to late September there are also opportunities to witness hatchling releases and nest excavations.

Numbers are limited to 17 people per night; bookings can be made through the website.

Örnek Holidays TOURS
(☑ 0533 888 4111; www.ornekholiday.com; Dedekorkut Plaza 13, Karakum; ☺ 9am-6pm Mon-Sat, from noon Sun) Specialists in Northern Cyprus hiking tours with excellent guides who have expertise in flora and bird life as well as history. Runs various small-group tours throughout the year, focused on themes such as cycling and culture as well as creating tailor-made tours for clients.

Eating

★ Tervetuloa Restaurant TURKISH €€
(Ufuk Sokak, Alsancak; meals 20TL; ☺ noon-11pm; 🕊) If you like your meze, don't miss Tervetuloa. It's a casual place with little pretension that serves up a parade of some of the tastiest meze dishes in Northern Cyprus, outshining the main dishes such as Cypriot classics and seafood. Just off the main coast road, it's about 10km west of Kyrenia. The full menu is only available after 6pm.

Jashan's INDIAN €€
(Karaoğlanoğlu Caddesi; mains 22-30TL; ☺ 6-11pm; 🕊) If you're hankering for a taste of the subcontinent, Jashan's is one of the area's top spots. To cater for its main customer-base, the menu is mostly British-style Indian food with the usual kormas and chicken tikkas but there's a few more authentic Punjabi dishes thrown in too. It's set back off the main road, approximately 4km west of Kyrenia.

Eminem Restaurant CYPRIOT €€€
(☑ 0548 881 1818; Böğürtlen Sokak 8, Çatalköy; meze per person (2 ppl minimum) 50-60TL; ☺ 5.30pm-midnight Tue-Sat, 12.15-10pm Sun; 🕊) If meze feasting tops your to-do list, then head to this family-run restaurant, just off the Kyrenia–Çatalköy (Agios Epiktitos)

highway. The fresh flavours of Cypriot cooking shine in the set menus, including creamy hummus, seasonal vegetables drizzled in olive oil and herbs, and mixed grill plates of *sheftalia* (*şeftalı kebap* in Turkish; sausages encased in caul fat) and chicken.

Buffavento Restaurant TURKISH €€€

(Beşparmak Pass; mains 35-50TL; ☺10am-11pm; 🛜) If you want views with your meal, this large, rustic wooden restaurant on the Beşparmak Pass – just opposite the turn-off to Buffavento Castle (p193) – is a great lunch choice. All the usual kebab suspects are represented and everything comes with a good meze selection to start. Service is super friendly.

🍷 Drinking & Nightlife

Club Locca CLUB

(www.escapebeachclub.com; Escape Beach, Alsancak; ☺10pm-late Fri-Sat; 🛜) Located right on the waterfront, Club Locca gets packed on Friday and Saturday nights with nightlife-lovers enjoying a mix of R&B, hip-hop and Turkish pop. It's at Escape Beach (p194), 10km west of Kyrenia, just off the main road.

Ice Lounge & Club CLUB

(☑0542 889 3333; off Karaoğlanoğlu Caddesi, Alsancak; ☺10.30pm-5am; 🛜) This club near Escape Beach (p194) is one of the most popular nightlife venues along the coast. Iridescent lights glow on its outdoor bars and stage and there are regular events hosted by international DJs during the summer.

Bellapais (Beylerbeyi)

Charmingly sleepy, the little village of Bellapais (Beylerbeyi) sits snugly into the mountainside, offering spectacular views of the Mediterranean coastline below. The impressive remnants of Bellapais Abbey (p197) are positioned on the village's lower flank, where narrow lanes rimmed by pot-plant-festooned houses creep up the hill. Just past the monastery there is a large car park on the left, so you can avoid stopping in the main street.

Bellapais found literary fame after being immortalised by British writer Lawrence Durrell, who lived here during the Ethniki Organosi tou Kypriakou Agona (EOKA; National Organisation for the Cypriot Struggle) uprising against British rule. His entertaining memoir of his time here, *Bitter Lemons*

of Cyprus, is a love letter to the village and a way of life now long gone.

Sights & Activities

★**Bellapais Abbey** HISTORIC SITE

(Zafer Caddesi; adult/student 9/5TL; ☺9am-6pm Jun-Sep, to 4pm Oct-May) The exquisite ruins of this Augustinian monastery are reason enough to drive up the mountain to Bellapais. It was built in the 12th century by monks fleeing Palestine after the fall of Jerusalem to Saladin (Selahaddin Eyyubi) in 1187. They called the monastery *Abbaye de la Paix* (Abbey of Peace), from which the corrupted version of the name, Bellapais, evolved.

The original structure, built between 1198 and 1205, was augmented between 1267 and 1284, during the reign of Hugh III. The cloisters and large refectory were added after that by Hugh IV (1324–59), and these embellishments are most of what remains today.

The 13th-century church is in fine condition, and remains much as it was in 1976, when the last of the stoic Orthodox faithful had to leave.

Behind is the 14th-century cloister lined with towering cypress trees and rimmed with Gothic-arched arcades that have survived the centuries almost intact. From here there are stairs up to the rooftop where you can savour tumbling views across the plains down to the sea. On the western side of the cloister is the kitchen court which has all but a few walls remaining.

The refectory on the north side of the cloister is frequently used for gatherings, events and wedding photos. Note the lintel above the main entrance with its Lusignan coat of arms.

Home of Lawrence Durrell NOTABLE BUILDING

(Acı Limon Sokak; ☺11.30am-1pm Sep) A yellow plaque above the door marks the house where British writer Lawrence Durrell lived in the early 1950s, marking Bellapais on the literary map with his descriptions of the village's idyllic, mixed-community life in his memoir *Bitter Lemons of Cyprus*.

To reach the house, follow the signs uphill for 200m on the main street, to the right of Huzur Ağaç (Tree of Idleness) Restaurant (p198). The house is now a private residence and is only open to visitors during September.

Bellapais Walk HIKING

Starting from the junction of Kemer and Tatlısu Sokaks in Bellapais, this circular day

KYRENIA (GIRNE) & THE NORTH BELLAPAIS (BEYLERBEYI)

hike takes you uphill to walk on the lofty ridge above the dinky village for astonishingly beautiful panoramas over the entire countryside.

✈ Festivals & Events

Bellapais Music Festival MUSIC
(www.bellapaisfestival.com; ⊘ May-Jun) Held annually during May and June, this festival of classical music, choirs, opera singers and brass-band concerts takes place in and around the atmospheric arches of Bellapais Abbey. Look out for event details in Kyrenia and around town.

✕ Eating

Cafe Oregano CAFE €€
(Şehit Enver Ali Sokak; sandwiches 18-25TL, cakes 12-14TL; ⊘ 10.30am-8pm; 🛜) This cafe's shaded outdoor terrace, decked out in geraniums and gerberas, is one of our favourite places to put our feet up after wandering Bellapais' lanes. The menu of European-style sandwiches (the smoked turkey and cranberry sauce can't be beaten) and calorific cakes and tarts makes for a relaxed lunch and there's decent coffee and plenty of tea options.

Tarihi Değirmen Historic Mill Cafe CAFE €€
(Değirmen Sokak; mains 15-25TL; ⊘ 11am-6pm) Follow the signs from the road up Bellapais hill from the abbey and you'll find this cafe, set in an old mill (with grinding machines on show) where locals once produced their olive oil. It's a good option for coffee or cold drinks as well as snacks and traditional Cypriot grills.

★ Bella Moon CYPRIOT €€€
(☑ 0542 851 6898; Zafer Caddesi; mains 25-35TL; ⊘ 6-11.30pm; 🛜) Head through the arch to the leafy courtyard to dine on meals of simple grilled-meat dishes which all come loaded down with plenty of homemade meze. This family-run restaurant has a charmingly old-fashioned atmosphere and warm and welcoming service. Pick-up and drop-off transfers from Kyrenia hotels can be arranged if you prebook.

Kybele INTERNATIONAL €€€
(☑ 0392 815 7531; Bellapais Abbey grounds; mains 35-54TL; ⊘ 11am-11pm; 🛜) Even if the food was so-so, the atmospheric garden setting and fantastic views of Bellapais Abbey next door would still make Kybele the prime spot for dining in the village. Luckily the menu of steaks, seafood and kebabs is top-notch.

Come for dinner to experience the romantic floodlit abbey ambience. The restaurant can provide free transfers from Kyrenia hotels.

Huzur Ağaç (Tree of Idleness) Restaurant INTERNATIONAL €€€
(☑ 0392 815 3380; Zafer Caddesi; sandwiches 19TL, mains 27-38TL; ⊘ 10am-11.30pm; 🛜 ☑) Across the road from Bellapais Abbey, the shady verandah at Huzur Ağaç is Bellapais' most famous lunch spot, with a large menu of sandwiches, kebabs and classic Cypriot favourites. Outside is the 200-year-old robinia which may (or may not) be Lawrence Durrell's famed 'Tree of Idleness'.

ℹ Getting There & Away

There's no public transport between Kyrenia and Bellapais. Taxis in Kyrenia charge around 25TL one-way. In Bellapais, taxis wait right beside the abbey. For those with sturdy legs and wanting some exercise, it's a straightforward 6km walk from Bellapais into the centre of Kyrenia, all downhill.

LAPTA (LAPITHOS)

The sprawling village of Lapta (Lapithos) winds up a hill in green, leafy lanes, rimmed by streams gurgling their way down the slope. Although the lower district along the coastline has been gobbled up by holiday-home complexes and big hotels, the old district, higher up the hill, still holds on to some traditional charm.

Lapta was one of the original city-kingdoms of Cyprus and a regional capital under Roman rule. Its abundant water supply and protected position have made it a favourite choice of foreign rulers and settlers for centuries.

A mixed village pre-1974, Lapta accommodated Greek Cypriots and Turkish Cypriots in harmony, until the skirmishes of the 1960s saw a mosque's bell tower spoiled in the wake of local differences. In the mid-1990s forest fires devastated much of the region but fortunately missed this town. Today the village population is a blend of Europeans, mainland Turks and Turkish Cypriots.

There are no real sights as such, but the **Lambousa Fish Ponds** (off Fevzi Çakmak Caddesi) FREE, hewn by fishermen in the ancient town of Lambousa as a place to store the day's catch, are an interesting oddity, and there are tombs cut into the rocky cliff behind.

Eating

Hanımeller CYPRIOT €€
(Fevzi Çakmak Caddesi; mains 18-30TL;
⊙10.30am-11pm) Grab yourself a table on the shoreside to make the most of the sea views, and dine on well-cooked and flavourful kebab dishes as well as all the usual Turkish Cypriot staples.

Charcos CYPRIOT €€€
(☑0533 876 3007; Şehit Celal Hassan Caddesi; mains 28-36TL; ⊙6-11pm) Trundle up Lapta's hill to find this atmospheric old house, festooned with local artwork. This is a good place to try Cypriot classics such as *kleftiko* (slow-cooked lamb, *küp kebap* in Turkish; it must be ordered in advance) and *stifado* (beef or rabbit stew with onions), or simply feast on lamb chops. Every meal comes with soup, chips, salad and dessert.

The Hut INTERNATIONAL €€€
(☑0533 874 9801; Fevzi Çakmak Caddesi; mains 25-35TL; ⊙11.30am-10pm May-Sep, to 6pm Apr & Oct; 🛜🅿) Good burgers, juicy steaks, a smattering of seafood, brunch favourites of eggs Benedict and French toast, plus cracking Mediterranean views. It's no wonder The Hut remains one of Lapta's most popular relaxed summer venues, with a great bar to boot. A good choice for when you're all kebabed out.

ⓘ Getting There & Away

Dolmuşes between Kyrenia and Lapta run every 30 minutes throughout the day (5.50TL, 20 minutes).

THE NORTHWEST

Away from the busy coastline around Kyrenia, traffic thins to a dribble and the road, rimmed by fields and citrus groves, leads into the northwest region of the Kyrenia Range. At the western tip is the Koruçam (Kormakitis) Peninsula, fringed at its eastern edge by the sandy sweep of Horseshoe Beach (p204), while to the south is the agricultural town of Morfou and its frescoed church. Head southwest from here along the coast to pass through the one-time mining port of Gemikonağı (Karavostasi) and little Lefke (Lefka) before making the final push onwards to the important archaeological sites of Ancient Soloi (p205) and Ancient Vouni (p205).

Distances here are relatively short, with the journey best made in a circular route, returning to North Nicosia via the peninsula and Kyrenia, or vice versa. There is also a Green Line crossing into the Republic of Cyprus, at Zodhia, near Morfou.

ⓘ Getting Around

Although the main towns have *dolmuş* services, the only way to get to the major historic sights such as Ancient Soloi and Ancient Vouni is with your own transport.

Dolmuşes run from North Nicosia every 30 minutes to Morfou (8TL), Gemikonağı (Karavostasi; 11TL) and Lefke (Lefka; 11TL).

Morfou (Güzelyurt)

POP 18,946

Once the centre of Cyprus' lucrative citrus industry, Morfou's vast groves begin shortly before the village of Şahinler (Masari),

---

TWO TREE HILL

When British writer Lawrence Durrell took up residence in Bellapais (Beylerbeyi) between 1953 and 1956, he little realised the minor controversy he would leave behind almost 50 years later. His famous book *Bitter Lemons of Cyprus* described life in the then blissfully bucolic mixed community and his trials and tribulations while purchasing and renovating a house in the village, along with the intrigues and gossip of local life.

Among the villagers' favourite activities was spending many hours in idle conversation under the so-called 'Tree of Idleness', which dominated the main square. However, throughout the book, Durrell never once mentioned what kind of tree it was. Maybe it was a plane, or a mulberry, or perhaps an oak?

Today there are two trees that vie for the title. One is a leafy mulberry tree, overshadowing the coffee shop next to the monastery ticket office. The other contender, hardly 20m away, is a robinia casting shade over the Huzur Ağaç (Tree of Idleness) Restaurant (p198). In fairness, both trees qualify for the role pretty well: both have their supporters and draw idle crowds of onlookers who like to sit and drink coffee or a cold beer, just as the villagers did in Durrell's day. So pick your tree, sit idly by, and ponder.

KYRENIA (GIRNE) & THE NORTH MORFOU (GÜZELYURT)

WHAT'S IN A NAME?

Since 1974, all the original Greek place names in Northern Cyprus have been replaced by Turkish names. Road signs to Kyrenia (Girne) and Famagusta (Gazimağusa) usually state both names but road signs for smaller towns and villages just display the Turkish name. Those only familiar with the pre-partition names may find it difficult to navigate without a new road map, available from the tourist information office (p192) in Kyrenia.

stretching all the way to the sea. Today, this quiet, provincial town of small shops and sputtering agriculture would be completely overlooked by tourism if it wasn't for the fine Agios Mamas Orthodox Church (p202), with its preserved frescos lording it up over the main square.

 Sights

 **Agios Mamas
Orthodox Church** CHURCH
(Main Square; combined admission with museum adult/student 7/5TL) Dedicated to the island's beloved tax-repelling patron saint, this church was formerly the site of a pagan temple. Before the 1974 Turkish invasion of the North, the faithful used to visit the ancient marble tomb of Saint Mamas here. Today, visitors come to see the lavish, blue-backed frescoes which cover the church's interior. The church is kept locked, but you can gain access by asking the staff at the Archaeological & Natural History Museum next door.

According to lore about Saint Mamas, a mysterious liquid is said to have oozed from his tomb when the Ottomans pierced it looking for treasure. The liquid, apparently flowing freely at irregular intervals, was supposed to have cured ear aches; as such, ear-shaped offerings can be seen around the tomb.

**Archaeological &
Natural History Museum** MUSEUM
(Güzelyurt Müzesi; Main Square; combined admission with church adult/student 7/5TL; ⏱9am-6pm May-Sep, to 3.30pm Oct-Apr) Next door to the Agios Mamas Orthodox Church, this little museum's upper floor displays some extraordinary finds from the archaeological site of Soloi (p205) and the nearby Bronze

Age site of Toumba tou Skourou, as well as an exceptionally beautiful Artemis statue unearthed at Salamis, near Famagusta.

The ground floor is given over to a bizarre taxidermy exhibit including a two-headed lamb and (oddly) a bunch of rabbits from New Zealand.

✕ **Eating**

There are some modern, generic-style restaurants dishing up kebabs and pizza in the centre but they're nothing to write home about. If you're out and about on a day trip of the northwest, you're better off heading a little further west, to the seafood restaurants near Gemikonağı.

ℹ **Getting There & Away**

There are hourly dolmuşes to Kyrenia (10TL, one hour) and every 30 minutes to North Nicosia (8TL, 45 minutes) throughout the day.

Gemikonağı (Karavostasi)

From the calm and secluded rough-pebble beach in Gemikonağı (Karavostasi), you can see the entire coast stretching northeast around Morfou Bay (Güzelyurt Körfezi). Although the beaches here are not as visually appealing as the softer, sandy ones found on the north coast, there are far fewer swimmers.

Pre-1974, local villagers from the Troödos foothills came to the bay to swim, and now with the passport checkpoints open, some are coming here again. The once-flourishing port of Gemikonağı dominates the bay, with its abandoned jetty slowly sagging by the port itself.

East of town, you'll notice the scarred hinterland, heavily mined by a large conglomerate. It ceased mining after 1974 and has left the town with a decidedly backwater appearance.

Nonetheless, the town supports a small local tourist industry, thanks to a few good restaurants dotted along the coast and its beaches. If you're heading to the ancient ruins of Soloi (p205) and Vouni (p205) this is the best place to stop for lunch. Both Karabetça King (☑0392 727 7350; Ecevit Caddesi, Yedidalga; mains 25-35TL; ⏱noon-11pm May-Oct; ☎) and Mardin Restaurant (☑0392 727 7527; Ecevit Caddesi, Gemikonağı; mains 25-35TL; ⏱11am-11pm May-Oct; ☎) have terraces overlooking the sea and offer seafood-strong menus.

MAVI KÖŞK

Probably the most eccentric sight in Northern Cyprus, the Mavi Köşk (Blue House; Çamlıbel; 3TL, credit/debit cards only; ☉ Tue-Sun 9am-4pm) in the village of Çamlıbel was supposedly built by Paulo Paolides, lawyer to Archbishop Makarios III. Lavishly fitted out in the retro-tastic style of the day, the rooms (which come in a rainbow of colours, not just blue) are a vision of kitsch tiles, plush mid-century-modern details and gaudy features such as an iguana-skin-covered custom-made drinks cabinet. The house sits in a military-controlled area and you'll need your passport to enter.

There are plenty of completely uncorroborated rumours about Mavi Köşk, the main one being that Paolides was involved with the Italian mafia, was smuggling guns into Cyprus for the uprising against British rule and the house acted as an ammunition depot. Various stories about secret tunnels under the house and rooms where mafia members once met are also swirled around. Paolides escaped (some say by using a secret tunnel) from the house during the 1974 Turkish invasion and died in 1986. Accordingly, his death is shrouded in myth as well, with some saying he was killed during a mafia meeting in Sicily. Whatever the truth, the house is a time capsule of highly kitsch design which would have been the height of chic for its day.

It's well-signposted from the main road on the outskirts of Çamlıbel (Myrtou). You leave your passport with the soldiers stationed at the booth just before the car park. The guards inside can give you an English-language information sheet, which walks you through each room describing the features. Unfortunately, no photographs are allowed inside, though you are allowed to take photos in the garden behind.

Nearby, to the east, is the 15th-century Agios Panteleimon Monastery (Çamlıbel), which is the subject of a UNDP- and EU-supported conservation project.

🏃 Beaches

The 12km stretch west of Gemikonağı has a mixture of sand and pebbly beaches, ending at the passport checkpoint with the South.

Asmalı Beach
BEACH

FREE Asmalı Beach is slap in front of the village of Yeşilirmak (Limnitis). It's a clean pebbled beach, with some surrounding it, catering to those who travel this far.

Yedidalga Beach
BEACH

(Yedidalga Plajı) FREE This pebbled public beach with stretches of imported sand has a wooden pier for diving and swimming, a small bar and restaurant, a changing room and toilet facilities. It is well signposted and easily found.

Lefke (Lefka)

A few kilometres from Gemikonağı, the road runs at a right angle to the hillside village of Lefke (Lefka). Its position amid limitless greenery and rolling hills gives it a pleasant and fresh feel.

The town's name is derived from the Greek word *lefka* (meaning 'poplar'). Today, with more orange groves and palm trees than poplars, the village is known for its superb citrus fruits.

Although Lefke is home to a large community of British expats, it is also regarded as a stronghold for the Islamic faith. It is the headquarters of the Naqshbandi order of Sufism and their charismatic leader Şeyh Nazım Kıbrıslı and his followers. This order follows the principles of Islam dutifully and urges less-strict Turkish Cypriots to do the same.

There is little to do in the village itself, save for taking in the Piri Osman Paşa Mosque and its courtyard, walking the windy streets, eating the delicious oranges and spotting pieces of broken aqueducts.

Ancient Soloi

One of Cyprus' ancient city-kingdoms, Soloi (Soli Harabeleri; adult/student 7/5TL; ☉ 8am-7pm May-Sep, to 3.30pm Oct-Apr) was originally referred to as Si-il-lu, on an Assyrian tribute list that dates from 700 BC.

The site consists of two main parts: the basilica near the entrance to the site, and the theatre, up the hill and south of the basilica. Most of the site has not yet been excavated but there are also some sparse ruins

KORUÇAM (KORMAKITIS) PENINSULA

A trip to the exposed northwestern tip of Northern Cyprus, known as Koruçam Burnu (Cape Kormakitis), is a fantastic day excursion from Kyrenia, with a number of deserted beaches on the way. Pack a picnic lunch, and enjoy the solitude at the cape and its surrounds. Apart from being the 'land's end', it is also home to one of Cyprus' least-known religious communities, the Maronites.

During the 4th century, Maronites broke away from the prevailing Orthodox religious theory of Christianity, which said God was both man and god. In contrast, they followed the Monophysite religious line, which states that God could only be viewed as one spiritual persona.

Persecuted by Orthodox Christians for their beliefs, they first sought refuge in Lebanon and Syria, before coming to Cyprus in the 12th century in the wake of the crusaders, whom they had helped as auxiliaries in the Holy Land campaign.

Post-1974 the Cypriot Maronites have clung to a tenuous existence in Koruçam village, where they still maintain a church. Over the years, the once-vigorous congregation has gradually left, and now barely 100 people remain to keep the old traditions and religion alive. The Maronites, like the Armenians and Latin religious communities, had to choose allegiance with either the Greek or Turkish communities in the 1960s. They chose the Greeks, and since '74 the youth from the village have gradually all but disappeared, crossing over into the South to study in Greek schools. Those who remained in the North have managed to tread the fine line between political and religious allegiances, with some degree of success. Pre-2003 their relatives from the South were even able to visit them on weekends. Since the passport checkpoints have opened, the South's Maronites visit for longer periods. Many hope that some of the younger generations will return to live here, preserving the village and its people's traditions.

Getting here is pretty simple, with a mostly paved road taking you almost all the way. It's best tackled as a loop starting from the northern end of the Kyrenia–Morfou (Güzelyurt) road, at the junction after the village of Karşıyaka (Vasileia).

From the junction follow the signs to Sadrazamköy (Livera). On your right you will see signs to petite Horseshoe Beach and Horseshoe Beach Restaurant (Horseshoe Beach; meals 20-35TL; ☉11am-8pm May-Oct), perfect spots for lunch and a swim.

To get to the cape, follow the winding road for 10km past Sadrazamköy; from here you find a 3.5km dirt track, which is easily driven with a conventional car. There are bare rocks, a solar-powered shipping beacon and a small rocky islet just offshore. This is the island's closest point to Turkey, which is a mere 60km across the sea.

For a different and interesting drive back, go via the picturesque inland loop road, through Koruçam village and past the massive Maronite Church of Agios Georgios, built in 1940 with funds raised by the villagers. The church is often kept closed.

Koruçam's Maronites have kept their dialect of Aramaic (the forgotten language of Christ) for hundreds of years, interlacing it with Greek, Turkish, French and Italian words, creating a richer version of their own language. While most communicate in this dialect or Turkish, some locals at the small coffee shop in Koruçam village speak Greek.

The final leg back to the Kyrenia–Morfou road is through a Turkish military area, with checkpoints at which you may be stopped. Once past, get on the main highway at Çamlıbel (Myrtou) and head back to Kyrenia. From here you can also go south to Morfou or turn southeast toward North Nicosia (Lefkoşa).

of a Roman-era agora north of the entrance, down the hill.

Soloi's grandest period began in 580 BC, when King Philokyprios moved his capital here, from Aepia, on the advice of his mentor, the Athenian philosopher Solon. Philokyprios promptly renamed the citadel Soloi in his honour.

In 498 BC, with the island under Persian rule, Soloi was part of the Ionian revolt, formed by Onesilous, king of Salamis. He had united all the city-kingdoms of Cyprus (except Amathous) in an attempt to overthrow the empire, but was ultimately defeated.

Soloi then languished until Roman times, when it flourished once again thanks to its rich copper mines. As was the case in many parts of Cyprus, Soloi and its wealth suffered sacking and looting by Arab raiders in the 7th century AD.

➡ **Soloi Basilica**

St Mark was baptised at Soloi by St Auxibius and its first church is thought to have been built in the 4th century. From what's left today it is difficult to appreciate the size and extent of the church, which by all accounts was impressive.

Most notable are the surviving decorated floors, including the mosaic of a swan with entwined floral patterns and small dolphin nearby.

➡ **Roman Theatre**

The Roman theatre is somewhat restored, after much of its original stonework, taken by the British in the late 19th century, was used to rebuild the dockside at Port Said.

The theatre is said to have been able to accommodate up to 4000 spectators in its day. The famous Roman statuette of Aphrodite of Soloi was discovered nearby. It is now on display in the Cyprus Museum in Nicosia (Lefkosia).

Ancient Vouni

The ruins may be sparse but the views at Ancient Vouni (Vouni Sarayı; adult/student 7/5TL; ☺ 8am-7pm May-Sep, to 3.30pm Oct-Apr)

are truly glorious and well worth the trip. On a superb hilltop location, this ancient site originally housed a palace and extensive building complex dating back to the 4th century BC.

The site consists of a discernible megaron (three-part rectangular room with central throne), private rooms and steps leading down to a courtyard and cistern. Here there's a pear-shaped stone believed to have supported a windlass (a machine for raising weights).

Vouni's origins and history are convoluted, but it's speculated that the palace was built by a Persian ruler from the nearby city-kingdom of Marion (today's Polis). The intent was to watch over the nearby Greek-aligned city of Soloi. However, this is unconfirmed at best, and based on scant entries by Herodotus in Book V of his *Histories*. It is true, however, that the stronghold does exhibit Persian palace architecture, which was added to and embellished later under Hellenistic rulers.

The palace was burned down in 380 BC (it's not known why or by whom) and was never re-established. Today the scant remains stand lonely on its hill, commanding excellent panoramic views across the region.

The site is reached by taking the signposted turn from the main road and following a narrow, steeply winding road all the way up the hill until you reach the car park and ticket office.

KYRENIA (GIRNE) & THE NORTH ANCIENT VOUNI

Famagusta (Gazimağusa) & the Karpas Peninsula

Best Places to Eat

➡ Othello's Meyhanesi (p215)

➡ Alevkayalı Restaurant (p223)

➡ Kiyi (p220)

➡ Oasis Restaurant (p224)

➡ Aspava Restaurant (p215)

Best Reminders of Old Cyprus

➡ Ancient Salamis (p217)

➡ Petek Confectioner (p214)

➡ Kantara Castle (p222)

➡ Monastery of Apostolos Andreas (p222)

Why Go?

The thin finger of the Karpas Peninsula (Karpasia in Greek; Karpaz in Turkish) is all rolling meadows, craggy cliffs and wild beaches with a handful of snoozy villages thrown in. It's a taste of old-style Cyprus that can't be beaten. Despite new roads and development, its agrarian soul still feels untouched by modern life.

When you've recharged your batteries with the Karpas' serene wilderness, turn back west to visit Ancient Salamis. This enigmatic window into the Hellenic world is the island's most impressive archaeological site.

Just to the south is the fortified city of Famagusta where you can climb the ramparts to walk the city walls. The city's faded long-lost grandeur can be found in lanes filled with gently dilapidated houses that sit beside crumbling ruins of once-majestic churches.

Brimming with history and full of mesmerising natural beauty, this is by far the island's most rewarding region to explore.

When to Go

➡ Wild orchids and flowers bloom on the Karpas Peninsula and bird life can be spotted from March to May.

➡ The International Famagusta Art & Culture Festival in July features performances amid the ruins of Salamis.

➡ Green and loggerhead turtles nest and hatch eggs on Karpas' wild beaches in August and September.

FAMAGUSTA (GAZIMAĞUSA)

POP 40,920

The walled city of Famagusta (Gazimağusa) was made for exploration. Winding lanes rimmed with terrace rows of houses suddenly give way to ruined Gothic churches where birds nest between roofless arches and scraps of faded frescos cling to stone walls. From atop the Venetian walls, the shattered shards of these once-grand churches punctuate the skyline of what was Cyprus' most lavish city.

Long since slumped into down-at-heel dilapidation, the area within the walls is endearingly shambolic. For years tourist infrastructure remained poor and most travellers only visited on day trips. Recently over €3 million in funding to preserve the walls and monuments has flooded in under the auspices of the Technical Committee on Cultural Heritage, the EU and the United Nations Development Programme. This spruce up has led to the opening of a clutch of guesthouses, finally allowing travellers a chance to sleep within the walled city itself.

History

Famagusta and its surroundings have an affluent and complex history. The wide sweep of Famagusta Bay and the sprawling Mesaoria plain was home to three major settlements over the ages: the Bronze Age city of Ancient Enkomi (Alasia), which existed during the 17th century BC; the Mycenaean settlement and tombs from the 9th century BC, described as a flourishing culture in Homer's *Iliad;* and the illustrious kingdom of Salamis, which prospered through the 6th century BC.

Founded by Ptolemy Philadelphus of Egypt in the 3rd century BC, Famagusta was originally known by its Greek name, Ammochostos, meaning 'buried in the sand'. For many years it was considered the bridesmaid to the famous city kingdom of Salamis, just to its north.

After Salamis was abandoned in AD 648, Famagusta's population greatly increased, but the city didn't truly bloom until the fall of Acre in 1291.

At this point, Christians fleeing the Holy Land took refuge in the city. In the late 13th century it became the region's main shipping stopover, gaining immense wealth almost overnight. A lavish and decadent lifestyle bloomed and more jewels and gold were said to be in Famagusta than in all of Europe's royal courts. This provoked scorn from the pious, who criticised what they felt were the loose morals of its citizens. To counteract this, a great number of churches were quickly built.

The great city's first decline began when the Genoese took control in the 14th century, prompting an exodus of its wealthiest and most illustrious citizens.

Although the town was recaptured by the Venetians 117 years later, its former fortune and decadence never really returned. During this time the huge walls and bastions were constructed, but this belated measure did little to prevent its capture by the Ottomans in 1571. In the bloody 10-month siege that ensued, an estimated 100,000 cannonballs were fired.

Under the Ottomans, Famagusta rotted like a bad tooth. Its ruined buildings were never repaired, leaving it in an almost Gothic time warp. The Old Town, Kaleici, became a Turkish Cypriot stronghold.

The region flourished again in the early 1960s. The renowned, predominantly Greek Cypriot resort district of Varosia (Maraş), just outside the southern side of the Old Town's walls, bloomed as the Mediterranean's new favourite holiday destination, annually pulling thousands of sun-seeking tourists to its stunning beaches. However, communal conflicts in 1964 saw more skirmishes in the area, resulting in the Turks essentially barricading themselves within the Old Town's walls and exiling any Greeks left to the confines of Varosia.

The island's invasion by the Turkish army in 1974 forced Famagusta, and more particularly Varosia, into the restricted border zone. Deserted by its Greek population in anticipation of the fast-approaching Turkish military, Varosia remains part of the large, uninhabited buffer zone and is now a ghost town. Haunting, with its gaping dark windows and abandoned tower blocks, and barricaded by oil drums and barbed wire, it is as it was in 1974, save for a few military outposts and occasional UN patrols.

◉ Sights

The eclectic mix of arched lanes, chapel ruins, Turkish baths, Byzantine and Knights Templar churches, and medieval quarters are best appreciated on foot. Allow the better part of a day to see the city properly.

★ **Lala Mustafa Paşa Camii**   MOSQUE
(St Nicholas Cathedral; Erenler Sokak; ⊙ outside prayer times) The former Cathedral of Agios Nikolaos (St Nicholas) is the finest example of

Famagusta & Karpas Peninsula Highlights

1 Ancient Salamis (p217) Exploring one of the most important cities of Cypriot antiquity.

2 Kantara Castle (p222) Savouring spectacular coastal views from this once-mighty Byzantine fortress.

3 Karpas Peninsula (p221) Road-tripping through scenery of undulating hills and patchwork fields to wild beaches, half-hidden church ruins and remote villages.

4 Famagusta (p207) Strolling atop the commanding walls then standing amid the shattered church fragments of Lusignan and Venetian splendour within the Old Town.

5 Golden Beach (p222) Swimming off one of the island's finest stretches of sand.

6 Church of Apostolos Varnavas (p218) Admiring the important icon collection kept within the soaring interior of this stately church.

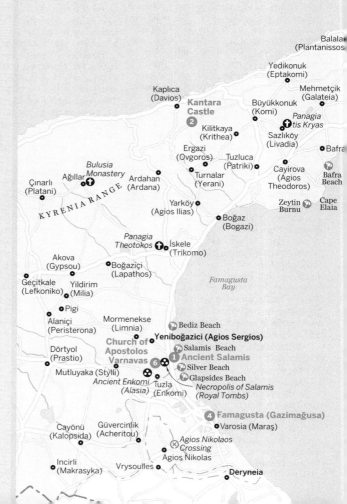

Zafer Burnu
(Cape Apostolos Andreas) **Kleides**
Kastros

Monastery of
Apostolos Andreas

Afendrika

Agios Filon
Beach
Agios Filon
Karpasia

5 Golden Beach
Nangomi Bay

Dipkarpaz
(Rizokarpaso)

Agios
Thyrsos

Panagia
Eleousa
Monastery

Yassi
Burnu Halk
Plajı

Basilica of
Agia Triada

Yenierenköy
(Yiallousa)

Sipahi Mt Pamboulos
(Agia (383m)
Triada)

Kaleburnu
(Galinoporni)

Yeşilköy
(Agios
Andronikos)

**Karpas
(Kırpaşa)
Peninsula**

3

Skoutari
(Üsküdar)

Kuruova
(Koroveia)

Panagia
Kanakaria Derince
(Vothylakas)

Avtepe
(Agios Simeon)

Nitovikla

Ziyamet
(Leonarisso)

Kumyalı
(Koma tou Gialou)

Kumyalı
(Koma tou Gialou)
Beach

MEDITERRANEAN SEA

(AKDENİZ)

N 0   20 km
      0   10 miles

ROAD TRIP > REMOTE RURAL VILLAGES OF THE KARPAS

The Karpas is Cyprus' most charming backwater, where peaceful silence replaces the sound of beach bars and car horns. This drive winds through sleepy villages where traces of Greek Cypriot culture live on in the Turkish north.

① Panagia Theotokos

Start the trip at the village of İskele (Trikomo), where the **Panagia Theotokos** (p220) houses an impressive collection of ancient icons, then take the main road into the Karpas, veering west to Turnalar (Yerani), where you can check out the church of Panagia Evangelistria, 1km to the town's west.

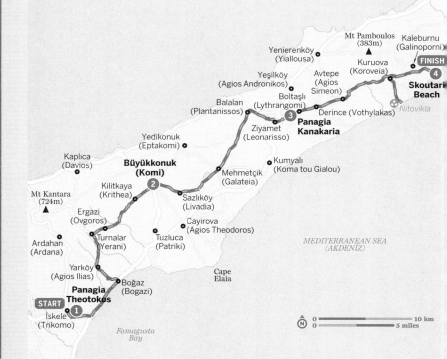

② Büyükkonuk (Komi)

From here go east (via Kutulus-Turnalar Yolu) through the traditional village of Ergazi (Ovgoros), then a further 9km northeast to Kilitkaya (Krithea). Another 2.5km along this road is the settlement of Büyükkonuk (Komi), Cyprus' first ecovillage, with restored traditional buildings and an old olive mill. After you've tried some local almonds and figs, take the old road east to the village of Sazlıköy (Livadia) and the 6th-century ruins of Panagia tis Kryas, which sits amid the fields 1km east of the village.

③ Panagia Kanakaria

The road northeast takes you to the vineyards of Mehmetcik (Galateia) village and its 95-proof *zivania* (Cypriot spirit). Leave via the main northeasterly road (not the stadium road) through the centre of the Karpas, and travel 16km through fields and groves to reach Balalan (Plantanissos). Continue southeast another 3km to Ziyamet (Leonarisso) then carry on past the Karpaz Yolu crossroad and through Gelincik (Vasili) to the village of Boltaşlı (Lythrangomi). Near the village entrance you'll find the church of Panagia Kanakaria. The church is famous as the original home of the Kanakaria Mosaics, which were looted a few years after the island was divided and repatriated to the Republic of Cyprus in the early 1990s. The church is usually kept locked but the village *muhtar* (elected leader) has the key. Ask around to find him.

④ Skoutari Beach

From here a road joins a string of small villages, Derince (Vothylakas), Avtepe (Agios Simeon) and Kuruova (Koroveia), with a series of unmarked tracks that lead to ancient cliff-tombs and the Bronze Age stronghold of Nitovikla (3km away) on the southern coast. Ask at the villages for the best paths to hike. Hop back in the car and go east to Kaleburnu (Galinoporni), where you can grab a bite and take the beach track to Skoutari Beach (Üsküdar) for a refreshing swim.

Famagusta (Gazimağusa)

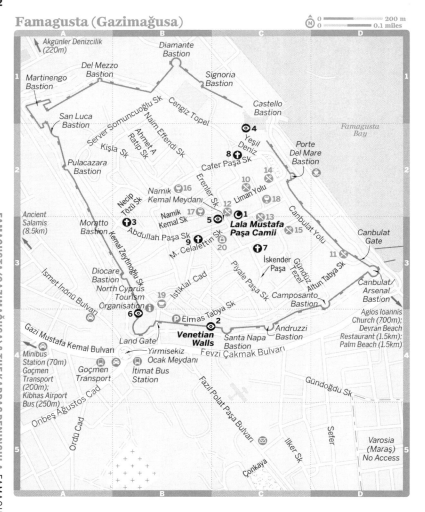

Lusignan Gothic architecture on the island, built between 1298 and 1326. Modelled on France's Cathedral of Reims, it outshines its sister church, the Church of Agia Sofia (now Selimiye Mosque) in North Nicosia (Lefkoşa).

Converted into a mosque (*camii* in Turkish) after 1571's Ottoman invasion, it still dominates the skyline of the Old Town. To enter, time your visit outside of prayer times and dress modestly.

During the Lusignan reign the church was Famagusta's centrepiece. As such, the last Lusignan king of Cyprus, Jacques II, and his infant son (Jacques III) were buried here.

The church was damaged considerably during the Ottoman siege of Famagusta and its twin towers were destroyed. The Ottomans added the minaret, stripped the church's interior of its Christian accoutrements and emptied the floor tombs.

The west-facing facade, now a pedestrian zone, is the most impressive part, with three gracious portals pointing towards a six-paned window, decorated with a circular rose.

Inside, the walls have been whitewashed in Islamic fashion, but the soaring Gothic architectural lines are still easy to follow.

Famagusta (Gazimağusa)

★ **Venetian Walls** HISTORIC SITE

Defining the Old Town, these imposing ramparts were constructed by the Venetians in the early 16th century. Although over 15m high and up to 8m thick, and surrounded by a now-waterless moat, the ramparts failed to keep the Ottomans at bay in 1571.

Like their counterpart in Nicosia (Lefkosia), Famagusta's walls comprised 14 bastions and five gates. Unlike in Nicosia, you can walk on sections of the walls here and get a sense of the sheer bulk of the fortifications.

Start your Famagusta wall tour at the southern end near the **Land Gate** on the **Ravelin (Rivettina) Bastion** (Akkule; Old Town entrance; ⊙9am-6pm Mon-Fri) **FREE**. It was here that the Ottomans first breached the fortifications. The Ravelin Bastion was being restored when we were last in town, but work should be finished by the time you arrive.

A set of stairs heads up onto the top of the walls on the eastern side of the Ravelin Bastion. From here, you can walk all the way along the top to the **Canbulat (Arsenal) Bastion** via the **Santa Napa**, **Andruzzi** and **Camposanto Bastions**. The Canbulat Bastion was renamed in honour of the Ottoman hero General Canbulat Bey, who died valiantly while attacking the walls on horseback during the bloody siege.

If restoration work on the eastern walls is still ongoing, take the path down the slope here, and walk down Canbulat Yolu until you reach **Porta del Mare** (the original Sea Gate). Here you can climb stairs up to the top again, although the views over the modern port are less than inspiring. This gate originally opened directly onto the sea; today the wharves have extended the land bridge considerably.

The next section of wall you can climb up on is at the **Diamante Bastion**, though you can't get very far as another restoration project is currently at work on the western walls. When this is finally finished, it is one of the most interesting sections of the walls to walk, starting from the steeply pitched **Martinengo Bastion** and passing the four minor bastions of **San Luca**, **Pulacazara**, **Moratto** and **Diocare** on your way back to the Ravelin Bastion.

Othello's Tower HISTORIC SITE

(Othello Kalesi; Canbulat Yolu; adult/student 9/5TL; ⊙9am-5.30pm Apr-Oct, 8am-3.30pm Nov-Mar) An extension of the Old Town's walls, Othello's Tower was constructed during Lusignan rule, in order to protect the harbour. In 1492 the Venetians further fortified the citadel and transformed it into an artillery stronghold.

In 2014 the building underwent a €1 million restoration carried out by the Technical Committee on Cultural Heritage. The restoration has sensitively preserved the tower's once-crumbling stonework.

The tower's name stems from a vague link to Shakespeare's play *Othello,* which has a modest stage note referring to 'a seaport in Cyprus'. Above the citadel's impressive entrance you'll see the Venetian Lion inscribed by its architect, Nicolò Foscarini. Leonardo da Vinci also apparently advised on the refurbishment of the tower during his visit to Cyprus in 1481.

The mix of Venetian and Lusignan architecture inside is a prime highlight of a visit here. The internal courtyard is bordered by the Great Hall, with beautiful vaults and corroded sandstone walls on its far side.

Ventilation shafts look out to the border ramparts, leading to Lusignan corridors and sealed chambers. Legend has it that fortunes still lie hidden here, buried by Venetian merchants in the face of the advancing Ottomans.

Palazzo del Provveditore   HISTORIC SITE
(Venetian Palace; Namık Kemal Meydanı) The ruined arches and supporting columns (taken from Salamis) of the Palazzo del Provveditore sit opposite Lala Mustafa Paşa mosque. The triple-arched entranceway is the best-preserved part.

St Peter & St Paul Church   CHURCH
(Sinan Paşa Camii; Abdullah Paşa Sokak) Although not open to the public, the magnificent facade of this mammoth 14th-century church, which has survived intact, gives you a good impression of what Famagusta would have looked like before most of its churches and monuments were ruined.

The church's construction was funded by a local merchant, Simon Nostrano, between 1358 and 1369. During the Ottoman period it served as a mosque and after the British arrived it was used as a wheat store.

St George of the Greeks Church   CHURCH
(Mustafa Paşa SM Ersu Sokak) The ruins of this once-stately and splendidly Gothic church are one of the most picturesque in the walled city. You can still make out the faint outlines of once-rich frescos upon the interior or stone walls. Beside it is the smaller, Byzantine St Simeon's Church where Salamis' archbishop St Epiphanios was said to have been first buried before his body was carted off to Constantinople by Emperor Leo in the 9th century.

St George of the Latins Church   CHURCH
(Cafer Paşa Sokak) Sitting incongruously amid a traffic intersection, St George of the Latins is one of Famagusta's oldest churches. The remaining walls with their distinctive lancet windows are a good example of early Gothic architecture.

Nestorian Church   CHURCH
(Abdullah Paşa Sokak) Built between 1360 and 1369 this Nestorian-order church has a sublimely well-preserved bell tower and squat golden-stoned facade.

According to local tradition, if you take soil from the church grounds and place it in your enemy's house, within one year they'll either die or leave Cyprus (it's probably best not to try out if this works on any enemies you have at home).

 Beaches

With Varosia being off limits, the best sand at Famagusta is at the south end of the city walls, at Palm Beach, or north of the city at Bediz Beach (p221) near Salamis.

Palm Beach   BEACH
(off Palmiye Sokak) The best strip of sand in Famagusta, and probably the weirdest beach you'll ever visit. The edge of the sand is rimmed with ruins of hotels with blown-out windows, and the southern end comes to an abrupt halt with a barricade of barbed wire and metal poles that run into the sea – with a soldier stationed in the watchtower above. Behind the barricade is the rest of Varosia's fine sweep of sand, backed by empty, decrepit hotel high-rises.

To get here, walk along the coast road (Havva Sentürk Caddesi) to the Palm Beach Hotel, head past the hotel and take the small alleyway signposted for the beach.

Festivals & Events

**International Famagusta
Art & Culture Festival**   MUSIC
(www.magusa.org/festival.aspx; ☉Jul) The festival takes place during July and includes a line-up of everything from classical and jazz to hip-hop, modern rock and reggae, performed by international and local artists. Concerts are usually staged near Othello's Tower within the Old Town and at Ancient Salamis' theatre.

Eating

Within the Old Town there are plenty of cafe-style places as well as a handful of more formal restaurants. Many places are open for lunch only due to the influx of day-trippers who leave once the sun has set.

★ **Petek Confectioner**   CAFE €
(☑0392 366 7104; Liman Yolu 1; cakes & desserts 4-10TL, ice cream 3-8TL; ☉10am-11pm; 🛜🍴) Famed throughout Northern Cyprus, Petek is a temple to all things sugary, with towers of *lokum* (Turkish delight), syrupy baklava, and what might be the best *dondurma* (ice cream) on the island. So pull up a pew and watch the world go by from Petek's verandah. Just make sure you've got enough money left over for the dentist bill afterwards.

Sweet Mama BAKERY €
(Mustafa Paşa SM Ersu Sokak 10; pastries & cakes 2-10TL; ⊙9am-6pm) Recover from trooping between the church ruins by grabbing a refreshing homemade lemonade and a börek (stuffed savoury pastry) or piece of cake, and relaxing in the leafy garden with its pots of colourful petunias and chirping birds.

Desdemona Bar & Restaurant TURKISH €€
(Canbulat Yolu 3; mains 25-30TL; ⊙6pm-midnight) There's a rough-and-ready look to this place but don't be put off, this restaurant-bar is superfriendly and serves excellent-value kebabs which come with plenty of meze. It's in an old stone building attached to the city walls. The dimly-lit interior is festooned with farming implements, instruments and oil paintings, and the bar area is a real local hang-out.

Ginkgo INTERNATIONAL €€
(✉0392 366 6660; Namık Kemal Meydanı; mains 22-35TL; ⊙11am-10pm; 🛜🍴) This friendly cafe-restaurant occupies an old *madrasa* (Islamic religious school) and arched Christian building right next to the Lala Mustafa Paşa mosque. The wide-ranging menu does everything from decent salads and sandwiches to kebabs, pasta and grilled fish. The lunch set menus are excellent value.

★**Othello's Meyhanesi** CYPRIOT €€€
(M. Celalettin Sokak; full meze per person 50TL; ⊙6pm-late; 🛜) It may not look fancy but this joint is where the locals go when they want

to indulge in full meze blow-outs. Pace yourself; this is the real-deal 30-plus-dish spread – don't expect to eat and run. If you are here on a weekend night, spontaneous folk dancing is likely to break out late in the evening.

★**Aspava Restaurant** CYPRIOT €€€
(✉0392 366 6037; Liman Yolu 19; set menu per person 60TL; ⊙11am-11pm; 🛜) Always bustling with tourists at lunchtime and locals during the evening, this vine-draped courtyard restaurant dishes up meze followed by a bevy of succulent grilled meats. Make sure you're hungry.

🍸 **Drinking & Nightlife**
The Old Town has a couple of really good bars and plentiful cafes where you can quaff a wine or two. To check out Famagusta's vibrant, modern youth scene, visit the cafes lining the New Town's main drag heading past the university towards Salamis.

De Molay BAR
(Kışla Sokak; ⊙noon-midnight; 🛜) Here's your chance to drink a beer in a Crusader church. The twin churches of the Knights Templars and Hospitallers were built in the 13th century and acted as headquarters for both orders in Cyprus. Where once swashbuckling knights prayed, now man-bun-toting cool kids hang out as the churches are now a bar.

One Shot Coffee CAFE
(Kemal Zeytinoğlu Sokak; ⊙9am-11pm; 🛜) Just opposite the Land Gate, this is hands down

VAROSIA (MARAŞ)

Before partition, Famagusta's new town district of Varosia (Maraş in Turkish) was a thriving community of Greek Cypriots and one of the liveliest beach resorts in the Mediterranean. All that changed in 1974, when Varosia's residents fled the Turkish invasion, leaving uncleared breakfast dishes and taking with them little more than the clothes they wore. Many left on the assumption that they would return within a few days, but Varosia has remained a ghost town ever since.

Behind the barricades, apartment blocks, shops and houses are caked in over 40 years of dust and sediment. A looted car dealership still stocks a single 1974 model, entombed in its showroom. The grand hotels that once played host to Elizabeth Taylor and Brigitte Bardot have been left to slowly decay like giant hollow sentinels on the coast. On rare occasions, access has been granted to **Agios Ioannis Church** (⊙9am-1pm Mon-Fri), 120m into the restricted area, but most of Varosia has been closed to the outside world since 1974.

However, there are signs that the Turkish administration may be rethinking its policy of isolation. In 2017 the military announced that part of the beach would be opened to Turkish Cypriots, as a prelude to more widespread access. However, the announcement was met by outcry from Greek Cypriots, who regard the move as a violation of the UN resolution guaranteeing right of return for the town's original inhabitants.

the best coffee in Famagusta. To be fair, it doesn't have much competition but One Shot serves up both excellent European-style coffees and *Türk kahve* (Turkish coffee) at reasonable prices and with friendly, on-the-ball service to boot. Also a good choice for a quiet beer.

Hamam Inn Bar
BAR
(Liman Yolu; ⊙noon-late; 🕾) This bar-cafe is inside the stately 17th-century Cafer Paşa Hamam (Turkish bath). An atmospheric and historic choice for a beer or wine at the end of the day in the Old Town.

Monks Inn
BAR
(⊙6pm-late; 🕾) Inside a medieval house, this well-stocked bar is all about relaxing and sampling the cocktails. It's tucked away in a side street just east of Lala Mustafa Paşa Camii.

Devran Beach Restaurant
CAFE
(Palm Beach; ⊙10am-11pm; 🕾) The place for a beer on Palm Beach, with sun loungers and umbrellas to rent in front of the terrace.

Shopping

Craft and souvenir shopping is limited. There's a glut of shops in the Old Town touting counterfeit brand-name watches, sneakers and apparel all brought over from Turkey.

Hoşgör
ANTIQUES
(M Celalettin Sokak 24/1; ⊙10am-2pm Mon-Sat) In this interesting antiques trove you can find traditional Cypriot ceramics, engravings, embroidery and gifts.

❶ Information

EMERGENCY
Police station (✆0392 366 5310; İlker Sokak Körler) Located just to the south of the old city along İlker Sokak.

MEDICAL SERVICES
Yaşam Hastanesi (✆0392 366 2876; Gazi Mustafa Kemal Bulvarı; ⊙24hr) The nearest hospital; 1.5km west of the Old Town.

MONEY
There are ATMs and a bank in the central Old Town around Namık Kemal Meydanı, opposite Lala Mustafa Paşa mosque.
Money-Exchange Office (İstiklal Caddesi; ⊙8am-5.30pm Mon-Fri)

POST
Post office (✆0392 366 2250; Fazıl Polat Paşa Bulvarı; ⊙8am-3.30pm Mon-Fri)

TOURIST INFORMATION
North Cyprus Tourism Organisation (NCTO; ✆0392 366 2864; Ravelin Bastion; ⊙8am-5pm) Just inside the Land Gate. English-speaking staff. Good free maps of the Old Town in English.

❶ Getting There & Away

AIR
Ercan Airport (p182) is 50km northwest of Famagusta.
Kibhas (✆0533 870 7847; www.kibhas.org; Famagusta Bus Terminal; ticket 17.50TL) runs airport shuttle buses between Famagusta and the airport (50 minutes) every two hours.

BOAT
Akgünler Denizcilik (www.akgunlerbilet.com; Eşref Bitlis Caddesi; adult/car TL115/190; ⊙9am-5pm Mon-Fri) run three services weekly at 11pm on Monday, Wednesday and Friday from Famagusta's **ferry terminal** (Famagusta Port) to Mersin, in Turkey.
Coming from Mersin the ferry sails at 11pm on Sunday, Tuesday and Thursday.
Its ticket office is next to the Port View Hotel.

BUS
Famagusta is well connected with both North Nicosia and Kyrenia (Girne) by bus.
From the **İtimat bus station** (İtimat Otogar; ✆0392 366 6666; Onbeş Ağustos Caddesi), buses to North Nicosia (Lefkoşa; 11TL, one hour) leave every 15 minutes between 6am and 7pm Monday to Saturday, and between 7am and 7pm on Sundays. There are also hourly buses to Kyrenia (12TL, 1¼ hours) between 6.20am and 6.20pm from here.
If you're coming from Kyrenia, the buses usually terminate at the **Goçmen Transport office** (✆0392 366 4313; www.gocmentransport.com; Gazi Mustafa Kemal Bulvarı) rather than at the bus station.

MINIBUS
There are *dolmuşes* to İskele (Trikomo; 5TL, 20 minutes) at 8.30am, 11am, 1pm, 4pm and 5pm. To Yenierenköy (Yiallousa; 5TL, one hour) there are three buses on weekdays at 1pm, 3.30pm and 5pm. All these services leave from the **minibus station** (Dolmuş Otogarı; Gazi Mustafa Kemal Bulvarı).

TAXI
Kombos (shared taxis) leave for Kyrenia (13TL, one hour) hourly between 7am and 5pm from the **Kontor Office** (Gazi Mustafa Kemal Bulvarı).
A regular taxi to Salamis should cost 30TL one way.

ℹ️ Getting Around

There are no public buses within the city as most major sights and services are within walking distance.

Taxi stands are dotted around the central town. **Raşıt Taxi** (✆ 0392 366 6636; Gazi Mustafa Kemal Bulvarı) and **Ada Taksi** (İsmet İnönü Bulvarı) both operate in and around Famagusta as well as further afield. Tariffs are generally fixed but check before accepting a ride.

Sur Car Hire (✆ 0533 841 7979, 0392 366 4796; İsmet İnönü Bulvarı; from €22 per day, 3 day min; ⏰ 9am-5pm) is a reliable car hire company.

AROUND FAMAGUSTA

The vast crumbled ruins of Ancient Salamis, overtaken by weeds and wild fennel, are the big-hitter sights here, but there's plenty more to explore. Both the Church of Apostolos Varnavas and Ancient Enkomi are close by and combining all three makes for an excellent day trip. Afterwards, there are a couple of decent beaches which make for good swim stops or you can head to Boğaz's dinky fishing harbour for dinner at one of the fish restaurants with platforms right over the sea.

◉ Sights

★ Ancient Salamis   ARCHAEOLOGICAL SITE
(Salamis Yolu; adult/student 9/5TL; ⏰ 9am-6pm Apr-Oct, to 5pm Nov-Mar) According to legend, Salamis was founded around 1180 BC by Teucer (Teukros), son of Telamon, king of Salamina, on the Greek mainland. Brother to the hero Ajax, he was unable to return home from the Trojan War after failing to avenge his brother's death.

Today the vast, scattered remnants of this ancient kingdom, 9km north of Famagusta on the seaward side of the Famagusta–Boğaz Hwy, are one of the island's premier archaeological sites.

After its legendary beginnings, Salamis later came under Assyrian rule; the first recorded mention of it is on an Assyrian stele dated to 709 BC.

After a land and sea battle between the Greeks and the Persians in 450 BC the city (and island) submitted. The city remained under Persian control until the great patriot king Evagoras fought for and obtained independence. During his reign Salamis flourished. It issued its own money and nurtured a thriving philosophical and literary scene, receiving noted Greek thinkers and poets.

Later, after Alexander the Great put an end to Persian domination across the island, the city saw a short period of peace. Nicocreon (the last king of Salamis) submitted to Alexander's rule and after Alexander's death, continued to cooperate with the subsequent Ptolemaic rulers, quelling uprisings in other Cypriot kingdoms. Nicocreon's death in 311 BC remains a mystery. Some texts says that he committed suicide while others hold that he was murdered. What is clear is that despite Ptolemy rule over Salamis lasting until 58 BC, the city began to flounder after Nicocreon's death.

It wasn't until Cyprus became a Roman colony that the city prospered again, through rebuilding and public works. It went on to suffer two earthquakes and a tidal wave, requiring rebuilding once more, courtesy of Emperor Constantine II. In AD 350 the city was renamed Constantia and declared Episcopal.

Constantia suffered similar problems to its predecessor and in the 7th and 8th centuries it suffered Saracen Arab raids.

Its silted-over harbour became unusable and the city was essentially forgotten. Many of its stones were later used to build Famagusta.

➜ **Gymnasium**

The remains of the city's gymnasium, with columned courtyard and adjacent pools, used for exercise and pampering, allude to Salamis' original grandeur. Its northerly portico is surrounded by headless statues despoiled by Christian zealots as symbols of pagan worship. Many that had survived numerous raids have disappeared since 1974. Fortunately, some made it to Nicosia's Cyprus Museum and are now prized exhibits.

➜ **Baths**

East of the portico are the Hellenistic and Roman baths, where you can see the exposed underfloor heating system. The southern entrance has a fresco of two faces, and in the south hall are two of the site's finest mosaics, dating from the 3rd and 4th centuries AD.

One mosaic depicts Leda and the Swan, the other Apollo and Artemis combating the Niobids. Some believe that the latter is a scene of a battle between warriors and Amazons.

➜ **Theatre**

Dating from the time of Augustus (31 BC to AD 14), the theatre once held 15,000 spectators. Much of it was destroyed by

FAMAGUSTA (GAZIMAĞUSA) & THE KARPAS PENINSULA AROUND FAMAGUSTA

ℹ️ TIPS FOR VISITING ANCIENT SALAMIS

➡ Allow at least half a day for your visit. There is about 7km of rambling to see it all.

➡ Once you pass the main entrance, stick to the site map so that you don't retrace your steps too much.

➡ On hot days take a hat and bottles of water with you as there's no shade.

➡ Be wary of snakes, especially in the more overgrown parts of the site. This is not a site for wearing flip-flops.

➡ The adjacent beach is perfect for a swim after a day's exploring. There's a good patch of sand right by the entrance car park or, for a mid-exploration dip, take the short trail down to the beach from the Kambanopetra Basilica.

➡ The handy restaurant at the site entrance car park dishes up excellent meze and grills. It's a top spot for lunch.

earthquakes, leaving stone raiders to seize its blocks for building projects elsewhere. Since then, it has been partially restored and occasionally hosts outdoor events.

➡ Roman Villa

South of the theatre, the villa was originally a two-storey structure made up of a reception hall and an inner courtyard with columned portico. The villa was utilised long after the city was finally abandoned and used as an olive-oil mill. The grinding stone can still be seen today.

➡ Kambanopetra Basilica

The vast remains of this 4th-century basilica are an entrancing spot with lonely columns backed by the sea. Originally it would have been an impressive church with three apses. In the complex behind the church (believed to have contained a bathhouse) there is an intricate, well-preserved mosaic floor.

➡ Basilica of Agios Epifanios

Once the largest basilica in Cyprus, this church was built during the episcopacy of Epifanios (AD 386–403) and completely destroyed during Arab raids in the 7th century.

➡ Reservoir

At the southern end of the site you come to the Roman-era reservoir, which stored the water brought to Salamis by a 50km aqueduct.

➡ Agora & Temple of Zeus

Just behind the reservoir are the sparse remains of Agora – the city's place of assembly during the Roman era – and the Temple of Zeus which the Romans built over an earlier Hellenistic temple. Not much remains from either complex, the stones having long been pilfered for other building projects.

Necropolis of Salamis   ARCHAEOLOGICAL SITE
(Royal Tombs, Salamis Mezarlık Alanı; adult/student 7/3TL; ⊙9am-5pm) This ancient cemetery dates back to the 7th and 8th centuries BC and consists of a scattering of 150 graves spread out over the wide field.

The arrangement of the burial chambers closely matches descriptions of Mycenaean tombs in Homer's *Iliad*. Kings and nobles were buried here with their favoured worldly possessions, food, drink, and even their sacrificed slaves.

The tombs are prominently signposted, south of the Salamis turn-off, along the road to the Church of Apostolos Varnavas.

⭐**Church of Apostolos Varnavas**   CHURCH
(☑0392 378 8331; adult/student 9/5TL; ⊙9am-6pm Jun-Sep, to 3.30pm Oct-Apr) This beautiful Orthodox church is dedicated to St Paul's good friend Varnavas (Barnabas), who was born in Cyprus and carried out his missionary work here. Although his name and work are listed in the Bible's 'Acts of the Apostles', he was never officially one of them.

Today the church is an icon museum with a wide selection of Greek Orthodox icons and some frescos on display, but its the stunningly well-preserved architecture of the building that is the true star.

Three monks (who were also brothers) called Barnabas, Stefanos and Khariton governed the church from 1917. They attempted to remain after 1974 but ultimately left in 1976, following constant searches of the premises and travel restrictions imposed by the Turkish authorities. They lived out their days at Stavrovouni Monastery.

The church was spared from the destruction and looting that befell many churches in the North when Turkish authorities turned it into a museum. Although many Greek Cypriots have objected to the site's use for monetary gain and not for worship, they are pleased the church has survived.

The original church was built in AD 477, beside the site of Varnavas' tomb. It was dis-

Ancient Salamis

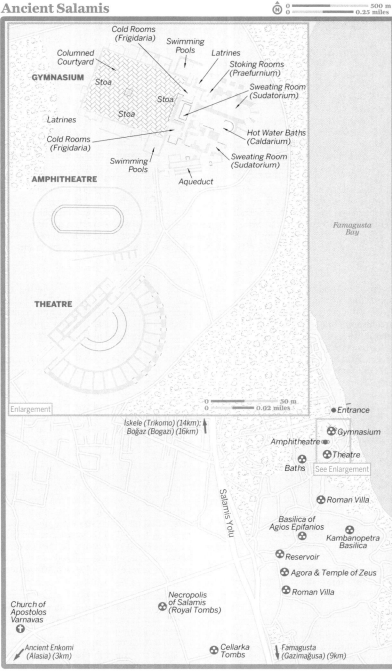

0 — 500 m
0 — 0.25 miles

GYMNASIUM

Cold Rooms (Frigidaria)

Columned Courtyard

Stoa

Stoa

Stoa

Swimming Pools

Latrines

Stoking Rooms (Praefurnium)

Sweating Room (Sudatorium)

Latrines

Cold Rooms (Frigidaria)

Swimming Pools

Hot Water Baths (Caldarium)

Sweating Room (Sudatorium)

Aqueduct

AMPHITHEATRE

THEATRE

Famagusta Bay

Enlargement

0 — 50 m
0 — 0.02 miles

İskele (Trikomo) (14km);
Boğaz (Bogazi) (16km)

● *Entrance*

Amphitheatre

🔀 *Gymnasium*

🔀 *Theatre*

Baths

See Enlargement

🔀 *Roman Villa*

Basilica of
Agios Epifanios
🔀

🔀 *Kambanopetra Basilica*

🔀 *Reservoir*

🔀 *Agora & Temple of Zeus*

🔀 *Roman Villa*

Salamis Yolu

Necropolis
of Salamis
🔀 (Royal Tombs)

Church of
Apostolos
Varnavas
✛

Ancient Enkomi
(Alasia) (3km)

🔀 Cellarka
Tombs

Famagusta
(Gazimağusa) (9km)

İSKELE (TRIKOMO) & AROUND

North of Famagusta (Gazimağusa), the crossroads village of İskele (Trikomo), birthplace of Ethniki Organosi tou Kypriakou Agona (EOKA; National Organisation for the Cypriot Struggle) leader Georgios Grivas, is noteworthy for its 12th-century church **Panagia Theotokos** (Church of the Blessed Virgin Mary) which is now an **icon museum** (İskele İkon Müzesi; Mustafa Orhan Caddesi; adult/student 7/5TL; ⊙ 9am-5pm Jun-Sep, to 3.30pm Oct-May) housing paintings of the Virgin Mary of the Annunciation and the Prayer of Joachim and Anna. It's easy to spot the domed building on the western edge of the village.

Northwest of İskele, you can tootle your way into the agricultural hills to blink-and-you-miss-them villages along roads where chugging tractors are the only traffic. The village of **Ağıller**, with crumbled stone buildings sitting amid the cottages, is a very typical example of this region's settlements. Follow the (signposted) road up behind the village that twists and turns for around 5km, through lush green scenery, to the **Bulusia Monastery**, which sits in splendid isolation overlooking the plains below.

Back down on the coast, stop off at **Boğaz** (Bogazi), about 24km north of Famagusta, for a meal at the harbour. Although the coastline here has been overtaken by villa-developments, the teensy harbour itself still has a local feel, packed with fishing boats rather than pleasure cruisers. The clutch of fish taverns here, right on the water's edge, serves up excellent fresh seafood. Head to **Kiyi** (mains 25-35TL; ⊙ 11am-11pm) for its friendly service, reasonable prices and the well-cooked, hearty portions of chips which come with the meals.

covered by Anthemios, the bishop of Constantia (Salamis), following a revelation in a dream. The current structure was built by Archbishop Philotheos in 1756 and incorporates much of the original church.

In the courtyard there is also a small archaeological museum, which contains some excellent finds from Salamis and nearby Enkomi. Some of its contents may have been moved from the now defunct Archaeological Museum (p215) in Varosia.

The artefacts and the rooms are not well signed. Clockwise from the entrance, the first room houses Bronze Age objects, the next has exhibits from the Venetian period, and there's a mixture of Ottoman and Classical periods in the final room. The most interesting exhibit is the statue of a woman holding a poppy, believed to be the goddess Demeter.

Slightly apart from the main church compound, down a trail just off the car park, is the little chapel said to contain Varnavas' tomb.

The church is 9km northwest of Famagusta, 2km down the well-signposted turn-off just south of Salamis.

Ancient Enkomi   ARCHAEOLOGICAL SITE
(Enkomi Ören Yeni; adult/student 7/5TL; ⊙ 9am-6pm May-Sep, to 3.30pm Oct-Apr) Settlement at Enkomi dates back as far as 1800 BC. The city rose to prominence when it became a large copper-producing centre during the late Bronze Age (1650–1050 BC). What remains of the present site dates from around 1200 BC, when the rectangular grid layout was established and its fine public buildings were erected.

The widespread site is 2km west from the Church of Apostolos Varnavas, along the same road.

Enkomi was known for its high standard of living and its wealthy merchants who conducted trade as agents of the Mycenaeans. Akkadian cuneiform slabs found in Tel el-Amarna, Egypt, contain promises of copper to the pharaoh from the king of Alasia, in return for silver and luxury items. It's still unclear whether the name Alasia referred to Cyprus as a whole or just Enkomi itself.

A fire and at least two earthquakes led to Enkomi's decline, and then its inland harbour silted up. Some speculate that its last residents headed to the coast and founded Salamis. Much of the site has been looted, but many of its tombs were said to have held gold, ivory and exquisite Mycenaean pottery.

➡ **Southern Site**

The southern end of the site (nearest the ticket office) is where excavations in the early 20th century unearthed some of Enkomi's most important finds.

From south to north you see the **House of Bronzes**, where bronze accoutrements were unearthed in 1934, the **House of Pil-**

lar, a public building, the Sanctuary of the Horned God, where a 60cm-tall bronze statue (now in the Cyprus Museum) was found, and Tomb 18, where most of the site's treasure was recovered.

→ **Cenotaph Mound**

The cenotaph mound, built on a rocky outpost, escaped most of the looting the rest of Enkomi suffered, with its funeral pyre concealing much of its contents from tomb robbers. Limestone statues, amphorae from Rhodes, an archaic bronze shield and clay effigies have all been recovered from here.

Archaeologists now contend that this probable tomb may have belonged to Nicocreon and that the plain between Enkomi and Salamis was once a significant connection between the two cities.

🏖 Beaches

Great stretches of beach can be found from Ancient Salamis, north of Famagusta, right around Famagusta Bay. The sea is knee deep to about 70m out and can be quite choppy on windy days.

Glapsides Beach BEACH
About 4km north of Famagusta, on the road to Salamis, this shallow sandy beach is perfect for swimming and snorkelling, and exploring the submerged harbour of the ancient city.

It's popular with locals and great for kids. There's a beach bar and restaurant, and you can hire sun loungers and umbrellas, as well as pedalos and kayaks. The beach is also a great birdwatching location during migratory seasons.

Glapsides is accessed via the path beside Golden Terrace restaurant.

Bediz Beach BEACH
Just past Salamis, this soft-sand beach offers all amenities, including sunbeds, umbrellas, showers and a restaurant-bar. If it's hot and you plan to see the ruins at Ancient Salamis, take a swim here afterwards.

🛈 Getting There & Away

The area is easiest seen with your own car, but most sites are close enough together for taxis to be affordable. A taxi from Famagusta to Ancient Enkomi or Ancient Salamis costs about 30TL.

Dolmuşes between Famagusta and İskele run at 8.30am, 11am, 1pm, 4pm and 5pm (5TL, 20 minutes) and can drop you near the Salamis turn off. They return from İskele at 7am, 8am, 9am, 1pm and 4.30pm.

KARPAS PENINSULA

A journey up the Karpas Peninsula – a Mediterranean rural idyll of rolling fields, olive groves and remote white-sand beaches licked by shallow turquoise water – is like watching the clocks wind themselves back to a time before investors and developers gobbled up much of the island's coast. East of Boğaz' forlorn tourism centre and Bafra's woefully bad-taste luxury resorts, you enter one of the island's last true wildernesses.

Set between a spine of undulating hills, country roads weave between forgotten archaeological sites, ruined churches and sleepy villages up to the thin tapering finger of land at the eastern tip where wild donkeys wander onto the roads and turtles nest on dune-backed Golden Beach. This region is a beacon for cyclists, hikers and anyone simply weary of matching lines of holiday villas.

Come in March when the fields erupt in a kaleidoscope of wild flower colours and rare orchids bloom.

🛈 Getting There & Around

In order to explore this region properly, you'll need your own wheels. Apart from the bus to Yenierenköy (5TL, 1¼ hours, three daily Monday to Friday), the only other option is to hire a taxi.

The main road (Karpaz Yolu) through the peninsula is first-rate for most of the way with excellent signage. Once you're off the main road, though, prepare for narrow, winding, unsigned roads, and expect to get lost periodically.

The last section of Karpaz Yolu – from Dipkarpaz (Rizokarpaso) to Apostolos Andreas Monastery – is narrow and riddled with potholes. It's also often roamed by the Karpas' wild donkeys. Take it slow here.

The South Coast

Sights in the Karpas are mainly strung out along the south coast of what locals euphemistically call the 'Panhandle'. The following sights are arranged in the order you reach them driving along the isthmus from Salamis.

◎ Sights

Kumyalı Beach BEACH
(Koma tou Gialou) This little beach–fishing harbour, just outside the village of Kumyalı (Koma tou Gialou), is ideal for a last stop and swim before you make the long drive up the western flank of the peninsula to the

WORTH A TRIP

KANTARA CASTLE

Perched above the coastal plain at 690m, **Kantara Castle** (Kantara Kalesi; adult/student 7/5TL; ⏱9am-5pm Jun-Sep, to 3.30pm Oct-May) is lowest of the three romantic Crusader castles that crown the ridge of the Kyrenia (Girne) mountain range, but it still offers 360-degree views across the island. On a clear day, you can see the coast of Turkey and even Syria. The castle's documented history dates back to 1191 when Richard the Lionheart seized it from Isaak Komninos, the Byzantine emperor of Cyprus, but its significance faded under the Venetians, and it was abandoned to the ravages of treasure-seeking raiders in the 16th century.

Although decayed by the centuries, the northern section of the castle stills stands resolutely above the forest, guarding the remains of the garrison and a deep water cistern. The roof of the north tower is narrow, unfenced and vertiginous, but the views are incredible. A free map of the site is provided but children should be accompanied at all times, as there are some dangerous drops and uncapped holes on the site.

From Kyrenia it takes about two hours to reach the castle; turn off the coastal highway at Kaplıca (Davios) and take the narrow, winding (but easily drivable) road upwards to the car park.

more exquisite beaches at the far end of the Karpaz.

★ Golden Beach
BEACH

(Nangomi Bay) Possibly the best on the island, Golden Beach is worth the trip to the Karpas in itself. Its white-sand dunes and gentle curves meet the calm, clear sea, and wild donkeys graze nonchalantly on the hills while you soak up the tranquillity. It's truly enchanting, with little development.

The beach is 5km before Zafer Burnu (Cape Apostolos Andreas), situated between scrubby headlands and stretching for several kilometres. There are some basic restaurants and accommodation options.

It's now part of a national park and also prime turtle-nesting ground. If you're visiting in September, contact the certified volunteers at the Society for the Protection of Turtles (SPOT; www.cyprusturtles.org) who monitor the progress of the turtles – you may even be lucky enough to witness baby turtles hatching.

★ Monastery of Apostolos Andreas
CHURCH

(donations accepted; ⏱8am-6pm) It's not as glitzy as other churches, with a plain, small interior holding an iconostasis with some lovely icons from the late 19th century. But the Monastery of Apostolos Andreas, sitting facing the sea near the tip of the Karpas, remains one the island's most important religious sites. On 15 August and 30 November, coachloads of Greek Cypriots make the long trek out here on pilgrimage to visit this monastery where miracles are reputed to take place.

The monastery's reputation for miracles was obtained during the time of St Andrew (the patron saint of sailors), who reputedly restored the sight of a ship's captain when he arrived from Palestine. Since then, attested-to miracles range from curing blindness and epilepsy to healing the crippled and granting extraordinary wishes.

Before 1974 the monastery was well supported by its devotees and pilgrims but since then – isolated from its patrons and with only a few Greek Cypriot caretakers – the great monastery has had a slow and steady deterioration. Turkish Cypriot authorities began to allow a small number of pilgrims to enter the North on organised visits to the monastery from 1996. Today, with the crossings opened, the pilgrimage is far simpler and the faithful can visit this site of holy miracles unescorted. A long overdue restoration project on the monastery buildings, carried out by the Technical Committee on Cultural Heritage, began in 2013. Although work is still ongoing on peripheral buildings, the main monastery church restoration was finished in 2016 and the church has been reopened to the public.

Zafer Burnu
(Cape Apostolos Andreas)
LANDMARK

A mere 3km from the Monastery of Apostolos Andreas, along a dirt track, is the easternmost tip of Cyprus. From here you can see the cluster of rocky isles known as the Kleides (The Keys).

The Neolithic site of Kastros was once located here. Later, the ancient Greeks built a temple to Aphrodite, of which nothing remains. If you have a 4WD, take the rougher northern track back to Dipkarpaz, though it can be particularly difficult in wet weather.

Yenierenköy (Yiallousa)

Formerly a predominantly Greek village, Yenierenköy was resettled by Turkish Cypriot residents of Erenköy (Kokkina) in the South. It's the peninsula's second-largest village and has a relaxed, friendly atmosphere.

At the tourist information office (☑ 0392 374 4984; ☺ 10am-6pm Jun-Sep, 9am-3pm Oct-May) the staff speak English and have lots of information on the peninsula.

⊙ Sights

Yenierenköy is a good base for exploring the little-visited cave tombs of the Karpas. The Kastros Cave Tombs near Avtepe (Agios Simeon) are thought to date from around the 5th century BC and are cut 20m high in the cliff. A metal spiral staircase allows access into the interconnected chambers.

Near here you can take the rough tracks down to the coast (4WD recommended) leading to the ruins of the ancient Bronze Age fort of Nitovikla.

Further east along the coast near Kaleburnu (Galinoporni) is the large Kastros Hill Cave Tomb, which still has shallow niches carved into the floor where the bodies of the dead once lay.

Agios Thyrsos   CHURCH
(Karpaz Yolu) The church of Agios Thyrsos sits majestically on the seafront, with waves lapping the black rocks of the coast below. Although the church's interior is plain, it's well worth stopping off here to walk on the narrow pier just behind the church for the coastal views.

Karpaz Gate Marina   MARINA
(☑ 0533 833 7878; www.karpazbay.com; Karpaz Yolu; beach club adult/child 15TL/free) Yenierenköy's luxury €15 million marina offers berthing for yachties in the Karpas Peninsula. For those not arriving on the island aboard their own yacht, the chief attraction is the marina's swish private beach club, complete with small white-sand beach, pool and an attractive bar-restaurant, draped in Caribbean-chic white curtains.

✖ Eating

★ **Alevkayalı Restaurant**   CYPRIOT €€€
(☑ 0533 876 0911; Karpaz Yolu; mains 30-35TL; ☺ 11am-10pm; ☎) Calamari cooked to perfection, superfresh fish and well-spiced *sheftalia* (grilled sausages wrapped in caul fat; *şeftali kebap* in Turkish); Alevkayalı is a top lunch spot. Generous mains come with a meze of hummus, haloumi (hellim in Turkish) and vegetables like broad beans in olive oil and pickled celery. Dine on the terrace with waves lapping the rocks below for the full experience.

ⓘ Getting There & Away

Monday to Friday there are three *dolmuşes* daily to Famagusta (5TL, one hour). Check current times at the tourist information office as the schedule tends to change. On weekends there are no bus services.

Sipahi (Agia Triada)

The small village of Sipahi (Agia Triada) is home to many mainland Bulgarian Turkish settlers and a tiny community of Karpas Greeks. Like the equally small group in Dipkarpaz, they refused to leave their homes in the North and have continued to live on the peninsula despite the political situation.

For travellers the village's main point of interest is the superb surviving mosaic floors of the ruined Basilica of Agia Triada (Sipahi; adult/student 7/5TL; ☺ 9am-5pm). Although only the foundations and a few battered half-columns of the 5th-century basilica survive to show the building's rough outline, the intricately patterned mosaic flooring has managed to withstand the ravages of time. The abstract, geometric designs on show here have even held onto much of their colour. Greek inscriptions at both the northern

CELEBRATE THE GRAPE!

All hail the grape! The surrounding vineyards of Mehmetçik (Galateia) are the inspiration for the Mehmetçik Grape Festival (Mehmetçik Üzüm Festivali; www.mehmetcikbelediyesi.org; Mehmetçik; ☺ Aug), which has been the Karpas' big annual event for over 50 years. Folk dancing, plenty of grape-related food products and music take over the village for one week in August.

PROTECTING THE WILDERNESS

In 1983, 150 sq km of the Karpas region, from the municipality of Dipkarpaz (Rizokarpaso) to Zafer Burnu (Cape Apostolos Andreas), was declared a national park by Turkish Cypriot authorities. Since then, however, encroaching development has continued to threaten this wilderness.

In a bid to introduce mass tourism to the Karpas region, investors have transformed Bafra, on the western edge of the peninsula, into a kind of Vegas-by-sea complete with themed luxury hotels and a high-roller casino. This rapid development has deeply concerned conservationists, who are worried about the sustainability of the region's greater environment, particularly its unique wildlife, plant life, undiscovered archaeological sites and rugged beaches.

Lobby groups, biologists and environmentalists have banded together to push for a commitment to adhere to stricter guidelines regarding the peninsula's use and further development. Most pressing are concerns over the building of new roadways and hotel developments, the scope of electrification plans for remote areas of the peninsula and the ongoing problem of litter.

and southern ends of the former nave reveal that the church's construction was partly financed by a local deacon on a personal vow of dedication.

Dipkarpaz (Rizokarpaso)

This is the peninsula's largest and most remote village, where a contemporary mosque sits next to an old Orthodox church. The church is a silent companion, as its bell is no longer tolled, although a small number of Greek Cypriots still live in the village. The once-thriving town is now mostly populated by mainland Turks and Kurds, who work the land and live in difficult rural conditions.

A small ring of shops, a couple of cafes where old men sit sipping tea all day and a petrol station form the tidy centre of town. Although there is little else in the way of facilities, thanks to a couple of great accommodation options it makes a pleasant, peaceful base for Karpaz forays.

Eating

Manolyam Restaurant   TURKISH €€
(Dipkarpaz; mains 20-30TL; ⊙ Apr-Oct) This restaurant dishes up traditional Turkish kebab plates and a small but filling array of mixed meze.

★ **Oasis Restaurant**   SEAFOOD €€€
(Oasis at Ayfilon, Agios Filon Beach; mains 25-40TL; ⊙ 11am-3pm & 6-11pm; ⑳ ✍) Looking over the cliffs and next door to the Agios Filon church, this little place serves up char-grills

and the peninsula's best freshly caught fish, marinated in olive oil.

Agios Filon & Afendrika

Grouped together on the north coast, close to the sleepy village of Dipkarpaz, the ruins at Agios Filon span several millennia of settlements, beside a small but lovely sand beach.

◉ Sights

Agios Filon Beach   BEACH
With its soft sand and big, flat sea rocks, this is a fantastic beach some 5km north of Dipkarpaz. It's also a turtle-hatching beach and a great place to watch the sunset. The 12th-century Agios Filon Church stands silently on the sparse coastline, next to the Oasis at Ayfilon hotel and restaurant. Its well-preserved outside walls were built over an earlier 5th-century Christian basilica. The conceptual mosaics from the basilica can be seen outside the walls of the later church.

Afendrika   RUINS
About 7km east of Agios Filon Beach is Afendrika, a major city in the 2nd century BC. What remains is a set of contiguous ruins comprising three churches: 6th-century Agios Georgios, Panagia Khrysiotissa and 10th-century Panagia Asomatos. Nearby are the necropolis and what remains of the citadel.

Understand Cyprus

Cyprus Today

Peace talks have been front and centre of Cypriot news as negotiations between the Republic and the North reach higher levels than ever before. Away from politics, the preservation of cultural heritage island-wide is receiving much-needed attention, while the prospect of exploratory drilling on the island's offshore gas reserves is both a cause for economic optimism and a major divisive issue on the road to peace.

Best on Film

Birds of a Feather (2012) Documentary exploring the different historical narratives of the Greek Cypriot and Turkish Cypriot communities.
Akamas (2006) Controversial film set in the 1960s about a Greek Cypriot and Turkish Cypriot who fall in love.

Best in Print

Gregory and other Stories (Panos Ioannides; 2014) War, guilt, duplicity and loss are explored in this short-story collection by the island's most lauded living writer.
Bitter Lemons of Cyprus (Lawrence Durrell; 1957) Durrell's famous memoir of Cypriot village life at the end of British rule.
The Sunrise (Victoria Hislop; 2015) Novel set in Famagusta during the Greek coup and following Turkish invasion in the 1970s.

Best Music

Sikoses (Monsieur Doumani; 2015) This second album from Cyprus' hottest band continues to invent fresh sounds while riffing on folk-music traditions.
East Meets West (Oytun Ersan Project; 2015) Funk and fusion jazz from bass player and composer Oytun Ersan.

Road Blocks on the Way to Reunification

Since Cyprus' division in 1974, talks to reunite it have taken place sporadically with little success. In April 2015 Mustafa Akinci came to power in the North on a pro-reunification platform, reigniting hope on both sides for the revival of talks and direct negotiations between the two leaders of the divided nation.

Talks between Akinci and the Republic's president Nicos Anastasiades began in 2015 and continued with surprising commitment from both sides, despite failures to agree on several complicated issues. In November 2016 the two leaders met in Switzerland, and for the first time, maps of potential territorial boundaries were presented and debated. Twenty months of talks culminated in January 2017's Geneva summit, when Anastasiades and Akinci were joined by representatives of Cyprus' three guarantor powers – Greece, Turkey and Great Britain – to attempt to hammer out a final solution. However, no deal was reached and both sides pledged to continue discussions.

The next round of talks in February 2017 broke down after the Republic's parliament voted to pass a bill on establishing a new annual commemoration for the 1950 *enosis* (union with Greece) referendum. Although negotiations recommenced in April, in the background disagreements flared over the Republic going ahead with its hydrocarbon exploration program without first putting a plan in place to equitably share gas-reserve profits, along with rhetoric from both sides about the other's commitment to a deal. Despite this, both sides signalled their willingness to work towards a new summit in June.

Relations in the run-up to the talks, however, were as fractious as ever, with both Anastasiades and Akinci disagreeing on the agenda for negotiations. Eventually, UN Secretary General Antonio Guterres persuaded the two sides to come together at the Swiss ski resort of Crans-Montana on 28 June, but the talks broke up without resolution on 7 July. Key sticking points in the impasse were the continued presence of Turkish troops on Cypriot soil, and the right of return of refugees. Before leaving for the G20 summit, a crestfallen Guterres gave a speech hopeful of 'other initiatives' to solve the Cyprus problem, but with with both sides no closer together on the core issues than in 1974.

Peace-Building: One Brick at a Time

Away from the quagmire of the political negotiation table, many normal Cypriots are making their own efforts to promote peace. The most significant example is the Technical Committee on Cultural Heritage (www.cy.undp.org), a bicommunal committee dedicated to restoring culturally significant monuments island-wide. Led by Greek Cypriot Takis Hadjidemetriou and Turkish Cypriot Ali Tuncay, the committee has restored 18 monuments across the island since its establishment in 2008, including Apostolos Andreas Monastery on the Karpas Peninsula, two mosques and two churches in the Pafos district and Famagusta's Othello Tower. The work, which uses joint teams of builders, engineers and architects from both the Greek Cypriot and Turkish Cypriot communities, has been rightfully praised internationally for its role in confidence-building between the two sides. In 2015 Hadjidemetriou and Tuncay jointly won the European Parliament's Citizen Prize for their leadership of the committee.

Wrangles over Resources

In the Republic of Cyprus optimism remains high for possible future revenues produced from oil and gas deposits offshore. The Republic is negotiating with energy consortiums to commence exploratory drilling in the waters off Cyprus in the near future. However, tensions regarding the sharing of potential offshore energy-resource revenues are both a major factor in spurring on reunification negotiation efforts and a major stumbling block.

In the North, the opening of the Northern Cyprus Water Supply Project in 2015 looks like it has finally solved (at least, in the short term) the North's water-scarcity woes. The project supplies the North with water from Turkey, via an undersea pipeline, not only fixing Northern Cyprus' water-shortage issues but also, it is hoped, boosting the economy by providing agricultural irrigation. In an area long plagued by lack of development due to its isolation on the world stage, the project is seen as a sign of economic improvement. But the pipeline's opening was not without controversy, with disagreements between Northern Cyprus and Turkey about management of water distribution.

POPULATION: **1,165,000 (300,000 ESTIMATED NORTHERN CYPRUS)**

AREA: **9251 SQ KM (3355 SQ KM NORTHERN CYPRUS)**

GDP: **REPUBLIC OF CYPRUS US$19.32 BILLION; NORTHERN CYPRUS US$4.03 BILLION**

if Cyprus were 100 people

71 would live in towns
29 would live in the country

belief systems
(% of population)

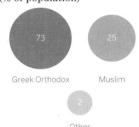

population per sq km

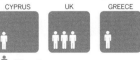

 ≈ 85 people

History

To gain some understanding of Cyprus' modern political and territorial situation, it's important to look back on the complicated weave of events which have helped shape the current climate. The island's position, at the nautical crossroads of the eastern Mediterranean basin, has been the catalyst for an extraordinarily turbulent history that more than equals its present-day problems, and stretches way back over the centuries with waves of invaders influencing and leaving their mark here.

Ancient Cyprus

City-kingdoms of Cyprus

Cyprus is one of the five richest copper-deposit areas in the world, and during the Copper and Bronze Ages, Cyprus was one of the world's richest countries.

Visitors to Cyprus today can see extraordinary remains of ancient city-kingdoms – excavations have revealed that they were both highly prosperous and influential during the Hellenistic period. These city-kingdoms were established at Kourion, Pafos, Marion (now Polis), Soloi, Lapithos, Tamassos and Salamis, with two others later established at Kition and Amathous. The Phoenicians, great traders from across the sea in Lebanon, also settled here during this time in Kition (Larnaka) and introduced the Greek alphabet to Cyprus (the Phoenician phonetic alphabet is believed to be the ancestor of virtually all modern alphabets).

Between 1400 and 1200 BC, Mycenaean and Achaean Greek settlers began to arrive en masse, bringing with them language, culture, art and gods. The Cypriots found a particular affiliation with the fertility goddess, Aphrodite, and Cyprus is her legendary birthplace – the rock near Pafos marks the spot and to this day remains firmly on the tourist trail.

From 750 BC to 475 BC, the city-kingdoms oversaw a period of advancement and increasing prosperity as demonstrated by the spectacular Necropolis of Salamis (Royal Tombs) which contain extravagant examples of wealth, and closely match Homer's descriptions of Mycenaean burials in *The Iliad*. Ancient Salamis is the most significant of the ancient city-kingdoms' archaeological sites that can be visited today.

During this time, Greek influence spread throughout the island, and Cyprus attracted a string of foreign rulers including the Assyrians, the Egyptians and the Persians. These powers sought control through

TIMELINE	Millions of years ago	10,000–8000 BC	6000 BC
	The island is forced to the surface from the Mediterranean ocean floor, revealing the Troödos Mountains, Kyrenia mountain ranges and Mesaoria plain. Scientists now study the seabed here.	Hunter-gatherers develop the first settlements. The world's earliest water wells are made and domesticated animals are introduced .	Stone buildings such as those of Choirokoitia are built in small enclosed villages. Inhabitants begin to form working societies with organised crops, stonework and domestic pets.

tribute more than settlement, essentially leaving the city-kingdoms to self-govern.

In 498 BC, under King Onesilos of Salamis, the city-kingdoms joined in the Ionian revolt against Persian rule, with the exception of Amathous, which aligned itself with the Phoenicians. The Persians landed their army just off Salamis and a ferocious battle raged. Ultimately the King of Kourion, Stesenor, betrayed the Greeks. Onesilos was killed and the revolt was crushed.

The island maintained its strong links with Hellenism, despite Persian hegemony. In 381 BC King Evagoras of Salamis tried to unite the city-kingdoms with the Greek states and attempted to overcome the Persians once more. He was defeated and assassinated seven years later, effectively ending the Classical Age of Greek influence (the remains of which are prevalent on the island to this day).

Hellenistic Cyprus

Alexander the Great's emphatic victory over Persian ruler Darius III at Issus in 333 BC released the island from the Persian empire. However, Alexander's control of Cyprus, as a part of the Greek empire, was fleeting. He asserted his authority by giving the city-kingdoms autonomy but refusing to allow them to make their own coins. After his death in 323 BC and after some quarrelling among his successors, the city-kingdoms were subjugated by Ptolemy I of Egypt, who took over the island as a part of Hellenistic Egypt.

The island's capital was moved from Salamis to Pafos, which was easily accessible by sea from Alexandria in Egypt. From this time, Egyptian influences prevailed, with local cults being introduced and assimilated with Egyptian gods and goddesses. Cyprus also grew to become an intermediary between the Greek world and the near east, with craftspeople, sculptors and merchants from throughout the eastern Mediterranean introducing ceramics, sculpture and jewellery.

Nicocreon, the last king of Salamis, assisted Ptolemy in centralising power away from the city-kingdoms to a single appointed governor general in Pafos. Later suspected of betrayal, he burned his opulent Salamis palace to the ground before committing suicide.

A *demos* (house and senate) version of parliament was subsequently established on the island and it remained a Ptolemaic colony (and relatively peaceful) for a further 200 years, languishing under the rule of an appointed governor general.

Romans & Rising Christianity

Cyprus was annexed by the expanding Roman Empire in 58 BC, orator and writer Cicero becoming one of its first proconsuls. Despite being

Top History Books

Cyprus: A Modern History (William Mallinson; 2008)

A Traveller's History of Cyprus (Tim Boatswain; 2011)

HISTORY ANCIENT CYPRUS

2500 BC	2300–1950 BC	1950–1650 BC	1650–1050 BC
Levantine immigrants bring new technologies and styles. Artistic achievements include the production of cross-shaped human figurines made from picrolite, a local Cypriot stone.	The early Bronze Age; objects are cast using imported tin, and imaginative pottery designs flourish, drawing noticeably on human and animal life in and around the villages.	Middle Bronze Age; sustained copper mining and the beginning of trading relationships with the Aegean. Settlements keep to the foothills and plains, in largely agrarian communities.	Writing in the form of a linear script known as Cypro-Minoan is adapted from Crete. Extensive foreign trade coincides with production of fine jewellery, carving and pottery.

In the 1st century BC, tin was imported from Lebanon to Cyprus and mixed with copper to make bronze. This composition was stronger and more durable, creating better tools and weapons.

briefly given to Cleopatra VII of Egypt by Mark Anthony (her lover) and subsequently handed back to Roman control, Cyprus enjoyed some 600 years of relative peace and prosperity under Roman rule, and many public buildings, aqueducts, harbours and roads date from this time; noteworthy among them were the theatre at Kourion, the colonnaded gymnasium at Salamis and the Sanctuary of Apollon Ylatis. Many of these ancient ruins can still be seen today, along with the many mosaic floors depicting scenes from Greek mythology. Trade also flourished, with exports including decorative pottery, copper and glassware.

Island of Saints

Christianity made its early appearance on the island in AD 45. It was during this period that the Apostle Paul began spreading the new religion on the island, accompanied by Barnabas, a Greek Jewish native of Salamis. He was later canonised St Barnabas (Agios Varnavas in Greek). The missionaries travelled across the island preaching the word of God and converting many locals. Once they reached Pafos, the Roman proconsul Sergius Paulus granted them an audience. A court magician mocked the Apostles upon their speech about Jesus, angering Paul, who is said to have temporarily blinded the sorcerer for his disbelief. The proconsul was so struck by this act that he was among the first to convert to Chris-

HOUSE OF STONE

Human habitation of the island began around 10,000 BC, when hunter-gatherers roamed the coastal caves of Akrotiri Aetokremnou (Vulture Cliff) and its peninsula in the South. These people may have brought about the extinction, via hunting, of the Pleistocene-era pygmy hippopotamus and dwarf elephant (a skeleton of the latter was discovered in a cave near Kyrenia in 1902).

Eventually, in around 6000 BC, these nomads built stone villages such as the Aceramic Neolithic settlement of Choirokoitia; a fascinating site near Larnaka which can be visited today.

Built on the side of a hill, beside the banks of a river, its more than 300 inhabitants lived in round, flat-roofed *tholoi* (huts) made of stones and mud. They were similar to the contemporary buildings found in Crete and Mesopotamia. The huts were organised within a protective rock wall, around a central courtyard, with some chambers dedicated to cooking and eating, others to sleeping and storage.

Evidence shows the inhabitants produced stone tools, weapons, containers and jewellery. They picked fruit, fished and kept sheep and goats. They even kept pets. The oldest known feline-human connection – a domesticated cat buried with its owner – was unearthed here, far predating similar ancient Egyptian finds.

1200 BC	1200–1100 BC	1200–1000 BC	11th century BC
The island enjoys an unprecedented level of prosperity and immigration. The first Greeks settle on the island, introducing new language, art, gods and culture.	Cities are built (or rebuilt) in a rectangular grid plan. Town gates and important buildings correspond to street systems. Increased social hierarchy and order are introduced.	The great Greek city-kingdoms of Salamis, Kourion, Pafos, Marion, Soloi, Lapithos and Tamassos flourish. The island enjoys a period of rapidly increasing advancement and prosperity.	Classical authors credit Greek heroes returning from the Trojan War with founding influential towns: Salamis is said to have been established by Teucer, and Pafos by Agapenor (of Tegea).

tianity. Cyprus became the first country in the world to be ruled by a Christian and Christianity flourished on the island.

The Apostles set up the Church of Cyprus, one of the oldest independent churches in the world, and the island quickly became known as 'The Island of Saints'.

A number of those involved in the early development of Christianity were sanctified, including Lazarus, raised from the dead by Jesus, who became the archbishop of Kition. St Helena also visited the island with pieces of the 'Holy Cross' that she left in the protection of Stavrovouni Monastery and at Tochni, where they can still be found today.

By the time of Constantine the Great, Christianity had almost completely supplanted paganism.

Byzantine Cyprus
Constantinople Calling

The Roman Empire was divided in AD 395 and Cyprus fell under its eastern half, the Byzantine Empire, with its capital in Constantinople. Byzantine rulers were sent to Cyprus to govern the island.

The island was able to keep a considerable degree of ecclesiastical autonomy when the Archbishop of Cyprus convinced the Byzantine emperor that the Church of Cyprus had been founded by the Apostles. In AD 488 the archbishop was granted the right to carry a sceptre instead of an archbishop's crosier. He was also given authority to write his signature in imperial purple ink, a practice which continues to this day.

During this period many of the stunning churches of the island were built, with frescoed walls, mosaics and domed roofs, including the church of St Barnabas, built over his grave in Famagusta (Gazimağusa).

This relative stability would not last long, as the island would soon be at the forefront of clashes between the Byzantines and the growing Islamic empire.

Arab Raids

Islamic expansion in the 7th century had a profound effect on the island. The lands of the Byzantine Empire were attacked by Muslim Arabs. Fleets of ships began a series of bloody raids starting in AD 647, killing many and destroying coastal cities. Salamis (Constantia) was ravaged and sacked heavily, never quite recovering. The city-kingdom of Kourion declined dramatically and coastal settlers moved inland.

In response, fortifications and castles were built, the three grandest being those of St Hilarion, Buffavento and Kantara in the Kyrenia mountains, defending the north coast.

During one such raid in Kition, Umm Haram, the wife of an Arab commander and the aunt of the Prophet Muhammad, fell from her mule

Historical Sites

Ancient Salamis, Famagusta (Gazimağusa)

Pafos Archaeological Site

Tombs of the Kings, Pafos

Ancient Kourion, Lemesos (Limassol)

HISTORY BYZANTINE CYPRUS

Greek Cypriots are mainly the descendants of early Mycenaean and Achaean settlers, who intermingled with the indigenous population around 1100 BC, and subsequent settlers up to the 16th century.

For a thorough rundown on all the Republic of Cyprus' historic monuments and archaeological sites, head to the Department of Antiquities section on www.mcw.gov.cy.

8th–3rd centuries BC	560–525 BC	499–450 BC	411–325 BC
The Assyrians become the first of a series of conquerors to control Cyprus, followed by the Egyptians under emperor Amasis (568–525 BC), and the Persians under King Cyrus.	The first Cypriot coins appear under the auspices of the King of Salamis. They are created out of base metals, using the Persian weight system.	The city-kingdoms of Cyprus join the Ionian revolt against the Persians. Salamis is punished for its role as the revolt is crushed. Kition becomes an important Phoenician trading post.	The Classical Age; Alexander the Great releases Cyprus from the Persians (351 BC). Cypriot art develops under strong Attic influence. Zenon the philosopher is born in Cyprus (334 BC).

The Stones of Famagusta is a 2008 documentary that traces the historical remains of Famagusta's beautiful, ruined architecture.

and died. The mosque at Hala Sultan Tekke was built at the site of her fall on the edge of Larnaka's salt lake. It is among the holiest places in the Muslim world.

In AD 688 a truce was called when Justinian II and the Arab caliph Abd-al-Malik signed an agreement for the joint rule of Cyprus. This agreement remained until AD 965, when Emperor Nikiforos Fokas sent an army of men to the island to regain complete control for the Byzantines.

New governors were sent to Cyprus as dukes. Due to the devastation of the coastal cities, the capital was moved inland to Nicosia and built on the remains of the old city of Ledra.

Richard I & the Crusades

Byzantine rule may well have continued had it not been for renegade governor Isaak Komninos, who proclaimed himself emperor of Cyprus in 1184.

On his way to the Holy Land as part of the Third Crusade, King Richard the Lionheart's fleet met with inclement weather and was forced to dock in Lemesos. The first ship to make port was that of the recently widowed Queen Joan of Sicily, Richard's sister, and his fiancée, Berengaria of Navarre.

Komninos attempted to capture the royal party and hold them to ransom. King Richard was outraged at this news and marched on Lemesos, overthrowing Komninos and seizing control of the island. This effectively brought an end to Byzantine rule.

Komninos fled to Kantara Castle in the north, and King Richard married his queen in Lemesos Castle's Agios Georgios chapel in 1191. To this

COPPER ISLAND

Once copper was discovered in around 2600 BC, it progressively replaced the old stone repertory and led to the excavation of abundant copper deposits in the Troödos Mountains. The country's production and export of copper became highly organised, and trade with Mediterranean islands and Egypt began in earnest. This gave Cyprus great commercial importance in the civilised Mediterranean world.

During the island's transition to the Bronze Age, around 2000 BC, a wave of foreign influence, from immigrants such as the Hittites, brought new technologies and styles. This age also saw new towns established around the coast, with overseas trade of pottery containers and copper ingots (shaped like oxhide) expanded further.

Cyprus enjoyed an unprecedented level of prosperity, accompanied by the movement of foreign goods and people into the island. It became a meeting point of Western and Eastern civilisations thanks to its location and natural wealth.

323 BC	323–58 BC	300 BC	289 BC
After the death of Alexander, Cypriot kings side with Ptolemy I against Antigonos. Ptolemy becomes ruler of Egypt, Syria, Pentapolis (Libya) and Cyprus (323–283 BC).	Strong commercial relationships with Athens and Alexandria maintain Hellenistic influence on the island. Carried out by administrators from Egypt, Ptolemaic rule continues until 58 BC.	Zenon's Stoic school of philosophy becomes dominant in Athens. Based on logic and formal ethics, it flourishes during the Hellenistic period through to the Roman era.	Ptolemy II becomes coregent of Egypt, Cyprus and the outlying areas. The important trade port of Famagusta (near Salamis) is founded during his reign (285–247 BC).

day Cyprus is the only foreign country to have held an English royal wedding.

Richard fell ill and stayed in Cyprus, postponing his campaign to the Holy Land. He was joined by the French knight Guy de Lusignan, who assisted him in defeating Komninos. Upon Komninos' capture, he was chained in silver, instead of iron, at his pleading.

Richard went on to conquer the entire island and stayed for a year until he was well enough to travel. He then sold Cyprus to the Knights Templar, to boost his coffers. The Knights ultimately were unable to afford the upkeep and, in turn, sold it to the dispossessed king of Jerusalem, Guy de Lusignan, in 1192.

Lusignan Dynasties

The French-speaking lord of Cyprus, Guy de Lusignan, established a lengthy dynasty that brought mixed fortunes to the island. He died in 1194 and was buried at the Church of the Templars in Nicosia and succeeded by his brother, Amalric.

Guy had invited Christian families who had lost property in the Holy Land to settle in Cyprus, many of whom were still concerned with the territorial affairs and disputes in Jerusalem. This proved to be a great economic strain on Cyprus, until the fall of Acre (Akko) in 1291.

For 100 years or so thereafter, Cyprus enjoyed a period of immense wealth and prosperity, with current-day Famagusta the centre of unrivalled commercial activity and trade. Many of the Byzantine castles were added to in grandiose style, and fine buildings and churches were erected. The Church of Agia Sofia in North Nicosia (Lefkoşa), Bellapais Abbey near Kyrenia and Kolossi Castle, near Lemesos (Limassol), were completed during this period.

Lusignan descendants continued to rule the Kingdom of Cyprus until 1474. The island's prosperity reached its zenith under King Peter I (r 1359–69), who spent much of his time overseas at war. He squashed many attempts at Turkish piracy raids, before mounting a counterattack in 1365. During this unsuccessful crusade, he only managed to sack the city of Alexandria. Upon his assassination at the hands of his nobles, the fortunes of the Lusignans took a turn for the worse.

Eyeing Cyprus' wealth and strategic position as an entrepôt, Genoa and Venice jostled for control. Genoa ultimately seized Famagusta and held it for 100 years; the fortunes of both Famagusta and the island declined as a result. The last Lusignan king was James II (r 1460–73), who managed to expel the Genoese from Famagusta. He married Caterina Cornaro, a Venetian noblewoman, who went on to succeed James. She was the last queen of Cyprus and the last royal personage from the Lusignan dynasty. Under pressure, she eventually ceded Cyprus to Venice.

60 BC	58 BC–AD 395	45	115–16
Noted Cypriot physician Apollonios of Kition is born. He would write several important medical books of antiquity. *Peri Arthron* (On Joints), with hand-painted sketches, is the only one to survive.	Romans take over from the Ptolemaic dynasty. Important public buildings are constructed, such as theatres and gymnasiums. Roads and vital aqueducts are built, bringing water to settlements.	Christianity is brought to the island by St Paul and St Barnabas. The Church of Cyprus is established. Cyprus is the first country to be ruled by a Christian.	A major Jewish revolt throughout Mesopotamia spreads to Cyprus and leaves thousands massacred. Roman emperor Trajan intervenes to restore peace and expels the Jews from Cyprus.

Venetian Forts

The citizens of Lusignan-era Famagusta were so rich and so debauched that a merchant is said to have once ground a large diamond to season his food, in front of all his guests.

The Venetians ruled Cyprus from AD 1489 to 1571. Their control was characterised by indifference to the Greek population, who fared no better under their new overlords than they had under the Genoese.

As excellent traders, the Venetians' chief concern was the expansion of their maritime empire. They used the island for its position along the vital Silk Route to China and as a defence against the growing Ottoman threat. They built heavy fortifications around the cities of Nicosia and Famagusta, believing the Ottomans would attempt to strike there.

The Ottomans first attacked Nicosia, defeating it swiftly and slaughtering the garrison. They then turned their attentions to Famagusta. The severed head of Nicosia's governor was sent as a grim message to Famagusta's Venetian captain-general Marcantonio Bragadino. He quickly prepared for the assault, with some 8000 men at the ready.

The Ottomans laid siege to the city with over 200,000 men and 2000 cannon. Bragadino held out for nearly a year, completely surrounded, with Famagusta Bay filled with Ottoman ships.

Upon his capture, Bragadino was tortured horrifically for his defiance. His ears and nose were cut off before he was skinned alive.

The fall of Famagusta signalled the end of a Western presence and Christian outpost in the Levant for the next 300 years.

THE CASE OF THE KANAKARIA MOSAICS

Resembling some Raymond Chandler crime thriller, one of the most famous cases of looting concerned the Kanakaria mosaics which were stolen, sometime between 1974 and 1979, from the Panagia Kanakaria church in the Karpas Peninsula. The priceless mosaics later turned up in Indianapolis, where an art dealer was hawking them around museums and galleries for a hefty $20 million or so. The wised-up curator at the J Paul Getty Museum in California became suspicious and contacted the Greek Cypriot authorities, who confirmed that these were, indeed, the stolen mosaics from the Panagia Kanakaria church. They were duly returned in 1991 and can be seen today at the Byzantine Museum in Nicosia (Lefkosia).

The Turkish art dealer, who was later identified as Aydın Dikmen, was eventually located in Munich in 1997 after an eight-month sting operation. His apartment was raided by police who discovered a further priceless collection of some 5000 Cypriot icons, frescos and other treasures concealed inside the walls and under the floorboards at his apartment. These included two priceless icons stolen from the monastery of St Chrysostomos.

The art treasures were eventually returned to Cyprus in 2010, after more than a decade of legal wrangling in the Bavarian courts.

4th century AD	350	395–647	647
A series of powerful earthquakes rock the island and many coastal cities are badly damaged or destroyed, including the prized city of Salamis. Drought and famine result.	Salamis is rebuilt by Constantius II, son of Constantine the Great. The site is lavishly decorated and renamed Constantia.	The island comes under Byzantine rule after the Roman Empire splits. The Church of Cyprus receives unprecedented ecclesiastical autonomy from Constantinople, a practice that continues today.	The first of the Arab raids causes great destruction and suffering. Salamis is destroyed and Kourion fades. Coastal inhabitants migrate inland to avoid constant pillaging and attacks.

Ottoman Rule

Over 20,000 Turks settled in Cyprus following its capture from the Venetians in 1571, but the island was not a high priority for the Ottomans. The ruling sultan sent Turkish governors to rule the island, who quickly suppressed the Latin church. They abolished serfdom and restored the Orthodox hierarchy and Church of Cyprus, to better appease and control the population.

From then on, taxes were arbitrarily increased for the Greek Cypriot population, and the Orthodox archbishop (considered the leader) was made responsible for their collection. In the wake of huge taxes, some Greeks converted to Islam to avoid oppression.

The Ottomans appointed a dragoman of the *serai* (translator to the governor's palace) to each town. They resided in opulent stone houses and acted as arbitrators for all business with Greek Cypriots.

In 1821, Greeks from the mainland were fighting the great war of liberation against the Ottomans. Cypriot Orthodox Archbishop Kyprianos sent money and support to Greece, in the hope that it would help to free Cyprus also. When the *paşa* (lord) Mehmed Silashor found out, he had the archbishop hanged in the public square in front of the *serai* (palace). Any support for the growing Greek revolution was quickly crushed. Another three bishops were beheaded on similar suspicions, and several priests, including the abbot of Kykkos, were put to death.

The Ottomans remained in control of the island until 1878, when the British sought authority in the region.

Modern Cyprus

Civil Struggle

In 1878 Turkey and Britain signed an agreement whereby Turkey would retain sovereignty of the languishing colony, while Britain would shoulder the responsibility for administering the island. Britain's aim was to secure a strategic outpost in the Middle East, from where it could monitor military and commercial movements in the Levant and the Caucasus. As part of the agreement, Britain would protect the sultan's Asian territories from threat by Russia. In 1914 the start of WWI meant the parties were at war. Britain assumed outright sovereignty of the island, but Turkey would not recognise the annexation of its territory until the 1923 Treaty of Lausanne. This treaty also included territorial claims with the newly independent Greece.

British control of Cyprus was initially welcomed by its mostly Greek population, since it was assumed that Britain would ultimately work with the Greeks to achieve enosis (union) with Greece. Turkish Cypriots,

688–965	1191	1191–92	1192
Justinian II and the Arab Caliph Abd-al-Malik agree to jointly rule Cyprus. Their agreement is broken in 965 and the Byzantines once again take over the island.	Richard the Lionheart is shipwrecked at Lemesos on his way to Acre; the English king conquers Cyprus and weds Princess Berengaria at Agios Georgios chapel, in the town.	Richard falls ill amid concerns for his coffers. After defeating Lemesos governor Isaak Komninos, he sells Cyprus to the Knights Templar to raise funds for a third Holy Crusade.	Guy de Lusignan takes Cyprus from the Knights Templar. Splendid churches and castles are built.

a 17% minority of the population, were less than enthusiastic at the prospect, fearing they would be ostracised.

Between 1955 and 1958 a Cypriot lieutenant colonel, Georgios 'Digenis' Grivas, founded the Ethniki Organosi tou Kypriakou Agona (EOKA; National Organisation for the Cypriot Struggle), and launched a series of covert attacks on the British military and administration. The EOKA began these attacks to show their frustration with the British for not helping to further their ultimate goal of enosis. Find out more about this tumultuous period by visiting the Agios Georgios Museum in Pafos.

The British came up with various proposals for limited home rule, but Turkish Cypriots began to demand *taksim* (partition), whereby the island would be divided between Greece and Turkey.

In 1959 Greek Cypriot ethnarch Archbishop Makarios III and Turkish Cypriot leader Faisal Küçük met in Zurich. They came to ratify a previously agreed plan where independence would be granted to Cyprus under conditions that would satisfy all sides.

The British were to retain two military bases and a number of other sites as part of the agreement. Cyprus also agreed not to enter into any political or economic unions with Turkey or Greece, or to be partitioned. Political power was to be shared on a proportional basis of 70% Greek and 30% Turkish. Britain, Turkey and Greece were named as the 'guarantor powers' of the island.

New Republic

The independent Republic of Cyprus was realised on 16 August 1960. Transition from colony to independent nation was difficult, with sporadic violence and protest, as extremists from both sides pushed opposing agendas.

Serious sectarian violence broke out in 1963, further dividing the Greek and Turkish communities. Turkish Cypriots withdrew from government, claiming that President Archbishop Makarios was pro-enosis, and wasn't doing enough to control radicals.

In 1964 the UN sent a peacekeeping force to the island headed by Major General Peter Young. The general drew a green line on a map of Nicosia separating the Greek and Turkish areas of the capital, thus forming the 'Green Line', which would go on to divide the entire island. Many Turkish Cypriots moved to enclaves around the island, separating themselves from the Greeks.

With the Cold War at its peak, Cyprus had strategic value for the British and Americans in monitoring Soviet activity. Makarios sought a position of political nonalignment and was suspected of being a communist. The Americans and their British allies feared another Cuban crisis – only in the Mediterranean – which added urgency to their interference.

Most Turkish Cypriots are descendants of the Ottoman settlers who arrived in Cyprus from 1570, following their conquest of the island over the ruling Venetians.

1194	1478	1571	1625–1700
The feudal system is introduced to the island by Amalric Lusignan upon the death of his younger brother Guy. He becomes King of Cyprus as Amalric I.	The last Lusignan king, James II, weds Venetian noblewoman Caterina Cornaro, who becomes the last queen of Cyprus. In 1489 she cedes Cyprus to Venice.	The Ottoman Empire crushes the Venetians and takes over Cyprus. Orthodox hierarchy is restored to assist in local taxation. Some 20,000 Turks settle on the island.	Plague wipes out over 50% of the estimated population. A string of bloody insurgencies against oppressive Ottoman rule are savagely quashed. Plague ends (1700).

While the island was still politically unstable, the situation on the ground quietened between 1964 and 1967, as Turkish Cypriots withdrew to consolidated areas. This included setting up a provisional government in North Nicosia.

Coup d'État & Invasion

Discussion of segregating the Greek and Turkish Cypriot communities stepped up again in 1967. A coup in Greece installed a right-wing military junta and Greece's relations with Cyprus cooled. Makarios had a number of diplomatic meetings with the Soviets, in keeping with his policy of nonalignment. Both the Greek junta and the Americans were suspicious of this and were fearful that the island would lean towards communism.

In July 1974 the CIA sponsored a Greek junta–organised coup in Cyprus, with the intention of installing a more pro-Western government.

On 15 July a renegade detachment of the National Guard (numbering a mere 180), led by officers from mainland Greece, launched an attempt to assassinate Makarios and establish enosis. Makarios narrowly escaped as the presidential palace was laid to waste. Cypriot Nikos Sampson, a former EOKA member with ties to the Greek junta, was proclaimed president of Cyprus.

Five days later, Turkish forces landed troops close to Kyrenia, using the right to restore a legal government as the pretext.

The regular Greek Cypriot army tried to resist the Turkish advance. However, once the Turks established the bridgehead around Kyrenia, they quickly linked with the Turkish sector of North Nicosia. From this point the Greek Cypriot army was outnumbered and could not stop the crushing Turkish assault.

On 23 July 1974, Greece's junta on the mainland fell and was replaced by a democratic government under Konstantinos Karamanlis. At the same time, the Cypriots removed Sampson and replaced him with Glafkos Clerides, president of the House of Representatives and a member of the democratic government.

The three guarantor powers – Britain, Greece and Turkey – met for discussions in Geneva, as required by the treaty, but it proved impossible to make the Turkish halt their advance. They pressed on for over three weeks until 16 August 1974. At that time Turkey controlled 37% of the northern part of the island. By the time Makarios returned to resume his presidency, having escaped the assassination attempt, Cyprus was divided.

A total of 190,000 Greek Cypriots who then lived in the northern third of Cyprus were displaced, losing their homes, land and businesses. Many were caught in the onslaught and killed; the rest fled south for safety. At

Colin Thubron's *Journey into Cyprus* (1975) is a classic travel tale. In 1972, two years before the Turkish invasion of the island, Thubron crossed almost 1000km on foot. His story weaves myth and history into the narrative and also serves as a poignant snapshot of Cyprus just before it was divided.

HISTORY MODERN CYPRUS

1821	1878–1923	1914–15	1923–25
Greek Cypriots side with Greece in a revolt against Turkish rule. The island's leading Orthodox clergy are executed as punishment, and 20,000 Christians flee the island.	Britain leases Cyprus from Turkey, as the administrator of the island. The British formally annex Cyprus in 1914. Turkey does not recognise the annexation until 1923.	Turkey sides with Germany in WWI. Britain offers Cyprus to Greece as incentive to support the British. King Constantine declines in an attempt to remain neutral.	Turkey is compensated by the British for its loss of the island. Cyprus becomes a Crown Colony (1925) and is governed by the British High Commissioner.

The Cyprus problem has been one of the major sticking points in Turkey's ongoing attempts to join the EU. Currently, Turkey does not recognise the Republic's Greek Cypriot government.

the same time around 50,000 Turkish Cypriots moved from the South to the Turkish-controlled areas in the North.

The human and economic cost to the island was catastrophic. The now-truncated Republic of Cyprus was deprived of some of its best land, two major cities, its lucrative citrus industry and the bulk of its tourist infrastructure. There was also widespread looting.

The invasion and forced division of Cyprus served convoluted political and military purposes. Reinstatement of the rightful government and dissipation of the military junta did not alter the Turkish government's stance. It forcibly continued its illegal occupation of the North and the Turkish troops remained.

The UN has maintained a peacekeeping force along the Green Line and the border that runs the length of the island ever since. They oversee the buffer zone that runs parallel to the Green Line with barbed wire and regular patrols. This no-man's land with its bombed-out buildings is a poignant reminder of the brutality of the conflict.

The declaration of a separate Turkish Republic of Northern Cyprus (TRNC), by President Rauf Denktaş, came in 1983. It is only officially recognised by Turkey.

THE CONTROVERSIAL RAUF DENKTAŞ

Viewed as the bane of Cypriot society by Greek Cypriots and saviour of the nation by many Turkish Cypriots, Rauf Denktaş was president of the self-proclaimed Turkish Republic of Northern Cyprus for an astonishing 31 years, before finally stepping down in 2005.

A mercurial character, Denktaş was born near Pafos on the island's southern coast and trained as a barrister in London before commencing his long political career. As well as leading the Turkish Communal Chamber in pre-partition Cyprus, Denktaş was instrumental in founding the armed Türk Mukavemet Teşkilatı movement, the Turkish Cypriot equivalent to Ethniki Organosi tou Kypriakou Agona (EOKA; National Organisation for the Cypriot Struggle).

As president of the North after partition, Denktaş became known for his dogged persistence and steadfast loyalty to the official position of his Turkish-mainland backers. UN-backed talks on reunification in 2003 failed to overcome Denktaş' insistence on a bizonal state, with continued separation between the two communities.

Yet, surprisingly, the same year, Denktaş made the unexpected announcement that he would ease border controls between the two parts of the island, thus allowing Cypriots from both sides to cross with immediate effect. This decision marked a major turning point in Cyprus' history, paving the way for more meaningful reunification negotiations.

1955–60	1963–64	1974	1975
Ethniki Organosi tou Kypriakou Agona (EOKA; National Organisation for the Cypriot Struggle) is founded. Guerrilla warfare is directed at the British. Archbishop Makarios III is first president of an independent Cyprus.	President Makarios proposes constitutional changes; intercommunal fighting ensues. Turkish Cypriots withdraw and UN peacekeeping forces arrive. The Green Line is first drawn across Nicosia.	Greek junta organises a coup. Turkish army invades, taking a third of the island. Archbishop's Palace is the scene of much fighting. Makarios resumes presidency. Cyprus is divided thereafter.	Turkish Cypriots establish an independent administration, with Rauf Denktaş as its leader. Denktaş and Glafkos Clerides then agree on a population exchange between North and South.

Unification Attempts

In the years since division, there have been several negotiation attempts to reunite the island, with both sides presenting entrenched and uncompromising points of view.

During the spring and summer of 2002, Cyprus and Turkey were seeking entry into the EU and the leaders of both the North and the South had thrice-weekly talks aimed at reunification. Again discussions got bogged down by the intricacies of land ownership and the real number of Turkish mainland settlers.

In April 2003 Northern Cyprus leader Rauf Denktaş made the surprise announcement that travel restrictions across the Green Line would be eased, allowing both Greek and Turkish Cypriots access to visit the opposite sides. Since then seven checkpoints have been opened and crossing the buffer zone has become a normal, everyday occurrence for some.

During this period Kofi Annan, the former UN secretary general, brokered an agreement allowing separate island-wide referendums on a reunification plan. The 'Annan Plan', as it was known, was designed to make Cyprus a federation of two constituent states, with shared proportional power. Political leaders on both sides campaigned for a 'no' vote. Greek Cypriots rejected the plan (76%), while Turkish Cypriots endorsed it (65%).

Peace talks were revived in 2008, however, when the Republic's president Demetris Christofias promised to work with Turkish Cypriot leader Mehmet Ali Talat, generating over 100 meetings. Their attempts at

Settlers from mainland Turkey began arriving in Northern Cyprus soon after the island's 1974 division. Many hail from Anatolia's poorer, rural areas and work in farming and the tourism sectors. Mainland Turks are now thought to make up about half of Northern Cyprus' population.

A GREEN LIGHT ON THE GREEN LINE

It all happened in a matter of hours. On 23 April 2003 Rauf Denktaş, then leader of the Turkish Cypriots, made the surprise announcement that the Green Line would open that day for all Cypriots to cross from 9am to midnight. The Greek Cypriot government, gobsmacked by the news, was silent. No one knew how the Cypriot people would react and what the consequences of this decision would be.

Starting with a few eager early-morning visitors, thousands of people crossed the UN Buffer Zone over the coming days. Friends and family met, and many tears were shed. Greeks and Turks visited their former homes and were welcomed by the current inhabitants. The two peoples treated each other with civility and kindness and, more than a decade after the checkpoints' opening, no major incidents have been reported.

Many Turkish Cypriots now cross the line every day on their way to work in the southern part of the island. Serdar Denktaş, the son of Rauf and the man behind the realisation of the Green Line opening, dubbed the events 'a quiet revolution'. Many compared it to the the fall of the Berlin Wall in 1989, minus the dramatic knocking down of the buffer zone, an event still to take place.

1977	1983	1999	2002
Archbishop Makarios dies suddenly at 63. Over 250,000 mourners pay respects during the funeral service. He is succeeded by Spyros Kyprianou.	Turkish Republic of Northern Cyprus is proclaimed by its leader. Its sovereignty is only recognised by Turkey. Thousands of mainland Turks settle in the North of the island.	The Republic of Cyprus (the South) starts to prosper economically and the standard of living booms. Northern Cyprus is supported largely by Turkey, in the wake of international economic sanctions.	Cyprus and Turkey both seek entry to the EU. The leaders of the Republic and the North attend intense talks, aimed at reunification. Talks stall and no agreement is reached.

camaraderie, aimed at creating a 'climate of peace', began to worry officials on the Turkish mainland. The situation was quickly blunted when the pro-Turkish Derviş Eroğlu came to power in 2010.

For the following few years there was the usual rhetoric regarding talks with UN mediators. However, in 2013 Nicos Anastasiades was elected as the new president in the Republic and in February 2014 it seemed a corner was turned when, for the first time in 55 years, talks took place in Athens and Ankara simultaneously. The talks ultimately failed and it wasn't until Mustafa Akinci won the Northern Cyprus election in 2015 that a peace plan was once again on the agenda.

Repairing the Damage

Many Greek Cypriots quickly regrouped after 1974, putting their energies into rebuilding their shattered nation. Within a few years the economy was on the mend and the Republic of Cyprus was recognised internationally as the only legitimate representative of the island. The economy pushed ahead through the 1980s. The opening of the Cyprus Stock Exchange in 1999 initially absorbed vast amounts of private funds, although in the early 2000s the stock exchange took a full-size nose dive and many lost huge amounts of money.

The first decade of the 21st century saw considerable changes in demographics, with foreign workers from Eastern Europe, Asia, Africa and India filling the labour markets, creating cheap labour. EU succession (2004) also changed the landscape in the Republic of Cyprus in a variety of areas, including skyrocketing prices of services and food.

Between 2012 and 2013, a combination of joining the eurozone and sharing close financial ties with Greece had a severe and negative impact on Cypriot banks (who were major holders of Greek government and corporate bonds). In March 2013 banks closed for 12 days while a deal was struck for a €10 billion bailout by the International Monetary Fund and the EU. The loan was conditional on Cyprus raising €5.8 billion through various austerity measures. Tourism remained stable throughout this period, however. The economy shrunk by just 5.4% (as opposed to the 20% predicted) and within a year there were cautious signs of recovery.

North of the Green Line is known by most foreigners simply as 'Northern Cyprus' and by the Greeks as the 'Occupied Territories' *(ta katehomena)*. This area, by comparison to the South, has developed at a snail's pace. An influx of Turkish mainlanders and international economic sanctions against the unrecognised Northern government has made progress difficult. It remains largely supported by its client and sponsor nation, Turkey, through direct funding and its use as a Turkish military outpost.

Even with its increasing economic expansion, the North is heavily dependent financially (and politically) on Ankara – to the sum of more than US$600 million a year.

2003	2004	2013	2015–17
The North's leader, Rauf Denktaş, announces a surprise decision to allow Cypriots from both sides to visit the opposing parts of the island. The first crossings in 29 years are peaceful.	The Greek Cypriot 'no' vote in the April referendum on the Annan Plan scuppers reunification hopes. One week later, in May, the Republic of Cyprus joins the EU.	Veteran centre-right politician Nicos Anastasiades is elected president in the Republic. In March the Republic's financial crash causes banks to close for 12 days while a €10-billion bailout deal is struck.	Mustafa Akinci wins Northern Cyprus' elections in April 2015, kick-starting the latest round of talks to reunify the island. Anastasiades and Akinci hold meetings throughout 2015–17.

The Cypriot Way of Life

Cypriot culture is a unique blend of Mediterranean and Middle Eastern; it has been moulded by centuries of rule by different nations that have coveted, fought over and possessed the island. Family life is considered of paramount importance and respect for the older generation remains strong. Despite an outwardly relaxed attitude towards religion, the traditions and values of the Orthodox church (in the South) and Islam (in the North) still play a key role in society as a whole.

The Great Divide

The daily lives of Cypriots are largely dominated by the domestic and international focus on the division that scores the island. For over 40 years, two generations have grown up with partition and the incessant political news and discussions on both sides of the Green Line regarding the 'Cyprus problem'. Nowadays, though there remains some allegiance to mainland Greece or Turkey, most people see themselves as Cypriot first and Greek or Turkish second. In recent years a significant number of the younger population on both sides of the divide, who were born after the island was split in two, have become increasingly tired of the political manoeuvring that dominates Cypriot headlines and are pressing for a final resolution.

When the first Green Line crossings between North and South opened in 2003, no one knew how the Cypriot people would react and what the consequences would be. Would there be riots or civil unrest? After all, no one had crossed the Green Line for 29 years, save for diplomatic reasons. Many still had friends, relatives and homes they missed on the 'other side'.

The newly opened checkpoints swelled with thousands of people crossing the buffer zone. Many Turkish Cypriots who came south were enchanted by the comparative wealth and the elegant shops and restaurants in streets of Nicosia (Lefkosia), while many Greek Cypriots wandered the streets of North Nicosia (Lefkoşa), surprised at the way time had stood still for 30 years. Old acquaintances met and tears were shed. Some Greek Cypriots visited their former homes and properties in the North, and in some cases existing inhabitants reportedly welcomed visitors cordially and even invited them in for coffee and gave them gifts of citrus fruit and flowers. It is estimated that more than 35% of Cyprus' population crossed in the first two weeks, and over 25,000 Turkish Cypriots applied for a Cypriot passport (from the Republic of Cyprus) in that year alone.

The people have treated each other with studied civility and kindness, and even now, years after the openings, no major incidents have been reported. Since the attitude to crossing the Green Line has normalised, over 20 million crossings have been recorded, with around 70% of those North to South. Indeed, many Turkish Cypriots now cross the buffer zone daily to shop or work in the southern part of the island. While Greek

Fast Facts

Sunshine: 326 days a year on average

Highest point: Mt Olympus (1952m)

Length of coastline: 648km

Etiquette

Driving Cypriots love to talk on mobile phones and not use indicators. Make eye contact at intersections before pulling out.

Tact Use it when discussing politics, division and the Green Line.

Eating out If invited for a meal, the host pays the bill. Offer to contribute, knowing you'll likely be scoffed at.

Cypriots make up less of the traffic, many do head over the line for Easter holidays and in particular to visit Apostolos Andreas church and for shopping bargains and casino visits.

While politics are discussed openly on both sides, travellers should always approach the subject with tact. Both Greek Cypriots and Turkish Cypriots may be forthright in discussing the issue, but it's still better to let them initiate the discussion. There are pockets of hardliners still on both sides of the island and for the older generation, especially those who experienced the trauma of partition first-hand, the sensitivity they feel in relation to this subject cannot be overstated.

Multiculturalism

Although immensely hospitable people by nature, some Cypriots regard outsiders with a little caution and wariness, perhaps understandably so given the island's long history of occupation and struggle for independence.

Patriotism is a strong force in people's identity. In the North, some Turkish Cypriots define settlers from mainland Turkey as outsiders and make a clear definition between the two. In the South, for a small number of locals, especially those who have never left the island, even expatriates and second-generation Cypriots from the UK, US, Canada and Australia are considered to be *xeni* (foreigners).

Both sides of the island have had an influx of foreign migrants over the past decade. Northern Cyprus' universities have attracted a large number of foreign students, many of whom have stayed on to work afterwards. In the South, a growing number of manual and service jobs are filled by migrant workers. This swift multicultural transformation has greatly changed the face of the island's population. Combine this with the lasting 'Britishness' that remains from the island's colonial past and from its present-day reliance on tourism and as such, rightly or wrongly, many locals feel bombarded by outsiders.

Much of the worry stems from the gradual loss of traditional lifestyle and culture. While this has caused some consternation and resentment, this expanded diversity has been welcomed by others, especially those Cypriots who have travelled and studied abroad.

Gradually most Cypriots are recognising the trend in their society towards greater multiculturalism. Indeed, this is reflected in the increasing number of Cypriots who are marrying foreigners (14% of marriages), particularly Europeans and Russians (many of whom belong to the Orthodox Church), creating a new generation of multicultural Cypriots. This phenomenon suggests that if racial and cultural barriers do linger – as some suspect they do – then their influence is diminishing.

Using first names alone is considered too familiar and is only done among friends. People greet each other with the title *kyrie* or *kyria* ('Mr' and 'Mrs' in Greek) before the person's name. In Turkish *bey* and *hanım* are used the same way, after naming the person.

Traditionally, ultimate relaxation for a Cypriot man in his courtyard or garden requires the use of seven time-honoured wooden chairs. One for his stick, one for his coffee, one for each arm, one for each leg and of course one to sit on.

THE KAFENEIO & THE TEA HOUSE

In the Republic's villages, the local *kafeneio* (coffee shop) is the central meeting point. Most will have two such places, distinguished by their political alignment (socialist or nationalist). In the North the village hub is the local tea house. In both South and North, these cafes are filled with men of all generations, sitting, serving or flipping beads. Many come and go on their way to and from work. The older men sit quietly, spread across chairs, waiting out the days like oracles, eating haloumi (hellim in Turkish) and olives or drinking coffee, tea and (in the South) *zivania* (fermented grape pomace). Good friends sit in pairs, smoking cigarettes and playing *tavli* (backgammon) in the shade of the vine leaves. Their dice rattle, while moves are counted and strategies are shaped in whispers. And come lunchtime, only the lingering smoke remains, as the men stampede home for their midday meal and siesta, returning in the evening to do it all again.

SUMMER SOUVLA

A favourite Cypriot pastime is enjoying a *souvla* (spit-roast) that's been roasting for hours over burning coals. It's especially fine on the beach. There's the joke that a Cypriot's favourite vehicle is a pick-up truck, because 20 chairs, a table and all the barbecue equipment can fit into the tray when the family heads out for the weekend. Indeed, part of the summer holidays for many Cypriots is often spent camping on beaches, where the sound of rotating skewers and the smell of soft lamb with herbs permeates the sea air.

This hangover of insularity is more than balanced by a natural tendency of hospitality towards guests. Most visitors to the island will find the Cypriots they meet to be amazingly friendly, welcoming and kind, regardless of whether they live in cities, villages or less-developed areas.

Orthodoxy & Islam

Almost 78% of Cypriots are Greek Orthodox, 18% are Muslims and the remaining 4% are Maronite, Armenian Apostolic and other Christian denominations. Due to the island's division, Muslims predominantly live in the North, while the Greek Orthodox live in the South.

The recent increase in asylum seekers from the Middle East, Africa and central and south Asia has increased the number of practising Muslims living in the Republic, particularly in the centres of Larnaka, Nicosia and Lemesos (Limassol), which all have mosques.

The presence of the Orthodox Church is ingrained in both politics and daily life in the South, with the Cypriot year centred on the festivals, celebrations and saint's days of the Orthodox calendar. Sundays in particular are popular for visiting monasteries and the Byzantine churches of the Troödos Mountains.

In the North, Turkish Cypriots are mostly secular Sunni Muslims. While religion plays an important part in Turkish Cypriot culture, the more conservative Islamic tradition practised in the Middle East is not so obvious in Cyprus. Alcohol, for example, is widely available and frequently consumed by Turkish Cypriots, and women dress far more casually than their counterparts in other countries where Islam is the main religion.

Changing Roles

Traditional ideas about the proper role of women – cooking, cleaning and tending to house and family – persist in some sectors of Cypriot society. However, modern Cypriot women, particularly those who live in cities, like to dress in designer labels, frequent beaches in bikinis, have careers and go out on the town.

Cypriot women have freedom and independence in many areas, but more needs to be done, especially when it comes to employment, as professional positions are still very much male-dominated.

Attitudes towards homosexuality have relaxed somewhat over the years, although open displays of affection are still frowned upon by the more socially conservative. The first Cyprus Pride Festival took place in Nicosia in 2014, and in 2015 civil-union partnerships between same-sex couples became legal in the Republic of Cyprus. In 2014 the North legalised same-sex sexual activity, becoming the last territory in Europe to decriminalise homosexuality.

While topless sunbathing is generally OK in the Republic, baring all is not. In Northern Cyprus, only sunbathe topless on private resort beaches (and check if it's OK before stripping off). Cyprus is a traditional country so across the island, when off the sand it's best to put on a T-shirt.

Landscapes & Wildlife

For a growing number of visitors, Cyprus' one-of-a-kind flora and fauna is the number-one reason for a trip here. Tiny rare orchids bloom amid the hillside wildflowers in early spring. Turtles nest on the beaches in their thousands during summer. Endemic bird species, along with seasonal visitors, can be spotted in the high forests and lowland salt lakes. This rich biodiversity makes it a nature-lover's paradise.

Lie of the Land

Above Troödos Mountains (p75)

Cyprus is an ophiolite that rose from the sea 20 million years ago. Shaped like a swordfish, with its sharp tip and flared fins, it is the third-largest island in the Mediterranean.

In the North, the 170km-long Kyrenia (Girne) Range was formed by upward-thrust masses of Mesozoic limestone. Its most famous feature is the five-ridged peak known as Five-Fingers Mountain (Pentadaktylos, in Greek; Beşparmak, in Turkish) that runs practically parallel to the northern coastline.

Directly south of this mountain range is the vast Mesaoria plain (which means 'In Between Mountains' in Greek), which stretches from Morfou (Güzelyurt) in the west to Famagusta (Gazimağusa) in the east, with the divided capital of Nicosia (Lefkosia) and North Nicosia (Lefkoşa) at its middle. The plain has over 1900 sq km of irrigation and is the island's primary grain-growing area.

Further south, the island is dominated by the vast range of the Troödos Mountains, created millions of years ago by rising molten rock in the deep ocean. It features the imposing Mt Olympus and its lower plateaus to the east. This area is rich in minerals and natural resources such as chromite, gypsum, iron pyrite, marble and copper. Mined for thousands of years, it was instrumental in the island's development during ancient times.

National Parks & Reserves

The upgrading of natural areas to national-park status has steadily increased. The declared list of parks in the South includes Akamas National Forest Park, Pafos region; Troödos National Park, declared in 1992; Cape Greco and the Peninsula Bay, east of Agia Napa; Athalassa National Forest Park, west of Nicosia; Polemidia National Forest Park, near Lemesos (Limassol); Rizoelia National Forest Park, near Larnaka; and Tripylos Natural Reserve, east of Pafos, which includes the wonderful Cedar Valley.

There's also one marine reserve: Lara Toxeftra Reserve, off the west coast near Lara, Pafos region, established to protect marine turtles and their nesting beaches.

In North Cyprus, 150 sq km of the Karpas (Kirpaşa) Peninsula have been declared a national park. Environmentalists were successful in having the vulnerable and precious area protected from development. Rare marine turtles that nest on the beaches on both sides of the peninsula are now benefiting from this decision.

A Plethora of Plant Life

The diversity of Cyprus' flora is not immediately obvious to first-time visitors. After the explosion of colour from endemic flora and wildflowers in spring, summer sees the island assume an arid appearance, with only a few hardy flowers and thistles.

The island is home to some 1800 species and subspecies of plants, of which about 7% are indigenous to Cyprus. Five major habitats characterise Cyprus' flora profile: pine forests, garigue and maquis (underbrush found in the Mediterranean), rocky areas, coastal areas and wetlands. One of the main places for indigenous plant species is the Troödos Mountains, where around 45 endemic species can be found.

The Karpas Peninsula has a further 19 endemic species that are found only in the North.

Over 40 species of orchid can be found on the island; many of these, such as the rare Punctate orchid, can be spotted in the lap of the Kyrenia Range. The best time to see Cyprus' wildflowers is in early spring (February to March) or in late autumn (October to November), when most of the species blossom, taking advantage of the moister climate.

Environmental Awareness

This beautiful island is unfortunately beset with environmental issues. True, some of its environmental concerns stem from tourism, but there is also the much deeper issue of littering on streets and beaches, and

Two handy field companions are *Butterflies of Cyprus* by Christodoulos Makris (2000) and *Butterflies of North Cyprus* by Dr Daniel H Haines and Dr Hilary M Haines (2010). Both comprehensive guides are available in paperback.

Search out *Wild Flowers of Cyprus* by George Sfikas (1994) and *The Floral Charm of Cyprus* by Valerie Sinclair (1992) for further information about the range of flora on the island.

LANDSCAPES & WILDLIFE ENVIRONMENTAL AWARENESS

Cyprus warbler

FLOWER POWER

For the best flower-spotting, enthusiasts will need to spend plenty of time trekking and searching, as many species are limited to small geographical areas. You'll need to enjoy a ramble and be patient.

Casey's larkspur This is a late-flowering species that carries a dozen or more deep-violet, long-spurred flowers atop a slender stem. Its habitat is limited to the rocky peaks 1.5km southwest of St Hilarion.

Cyprus crocus A delicate white and yellow flower from the iris family. An endangered species, it's protected by law and is generally found at high altitudes in the Troödos Mountains.

Cyprus tulip Delicate and dark red, this is another rare, protected species found in the Akamas Peninsula, the Koruçam (Kormakitis) Peninsula and remote parts of the Kyrenia Range.

Orchids The most popular wildflowers for enthusiasts. The one endemic orchid, Kotschy's bee orchid, is an exquisite species that resembles a bee, both in its shape and patterning. While fairly rare, it's found in habitats all over the island. Other varieties found on the slopes of Mt Olympus include the slender, pink Troödos Anatolian orchid, the cone-shaped pyramidal orchid, the giant orchid and the colourful woodcock orchid.

St Hilarion cabbage This unlikely sounding beauty grows in the North, mainly on rocky outcrops near St Hilarion Castle. This large endemic cabbage flower grows to 1m high and has spikes of creamy white flowers.

Troödos golden drop A member of the borage family, this is an endemic yellow bell-shaped flower appearing in leafy clusters. Another endangered species, it's confined to the highest peaks of the Troödos Mountains.

Mouflon in the wild

garbage dumping on roadsides. Industrial waste, fridges, rubble and all sorts of debris are often dumped in forests and near natural salt lakes.

In an attempt to remedy this situation, the Republic's government has responded with advertisements encouraging people to put rubbish in bins and stop discarding cigarette butts on beaches, and by introducing recycling points. On a more grassroots level, educational programs have been launched in primary schools to encourage the next generation to be more aware of their environment and the benefits of recycling. Local councils have joined in, providing skips near and around natural habitats where dumping regularly occurs. Positive actions such as these are providing new hope and putting a much-needed focus on the issue.

Cyprus has 140 unique flowering plants only found in the Troödos Mountains, 390 different migratory bird species during spring and autumn, and over 80 nesting sites for rare and protected turtles.

Water, Water, Everywhere...

A significant ongoing issue for the island is the shortage of water. Population growth, mismanagement of underground aquifers and years of drought, which depleted water reserves in dams and reservoirs, have all added to Cyprus suffering a severe water crisis.

Looking for a permanent and sustainable solution, the South opted to begin building desalination plants in the 1990s. There are now four installations (which each produce 40,000 cu metres of water per day) supplying over 50% of domestic water, and another being built.

In the North, the ambitious Northern Cyprus Water Supply Project became operational in October 2015. The project transports water from the Alaköprü Dam in Turkey to the Geçitköy Dam, near Kyrenia (Girne), via an 80km underwater pipeline, and cost 1.2 billion Turkish lira to implement.

Island Animals

Birds

Cyprus is a major overwintering stop on the north–south migration routes and is also home to two endemic bird species. The Cyprus warbler and Cyprus wheatear are found nowhere else in the world and many bird enthusiasts come to the island solely to tick them off their spotting list.

Although only approximately 50 species of birds are resident in Cyprus year-round, during the major Mediterranean migration period over 200 species utilise the island as one of their stops along the route.

October through to April are all good birding months but spring, particularly April, is peak time for birdwatching.

Mammals

While the most famous Cypriot wild animal is still the mouflon (the native wild mountain sheep), a scattering of twitchy wild donkeys can be seen on the Karpas Peninsula. They are believed to be descendants of the domesticated donkeys that escaped or were abandoned in 1974.

In the island's differing forest environs you may also see smaller animals such as foxes, rabbits, hares, hedgehogs, squirrels and fruit bats.

Reptiles

The island's dry, hot summer landscape is a natural home for lizards, geckos, chameleons and snakes, of which only the Montpellier snake and blunt-nosed viper are poisonous.

Lizards and geckos, in particular, pop up everywhere, sunbathing on rocks, ruins and concrete walls. Keep your eyes peeled to spot the particularly common, grey-green striped Troödos lizard and brown-yellow ocellated skink.

For those wanting to be immersed in the island's natural habitat, the Republic's agrotourism network (www.agrotourism.com.cy) offers an ever-growing range of rural retreats in the mountains and traditional villages.

Birding Resources

Bird Life Cyprus (www.birdlife cyprus.org; Republic of Cyprus)

Birds of Cyprus (Jane Stylianou; 2009)

North Cyprus Society for the Protection of Birds & Nature (www.kuskor.org; Northern Cyprus)

WHERE TO WATCH

Birds travelling between Africa and Europe use Cyprus as a stepping stone on their migratory path. Birdwatchers have an excellent window into both more exotic migratory species and local birds. Here are some of the best birdwatching locations on the island.

Larnaka Salt Lake An important migratory habitat that fills with flamingos and waterfowl from February to March. There are lookout posts (with seats) at various intervals along the airport road to Larnaka. You can also walk the nature trails around the lakes past the Hala Sultan Tekkesi mosque.

Troödos Mountains The ranges offer excellent vantage points along the many nature trails in the region. Take binoculars to catch the likes of griffon vultures, falcons and kestrels. One of the best birdwatching spots is the Kaledonia Trail, which showcases large amounts of Cyprus and Sardinian warblers and nightingales.

Cape Greco Peninsula In addition to being the home of wonderful sea caves, the cape, with its scrubland and rocky outcrops, is one of the prime migration zones for birds from across the seas. Expect to see a range of birds, from chukars and spectacled warblers to pallid harriers and red-rumped swallows.

Kyrenia Range Bonelli's eagles nest amid the rugged rock faces and Cyprus warblers and wheatears are easy to spot. Sightings of black-headed bunting, spectacled warblers and blue rock thrush are common.

Famagusta Wetlands Like Larnaka Salt Lake in the South, the Famagusta wetlands in the North are home to a host of waterbirds. It's also the island's only glossy ibis breeding site. Likely sightings include pelicans, flamingos, Demoiselle cranes and spoonbills.

Top Kyrenia Range from St Hilarion Castle (p194)

Bottom Wild white crocus flowers

Sea Fauna

Cyprus' warm, clear waters are home to over 260 different kinds of fish, and the coves and underwater reefs along its coasts are teeming with sea-life such as corals, sponges, mussels and sea anemones, making it a haven for diving and snorkelling.

Schools of grouper, jack, tuna, barracuda, rays and parrotfish are commonly seen by divers here, while the seas surrounding the island are also home to moray eels, octopus, and green and loggerhead turtles.

Endangered Species

Mouflon are timid, nimble and skilled at climbing. The males have enormous curved horns and were hunted for sport by nobles in Lusignan times. By the early 20th century widespread shooting by farmers and hunters had nearly reduced them to extinction. However, awareness of the plight of the island's national emblem increased, and now they are protected at sites such as Stavros tis Psokas forest station, in Pafos, which shelters a small herd. In the wild, mouflon are only found in remote parts of the mountain ranges and are rarely spotted.

Green and loggerhead turtles have bred and lived on Cypriot beaches for centuries, but tourism and beach development have encroached on vital nesting areas. They nest in the soft sands of the northern beaches in particular, which are now signed and closed at night (hatching times). Look out for conservation programs in coastal areas. Follow the rules, stick to allocated swimming times and plant your umbrellas as close to the water's edge as possible to avoid crushing eggs.

Monk seals are rarely spotted off the coast and had been considered extinct as recently as 10 years ago. However, sightings off the eastern coast and at Cape Greco's sea caves revived hope and a monitoring program was implemented in 2011. It's currently thought that a very small population of monk seals still survives in remote locations around the island's shores.

Although years of meagre rainfall is the main cause of Cyprus' water woes, the influx of over three million tourists every year has added to the problem. Travellers should be extra aware of their water usage while here.

Above Lacemaking, Lefkara village (p135)

The Arts

Cyprus' heritage reflects a rich and diverse love of the arts. Cypriots, overall, have an aesthetic deep-rooted artistic sensibility towards both visual and creative arts. Examples range from dazzling icons painted in punchy primary colours to delicate embroidery with minute intricate stitchery, . Music is also an important facet of life here and tradition still strikes a resounding chord, particularly in the continuing popularity of the urban Greek folk music, *rebetiko.*

Visual Arts

The art of Cyprus has long reflected both Eastern and Western influences. Political turmoil and the division of the island have similarly had an inevitable impact.

From Frescos to Folk Painters

During the neolithic age, decorative ceramics and mosaics reflected a desire for ornamentation, which continued with the conversion of the island to Christianity in AD 45 and the emergence of Byzantine art. This religious expression was represented most vividly in frescos, mosaics and icons, many of which are still in evidence today in the monasteries and churches. For the most comprehensive collection of stunning artwork from this period, visit the Byzantine Museum at the Makarios Cultural Foundation in Nicosia (Lefkosia), home to the largest collection of icons relating to Cyprus, and the Kykkos Monastery near Pedoulas in the Troödos Mountains. Kykkos is just one of several monasteries where you can also see richly coloured and complex mosaics. Other recommended monasteries and churches, particularly for Byzantine frescos, include Agios Nikolaos tis Stegis, Panagia tis Podythou, Panagia Forviotissa and Timios Stavros.

Little remains of the Frankish (1192–1489) and Venetian (1489–1571) periods, due to the looting and plundering of numerous invaders. This sorry situation continued after the conquest of the Ottomans in 1570, when physical survival took precedence over art.

The 19th century saw the emergence of folk painters and sculptors who were the forerunners of contemporary Cypriot art. They painted friezes in coffee shops and decorated glass and furniture, particularly traditional iron beds, which were adorned with plant motifs or similar.

Twentieth- to 21st-Century Painting

In the 1950s artists began to return to Cyprus after studying abroad. Important artists who emerged during this period include Christofors Savva (1924–68), who was strongly influenced by the cubist and expressionist movements, and abstract artists Costas Joachim (b 1936), Nicos Kouroussis (b 1937) and Andreas Ladommatos (b 1940). One of the best-known design artists of this period is İsmet Güney (1923–2009), who designed the Cyprus flag (now used by the Republic of Cyprus) in 1960.

The 1974 division of the island had a significant influence on trends in art, with a rise in symbolism and subject matter that reflected the spiritual anguish of the time. Important artists from this period include Angelos Makrides (b 1942), who represented Cyprus in the 1988 Venice Biennale, and Emin Chizenel (b 1949), who has exhibited on both sides of the divide.

Female artist Haris Epaminonda, born in Nicosia in 1980 and known for her collages, installations and videos, has exhibited in Europe and North America, while British Cypriot Mustafa Hulusi had a solo show at London's Tate Modern in 2010 and contributed to the Terra Mediterranea in Crisis exhibition at the Nicosia Municipal Arts Centre in 2012.

In 2014 the AG Leventis Gallery opened in Nicosia with a collection that includes some of the island's most iconic contemporary artworks. At its heart is the monumental *The World of Cyprus* by the famous late Cypriot painter Adamantios Diamanis. The work is based on 75 drawings depicting the landscape and people of the island. Another art museum that provides an excellent insight into Cypriot art is the State Gallery of Cypriot Contemporary Art, also located in Nicosia.

Icons

Although some Cypriot churches and several museums still house magnificent Byzantine icons, many have been looted and their treasures sold on the open market. These are often unwittingly bought by collectors and, occasionally, celebrities. Singer Boy George had an icon of Jesus Christ hung proudly over his fireplace for decades before it was spotted by an expert during a televised interview. The icon was duly returned to

Mosaic, Kykkos Monastery (p90)

the Church of St Charalambos in Chorio Kythrea in 2011, from where it had been stolen in 1974.

Icons are still produced in many monasteries today. The most justifiably famous contemporary icon painter was Father Kallinikos Stavrovounis (1920–2011) of Stavrovouni Monastery, who is credited with being a key figure in reviving the Orthodox Byzantine style of icon painting in Cyprus.

Traditional Crafts

Cyprus continues its healthy tradition of folk arts, ranging from basket making to lacework. Head for a branch of the Cyprus Handicrafts Centre (p165) in Nicosia, Lemesos (Limassol) or Pafos to guarantee authenticity and a fair price.

The theft and sale of Cypriot works of art that followed the Turkish invasion has been described as the greatest looting of art since WWII.

Pottery

Decorative pottery is worth seeking out. You can't miss the enormous *pitharia* (earthenware storage jars), often used as stylish plant pots. Originally used for storing water, oil or wine, their sheer size renders them impossible to transport home. One of the best places to learn about the history of the *pitharia* is at the Folk Art Museum in Foini in the Troödos Mountains. Curator Theophanis Pilavakis, now in his 90s, is famed for making an enormous *pitharia* (on display here) that holds 2000 litres and made the *Guinness Book of Records*. The village of Kornos, between Lemesos and Larnaka, is also famous for its pottery, as is Pafos and the southwest region of the Republic.

Basket Making

One of the oldest handicrafts, basket making was traditionally learned by everyone in the family. Today baskets are still usually made from reeds

Street musician, Lemesos (Limmasol; p56)

found growing next to streams, though in the Akamas Peninsula, villages such as Kritou Terra are famous for their intricately woven twig baskets. Palm leaves and straw are used for creating the distinctive brightly coloured *tsestos* (*sestas* in Turkish; decorative 'platters' with geometric designs). These are more prevalent in Northern Cyprus, especially in the Karpas Peninsula and Mesaoria (Mesarya) regions. Be wary of synthetic copies made from plastic, which are fortunately easy to spot.

Lacework

One of the most famous folk-art exports is the exquisite Lefkara lacework, from the same-name village, located in the southern Troödos foothills. Be wary of cheap Chinese imports. The village of Fyti in the Pafos region is also famous for its needlework, particularly woven and embroidered silk and cotton, and is, to date, not on the coach-tour trail. Also check out the Museum for the Preservation of Lace at Timiou Stavrou (Holy Cross) Monastery in Omodos. In the North, look out for the delicate cross-stitch motifs of Lapithos (Lapta). Traditionally embroidered on to clothing, they now more commonly decorate household linens.

The International Festival of Ancient Greek Theatre in July is one of the best opportunities to watch productions of the dramas, tragedies and comedies of classical Greece and takes place in venues across the Republic.

Music & Dance

Cypriot music and dance is diverse and reflects Greek, Turkish and Arabic influences. Traditional music continues to have an enduring appeal – as evidenced by the distinctive bouzouki twanging out from all those open car windows – and both Greek Cypriot and Turkish Cypriot musical cultures share a remarkable overlap in sounds and instrumentation.

Music

The bouzouki, which you will hear all over Cyprus, is a mandolin-like instrument similar to the Turkish *saz* and *bağlama*. It's one of the main instruments of *rebetiko* music – the Greek equivalent of American blues. The name *rebetiko* may come from the Turkish word *rembet,* which means 'outlaw'. Opinions differ as to the origins of *rebetiko,* but it is probably a hybrid of several different types of music. One source was the music that emerged in the 1870s in the 'low-life' cafes called *tekedes* (hashish dens) in urban areas and ports. Today's music scene is a mix of old and new, traditional and modern, with young Greek Cypriots as happy with *rebetiko* as they are with contemporary rock.

Although Greek rock from mainland Greece is hugely popular, the Republic of Cyprus has a small but vibrant modern-music scene all of its own which is producing eclectic, original bands and musicians, some of whom have received international acclaim.

For more traditional sounds, Cypriot singer and lyricist Evagoras Karageorgis has produced some excellent music including *Topi se Hroma Loulaki* (Places Painted in Violet), a nostalgic and painful look at the lost villages of Northern Cyprus sung in a mixture of Cypriot dialect and standard Greek. Alkinoos Ioannidis is one of Cyprus' most prolific and popular artists, with 11 albums which merge traditional Cypriot and Greek music with rock and classical influences.

Of the newer names on the scene, Monsieur Doumani's debut *Grippy Grappa* and follow-up album *Sikoses* have both won plaudits in the global music scene for the Nicosia trio's quirky, contemporary interpretations of traditional folk music. Jazz trio Tricoolore bring a melodic Mediterranean vibe and swags of stylish improvisation to their instrumental tunes, and blues-band The Zilla Project (who sing in English) remain firm favourites locally for their authentic gravelly sound.

In the North, musical trends tend to mirror those of mainland Turkey, with *arabesk* (a melancholy, Arabic-influenced musical style) and Turkish pop and rock dominating the scene. Turkish Cypriot folk music, played at weddings and other important events, with the *darbuka* (goblet-drum) marking out the beat, was traditionally played to accompany folk dances.

Although most Turkish Cypriot musicians remain unknown off the island, a handful have found acclaim overseas. In particular, concert pianist Rüya Taner is highly regarded in the classical-music world, while jazz-fusion bass guitarist and composer Oytun Ersan has released two albums which feature collaborations with some of jazz's top names.

Karagöz shadow-puppet theatre spread throughout Cyprus during the Ottoman era, though today this art form is dying. The only theatre (in North Nicosia) which regularly hosted performances of this centuries-old art form closed in 2014 when puppeteer Mehmet Ertuğ retired due to illness.

THE ARTS MUSIC & DANCE

Dance

Traditional Cypriot dances are commonly 'confronted pair' dances of two couples, or vigorous solo men's dances in which the dancer holds an object such as a sickle, knife, sieve or tumbler. Shows at popular tourist restaurants frequently feature a dance called *datsia* where the dancer balances a stack of glasses full of wine on a sieve.

Dances in the North share very similar patterns of development and execution to those in the South, the only real difference being the names. Thus the *tsifteteli* (a style of belly dancing) is the *ciftetelli* in the North. In addition there is the *testi* and the *kozan,* both wedding dances, and the *kaşıklı oyunları,* a dance performed with wooden spoons. Restaurants with floor shows are most likely your best opportunity to sample northern variants of Cypriot dancing.

Dancecyprus (www.dancecyprus.org) is Cyprus' ballet company. It produces inspiring modern and classical works to a European standard with a distinctive Cypriot influence. Venues include the prestigious Rialto Theatre in Lemesos.

Top Music Festivals

Bellapais Music Festival

International Pharos Chamber Music Festival, Nicosia (Lefkosia)

Fengaros Music Festival, Kato Drys

Pafos Aphrodite Festival

International Famagusta Art & Culture Festival

Literature

Cyprus has produced a sprinkling of literary stars and the literature scene is actively promoted and encouraged in both the Republic and Northern Cyprus. Novels and nonfiction books by local writers are often translated from Greek to Turkish and vice versa.

Home-grown literary talent of the 20th century includes Loukis Akritas (1932–65), who made his mark mainly in Greece as a journalist and writer, and later championed the cause of Cypriot independence through letters rather than violence. His works include novels, plays, short stories and essays. Theodosis Pierides (1908–67) is one of Cyprus' most respected poets. His *Cypriot Symphony* is considered to be one of the island's finest epics. Also important is his contemporary fellow poet Tefkros Anthias (1903–68). Anthias was excommunicated by the Orthodox Church and internally exiled by the British administration in 1931 for his poetry collection *The Second Coming*. He was arrested during the liberation struggle of 1955–59 and imprisoned. While in prison he wrote a collection of poems called *The Diary of the CDP*, which was published in 1956.

Novelist, poet and playwright Panos Ioannides (b 1935) is one of the biggest names on the contemporary literary scene and has won the National Prize for Literature five times. His most recent short-story collection, *Gregory and Other Stories,* was translated into English in 2014.

The North supports a small but healthy literary scene with more than 30 'name' personages. Neşe Yaşın (b 1959) is a writer, journalist and poet, and a founding member of a movement known as the '74 Generation Poetry Movement. This was a postdivision literary wave of writers that sought inspiration from the climate generated after Cyprus was divided. Yaşın's poems have been translated and published in magazines, newspapers, anthologies and books in Cyprus, Turkey, Greece, Hungary, the Netherlands, Germany and the UK.

Survival Guide

Directory A–Z

Accommodation

See the Accommodation chapter for more information on where to stay in Cyprus.

Customs Regulations

Republic of Cyprus

General EU customs rules apply. You are allowed to bring in or out an unrestricted amount of (legal) goods, as long as they are for your own consumption.

Northern Cyprus

Limits for entering or leaving Northern Cyprus:

➡ 200 cigarettes

➡ 1L of spirits or wine

➡ €100 worth of other goods

The importation of agricultural products is subject to strict quarantine control and requires prior approval by the Ministry of Agriculture & Natural Resources.

When travelling, be aware that you become subject to both British and the Republic of Cyprus customs regulations when crossing passport control at Pergamos (Larnaka) and Agios Nikolaos (Famagusta), as those two checkpoints are in the Dekelia Sovereign Base Area (Great Britain). The regulations are the same, but it might take a bit more time.

Discount Cards

Senior Discounts

Reduced prices for people over 60 or 65 (depending on location) at various museums.

Student Cards

Students usually receive discounts of half the normal admission fee. You will need some kind of identification (eg an International Student Identity Card; www.isic.org) to prove student status. Not accepted everywhere.

Electricity

Type G
230V/50Hz

Embassies & Consulates

Republic of Cyprus

Countries with diplomatic representation in the Republic of Cyprus are in Nicosia.

Australian High Commission (☑2275 3001; www.cyprus. embassy.gov.au; 7th fl, Alpha Business Centre, Pindarou 27)

Canadian Consulate (☑2277 5508; www.canadainternational.gc.ca/greece-grece_draft/contact-cyprus-chypre-contactez.aspx?lang=eng; Suite 402, 4th fl, Margarita House, Themistocles Dervi 15; ⊗9am-noon Mon-Fri)

French Embassy (☑2258 5300; www.ambafrance-cy.org; Leoforos Demestheni Severi 34; ⊗8.30-10.30am Mon-Fri)

German Embassy (☑2245 1145; www.nikosia.diplo.de; Nikitara 10; ⊗9am-noon Mon-Fri)

Greek Embassy (☑2244 5111; www.mfa.gr/nicosia; Leoforos Lordou Vyronos 8-10; ⊗9am-1pm Mon-Fri)

Irish Embassy (☑2281 8183; www.embassyofireland.com.cy; Aiantas 7 ⊗9am-noon Mon-Fri)

Netherlands Embassy (☑2287 3666; www.nederlandwereldwijd.nl/landen/cyprus; Dimosthenis Severis 34; ⊗10.30am-12.30pm)

UK High Commission (☑2286 1100; www.gov.uk/government/world/cyprus; Alexandrou Palli,

Climate
Lefkosia/North Nicosia

Lemesos

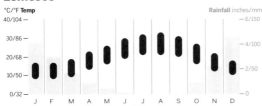

Nicosia; ⊘7.30am-2.30pm
Mon-Fri)

US Embassy (☑2239 3939;
http://cyprus.usembassy.gov;
cnr Metohiou & Agiou Ploutarhou, Engomi, Nicosia; ⊘8am-
4pm Mon-Fri)

Northern Cyprus

Countries with diplomatic
representation in Northern
Cyprus are all located in
North Nicosia (Lefkoşa).

Australian High Commission
(☑0392 227 7332; http://
cyprus.embassy.gov.au; Güner
Türkmen Sokak 20; ⊘8am-1pm
Thu)

Turkish Embassy (☑0392 600
3100; www.nicosia.emb.mfa.
gov.tr; Bedrettin Demirel Caddesi; ⊘8.30am-noon Mon-Fri)

UK High Commission (☑in
Nicosia (Lefkosia) +357 2286
1100; www.gov.uk/government/
world/cyprus; Mehmet Akif
Caddesi 29; ⊘9.30am-12.30pm
Wed)

Food

See the Eat & Drink Like a
Local chapter for more infor-
mation on food and drink in
Cyprus.

Gay & Lesbian Travellers

Homosexuality is legal in the
Republic. You will find interesting discussions, tips and
contacts on anything gay in
Cyprus at www.gay-cyprus.
com.

In Northern Cyprus,
homosexuality, which had
long been officially banned,
was decriminalised in 2010.
However, you may still find an
overall conservative attitude,
and overt public displays of
affection may be frowned
upon. To date there are no
organised support groups in
the North, though there is a
handful of gay forums, including www.turkeygay.net/
cyprus.html.

Health
Before You Go
HEALTH INSURANCE

➡ Citizens of EU countries
are currently (ie pre-Brexit
enforcement) entitled to
free or cheaper medical care
in the Republic, but not in
Northern Cyprus.

➡ EU citizens must carry
proof of their entitlement
in the form of the European
Health Insurance Card
(EHIC).

➡ Citizens from other
countries should find out
if there is a reciprocal
arrangement for free
medical care between their
country and Cyprus, though
travel insurance is always
recommended.

VACCINATIONS

No jabs are required to travel
to Cyprus, but the World
Health Organization (WHO)
recommends that all trav-
ellers should be covered for
diphtheria, measles, mumps,
rubella and polio.

In Cyprus
AVAILABILITY & COST OF HEALTH CARE

➡ If you need an ambulance,
call ☑119 in the Republic of
Cyprus or ☑112 in Northern
Cyprus.

➡ Pharmacies can dispense
basic medicines without a
prescription. You can consult
a pharmacist for minor
ailments.

➡ Emergency medical
treatment and assistance
is provided free of charge
at government hospitals
or medical institutions.
However, payment of the
prescribed fees is required
for outpatient and inpatient
treatment.

TAP WATER

Tap water is perfectly safe to
drink in the South, although
most locals drink bottled

BOOK YOUR STAY ONLINE

For more accommodation reviews by Lonely Planet
authors, check out http://lonelyplanet.com/hotels/.
You'll find independent reviews, as well as recommendations on the best places to stay. Best of all, you can
book online.

PRACTICALITIES

Local newspapers & magazines The Republic of Cyprus' English-language newspapers are the *Cyprus Mail* (www.cyprus-mail.com) and the *Cyprus Weekly* (www.incyprus.com.cy). In Northern Cyprus, look for the *Turkish Daily News, Hurriyet Daily News* (www.hurriyetdailynews.com) and *Cyprus Today* (www.cyprustoday.net).

Radio Cyprus Broadcasting Corporation (CyBC) has programs and news bulletins in English on Radio 2 (91.1FM). British Forces Broadcasting Services (BFBS) 1 broadcasts 24 hours a day in English on 89.7FM (Nicosia), 92.1FM (west Cyprus) and 99.6FM (east Cyprus). Bayrak FM is the voice of the North and has a lively English-language program on 87.8FM and 105FM.

TV CyBC TV has news in English at 8pm on Channel 2. Midrange to top-end hotels will probably have satellite TV.

Weights & measures Cyprus uses the metric system.

water, as it is very hard. However, the glass of water you automatically receive with your Cypriot coffee will undoubtedly be tap water. It is advisable to drink bottled water in the North.

Insurance

➡ A travel-insurance policy to cover theft, loss and medical problems as well as cancellation or delays to your travel arrangements is a good idea.

➡ Paying for your ticket with a credit card can often provide limited travel-accident insurance and you may be able to reclaim the payment if the operator doesn't deliver.

➡ Worldwide travel insurance is available at www.lonelyplanet.com/bookings. You can buy, extend and claim online anytime – even if you're already on the road.

Internet Access

Wi-fi is increasingly available at most hotels and in many cafes, restaurants and airports, particularly in the Republic. Internet cafes are difficult to find in the Republic but more common in Northern Cyprus.

EATING PRICE RANGES

The following price ranges refer to a standard main course.

Republic of Cyprus

€ less than €7

€€ €7–12

€€€ more than €12

Northern Cyprus

€ less than 20TL

€€ 20–26TL

€€€ more than 26TL

Legal Matters

If you are arrested, you are entitled to make one phone call. If you use this to call your embassy or consulate, the staff should be able to refer you to an English-speaking lawyer. Be cautious around military areas and take 'No Photography' signs seriously or risk having your camera confiscated.

Drinking & Driving

Driving while under the influence of alcohol is strictly controlled, and being over the limit can result in a stiff fine and a night behind bars.

Drugs

The Cypriot authorities in both Northern Cyprus and the Republic show zero tolerance towards drugs. Although, strictly speaking, a small amount of cannabis for personal use should be permissible (under EU law) in the South, it is just not worth the risk.

Money

The unit of currency in Northern Cyprus is the Turkish lira (Turkye Lira; TL). Exchange rates for the new Turkish lira are subject to fluctuations due to a high inflation rate.

The Republic's unit of currency is the euro (€).

Banks in Cyprus exchange all major currencies in cash (travellers cheques are becoming increasingly rare). Most shops and hotels in Northern Cyprus accept hard currencies such as UK pounds, US dollars and euros.

ATMs

You will find ATMs in most towns and larger villages throughout the island.

Bargaining

Overall, haggling is not part of the Cypriot culture, although gentle bartering is common in markets if prices are not marked.

Cash

In the Republic, you can get a cash advance on Visa, MasterCard, Diners Club, Eurocard and American Express at a number of banks, and there are plenty of ATMs. In the North, cash advances are given on Visa cards at the Vakıflar and Kooperatif banks in North Nicosia and Kyrenia (Girne); major banks (such as İş Bankası) in large towns will have ATMs, while there is an increasing number of petrol stations with ATMs attached. Do carry some cash with you though, especially if you're travelling up to the Karpas (Kırpaşa) Peninsula.

Foreign-currency notes may be all right to use in major tourist centres in Cyprus, but are not much use in villages in the Troödos Mountains. In the North, foreign currency is more likely to be widely accepted in lieu of new Turkish lira.

Currency-exchange bureaus in tourist centres operate over extended hours and most weekends.

Credit & Debit Cards

As ubiquitous as ATMs, credit cards can be used in stores, restaurants, supermarkets and petrol stations. In the latter, you can even buy petrol after hours from automatic dispensers with your credit card.

The Republic of Cyprus is more credit-card friendly than Northern Cyprus, though the main restaurants, hotels and car-hire companies in the North will happily take plastic.

International Transfers

If you need to access your funds, international transfers are possible from your home bank to any of Cyprus' major banks. While this method is reliable, it is usually slow – taking a week or more – and not helpful if you need a cash infusion quickly.

Telegraphic transfers are nominally quicker (and cost more) but can still take up to three working days to come through.

Private financial agencies such as Western Union are usually the best bet, as you can often obtain your transferred money the same day.

Tipping

➡ In the North and South, a 10% service charge is often added to a restaurant bill; if not, then a tip of a similar percentage is expected.

➡ Taxi drivers and hotel porters always appreciate a small tip.

Taxes & Refunds

Value-added tax (VAT) is 19% sales tax levied on most goods and services. Restaurants must include VAT in their prices, but it's not always included in hotel room prices – check when booking. Non-EU residents can claim a refund on VAT paid on goods costing more than €50. When paying for your purchase request a Tax Free Form: customs must stamp it at the airport. You'll need to produce the relevant purchases in their original packaging.

Travellers Cheques

Increasingly overlooked by card-wielding travellers, travellers cheques are a dying breed. They should not, however, be written off entirely as they're an excellent form of backup.

Amex, Visa and Travelex cheques are the easiest to cash, particularly if in US dollars, British pounds or euros. Banks can charge hefty commissions, though, even on cheques denominated in euros. Whatever currency they are in, travellers cheques can be difficult to exchange in smaller towns. Always take your passport as identification when cashing travellers cheques.

Opening Hours

The following hours are for high season and tend to decrease outside that time. They apply to the North and South, unless otherwise specified.

Banks Republic of Cyprus 8.30am to 12.30pm Monday to Friday; some also 3.15pm to 4.45pm Monday; Northern Cyprus 8am to noon and 2pm to 5pm Monday to Friday, 8am to noon Saturday and Sunday

Entertainment 9pm to 3am Thursday to Saturday

Restaurants 11am to 2pm and 7.30pm to 11pm daily

Shops 9am to 7pm weekdays, closing 2pm Wednesday, 9am to 2pm Saturday

Tourist offices 8.30am to 2.30pm and 3pm to 6.30pm Monday to Friday, 8.30am to 2.30pm Saturday and Sunday

Photography

In general, you can photograph anywhere in Cyprus, with the following fairly obvious exceptions.

➡ You cannot normally photograph anywhere near the Green Line. In practice, this is rarely monitored other than on both sides of the Green Line in Nicosia, where sensitivities run high. Warning signs, usually a camera with a line through it, are normally displayed prominently, so heed them.

➡ Military camps are another no-go area, and while there are military installations in both parts of Cyprus, you will be more aware of them in the North. Do not even get a camera out if you see a warning sign.

➡ Airports, ports and other government installations are normally touchy photo subjects, so you are advised to keep your camera out of sight near these places too. Museums do not normally allow you to photograph exhibits unless you have written permission.

➡ Churches with icons do not allow the use of a flash and, depending on the commercial value of the pictures you take, may not allow photos at all.

➡ Cypriots are often willing subjects for photos. However, it is bad form to simply point a camera at someone without at least acknowledging them.

➡ It is not culturally appropriate to take photographs in mosques when people are praying. Lonely Planet's *Guide to Travel Photography* is full of helpful tips for photography while on the road.

Post

Postal services on both sides of the island are generally very efficient. Post offices are located in all major towns and villages. Services are normally only related to selling stamps and some packing materials. Stamps can also be bought at newsagents and street kiosks. Post boxes are everywhere (in the South they are yellow and in the North, red).

If you send mail to any address in Northern Cyprus, ensure that you use the suffix 'Mersin 10, Turkey', not 'Northern Cyprus'.

Public Holidays

Republic of Cyprus

Holidays in the Republic of Cyprus are the same as in Greece, with the addition of Greek Cypriot Day (1 April) and Cyprus Independence Day (1 October). Kids are on holidays in August and over the New Year.

New Year's Day 1 January

Epiphany 6 January

First Sunday in Lent February

Greek Independence Day 25 March

(Orthodox) Good Friday March/April

(Orthodox) Easter Sunday March/April

Greek Cypriot Day 1 April

Spring Festival/Labour Day 1 May

Kataklysmos June

Feast of the Assumption 15 August

Cyprus Independence Day 1 October

Ohi Day 28 October

Christmas Day 25 December

St Stephen's Day 26 December

Northern Cyprus

Northern Cyprus observes Muslim religious holidays. These holidays change each year, since they are calculated by the lunar system. The two major holidays are Kurban Bayramı and Şeker Bayramı, both coming at the end of the month-long Ramadan (Ramazan in Turkish) fast. The fast itself is not strictly observed in the North, and restaurants and cafes are open as normal. As in the South, children are on holiday in August and over the New Year.

New Year's Day 1 January

Peace & Freedom Day 20 July

Victory Day 30 August

Turkish National Day 29 October

Proclamation of the Turkish Republic of Northern Cyprus 15 November

Safe Travel

Cyprus is a relatively safe place for visitors. The main thing to be aware of is petty theft, especially in main tourist sights. Be careful but don't be paranoid. Organised crime, mainly from Eastern Europe, is a factor to be aware of and has had particular impact on prostitution, mainly confined to cabarets, in clearly defined areas of larger towns.

Scams

You may come across time-share touts if you hang around the main resorts in Cyprus, and in particular Pafos. If you like the island enough, a time share may be worth considering, but be careful about how and what you choose. You need to have all your rights and obligations in writing, especially where management companies promise to sell your time share for you if you decide to buy a new one.

Smoking

Prohibited in all bars and restaurants, though some owners turn a blind eye and Cyprus hasn't adopted the antismoking mentality as strongly as the UK or US. That said, a smoking bill in February 2017 bans smoking in all work areas, schools and playgrounds in the South; North Cyprus is still marginally more lax. Hotels throughout the island have nonsmoking rooms. E-cigarettes face similar restrictions to tobacco in the South but are accepted more readily in the North.

Telephone

There are no area codes as such in Cyprus; they are an integral part of the telephone number.

Payphones are common in both the Republic and Northern Cyprus and take phonecards, available from kiosks, post offices and offices of the national telephone companies.

Mobile Phones

REPUBLIC OF CYPRUS

In the South, mobile-phone numbers begin with 95, 96 or 97. If you plan to spend any time here, you may want to buy a SIM card for your (unlocked) mobile phone. Check out long-established CYTA (www.cyta.com.cy) for costs and top-up validity periods.

NORTHERN CYPRUS

In the North, mobile-phone numbers start with either 0542 (Telsim) or 0533 (Turkcell). To call a local number, you'll need to dial the full 11-digit number, ie including the Northern Cyprus code of 0392.

Turkcell has good coverage and it costs about 20TL for a pay-as-you-go SIM with enough credit to start you off.

Calls Between Northern Cyprus & the Republic

➡ If you have a mobile phone from outside Cyprus with global roaming activated, it's possible to tune into the GSM networks of either side.

➡ If you have bought a pay-as-you-go Cypriot card from either side, it will only pick up its own network in Nicosia or North Nicosia. Go any further from the Green Line and you will have to revert to your international card, as roaming is not supported between the two local mobile networks.

➡ Text messaging between the North and the South is not possible.

Time

Time Zone

Cyprus is normally two hours ahead of GMT and seven hours ahead of EST.

Daylight Saving

Republic of Cyprus Uses daylight saving time during summer. Clocks go forward one hour on the last weekend in March and back one hour on the last weekend in October.

Northern Cyprus In 2016 Northern Cyprus followed Turkey in scrapping daylight saving time. This means from late October to March, Northern Cyprus is one hour ahead of the Republic.

Current Time

A recorded time message can be heard by dialling ☎193 in the Republic of Cyprus.

Toilets

➡ Most toilets will display a sign requesting you do not flush toilet paper as due to poor island-wide plumbing, this can easily cause a blockage. Wastepaper baskets are provided.

➡ It is wise to carry a small packet of tissues when you are out and about.

➡ Most public toilets are free, while some charge a small fee. You can also use the public facilities in a bar or cafe, although it is standard to offer a small sum or buy a drink in return.

Tourist Information

As well as the tourist authorities listed below, you can pick up maps and brochures at travel and tour agencies, and hotels generally can provide guests with a map and information on tours and car hire.

Cyprus Tourism Organisation (CTO; Map p152; ☎2267 4264; www.visitcyprus.com; Aristokyprou 11; ◷8am-4pm Mon-Fri, to 2pm Sat) Headquarters are in Nicosia with branch offices in major towns in Cyprus (Agia Napa, Lemesos, Larnaka, Pafos, Polis and Platres).

North Cyprus Tourism Organisation (NCTO; Map p176; ☎0392 227 299; www.north-cyprus.org; Kyrenia Gate, Girne Caddesi; ◷8am-5pm) Located in North Nicosia at Kyrenia Gate (Girne Kapısı) with another branch at the Ledra Palace Hotel crossing point. It also maintains tourist offices in Famagusta (Gazimağusa), Kyrenia and Yenierenköy (Yiallousa), which have free country and town maps, plus an increasing number of brochures.

Travellers with Disabilities

Overall Cyprus is not geared towards smooth travel for people with disabilities, sadly. Most restaurants, shops and tourist sights are not equipped to handle wheelchairs, though midrange and top-end accommodation options generally have wheelchair ramps, plus rooms with appropriate facilities. Transport is tricky, but you should be able to organise a specially modified hire car from one of the international car-rental companies with advance warning. In fact, advance warning is always a good idea; start with your travel agent and see what they can offer in terms of information and assistance.

One positive development is the addition of ramps at 26 of the Republic's beaches, allowing wheelchair access directly into the water, with modified beach wheelchairs available at a further 21 beaches. Contact the CTO (p263) for details. Useful organisations include the following:

Accessible Cyprus (www.accessible-cyprus.com) Overseen by the CTO and lists hotels

GOVERNMENT TRAVEL ADVICE

The following government websites offer travel advisories and information for travellers.

➡ **Australian Department of Foreign Affairs** (www.smartraveller.gov.au)

➡ **British Foreign Office** (www.fco.gov.uk/countryadvice)

➡ **Canadian Department of Foreign Affairs** (www.voyage.gc.ca)

➡ **US State Department** (www.travel.state.gov)

AUDIO GUIDES

The **Cyprus Tourism Organisation** (CTO; www.visit-cyprus.com) has introduced a series of audio guides, which you can download from the website in mp3 or mobile-phone format with a choice of six languages. Sights covered include the following:

Nicosia (Lefkosia) Cyprus Museum, House of Hatzigeorgakis Kornesios, Omeriye Mosque and Makarios Cultural Foundation Byzantine Museum.

Troödos area Ten Byzantine churches.

Lemesos (Limassol) area Archaeological site of Kourion, Kolossi Castle and Petra tou Romiou.

Larnaka area Agios Lazaros, Hala Sultan Tekkesi and Choirokoitia.

Pafos area Pafos Archaeological Site, Pafos Castle, Tombs of the Kings and Baths of Aphrodite.

with facilities for people with disabilities.

Para-Quip (www.paraquip.com.cy) Rents out mobility scooters and similar.
Download Lonely Planet's free Accessible Travel guide from http://lptravel.to/AccessibleTravel

Visas

➡ In both the Republic of Cyprus and Northern Cyprus, nationals of the US, Canada, Australia, New Zealand and Singapore can enter and stay for up to three months without a visa.

➡ Citizens of South Africa may enter for up to 30 days without a visa.

➡ You must have your passport to cross from one side to the other.

➡ The same passport-control crossing rules apply for Greek and Turkish travellers as for everyone else.

Volunteering

Aside from international volunteering agencies, there is not a lot of scope for volunteer work in Cyprus. You can check out the following.

Grol Garden (www.grolgarden.info) Organic permaculture garden in Northern Cyprus which accepts local and international volunteers.

Transitions Abroad (www.transitionsabroad.com) A good website to start your research.

Turtle Conservation Project (www.seaturtle.org/mtrg/projects/cyprus/volunteer) Voluntary opportunities for the marine-turtle conservation project on the Karpas Peninsula.

Women Travellers

Women travellers will encounter little sexual harassment, though you'll get more or less constant verbal 'approaches' from Cypriot men. This is common for both foreign and Cypriot women, but foreign women merit particular attention from these verbal Romeos. This can get rather tiresome, if not outright offensive. It is best to ignore the advances.

Solo women travellers should take reasonable care at rowdy nightclub resorts, such as in Agia Napa, where inebriated foreign males may be a nuisance.

Work

Nationals of EU countries, Switzerland, Norway and Iceland may work freely in the Republic of Cyprus. If you are offered a contract, your employer will normally steer you through any bureaucracy.

Virtually everyone else is supposed to obtain a work permit, and if they plan to stay more than 90 days, a residence visa. These procedures are well-nigh impossible unless you have a job contract lined up before you begin.

Transport

GETTING THERE & AWAY

Most visitors to Cyprus arrive by air. Many of them come on charter flights or inexpensive flights operated by budget airlines, particularly from the UK.

Flights, cars and tours can be booked online at lonelyplanet.com/bookings.

Crossing the Border

Travelling between the Republic and Northern Cyprus is easy nowadays, since the restrictions on crossing through passport control have been eased; however, you are only allowed to cross at designated checkpoints. Don't forget your passport.

Entering the Country

Citizens of EU member states and Switzerland can travel to the Republic with just their national identity card. Nationals of the UK have to carry a full passport (UK visitor passports are not acceptable) and all other nationalities must have a full valid passport. In Northern Cyprus, EU citizens can stay for up to three months.

You will need a valid passport to cross between the North and South. You'll need to produce your passport or ID card every time you check into a hotel in Cyprus and when you conduct banking transactions.

Air

There are scheduled flights and an ever-increasing number of charter and budget flights to Cyprus from most European cities and the Middle East. Flights are heavily booked in high season (midsummer). Tickets on scheduled flights tend to be expensive, but Europe-based travellers may be able to pick up cheaper tickets with budget companies. If you're in Greece, you can usually find reasonably priced one-way or return tickets to the Republic from travel agents in Athens, Thessaloniki or Iraklio.

Airports & Airlines
REPUBLIC OF CYPRUS

Two airports handle international flights in the Republic. Note that on most airline schedules, Larnaka is listed as 'Larnaca' and Pafos as 'Paphos'. This is particularly important to know when making online bookings. Cyprus Airways (www.cyprus airlines.com) is the national carrier of the Republic of Cyprus.

CLIMATE CHANGE & TRAVEL

Every form of transport that relies on carbon-based fuel generates CO_2, the main cause of human-induced climate change. Modern travel is dependent on aeroplanes, which might use less fuel per kilometre per person than most cars but travel much greater distances. The altitude at which aircraft emit gases (including CO_2) and particles also contributes to their climate change impact. Many websites offer 'carbon calculators' that allow people to estimate the carbon emissions generated by their journey and, for those who wish to do so, to offset the impact of the greenhouse gases emitted with contributions to portfolios of climate-friendly initiatives throughout the world. Lonely Planet offsets the carbon footprint of all staff and author travel.

Larnaka International Airport (www.cyprusairports.com.cy)

Pafos International Airport (www.cyprusairports.com.cy)

NORTHERN CYPRUS

Ercan Airport, covering Northern Cyprus, is 14km east of North Nicosia (Lefkoşa). It is not recognised by the international airline authorities, so you can't fly there direct. Airlines must touch down first in Turkey and then fly on to Northern Cyprus.

Ercan Airport (www.flyercan.com)

Tickets

Tickets to Cyprus are most expensive in August. Try picking up flight-only deals with package-holiday companies during this time or scour the budget airlines (though these are hardly budget in summer). Prices depend on the season, and to a lesser degree on the day of the week or even the time you fly.

CHARTER FLIGHTS

Vacant seats on charter flights block-booked to Cyprus by package-tour companies are cheap, but conditions apply. First, you can rarely get more than two weeks for your itinerary and, second, the departure and arrival times are quite inflexible once booked. That said, a percentage of all package-tour seats is given over to flight-only travellers, so give it a go.

Departure Tax

Departure tax is included in the price of a ticket.

Sea

The only way to arrive in the Republic by sea is aboard a cruise boat; there are no longer any passenger ferries. Lemesos (Limassol) is the South's main arrival and departure port, and the port, complete with new marina, is 3km southwest of the town centre.

In Northern Cyprus, two Turkish ferry companies run regular boats, from the New Harbour in Kyrenia (Girne), to Taşucu in Turkey.

Akgünler Denizcilik (www.akgunlerbilet.com) Runs three boats every week with sailings at 6pm on Monday and Friday and 11.30pm on Thursday (adult/child/car 105/40/181TL including all port departure taxes).

Filo Shipping (www.filoshipping.com/tr) Runs three car ferries per week on Monday, Wednesday and Friday at midnight (adult/child/car 105/40/206TL including all port departure taxes).

Akgünler Denizcilik also runs a regular ferry service from Famagusta (Gazimağusa) to Mersin in Turkey. There are three car ferries weekly at 11pm on Monday, Wednesday and Friday from (adult/car TL115/190).

Salamis Tours (☑2535 5555; www.salamisinternational.com; Salamis House, Oktovriou 28; ⊙9am-6pm Mon-Fri) is a long-standing travel agency that organises cruises to Greece and can issue tickets to transport your vehicle by boat to Greece or Israel.

GETTING AROUND

Cyprus is small enough for you to get around easily. Roads are good and well-signposted, and traffic moves smoothly.

Public transport is limited to buses and service taxis (stretch taxis that run on predetermined routes). There is no train network and no domestic air services in either the North or the South. Four-lane motorways link Nicosia (Lefkosia) with Lemesos and Larnaka, expanding west to Pafos and east to Agia Napa. In Northern Cyprus there is only one motorway, which runs between North Nicosia and Famagusta.

Bicycle

Cycling is a cheap, convenient, healthy, environmentally sound and, above all, fun way of travelling. In the Republic of Cyprus, the Cyprus Tourism Organisation (CTO) produces a helpful brochure

---

CROSSING THE GREEN LINE

Crossing freely between the North and the South has become pretty straightforward since the easing of restrictions in 2003. It is now possible to cross at seven points on the island and there are ongoing negotiations between the two sides about opening more. Crossings at Ledra Palace Hotel and Ledra St are for pedestrians only, while crossings at Agios Dometios, Pergamos, Agios Nikolaos, Limnitis-Yeşilirmak and Zodhia are for vehicles. If you don't have your own transport, a taxi will take you across and then to anywhere you want to go.

EU citizens are allowed to cross into the Republic if their point of entry into the country is in the North. For all other nationalities, the situation is murkier. Officially, the Republic regards Ercan Airport and the ferry ports of Famagusta (Gazimağusa) and Kyrenia (Girne) as illegal points of entry and can refuse you entry. In practice, for US, Canadian, New Zealand, Japanese and Australian citizens this is rarely enforced, but we know of at least two occasions in 2017 when non-EU passport holders were refused entry into the South.

entitled *Cyprus for Cycling*, which lists 19 recommended mountain-bike rides around the South. These range from 2.5km to 19km from the Akamas Peninsula in the west to Cape Greco in the east. Bicycles can be hired in most areas. Rates start from around €15 a day and local tourist offices can provide you with a list of reputable local operators.

Prospective cyclists are advised to consider the following:

➡ It's best to stick to cycling on ordinary roads, many of which parallel motorways, where cycling is not allowed. The roads are generally good, but there is rarely extra roadside room for cyclists, so you will have to cycle with care.

➡ You will need a bicycle with good gears to negotiate the long hauls up and around the Troödos Mountains and Kyrenia (Girne) Range.

➡ Towns and cities in general are much more cyclist friendly than their counterparts in other parts of the Mediterranean. In some tourist centres, such as Protaras and Agia Napa, there are urban bicycle paths, as well as beachside boulevards that incorporate space for bike riding.

➡ You cannot take bicycles on all buses.

Bus

Buses in the South are frequent and run from Monday to Saturday, with limited services on Sunday. Five companies cover their respective districts and all have comprehensive websites.

Emel (www.limassolbuses.com) Lemesos district.

Osea Buses (www.osea.com.cy) Larnaka district.

Osel Buses (www.osel.com.cy) Nicosia district.

Pafos Buses (www.pafosbuses.com) Pafos district.

Zinonas Buses (www.zinonas-buses.com) Famagusta district.

A useful website that does a good job pulling together all the routes is www.cyprusbybus.com. Buses that connect the cities are run by the InterCity Bus Company (www.intercity-buses.com), which offers discounted fares on multiple journeys.

Buses in the North are a varied mix of old and newer privately owned buses too numerous to list here.

Costs
Fares cost €1.50 per ride, €5 per day, €15 per week and €40 for a month of unlimited journeys within a district, which includes rural villages. InterCity Buses are government subsidised and surprisingly reasonable, given the distances involved.

Bus prices in the North generally cost between 4TL and 8TL.

Reservations
Bus reservations are not normally required in either the South or the North.

Car & Motorcycle
First, and most important: drive defensively. Cyprus has one of the highest accident rates in Europe, despite the overall good state of its roads, often due to reckless driving. In the Republic of Cyprus *autopistas* (motorways) connect the airport to major resorts and towns, while secondary roads are normally well surfaced with a minimum of potholes.

Automobile Associations
Cyprus Automobile Association (www.caa.com.cy). Covers the South. The 24-hour emergency road assistance number is 2231 3131.

There is no equivalent organisation in Northern Cyprus.

Driving Licences
To rent a car in Cyprus, you'll need to be aged 21 and over (Republic) or 18 and over (Northern Cyprus). You'll also need the following.

➡ Driver's licence. Note that a licence is required for any vehicle over 50cc.

➡ A credit or debit card (for the major companies at least).

Fuel
Service stations selling lead-free petrol and diesel are common on major roads and in big cities, but sparse in the mountainous interior and the Akamas and Karpas Peninsulas.

Hire
It's a good idea to arrange car rental prior to arrival; not only is it generally cheaper but in high season you may find it difficult to find a car, particularly in Northern Cyprus. It's common practice for the rental agency to leave your vehicle at the airport, unlocked, with the key waiting for you under the floor mat. Don't be surprised: with the obvious red hire-car plates and a nonexistent car-theft record, the car is as safe as can be.

➡ Cars and 4WDs are widely available for hire and cost

BUS TRAVEL IN THE LOW SEASON
Most bus transport times listed by us are for peak season (June to October). Public-transport frequency decreases, together with tourist demand, during off-peak times. This is particularly problematic with mountain destinations, where the buses sometimes don't run at all. So before departure in quieter months be sure to check all transport times via the bus company's website.

around €25 per day for a week's rental.

➡ In some towns, you can also rent motorcycles (from €10) or mopeds (€10).

➡ Rental cars are usually in good condition, but inspect your vehicle before you set off.

➡ Open-top 4WDs are popular options. If you hire a 2WD, make sure it has air-conditioning and enough power to get you up hills.

Insurance

The Republic of Cyprus issues full car insurance when you rent a car. The North also issues full insurance to cars rented in the North, but has a special third-party insurance for cars coming from the South.

Road Rules

Blood-alcohol limit The legal limit is 50 mg of alcohol per 100mL of blood. Random breath testing is carried out. If you are found to be over the limit you can be fined and deprived of your licence.

Front seat belts Compulsory. Children under five years of age must not sit in the front seat.

Legal driving age for cars Twenty-one (Republic), 18 (Northern Cyprus).

Legal driving age for motorcycles and scooters Eighteen (80cc and over) or 17 (50cc and under). A licence is required.

Motorcyclists Must use headlights at all times and wear a helmet if riding a bike of 125cc or more.

Road distances Posted in kilometres only. Road signs are in Greek and Latin script in the Republic of Cyprus; in Northern

Cyprus, destinations are given in Turkish only.

Roundabouts (traffic circles) Vehicles already in the circle have right of way.

Side of the road Drive on the left.

Speed limits In built-up areas, 50km/h, which increases to 80km/h on major roads and up to 100km/h on motorways. Speed limits in the North are 100km/h on open roads and 50km/h in towns.

Service Taxi

Taking up to eight people, service taxis are a useful transport option between major cities in the South.

Travel & Express (www.travel express.com.cy) is run by an amalgamation of private companies with one national phone number. The individual offices can be contacted directly.

The North has *dolmuşes* (minibuses) between North Nicosia and the main towns, and Kyrenia and the main towns (fares between 5TL and 11TL, depending on the route). It also has service taxis (*kombos*) between North Nicosia and Kyrenia and Famagusta.

Walking

Cyprus is a popular destination for long-distance walkers, with some spectacular routes running along the ridge of the Troödos Mountains. European Long Distance Path E4 (p91) runs through Cyprus as part of its grand tour across Europe, tracing a 640km path from Pafos airport, across the Troödos and down to the Ammochostos region and Larnaka Airport. Popular bases for shorter walks include Troödos, Platres and the villages in the Pitsylia region.

In Northern Cyprus, the mountains of the 170km-long Kyrenia Range offer plentiful walking opportunities, though some areas are off

---

ELUSIVE CROSS-BORDER INSURANCE

Since the 2003 border-crossing changes, there has been a lot of talk of the North's car insurance, issued upon entry from the Republic. And after all this talk, things are still as clear as mud. If you ask about the insurance, you are likely to get numerous reactions and conflicting information. This is because the insurance 'law' concerning vehicles and drivers from the South is full of holes and open to interpretation (mainly by the North's police force).

When you enter the North by car (privately owned or rented) at any checkpoint, your own car insurance will no longer be valid and you will have to purchase Turkish car insurance. It is third-party cover only, so do check exactly what is covered (and the cost) should you be unfortunate enough to be involved in an accident, and whatever you do, do not move your car until a police report has been made.

If you're driving a rented car, keep in mind that while the Republic's car-rental agencies have no objections to you taking rented cars to the North (although they don't condone it), it's up to you to decide whether this risk is worth taking. Establishing who is at fault in an accident can sometimes take a lot longer than you may think and be subject to many twists and turns.

Turkish-owned cars crossing into the South have to get the standard insurance, similar to that in other EU countries. At the time of research, the North's car-rental agencies did not allow rented cars to be taken into the Republic.

limits due to the presence of Turkish army bases. The hike linking the castles of Kantara, Buffavento and St Hilarion is particularly dramatic.

Local Transport

Bus

While urban bus services exist in Nicosia, Lemesos, Larnaka, Pafos and Famagusta, about the only places where they are of any practical use are Larnaka and Pafos (to get to and from the airport) and Lemesos, where frequent local buses trundle between the tourist area and old harbour, and where there are also regular services to Kourion and Kolossi from the local bus station; and Ayia Napa, where there are regular services to Paralimni and Protaras.

Taxi

In the South, taxis are extensive and available on a 24-hour basis; they can either be hailed from the street or a taxi rank, or booked over the phone. Taxis are generally modern, air-conditioned vehicles, usually comfortable Mercedes, and, apart from outside major centres, equipped with meters that the drivers are obliged to use.

'Taxi sharing', which is common in Greek cities such as Athens, is not permitted in Cyprus. Taxi drivers are normally courteous and helpful.

In the North, taxis do not sport meters, so agree on the fare with the driver beforehand. As a rough guide, expect to pay around 10TL to 15TL for a ride around any of the towns. A taxi ride from North Nicosia to Kyrenia will cost between 80TL and 100TL, and from North Nicosia to Famagusta, 120TL to 150TL.

Language

Visitors to Cyprus are unlikely to encounter any serious language difficulties since many people in both the North and the South speak English. Neither Greek nor Turkish Cypriots will expect a visitor to be able to speak their respective languages – let alone the Cypriot variants. However, trying a few of the words in the local lingo will go a long way to breaking the ice. The Greek and Turkish spoken in Cyprus differs somewhat from that spoken in Greece and Turkey. However, if you use the mainland varieties – which is what we've included below – you'll be understood just fine.

GREEK

Greek is the official language of Greece and co-official language of Cyprus (alongside Turkish).

The Greek alphabet is explained on the next page, but if you read the blue pronunciation guides given with each phrase in this chapter as if they were English, you'll be understood. Note that dh is pronounced as the 'th' in 'there', gh is a softer, slightly throaty version of 'g', and kh is a throaty sound like the 'ch' in the Scottish 'loch'. All Greek words of two or more syllables have an acute accent ('), which indicates where the stress falls. In our pronunciation guides, stressed syllables are in italics.

In Greek, all nouns, articles and adjectives are either masculine, feminine or neuter – in this chapter these forms are included where necessary, separated with a slash and indicated with 'm/f/n'.

Basics

Hello.	Γειά σας.	ya·sas (polite)
	Γειά σου.	ya·su (informal)
Good morning.	Καλή μέρα.	ka·li me·ra
Good evening.	Καλή σπέρα.	ka·li spe·ra
Goodbye.	Αντίο.	an·di·o

Yes./No.	Ναι./Οχι.	ne/o·hi
Please.	Παρακαλώ.	pa·ra·ka·lo
Thank you.	Ευχαριστώ.	ef·ha·ri·sto
That's fine./	Παρακαλώ.	pa·ra·ka·lo
You're welcome.		
Sorry.	Συγγνώμη.	sigh·no·mi

What's your name?
Πώς σας λένε;   pos sas le·ne
My name is ...
Με λένε ...   me le·ne ...
Do you speak English?
Μιλάτε αγγλικά;   mi·la·te an·gli·ka
I (don't) understand
(Δεν) καταλαβαίνω.   (dhen) ka·ta·la·ve·no

Accommodation

campsite	χώρος για κάμπινγκ	kho·ros yia kam·ping
hotel	ξενοδοχείο	kse·no·dho·khi·o
youth hostel	γιουθ χόστελ	yuth kho·stel
a ... room	ένα ... δωμάτιο	e·na ... dho·ma·ti·o
single	μονόκλινο	mo·no·kli·no
double	δίκλινο	dhi·kli·no
How much is it ...?	Πόσο κάνει ...;	po·so ka·ni ...
per night	τη βραδυά	ti·vra·dhya
per person	το άτομο	to a·to·mo
air-con	έρκοντίσιον	er·kon·di·si·on
bathroom	μπάνιο	ba·nio
fan	ανεμιστήρας	a·ne·mi·sti·ras
TV	τηλεόραση	ti·le·o·ra·si
window	παράθυρο	pa·ra·thi·ro

Directions

Where is ...?
Πού είναι ...;   pu *i*·ne ...

Turn left.
Στρίψτε αριστερά.   *strips*·te a·ri·ste·*ra*

Turn right.
Στρίψτε δεξιά.   *strips*·te dhe·*ksia*

at the next corner
στην επόμενη γωνία   stin e·*po*·me·ni gho·*ni*·a

at the traffic lights
στα φώτα   sta *fo*·ta

behind	πίσω	*pi*·so
in front of	μπροστά	bro·*sta*
far	μακριά	ma·kri·*a*
near (to)	κοντά	kon·*da*
next to	δίπλα	*dhi*·pla
opposite	απέναντι	a·*pe*·nan·di
straight ahead	ολο ευθεία	o·lo ef·*thi*·a

Eating & Drinking

What would you recommend?
Τι θα συνιστούσες;   ti tha si·ni·*stu*·ses

What's in that dish?
Τι περιέχει αυτό το φαγητό;   ti pe·ri·e·hi af·*to* to fa·ghi·*to*

I'm a vegatarian.
Είμαι χορτοφάγος.   *i*·me khor·to·*fa*·ghos

That was delicious.
Ήταν νοστιμότατο!   *i*·tan no·sti·*mo*·ta·to

Cheers!
Εις υγείαν!   is i·*yi*·an

Please bring the bill.
Το λογαριασμό, παρακαλώ.   to lo·*ghar*·ya·*zmo* pa·ra·ka·*lo*

a table for ...	Ενα τραπέζι για ...	*e*·na tra·*pe*·zi ya ...
(two) people	(δύο) άτομα	(*dhi*·o) a·to·ma
(eight) o'clock	τις (οχτώ)	stis (okh·*to*)
I don't eat ...	Δεν τρώγω ...	dhen *tro*·gho ...
fish	ψάρι	*psa*·ri
(red) meat	(κόκκινο) κρέας	(*ko*·ki·no) *kre*·as
peanuts	φυστίκια	fi·*sti*·kia
poultry	πουλερικά	pu·le·ri·*ka*

GREEK ALPHABET

The Greek alphabet has 24 letters, shown below in their upper- and lower-case forms. Be aware that some letters look like English letters but are pronounced very differently, such as B, which is pronounced 'v'; and P, pronounced like an 'r'. As in English, how letters are pronounced is also influenced by how they are combined, for example the ou combination is pronounced 'u' as in 'put', and οι is pronounced 'ee' as in 'feet'.

Α α	a	as in 'father'	**Ξ ξ**	x	as in 'ox'	
Β β	v	as in 'vine'	**Ο ο**	o	as in 'hot'	
Γ γ	gh	a softer, throaty 'g'	**Π π**	p	as in 'pup'	
	y	as in 'yes'	**Ρ ρ**	r	as in 'road',	
Δ δ	dh	as in 'there'			slightly trilled	
Ε ε	e	as in 'egg'	**Σ σ, ς**	s	as in 'sand'	
Ζ ζ	z	as in 'zoo'	**Τ τ**	t	as in 'tap'	
Η η	i	as in 'feet'	**Υ υ**	i	as in 'feet'	
Θ θ	th	as in 'throw'	**Φ φ**	f	as in 'find'	
Ι ι	i	as in 'feet'	**Χ χ**	kh	as the 'ch' in the	
Κ κ	k	as in 'kite'			Scottish 'loch', or	
Λ λ	l	as in 'leg'		h	like a rough 'h'	
Μ μ	m	as in 'man'	**Ψ ψ**	ps	as in 'lapse'	
Ν ν	n	as in 'net'	**Ω ω**	o	as in 'hot'	

Note that the letter **Σ** has two forms for the lower case – **σ** and **ς**. The second one is used at the end of words. The Greek question mark is represented with the English equivalent of a semicolon (;).

KEY PATTERNS

To get by in Greek, mix and match these simple patterns:

When's (the next bus)?
Πότε είναι
(το επόμενο
λεωφορείο);
*po·te i·ne
(to e·po·me·no
le·o·fo·ri·o)*

Where's (the station)?
Πού είναι (ο σταθμός); *pu i·ne (o stath·mos)*

I'm looking for (...).
Ψάχνω για (...). *psakh·no yia (...)*

Do you have (a local map)?
Έχετε οδικό
(τοπικό χάρτη);
*e·he·te o·dhi·ko
(to·pi·ko khar·ti)*

Is there a (lift)?
Υπάρχει (ασανσέρ); *i·par·hi (a·san·ser)*

Can I (try it on)?
Μπορώ να
(το προβάρω);
*bo·ro na
(to pro·va·ro)*

I have (a reservation).
Έχω (κλείσει
δωμάτιο).
*e·kho (kli·si
dho·ma·ti·o)*

I'd like (to hire a car).
Θα ήθελα (να
ενοικιάσω ένα
αυτοκίνητο).
*tha i·the·la (na
e·ni·ki·a·so e·na
af·to·ki·ni·to)*

Key Words

appetisers	ορεκτικά	*o·rek·ti·ka*
bar	μπαρ	bar
beef	βοδινό	*vo·dhi·no*
bottle	μπουκάλι	*bu·ka·li*
bowl	μπωλ	bol
bread	ψωμί	*pso·mi*
breakfast	πρόγευμα	*pro·yev·ma*
cafe	καφετέρια	*ka·fe·te·ri·a*
cheese	τυρί	*ti·ri*
chicken	κοτόπουλο	*ko·to·pu·lo*
cold	κρυωμένος	*kri·o·me·nos*
cream	κρέμα	*kre·ma*
delicatessen	ντελικατέσεν	*de·li·ka·te·sen*
desserts	επιδόρπια	*e·pi·dhor·pi·a*
dinner	δείπνο	*dhip·no*
egg	αβγό	*av·gho*
fish	ψάρι	*psa·ri*
food	φαγητό	*fa·yi·to*
fork	πιρούνι	*pi·ru·ni*
fruit	φρούτα	*fru·ta*
glass	ποτήρι	*po·ti·ri*
grocery store	οπωροπωλείο	*o·po·ro·po·li·o*
herb	βότανο	*vo·ta·no*

high chair	καρέκλα για μωρά	*ka·re·kla* *yia mo·ro*
hot	ζεστός	*ze·stos*
knife	μαχαίρι	*ma·he·ri*
lamb	αρνί	*ar·ni*
lunch	μεσημεριανό φαγητό	*me·si·me·ria·no* *fa·yi·to*
main courses	κύρια φαγητά	*ki·ri·a fa·yi·ta*
market	αγορά	*a·gho·ra*
menu	μενού	*me·nu*
nut	καρύδι	*ka·ri·dhi*
oil	λάδι	*la·dhi*
pepper	πιπέρι	*pi·pe·ri*
plate	πιάτο	*pia·to*
pork	χοιρινό	*hi·ri·no*
restaurant	εστιατόριο	*e·sti·a·to·ri·o*
salt	αλάτι	*a·la·ti*
souvlaki	σουβλάκι	*suv·la·ki*
spoon	κουτάλι	*ku·ta·li*
sugar	ζάχαρη	*za·kha·ri*
vegetable	λαχανικά	*la·kha·ni·ka*
vegetarian	χορτοφάγος	*khor·to·fa·ghos*
vinegar	ξύδι	*ksi·dhi*
with	με	me
without	χωρίς	*kho·ris*

Drinks

beer	μπύρα	*bi·ra*
coffee	καφές	*ka·fes*
juice	χυμός	*hi·mos*
milk	γάλα	*gha·la*
soft drink	αναψυκτικό	*a·nap·sik·ti·ko*
tea	τσάι	*tsa·i*
water	νερό	*ne·ro*
(red) wine	(κόκκινο) κρασί	*(ko·ki·no) kra·si*
(white) wine	(άσπρο) κρασί	*(a·spro) kra·si*

Emergencies

Help!	Βοήθεια!	*vo·i·thya*
Go away!	Φύγε!	*fi·ye*
I'm lost	Έχω χαθεί.	*e·kho kha·thi*
I'm ill.	Είμαι άρρωστος.	*i·me a·ro·stos*
There's been an accident.	Έγινε ατύχημα.	*ey·i·ne a·ti·hi·ma*
Call ...!	Φωνάξτε ...!	*fo·nak·ste ...*
a doctor	ένα γιατρό	*e·na yi·a·tro*
the police	την αστυνομία	*tin a·sti·no·mi·a*

Numbers

1	ένας/μία	e·nas/mi·a (m/f)
	ένα	e·na (n)
2	δύο	dhi·o
3	τρεις	tris (m&f)
	τρία	tri·a (n)
4	τέσσερεις	te·se·ris (m&f)
	τέσσερα	te·se·ra (n)
5	πέντε	pen·de
6	έξη	e·xi
7	επτά	ep·ta
8	οχτώ	oh·to
9	εννέα	e·ne·a
10	δέκα	dhe·ka
20	είκοσι	ik·o·si
30	τριάντα	tri·an·da
40	σαράντα	sa·ran·da
50	πενήντα	pe·nin·da
60	εξήντα	ek·sin·da
70	εβδομήντα	ev·dho·min·da
80	ογδόντα	ogh·dhon·da
90	ενενήντα	e·ne·nin·da
100	εκατό	e·ka·to
1000	χίλιοι/χίλιες	hi·li·i/hi·li·ez (m/f)
	χίλια	hi·li·a (n)

Shopping & Services

I'd like to buy ...
Θέλω ν' αγοράσω ...   the·lo na·gho·ra·so ...

I'm just looking.
Απλώς κοιτάζω.   ap·los ki·ta·zo

I don't like it.
Δεν μου αρέσει.   dhen mu a·re·si

How much is it?
Πόσο κάνει;   po·so ka·ni

It's too expensive.
Είναι πολύ ακριβό.   i·ne po·li a·kri·vo

Can you lower the price?
Μπορείς να κατεβάσεις   bo·ris na ka·te·va·sis
την τιμή;   tin ti·mi

ATM	αυτόματη	af·to·ma·ti
	μηχανή	mi·kha·ni
	χρημάτων	khri·ma·ton
bank	τράπεζα	tra·pe·za
credit card	πιστωτική	pi·sto·ti·ki
	κάρτα	kar·ta
internet cafe	καφενείο	ka·fe·ni·o
	διαδικτύου	dhi·a·dhik·ti·u

mobile phone	κινητό	ki·ni·to
post office	ταχυδρομείο	ta·hi·dhro·mi·o
toilet	τουαλέτα	tu·a·le·ta
tourist office	τουριστικό	tu·ri·sti·ko
	γραφείο	ghra·fi·o

Time & Dates

What time is it?	Τι ώρα είναι;	ti o·ra i·ne
It's (2 o'clock).	είναι	i·ne
	(δύο η ώρα).	(dhi·o i o·ra)
It's half	(Δέκα) και	(dhe·ka) ke
past (10).	μισή.	mi·si
today	σήμερα	si·me·ra
tomorrow	αύριο	av·ri·o
yesterday	χθες	hthes
morning	πρωί	pro·i
(this)	(αυτό το)	(af·to to)
afternoon	απόγευμα	a·po·yev·ma
evening	βράδυ	vra·dhi
Monday	Δευτέρα	dhef·te·ra
Tuesday	Τρίτη	tri·ti
Wednesday	Τετάρτη	te·tar·ti
Thursday	Πέμπτη	pemp·ti
Friday	Παρασκευή	pa·ras·ke·vi
Saturday	Σάββατο	sa·va·to
Sunday	Κυριακή	ky·ri·a·ki
January	Ιανουάριος	ia·nu·ar·i·os
February	Φεβρουάριος	fev·ru·ar·i·os
March	Μάρτιος	mar·ti·os
April	Απρίλιοςq	a·pri·li·os
May	Μάιος	mai·os

SIGNS

ΕΙΣΟΔΟΣ	Entry
ΕΞΟΔΟΣ	Exit
ΠΛΗΡΟΦΟΡΙΕΣ	Information
ΑΝΟΙΧΤΟ	Open
ΚΛΕΙΣΤΟ	Closed
ΑΠΑΓΟΡΕΥΕΤΑΙ	Prohibited
ΑΣΤΥΝΟΜΙΑ	Police
ΑΣΤΥΝΟΜΙΚΟΣ ΣΤΑΘΜΟΣ	Police Station
ΓΥΝΑΙΚΩΝ	Toilets (women)
ΑΝΔΡΩΝ	Toilets (men)

QUESTION WORDS

How?	Πώς;	pos
What?	Τι;	ti
When?	Πότε;	po·te
Where?	Πού;	pu
Who?	Ποιος;/Ποια;	pi·os/pi·a (m/f)
	Ποιο;	pi·o (n)
Why?	Γιατί;	yi·a·ti

June	Ιούνιος	i·u·ni·os
July	Ιούλιος	i·u·li·os
August	Αύγουστος	av·ghus·tos
September	Σεπτέμβριος	sep·tem·vri·os
October	Οκτώβριος	ok·to·vri·os
November	Νοέμβριος	no·em·vri·os
December	Δεκέμβριος	dhe·kem·vri·os

Transport

Public Transport

boat	πλοίο	pli·o
(city) bus	αστικό	a·sti·ko
(intercity) bus	λεωφορείο	le·o·fo·ri·o
plane	αεροπλάνο	ae·ro·pla·no
train	τραίνο	tre·no

Where do I buy a ticket?
Πού αγοράζω εισιτήριο;   pu a·gho·ra·zo i·si·ti·ri·o

I want to go to ...
Θέλω να πάω στο/στη ...   the·lo na pao sto/sti...

What time does it leave?
Τι ώρα φεύγει;   ti o·ra fev·yi

Do I need to change?
Χειάζεται να αλλάξω;   khri·a·ze·te na a·lak·so

Is it direct/express?
Είναι κατ'ευθείαν/   i·ne ka·tef·thi·an/
εξπρές;   eks·pres

Does it stop at (...)?
Σταματάει στο (...);   sta·ma·ta·i sto (...)

I'd like to get off at (...).
Θα ήθελα να κατεβώ   tha i·the·la na ka·te·vo
στο (...).   sto (...)

I'd like (a) ...	Θα ήθελα (ένα) ...	tha i·the·la (e·na) ...
one-way ticket	απλό εισιτήριο	a·plo i·si·ti·ri·o
return ticket	εισιτήριο με επιστροφή	i·si·ti·ri·o me e·pi·stro·fi
1st class	πρώτη θέση	pro·ti the·si
2nd class	δεύτερη θέση	def·te·ri the·si

cancelled	ακυρώθηκε	a·ki·ro·thi·ke
delayed	καθυστέρησε	ka·thi·ste·ri·se
platform	πλατφόρμα f	plat·for·ma
ticket office	εκδοτήριο εισιτηρίων	ek·dho·ti·ri·o i·si·ti·ri·on
timetable	δρομολόγιο	dhro·mo·lo·gio
train station	σταθμός τρένου	stath·mos tre·nu

Driving & Cycling

I'd like to hire a ...	Θα ήθελα να νοικιάσω ...	tha i·the·la na ni·ki·a·so ...
car	ένα αυτοκίνητο	e·na af·ti·ki·ni·to
4WD	ένα τέσσερα επί τέσσερα	e·na tes·se·ra e·pi tes·se·ra
jeep	ένα τζιπ	e·na tzip
motorbike	μια μοτοσυκλέττα	mya mo·to·si·klet·ta
bicycle	ένα ποδήλατο	e·na po·dhi·la·to

Do I need a helmet?
Χρειάζομαι κράνος;   khri·a·zo·me kra·nos

Do you have a road map?
Έχετε οδικό χάρτη;   e·he·te o·thi·ko khar·ti

Is this the road to ...?
Αυτός είναι ο   af·tos i·ne o
δρόμος για ...   dhro·mos ya ...

Can I park here?
Μπορώ να παρκάρω   bo·ro na par·ka·ro
εδώ;   e·dho

The car/motorbike has broken down (at ...).
Το αυτοκίνητο/   to af·to·ki·ni·to/
η μοτοσυκλέττα   i mo·to·si·klet·ta
χάλασε στο ...   kha·la·se sto ...

I have a flat tyre.
Έπαθα λάστιχο.   e·pa·tha la·sti·cho

I've run out of petrol.
Έμεινα από βενζίνη.   e·mi·na a·po ven·zi·ni

Where's a petrol station?
Πού είναι ένα πρατήριο   pu i·ne e·na pra·ti·ri·o
βενζίνας;   ven·zi·nas

TURKISH

Turkish is co-official language of Cyprus (alongside Greek).

Turkish pronunication is not difficult as most sounds are also found in English. There are just a few simple things to watch out for.

The Turkish letter ı – undotted in both lower and upper case (eg Isparta uhs·par·ta) – is pronounced as uh (a sound similar to the 'i' in 'habit'), while the i – with dots in both cases (eg İzmir *eez·meer*) – is pronounced as ee . Similarly, o is pronounced o as in 'go', ö as er in 'her' (without 'r' sound), u as oo in 'moon' and ü as ew in 'few'. Also note that ğ is a silent letter which extends the vowel before it – it acts as the 'gh' combination in 'weigh', and is never pronounced. The letter h is always pronounced h as in 'house'. The letter j is pronounced zh (as the 's' in 'pleasure'), ç as ch in 'church', and ş as in the sh in 'ship'.

Don't worry about these spelling and pronunciation idiosyncracies – if you read the blue pronunciation guides given with each phrase in this chapter as if they were English, you'll be understood.

Basics

Hello.	Merhaba.	mer·ha·ba
Hi.	Selam.	se·lam
Good morning.	İyi sabahlar.	ee·yee sa·bah·lar
Good evening.	İyi akşamlar.	ee·yee ak·sham·lar
Goodbye. (when leaving)	Hoşçakal. Hoşçakalın.	hosh·cha·kal (inf) hosh·cha·ka·luhn (pol)
Goodbye. (when staying)	Güle güle.	gew·le gew·le
Yes./No.	Evet./Hayır.	e·vet/ha·yuhr
Please.	Lütfen.	lewt·fen
Thank you (very much).	(Çok) Teşekkür ederim.	(chok) te·shek·kewr e·de·reem
Thanks.	Teşekkürler.	te·shek·kewr·ler
You're welcome.	Birşey değil.	beer·shay de·eel
Sorry.	Özür dilerim.	er·zewr dee·le·reem

What's your name?
Adınız ne? — a·duh·nuhz ne (inf)
Adınız nedir? — a·duh·nuhz ne·deer (pol)

My name is ...
Benim adım ... — be·neem a·duhm ...

Do you speak English?
(İngilizce) konuşuyor musunuz? — (een·gee·leez·je) ko·noo·shoo·yor moo·soo·nooz

I understand.
Anlıyorum. — an·luh·yo·room

I don't understand.
Anlamıyorum. — an·la·muh·yo·room

Accommodation

campsite	kamp yeri	kamp ye·ree
hotel	otel	o·tel
youth hostel	gençlik hosteli	gench·leek hos·te·lee

Do you have a ... room?	... odanız var mı?	... o·da·nuhz var muh
single	Tek kişilik	tek kee·shee·leek
double	İki kişilik	ee·kee kee·shee·leek

How much is it per ...?	... ne kadar?	... ne ka·dar
night	Geceliği	ge·je·lee·ee
person	Kişi başına	kee·shee ba·shuh·na

air-con	klima	klee·ma
bathroom	banyo	ban·yo
fan	fan	fan
TV	TV	te·ve
window	pencere	pen·je·re

Directions

Where is ...?	... nerede?	... ne·re·de
Turn left.	Sola dön.	so·la dern
Turn right.	Sağa dön.	sa·a dern
It's ...		
behind ...	... arkasında.	... ar·ka·suhn·da
in front of ...	... önünde.	... er·newn·de
near ...	... yakınında.	... ya·kuh·nuhn·da
next to ...	... yanında.	... ya·nuhn·da
opposite ...	... karşısında.	... kar·shuh·suhn·da

KEY PATTERNS

To get by in Turkish, mix and match these simple patterns:

When's (the next bus)?
(Sonraki otobüs) ne zaman? — (son·ra·kee o·to·bews) ne za·man

Where's (the market)?
(Pazar yeri) nerede? — (pa·zar ye·ree) ne·re·de

Do you have (a map)?
(Haritanız) var mı? — (ha·ree·ta·nuhz) var muh

Is there (a toilet)?
(Tuvalet) var mı? — (too·va·let) var muh

I have (a reservation).
(Rezervasyonum) var. — (re·zer·vas·yo·noom) var

I'd like (the menu).
(Menüyü) istiyorum. — (me·new·yew) ees·tee·yo·room

I need (assistance).
(Yardıma) ihtiyacım var. — (yar·duh·ma) eeh·tee·ya·juhm var

QUESTION WORDS

How?	Nasıl?	na·suhl
What?	Ne?	ne
When?	Ne zaman?	ne za·man
Where?	Nerede?	ne·re·de
Who?	Kim?	keem
Why?	Neden?	ne·den

It's ...

at the traffic lights	Trafik ışıklarından.	tra·feek uh·shuhk·la·ruhn·dan
close	Yakın.	ya·kuhn
here	Burada.	boo·ra·da
on the corner	Köşede.	ker·she·de
straight ahead	Tam karşıda.	tam kar·shuh·da
there	Şurada.	shoo·ra·da

Eating & Drinking

What would you recommend?
Ne tavsiye edersiniz? — ne tav·see·ye e·der·see·neez

What's in that dish?
Bu yemekte neler var? — boo ye·mek·te ne·ler var

I'm a vegetarian.
Ben vejeteryanım. — ben ve·zhe·ter·ya·nuhm

That was delicious.
Nefisti! — ne·fees·tee

Cheers!
Şerefe! — she·re·fe

Could I have the bill, please?
Lütfen hesabı getirir misiniz? — lewt·fen he·sa·buh ge·tee·reer mee·see·neez

I'd like to reserve a table for ...	... bir masa ayırtmak istiyorum.	... beer ma·sa a·yuhrt·mak ees·tee·yo·room
(two) people	(İki) kişilik	(ee·kee) kee·shee·leek
(eight) o'clock	Saat (sekiz) için	sa·at (se·keez) ee·cheen

I don't eat ...	... yemiyorum.	... ye·mee·yo·room
fish	Balık	ba·luhk
(red) meat	(Kırmızı) Et	kuhr·muh·zuh et
peanuts	Fıstığa	fuhs·tuh·a
poultry	Tavuk eti	ta·vook e·tee

Key Words

appetisers	mezeler	me·ze·ler

bar	bar	bar
beef	sığır eti	suh·uhr e·tee
bottle	şişe	shee·she
bowl	kase	ka·se
bread	ekmek	ek·mek
breakfast	kahvaltı	kah·val·tuh
cafe	kafe	ka·fe
cheese	peynir	pay·neer
chicken	tavuk	ta·vook
cold	soğuk	so·ook
cream	krema	kre·ma
delicatessen	şarküteri	shar·kew·te·ree
desserts	tatlılar	tat·luh·lar
dinner	akşam yemeği	ak·sham ye·me·ee
drinks	İçecekler	ee·che·jek·ler
egg	yumurta	yoo·moor·ta
fish	balık	ba·luhk
food	yiyecek	yee·ye·jek
fork	çatal	cha·tal
fruit	meyve	may·ve
glass	bardak	bar·dak
greengrocer	manav	ma·nav
herb	bitki	beet·kee
high chair	mama sandalyesi	ma·ma san·dal·ye·see
hot	sıcak	suh·jak
ice cream	dondurma	don·door·ma
kebab	kebab	ke·bab
knife	bıçak	buh·chak
lamb	kuzu	koo·zoo
lunch	öğle yemeği	er·le ye·me·ee
main courses	ana yemekler	a·na ye·mek·ler
market	pazar	pa·zar
menu	yemek listesi	ye·mek lees·te·see
nut	çerez	che·rez
oil	yağ	ya
pepper	kara biber	ka·ra bee·ber
plate	tabak	ta·bak
pork	domuz eti	do·mooz e·tee
restaurant	restoran	res·to·ran
salad	salata	sa·la·ta
salt	tuz	tooz
soup	çorba	chor·ba
spoon	kaşık	ka·shuhk
sugar	şeker	she·ker
vegetable	sebze	seb·ze
vegetarian	vejeteryan	ve·zhe·ter·yan

vinegar	*sirke*	seer·*ke*
with	*ile*	ee·*le*
without	*-sız/-siz/ -suz/-süz*	·suhz/·seez/ ·sooz/·sewz

Drinks

beer	*bira*	bee·ra
coffee	*kahve*	kah·ve
juice	*suyu*	soo·yoo
milk	*süt*	sewt
soft drink	*meşrubat*	mesh·roo·bat
tea	*çay*	chai
water	*su*	soo
wine	*şarap*	sha·rap
white	*beyaz*	be·yaz
red	*kırmızı*	kuhr·muh·zuh

Emergencies

Help!	*İmdat!*	eem·dat
Go away!	*Git burdan!*	geet boor·dan
I'm lost.	*Kayboldum.*	kai·bol·doom
I'm ill.	*Hastayım.*	has·ta·yuhm
There's been an accident.	*Bir kaza oldu.*	beer ka·za ol·doo

Call ...!	*... çağırın!*	... cha·uh·ruhn
a doctor	*Doktor*	dok·tor
the police	*Polis*	po·lees

Numbers

0	*sıfır*	suh·fuhr
1	*bir*	beer
2	*iki*	ee·kee
3	*üç*	ewch
4	*dört*	dert
5	*beş*	besh
6	*altı*	al·tuh
7	*yedi*	ye·dee
8	*sekiz*	se·keez
9	*dokuz*	do·kooz
10	*on*	on
20	*yirmi*	yeer·mee
30	*otuz*	o·tooz
40	*kırk*	kuhrk
50	*elli*	el·lee
60	*altmış*	alt·muhsh
70	*yetmiş*	yet·meesh
80	*seksen*	sek·sen
90	*doksan*	dok·san
100	*yüz*	yewz
1000	*bin*	been

Shopping & Services

I'd like to buy ...
... almak istiyorum.	... al·mak ees·tee·yo·room

How much is it?
Ne kadar?	ne ka·dar

It's too expensive.
Bu çok pahalı.	boo chok pa·ha·luh

Do you have something cheaper?
Daha ucuz birşey var mı?	da·ha oo·jooz beer·shay var muh

ATM	*bankamatik*	ban·ka·ma·teek
bank	*banka*	ban·ka
credit card	*kredi kartı*	kre·dee kar·tuh
internet cafe	*internet kafe*	een·ter·net ka·fe
mobile phone	*cep telefonu*	jep te·le·fo·noo
post office	*postane*	pos·ta·ne
toilet	*tuvalet*	too·va·let
tourist office	*turizm bürosu*	too·reezm bew·ro·soo

Time & Dates

What time is it?	*Saat kaç?*	sa·at kach
It's (ten) o'clock.	*Saat (on).*	sa·at (on)
It's half past (ten).	*(On) buçuk.*	(on) boo·chook
today	*bugün*	boo·gewn

SIGNS

Giriş	gee·reesh	Entrance
Çıkış	chuh·kuhsh	Exit
Açık	a·chuhk	Open
Kapalı	ka·pa·luh	Closed
Danışma	da·nuhsh·ma	Information
Yasak	ya·sak	Prohibited
Tuvaletler	too·va·let·ler	Toilets
Erkek	er·kek	Men
Kadın	ka·duhn	Women

tomorrow	yarın	ya·ruhn
yesterday	dün	dewn
morning	sabah	sa·bah
(this)	(bu)	(boo)
afternoon	öğleden sonra	er·le·den son·ra
evening	akşam	ak·sham
Monday	Pazartesi	pa·zar·te·see
Tuesday	Salı	sa·luh
Wednesday	Çarşamba	char·sham·ba
Thursday	Perşembe	per·shem·be
Friday	Cuma	joo·ma
Saturday	Cumartesi	joo·mar·te·see
Sunday	Pazar	pa·zar

January	Ocak	o·jak
February	Şubat	shoo·bat
March	Mart	mart
April	Nisan	nee·san
May	Mayıs	ma·yuhs
June	Haziran	ha·zee·ran
July	Temmuz	tem·mooz
August	Ağustos	a·oos·tos
September	Eylül	ay·lewl
October	Ekim	e·keem
November	Kasım	ka·suhm
December	Aralık	a·ra·luhk

Transport

Public Transport

boat	vapur	va·poor
(city) bus	şehir otobüsü	she·heer o·to·bew·sew
(intercity) bus	şehirlerarası otobüs	she·heer·ler·a·ra·suh o·to·bews
plane	uçak	oo·chak
train	tren	tren

Where do I buy a ticket?
Nereden bilet alabilirim? — ne·re·den bee·let a·la·bee·lee·reem

What time does it leave?
Ne zaman kalkacak? — ne za·man kal·ka·jak

Do I need to change?
Aktarma yapmam gerekli mi? — ak·tar·ma yap·mam ge·rek·lee mee

Does it stop at ...?
... durur mu? — ... doo·roor moo

What's the next stop?
Sonraki durak hangisi? — son·ra·kee doo·rak han·gee·see

I'd like to get off at ...
... inmek istiyorum. — ... een·mek ees·tee·yo·room

A one-way ticket, please.
Gidiş bileti lütfen. — gee·deesh bee·le·tee lewt·fen

A ... ticket, please.	... bilet lütfen.	... bee·let lewt·fen
1st-class	Birinci mevki	bee·reen·jee mev·kee
2nd-class	Ikinci mevki	ee·keen·jee mev·kee
return	Gidiş-dönüş	gee·deesh·der·newsh

cancel v	iptal etmek	eep·tal et·mek
delay n	gecikme	ge·jeek·me
platform	peron	pe·ron
ticket office	bilet gişesi	bee·let gee·she·see
timetable	tarife	ta·ree·fe
train station	tren istasyonu	tren ees·tas·yo·noo

Driving & Cycling

I'd like to hire a/an ...	Bir ... kiralamak istiyorum.	beer ... kee·ra·la·mak ees·tee·yo·room
4WD	dört çeker	dert che·ker
car	araba	a·ra·ba
motorbike	motosiklet	mo·to·seek·let
bicycle	bisiklet	bee·seek·let

Do I need a helmet?
Kask takmam gerekli mi? — kask tak·mam ge·rek·lee mee

Is this the road to ...?
... giden yol bu mu? — ... gee·den yol boo moo

How long can I park here?
Buraya ne kadar süre park edebilirim? — boo·ra·ya ne ka·dar sew·re park e·de·bee·lee·reem

The car/motorbike has broken down (at ...).
Arabam/ motosikletim ... bozuldu. — a·ra·bam/ mo·to·seek·le·teem ... bo·zool·doo

I have a flat tyre.
Lastiğim patladı. — las·tee·eem pat·la·duh

I've run out of petrol.
Benzinim bitti. — ben·zee·neem beet·tee

GLOSSARY

For words dealing with Cypriot cuisine, see p41.
Abbreviations
(Fr) = French
(Gr) = Greek
(Tr) = Turkish
(m) = masculine
(f) = feminine
(n) = neutral

agios (m), **agia** (f; Gr) – saint

bedesten (Tr) – covered market
belediye (Tr) – town hall
bulvarı (Tr) – boulevard, avenue
burnu (Tr) – cape
Byzantine Empire – Hellenistic, Christian empire lasting from AD 395 to 1453, centred on Constantinople (Istanbul)

caddesi (Tr) – road
camii (Tr) – mosque
commandery – a district under the control of a commander of an order of knights
CTO – Cyprus Tourism Organisation, the Republic of Cyprus' official tourism promotion body

dolmuş (Tr) – minibus, shared taxi (literally 'stuffed')

enosis (Gr) – union (with Greece); the frequent demand made by many Greek Cypriots before 1974
entrepôt (Fr) – commercial centre for import and export
EOKA – Ethniki Organosi tou Kypriakou Agona (National Organisation for the Cypriot Struggle); nationalist guerrilla movement that fought for independence from Britain
EOKA-B – post-independence reincarnation of *EOKA*, which mostly fought Turkish Cypriots
ethnarch (Gr) – leader of a nation

garigue (Fr) – low, open scrubland with evergreen shrubs, low trees, aromatic herbs and grasses, found in poor or dry soil in the Mediterranean region
Green Line – the border that divides Greek Cypriot Nicosia (Lefkosia) from Turkish Cypriot North Nicosia (Lefkoşa); also the whole border between North and South

hammam (Tr) – public bathhouse

kafeneio (Gr) – coffee shop
kalesi (Tr) – castle
kato (Gr) – lower, eg Kato Pafos (Lower Pafos)
KKTC (Tr) – Kuzey Kıbrıs Türk Cumhuriyeti (Turkish Republic of Northern Cyprus)
KOT (Gr) – Kypriakos Organismos Tourismou; the official tourist organisation of the Republic of Cyprus; see *CTO*

leoforos (Gr) – avenue
Lusignan – Cypriot dynasty founded by French nobleman Guy de Lusignan in 1187, which lasted until 1489

maquis (Fr) – thick, scrubby underbrush of Mediterranean shores, particularly of the islands of Corsica and Cyprus
Maronites – ancient Christian sect from the Middle East
Mesaoria (Gr), **Mesarya** (Tr) – the large plain between the Kyrenia (Girne) Range and the Troödos Mountains
meydanı (Tr) – square
meze (s), **mezedes** (pl) – literally 'appetiser'; used in Cyprus to mean dining on lots of small plates of appetisers
mouflon (Fr) – endangered indigenous wild sheep of Cyprus

narthex (Gr) – railed-off western porch in early Christian churches used by women and penitents
NCTO – North Cyprus Tourism Organisation; Northern Cyprus' tourism-promotion body

neos (m), **nea** (f), **neo** (n; Gr) – new; common prefix to place names

Ottoman Empire – Turkish empire founded in the 11th century AD, which ruled Cyprus from 1571 to 1878; it was abolished in 1922

panagia (Gr) – church
panigyri (Gr) – feast or festival
Pantokrator (Gr) – the 'Almighty'; traditional fresco of Christ, painted in the dome of Orthodox churches
paşa (Tr) – Ottoman title roughly equivalent to 'lord'
pitta (Gr) – flat, unleavened bread
plateia (Gr) – square
Ptolemies – Graeco-Macedonian rulers of Egypt in the 4th century BC

rembetika (Gr) – Greek equivalent of American blues music, believed to have emerged from 'low-life' cafes in the 1870s

sokak (Tr) – street
Sufi (Tr) – adherent of the Sufi variant of Islam

taksim (Tr) – partition (of Cyprus); demanded by Turkish Cypriots in response to Greek Cypriots' calls for *enosis*
taverna (Gr) – traditional restaurant that serves food and wine
tekkesi (Tr) – gathering place of the Sufi; mosque
tholos (Gr) – the dome of an Orthodox church
TRNC (Tr) – Turkish Republic of Northern Cyprus; see KKTC

Unesco – United Nations Educational, Scientific and Cultural Organization

Behind the Scenes

SEND US YOUR FEEDBACK

We love to hear from travellers – your comments keep us on our toes and help make our books better. Our well-travelled team reads every word on what you loved or loathed about this book. Although we cannot reply individually to your submissions, we always guarantee that your feedback goes straight to the appropriate authors, in time for the next edition. Each person who sends us information is thanked in the next edition – the most useful submissions are rewarded with a selection of digital PDF chapters.

Visit **lonelyplanet.com/contact** to submit your updates and suggestions or to ask for help. Our award-winning website also features inspirational travel stories, news and discussions.

Note: We may edit, reproduce and incorporate your comments in Lonely Planet products such as guidebooks, websites and digital products, so let us know if you don't want your comments reproduced or your name acknowledged. For a copy of our privacy policy visit lonelyplanet.com/privacy.

OUR READERS

Many thanks to the travellers who used the last edition and wrote to us with helpful hints, useful advice and interesting anecdotes:

Alan Martin, Anne Werner, Arkadiusz Rubajczyk, Barney Smith, Chris Tozer, Colin Stevenson, Dan Livney, Gloria Ridley, Liesl Marelli, Lynne Mackey, Nicolas Kefalas, Paul Charman, Rita Cordes, Robert Power, Russell Pepper, Ruth Keshishian, Shauna Brown, Simon Godfrey

WRITER THANKS

Joe Bindloss

A big thanks to Brana Vladisavljevic for the welcome opportunity to cover the country where I was born, and to Jessica Lee and Josephine Quintero for providing such excellent material to work with.

Jessica Lee

A big thanks to Kris in Larnaka; Yiannis and Lefteris in Lefkosia; to Angela and Özgür Gökaşan in Kyrenia for loads of tips and even more coffee; to Vicky Burke and François Hameon in Famagusta; and to the friendly staff at the CTO offices in Agia Napa and Lefkosia. At Lonely Planet, a huge thank you to Brana, fellow author Jo, and to cartographer Anthony for helping to solve a mapping conundrum.

Josephine Quintero

First and foremost thanks to Brana Vladisavljevic from Lonely Planet for commissioning me to re-search these fascinating regions of Cyprus. Also to the numerous helpful CTO folk throughout the island. Thanks too to Victoria Oliver in Lemesos for her insight into the local restaurant scene and to George Anagnos for being my hiking companion in the Troödos.

ACKNOWLEDGEMENTS

Climate map data adapted from Peel MC, Finlayson BL & McMahon TA (2007) 'Updated World Map of the Köppen-Geiger Climate Classification', Hydrology and Earth System Sciences, 11, 163344.

Cover photograph: Beach at Aphrodite's Rock, Pafos, advertize/Getty Images©

THIS BOOK

This 7th edition of Lonely Planet's *Cyprus* guidebook was curated by Joe Bindloss and researched and written by Jessica Lee and Josephine Quintero. The 6th edition was also written by Jessica Lee and Josephine Quintero, while the 5th edition was written by Josephine Quintero and Matthew Charles. This guidebook was produced by the following:

Destination Editor Branislava Vladisavljevic

Product Editors Bruce Evans, Anne Mason

Senior Cartographers Anthony Phelan, Corey Hutchison

Book Designer Nicholas Colicchia

Assisting Editors James Bainbridge, Jennifer Hattam, Kellie Langdon, Lou McGregor, Charlotte Orr, Susan Paterson, Tamara Sheward, Saralinda Turner

Assisting Cartographer Rachel Imeson

Cover Researcher Naomi Parker

Thanks to Shona Gray, Ellie Simpson, Tony Wheeler

282

Index

Map Legend

Sights
- Beach
- Bird Sanctuary
- Buddhist
- Castle/Palace
- Christian
- Confucian
- Hindu
- Islamic
- Jain
- Jewish
- Monument
- Museum/Gallery/Historic Building
- Ruin
- Shinto
- Sikh
- Taoist
- Winery/Vineyard
- Zoo/Wildlife Sanctuary
- Other Sight

Activities, Courses & Tours
- Bodysurfing
- Diving
- Canoeing/Kayaking
- Course/Tour
- Sento Hot Baths/Onsen
- Skiing
- Snorkelling
- Surfing
- Swimming/Pool
- Walking
- Windsurfing
- Other Activity

Sleeping
- Sleeping
- Camping
- Hut/Shelter

Eating
- Eating

Drinking & Nightlife
- Drinking & Nightlife
- Cafe

Entertainment
- Entertainment

Shopping
- Shopping

Information
- Bank
- Embassy/Consulate
- Hospital/Medical
- Internet
- Police
- Post Office
- Telephone
- Toilet
- Tourist Information
- Other Information

Geographic
- Beach
- Gate
- Hut/Shelter
- Lighthouse
- Lookout
- Mountain/Volcano
- Oasis
- Park
- Pass
- Picnic Area
- Waterfall

Population
- Capital (National)
- Capital (State/Province)
- City/Large Town
- Town/Village

Transport
- Airport
- Border crossing
- Bus
- Cable car/Funicular
- Cycling
- Ferry
- Metro station
- Monorail
- Parking
- Petrol station
- S-Bahn/Subway station
- Taxi
- T-bane/Tunnelbana station
- Train station/Railway
- Tram
- Tube station
- U-Bahn/Underground station
- Other Transport

Routes
- Tollway
- Freeway
- Primary
- Secondary
- Tertiary
- Lane
- Unsealed road
- Road under construction
- Plaza/Mall
- Steps
- Tunnel
- Pedestrian overpass
- Walking Tour
- Walking Tour detour
- Path/Walking Trail

Boundaries
- International
- State/Province
- Disputed
- Regional/Suburb
- Marine Park
- Cliff
- Wall

Hydrography
- River, Creek
- Intermittent River
- Canal
- Water
- Dry/Salt/Intermittent Lake
- Reef

Areas
- Airport/Runway
- Beach/Desert
- Cemetery (Christian)
- Cemetery (Other)
- Glacier
- Mudflat
- Park/Forest
- Sight (Building)
- Sportsground
- Swamp/Mangrove

Note: Not all symbols displayed above appear on the maps in this book

OUR STORY

A beat-up old car, a few dollars in the pocket and a sense of adventure. In 1972 that's all Tony and Maureen Wheeler needed for the trip of a lifetime – across Europe and Asia overland to Australia. It took several months, and at the end – broke but inspired – they sat at their kitchen table writing and stapling together their first travel guide, *Across Asia on the Cheap*. Within a week they'd sold 1500 copies. Lonely Planet was born.

Today, Lonely Planet has offices in Franklin, London, Melbourne, Oakland, Dublin, Beijing and Delhi, with more than 600 staff and writers. We share Tony's belief that 'a great guidebook should do three things: inform, educate and amuse'.

OUR WRITERS

Joe Bindloss

Joe was born in Cyprus and has contributed to more than 50 Lonely Planet guidebooks since 1999, covering everywhere from Australia to the high reaches of the Himalaya. Joe currently works as Lonely Planet's Destination Editor for the Indian subcontinent.

Jessica Lee

Jess high-tailed it for the road at the age of 18 and hasn't looked back since. In 2011 she swapped a career as an adventure-tour leader for travel writing and since then her travels for Lonely Planet have taken her across Africa, the Middle East and Asia. She has lived in the Middle East since 2007. Jess has contributed to Lonely Planet's *Egypt, Turkey, Cyprus, Marrakesh, Middle East, Europe, Africa, Cambodia* and *Vietnam* guidebooks, and her travel writing has appeared in *Wanderlust* magazine, the *Daily Telegraph,* the *Independent,* BBC Travel and lonelyplanet.com.

Josephine Quintero

Josephine first got her taste of travel when she slung a guitar on her back and travelled in Europe in the early 70s. After moving to the US she went to Kuwait where she worked as the Editor of a Kuwait Oil Company magazine. After Iraq invaded, she went to the relaxed shores of Andalucia in southern Spain where she writes regularly for in-flight magazines. Josephine primarily covers Spain and Italy for Lonely Planet, as well as Mexico City, Australia, Portugal and Cyprus.

Published by Lonely Planet Global Limited
CRN 554153
7th edition – February 2018
ISBN 978 1 78657 349 0
© Lonely Planet 2018   Photographs © as indicated 2018
10 9 8 7 6 5 4 3 2 1
Printed in China